GLOBAL
MEMBER CARE

Isn't it great when you find a book that compiles relevant materials needed for your own work? *Crossing Sectors* does just that. It provides a large amount of information that can stimulate those of us in the humanitarian or mission sectors to learn more from others. The more we understand the roles and concerns of our colleagues, other organisations, and beneficiaries, the better we will all be able to serve humanity—together. For example, the inclusion of human resource specialists as 'business partners' within operational departments can facilitate humanitarian planning and response. Over the years, Kelly and Michèle have continually championed the key role of staff and volunteers for accomplishing the demanding tasks of humanitarian work. Their ongoing focus on linking health and human resources is a significant contribution to our sector.

– Jonathan Potter
Executive Director
People In Aid

This book is full of helpful insights to further develop the broad and strategic world of global member care. Kelly and Michèle do a great job in presenting a foundational model for our work, demonstrating the crucial need for cross-sectoral collaboration, and presenting a wealth of tools from other sectors that can support member care. Crossing sectors is indeed challenging, but the payoffs are great! There are so many opportunities to work jointly towards the same end—the wellbeing of humanity. This inspired book guides us into many of the complex challenges facing humanity and highlights the increasing relevance of *multi-sectoral member care* in addressing these challenges.

– Alison Schafer
Senior Program Advisor for Mental Health and Psychosocial Support (MHPSS)
World Vision Australia/International

The last decade has seen substantial increase in analysis and professionalization of the international humanitarian and development assistance sector. As a result, there has been both an upsurge in documentation of policies and proposed best practices and a growth in awareness of the range of disciplines and perspectives relevant to such trends. This book does a great job of assisting workers and organizations in international settings by bringing together a selection of key writings and documents. Together this material asserts not only the complexity and challenge of our sector, but also the emergence of key principles to secure its appropriate advance.

– Alastair Ager, PhD
Professor of Clinical Population and Family Health
Mailman School of Public Health, Columbia University

This volume is a unique contribution—even beyond its success in moving across traditional sectoral boundaries. The book is animated by, indeed founded on, an often overlooked linkage between human rights and the helping vocation. We all embrace the dignity and agency of those who are on the receiving end of our services. But coming to grips with the consequences and inevitable tensions accompanying a human rights approach to member care, as *Crossing Sectors for Humanity* does, is both brave and essential to the task. Thank you for this unique and comprehensive contribution to advancing human dignity in humanitarian practice.

– Leonard Rubenstein
Director, Program on Human Rights, Health and Conflict
Center for Public Health and Human Rights
Bloomberg School of Public Health, Johns Hopkins University

Crossing Sectors for Serving Humanity is a ground-breaking book that presents a multi-sectoral framework to understand and develop global member care. It also showcases how the diversity of international organizations can share strategies for supporting their members who work in cross-cultural settings. The O'Donnells excel yet again in selecting a variety of readings that are well-organised, creative, scholarly, directional, trend setting, and highly relevant for expanding our thinking and skill sets. Get ready to head into the next phase of member care—and into the heart of global issues and opportunities!

– Ruth E. Van Reken

co-author *Third Culture Kids: Growing Up Among Worlds*,
co-founder Families in Global Transition conference

Crossing Sectors for Serving Humanity, edited by renowned authors and psychologists Kelly and Michèle O'Donnell, makes a profound contribution to all who are helping to make the world a better, safer, and healthier place. Its multiple authors and wide-ranging topics help us to cross the boundaries of cultures, disciplines, organizations, and sectors in order to more effectively address the health and wellbeing of staff and their agencies. This new book also effectively builds upon the authors' previous volumes which helped set the norm for good practice in the member care movement, including *Doing Member Care Well* (2002). At last we have a member care book written for and by members of several sectors who are involved in the care of our planet and its people. The member care movement has truly come of age with this book.

– Ted Lankester, MD

Director of Health Services, InterHealth Worldwide,
Director of Community Health Global Network

– EDITORS –

Kelly O'Donnell & Michèle Lewis O'Donnell

GLOBAL MEMBER CARE

VOLUME TWO

Crossing Sectors for Serving Humanity

WILLIAM CAREY
LIBRARY

Global Member Care: Crossing Sectors for Serving Humanity
Copyright © 2013 by Kelly O'Donnell and Michèle Lewis O'Donnell

Disclaimer: The opinions and recommendations expressed in these multimedia materials do not necessarily reflect those of the publishers or editors. Readers are strongly encouraged to obtain the full versions of the materials included in this volume and to review them thoroughly. The responsibility for the interpretation and use of the material lies with the reader, and neither the publishers nor editors shall be held liable for damages arising from its use.

For updates on the Global Member Care series, including new links and resources, visit https://sites.google.com/site/globalmca/.

Kelley K. Wolfe, editor
Brad Koenig, copyediting
Hugh Pindur, graphic design
Rose-Lee Norman, indexing

Published by
William Carey Library
1605 E. Elizabeth Street
Pasadena, CA 91104 | www.missionbooks.org

William Carey Library is a ministry of the
U.S. Center for World Mission
Pasadena, CA | www.uscwm.org

17 16 15 14 13   5 4 3 2 1 BP300/SF

Printed in the United States of America

Library of Congress Cataloging-in-Publication Data

O'Donnell, Kelly S.
Global member care : crossing sectors for serving humanity / [Kelly O'Donnell and Michèle Lewis O'Donnell].
p. cm.
Includes bibliographical references and index.
ISBN 978-0-87808-122-6
1. Personnel management. 2. Mission. 3. Humanitarian assistance. I. Title.
BV2091.O36 2010
266.0068'3--dc22
2010017126

AD MAJOREM DEI GLORIAM

Contents

Preface

We the peoples of the United Nations determined: to save suc-
ceeding generations from the scourge of war, which twice in our
lifetime has brought untold sorrow to mankind, and to reaffirm
faith in fundamental human rights, in the dignity and worth of
the human person, in the equal rights of men and women and of
nations large and small, and to establish conditions under which
justice and respect for the obligations arising from treaties and other
sources of international law can be maintained, and to promote
social progress and better standards of life in larger freedom . . .
(Preamble, Charter of the United Nations, 1945)

If you are interested in seeing the world in new ways, expanding your global reach,
developing your member care skills, and staying current with good practice in order
to work in tough places, then you have come to the right place. This second book
and all the books in the *Global Member Care* series are for you. Welcome!

Member care is an interdisciplinary, international, and transcultural field that
focuses on supporting the diversity of mission/aid personnel and sending groups. It
is also increasingly becoming a *cross-sectoral* field, and one which relevantly relates
to the aspirations of humanity, as summarized in the Preface's opening and closing
quotes from the Charter of the United Nations.

The member care field has clear roots that can be traced back to the 1960s and
1970s, although its phenomenal growth has occurred during the last two decades.
Just about everyone is aware of the notion of member care, albeit perhaps by different names such as personnel development, human resource management, staff
well-being, worker health, etc. The wealth of concepts, resources, practices, and
practitioners have contributed greatly to the people and purposes of the mission/
aid community—and beyond. These contributions will only increase in the coming
years as the member care field further expands and develops globally. We are entering into a new season for member care marked by a diversity of good practitioners
with both multicultural and multisectoral competencies.

This *Global Member Care* series is dedicated to the diversity of people around the world in mission/aid who have member care responsibility. This includes people who are probably very much like you: field and team leaders, mission/aid workers themselves, personnel department staff, professionally trained caregivers, educators, researchers, health advocates, and many others in formal or informal member care roles. The three books in the series build especially upon the fifty chapters in the 2002 book *Doing Member Care Well: Perspectives and Practices from Around the World*. Together they represent the ongoing efforts to help all of us in the mission/ aid community, and beyond into other sectors, get a better sense of the vast domain of member care. The series is designed to further equip us all with the knowledge and skills necessary for good practice.

Volume 1 (*The Pearls and Perils of Good Practice*) reviewed member care history and future directions, the crucial issues of health/dysfunction, and guidelines for ethics / human rights. This second volume (*Crossing Sectors for Serving Humanity*) continues the emphasis on good practice by encouraging us to intentionally con-nect and contribute to different sectors, especially humanitarian assistance, human resources, and health-care sectors. We thus encourage member care to expand in new ways and to take advantage of the many opportunities for serving humanity. Volume 3 will advocate for member care to go to and from all people groups and will include examples and stories from around the world. We have endeavored to make the *Global Member Care* series as practical, cutting edge, and interesting as possible. For updates on the series, including new links and resources, visit the *Global MCA* website: https://sites.google.com/site/globalmca/. Most of the URLs at the end of the chapters (References, Notes, Sources, and Related Resources) are also located on the Global MCA website.

We emphasize the importance of both personal and professional growth in this series. Our perspective (as described in chapter 10 of volume 1) is that character and competence, permeated with compassion, are needed in order to provide good practice. This focus on growth is seen in the many exercises and resources that are included throughout the books. We encourage you to use them for your own reflection and when possible for group discussions. Grow deeply and go broadly.

We want to express our gratitude to our many colleagues and friends over the years that have helped to shape our practice in global member care and mental health. We also sincerely appreciate the various colleagues around the world who have provided helpful feedback on the materials included in *Crossing Sectors*. In addition, our work would not be possible without the generosity of donors and the encouraging support of our friends and family. Our heartfelt thanks for traveling together with us on this global journey!

Member care involves the transcultural practice of fervently loving one another. It is both sacrificial and celebratory. It is both duty and desire—and hopefully more of the latter! Such love, as affirmed in the multilingual epigraph (next page), never ceases. We grow together in the mission/aid community and beyond, we celebrate life together, and as human vessels full of strengths and weaknesses, we do our utmost to stay close together. Resilient love is the ultimate measure of the effectiveness of member care in our service to humanity.

> And for these ends: to practice tolerance and live together in peace with one another as good neighbors, and to unite our strength to maintain international peace and security, and to ensure, by the acceptance of principles and the institution of methods, that armed force shall not be used, save in the common interest, and to employ international machinery for the promotion of the economic and social advancement of all peoples, have resolved to combine our efforts to accomplish these aims. (Preamble, Charter of the United Nations, 1945)

Kelly and Michèle O'Donnell
Geneva, Switzerland
September 2013

사랑은 언제까지든지 떨어지지

Axebbeṛ n wayen i d-yeṭṭasen

Kasih tidak berkesudahan

Anbu orukallum ozliyathu

Хайр хэзээ ч дуусдаггүй

Ljubav nikad ne prestaje

ٱلْمَحَبَّةُ فَتَدُومُ وَلَا تَنْتَهِي

Armastus ei hävi ilmaski

ความรักไม่มีวันสูญสิ้น

לעולם תבל לא האהבה

Ime eque carpis

爱 是 永 不 止 息

Սէրը բնաՙւ չիյնամը

Mbëggeel amul àpp

Uthando aluze lutshitshe

ፍቅር ለዘወትር ኢይወድቅም

Dashuria nuk ligshtohet kurrë

Kærleikurinn fellur aldrei úr gildi

Die liefde vergaan nimmermeer

Quintlasohtla nochipa in oc sequin

愛はいつまでも絶えることがない

Любовь никогда не перестает

Upendo hauna kikomo kamwe

A szeretet soha el nem fogy

E kore rawa te aroha e taka

Die Liebe höret nimmer auf

La charité ne périt jamais

Caritas numquam excidit

Miłość nigdy nie ustaje

O amor jamais acaba

Renmen pa janm fini

Kärleken förgår aldrig

Sevgi asla son bulmaz

Láska nikdy nevypadá

Meilė niekada nesibaigia

Kasih tidak berkesudahan

El amor nunca deja de ser

Charitatea nehoiz-ere ezta erorten

Tình yêu thương chẳng hề hư mất bao giờ

Ang pagibig ay hindi nagkukulang kailan man

ἡ ἀγάπη οὐδέποτε πίπτει

Love never fails.

1 Cor 13:8

INTRODUCTION

Growing Broadly
in Mission/Aid—and Beyond

THIS BOOK IS A SUMMONS, A STIMULUS, AND A SPRINGBOARD:
FOR CROSSING SECTORS TO FURTHER DEVELOP GOOD PRACTICE IN MEMBER CARE
AND FOR SERVING HUMANITY IN NEW WAYS THROUGH THE
MEMBER CARE FIELD.

Volume 2 in the *Global Member Care* series, *Crossing Sectors*, is part of an ongoing effort to help us keep current with both our globalizing world and the global field of member care. It is designed for those with member care responsibility who want to develop their member care skills in light of the major challenges affecting the world. The goal is to encourage us all to "broaden our experiential boundaries": to take advantage of the wealth of opportunities for *connecting and contributing* to various international sectors on behalf of the diversity of remarkable people who serve in mission/aid as well as on behalf of humanity itself.

A GRID FOR THE BOOK

A major emphasis in this book is on *sectors*. Sectors are large, amorphous yet recognizable entities that bring together people and resources for a broad purpose to benefit society. Chapter 2, "Charting Your Course through the Sectors," goes into more detail about sectors and their relevance for good practice. We have carefully selected materials for this book from three highly diverse human sectors based on our experience in them and with input from colleagues. We refer to these sectors as being "human," not only because they contain the word "human" or are comprised of humans, but because, like the mission/aid sector, they focus on the well-being of fellow humans. These three human sectors overlap with each other and are particularly relevant for the member care field in mission/aid.

Humanitarian Sector: relevant in the common commitment for supporting and managing international and local staff, in maintaining effective organizations, and in offering a variety of relief and development services to vulnerable populations.

Human Health Sector: relevant in the common commitment to promote human wellness through research, resources, advocacy, and policies at all levels of society, and applicable to staff and those with whom staff work.

Human Resource Sector: relevant in the common commitment to fulfill organizational objectives by developing and managing human resource systems and by promoting staff/volunteer well-being and effectiveness (with some emphasis on organizational development).

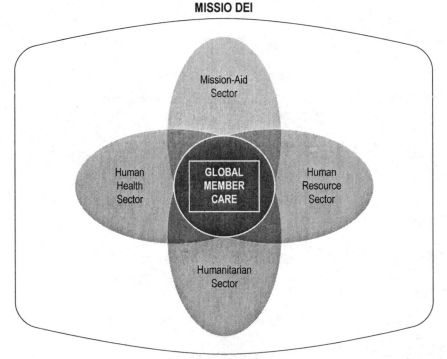

Figure 1
Member care's expanding role in serving humanity, highlighting the influence of four key sectors

Here is a grid (see fig. 1) to help visualize how these three sectors, along with the mission/aid sector, are influential for member care. Note that member care, while historically being primarily part of the mission/aid sector, is influenced here by all four sectors. The grid also shows that member care likewise influences these four sectors (with the main one being, of course, the mission/aid sector) since crossing into sectors is meant to be a two-way street for mutual learning and sharing of resources. The grid has a significant philosophical overlay as well: the outer permeable brackets represent the sectors as being part of both the *missio Dei* (from a theological perspective, the overall mission of God on behalf of humanity) and the *missio mundi* (from a secular perspective, the overall mission of humans on behalf of humanity). *This grid forms the conceptual framework for the book and an important direction for the global member care field to pursue in mission/aid and beyond.*

BOOK OVERVIEW

Crossing Sectors is divided into four parts. Part 1 overviews the relevance, key concepts, and experience of crossing sectors (five chapters). It also includes the Universal Declaration of Human Rights as a foundational reference point for human worth, dignity, and well-being as well as for our work within and across sectors. We offer a variety of materials related to good practice in the Humanitarian Sector (part 2, ten chapters), the Human Health Sector (part 3, ten chapters), and the Human Resource Sector (part 4, ten chapters). You will find guidelines, codes, resolutions, perspectives, principles, resources, case examples, tools, Internet links to videos, human rights emphases, and more. Most of the materials are published in the Global North(s), such as by Geneva-based, international nongovernmental organizations (NGOs) and intergovernmental bodies (e.g., United Nations, World Health Organization). Nonetheless the influence of the Global South(s) in developing many of these materials is substantial. The playing field must continue to become increasingly level for all stakeholders.

All of the material in parts 2–4 (thirty chapters) has been previously published, about half within the past few years. We have selected this material because of its practical relevance for good practice in member care and because it is easily accessible online, often in many languages. In addition, about half of the chapters are comprised of core sections or excerpts due to the length of the source material. Many other superb materials and vital sector-related topics could not be included due to space limitations. There is, though, plenty reproduced to inform and inspire you, and to encourage you to read the full versions and further explore these sectors.

Finally, most of the chapters conclude by listing at least five additional resources, including a short video related to the chapter topic.

MAKING THE MOST OF THE MATERIAL

We suggest that you keep in mind the five goals below for crossing sectors as you go through the material in the book. Underlying these goals is the process of mutual learning, exchanging of resources, and building relationships as we seek to connect and contribute across sectors.

- To support mission/aid workers in their well-being and effectiveness
- To support colleagues in other sectors via materials in the member care field
- To equip mission/aid workers with tools and opportunities for their work with others
- To equip member caregivers who directly work with vulnerable populations and others
- To stay informed as global citizens about current and crucial issues facing humanity

Crossing Sectors can be used as a state-of-the-art text for training purposes in universities, seminaries, and mission/aid settings, formally or informally, and as a handbook for member care workers, sending groups, and those with member care responsibility. It not only provides valuable content but also models the value of stretching our mentalities and practices by crossing into other sectors. The intended audience includes people in the mission/aid and other international sectors who focus on making the world a more just and healthier place for all.

FIVE IMPORTANT PERSPECTIVES

1. Historical continuity and ongoing opportunity in crossing sectors. Involvement in sectors is not new to member care or to mission/aid. Nonetheless, this is the first book in the member care literature to explicitly focus in detail on the importance of different *sectors* for supporting and managing mission/aid workers. Engaging with other sectors was previously emphasized in two of our other books, *The Pearls and Perils of Good Practice* (O'Donnell 2011) and *Doing Member Care Well* (O'Donnell 2002). The more recent book built upon member care foundations by exploring the input from other sectors for such areas as psychosocial support for victims in conflicts/calamities, good management practices in sending organizations, and human rights principles for staff development. In the earlier book a major emphasis was to "launch into and learn from new areas . . . pushing the usual borders of member care into several additional realms" (O'Donnell 2002, 3). These new areas included contributions from travel health (preventing accidents), personnel programs (supporting military families), human rights (advocating for religious liberty), and human resources (supporting national staff, developing codes of good practice). In *Crossing Sectors*, we continue this emphasis for the member care field by highlighting the opportunity for mutual contributions and connections with relevant sectors.

2. **Mission/aid as an inclusive term and a practical reality.** We use the term "mission/aid" throughout the book. This is a broad, inclusive term that represents the increasing focus and contributions of faith-based, Christian work around the world. By "mission" we are referring to the efforts of both Christian workers serving in cross-cultural settings and national Christian workers located in their home/passport countries. The former group is estimated to be about 426,000 and the latter group about 12.3 million people (Johnson and Crossing 2013). This term also includes the efforts of Christians who relocate for economic, sociopolitical, and other reasons (e.g., tentmakers, international workers, refugees) and in the process bring their faith and good works with them. Mission/aid as mentioned earlier is seen as a core part of the broader theological concept of *missio Dei*—the extensive and multifaceted mission of God in the world. It is not meant to minimize the important roles that people with other faith/no faith commitments are playing in the service of humanity. By "aid" we refer to the extensive area of humanitarian *assistance*. This area encompasses relief and development operations by civil society, NGOs, the United Nations, faith-based groups, etc. (e.g., there are an estimated 274,000 humanitarian workers and 4,400 NGOs undertaking humanitarian action; ALNAP 2012, p. 9). It is not meant to imply a service providers / service receivers dichotomy but rather reflects the respectful commitment to work together with those in need, who are often referred to as beneficiaries and vulnerable populations. Mission and aid overlap with each other, and using the term "mission/aid" reflects this practical reality.

3. *Global* **is small and all.** Global, as in *global* member care, or global anything for that matter, does not necessarily mean globe-*all*. In fact, we find that the word global is overused and that often a much smaller part of an important global area is actually involved. What we mean by it in the *Global Member Care* series is that member care is a growing field, expanding across nations, cultures, sectors, and issues. Although it is "international," it is not everywhere in the world. Yet it is certainly

increasing its worldwide influence. To continue in a truly global direction, we must especially engage with *all* of our colleagues, listening to each other and learning from our varieties of experience and expertise (especially since the vast majority of aid/development workers are not "internationals"), being willing to incorporate various contributions (concepts and practices) into our health/member care approaches as well as to encourage the development of truly indigenous approaches which might be quite different from those that significantly influence health/member care currently.

4. Good practice is essential yet aspirational. Note also that "good practice," as used in this book, does not mean "perfect" practice. It rather endeavors to reflect the best attempts to date, consensually derived and evidence-based, to guide practice. In some cases it may actually be more aspirational yet worthy objectives for which to strive. Helping to set benchmarks for good practice in a field is always challenging. It requires doing the hard work of setting "trenchmarks"—learning by serving in the trenches and not just in the relatively safe towers. Further, and in view of the major problems affecting humanity (such as those outlined in the eight Millennium Development Goals—poverty, gender equity, education, nutrition, etc. as they emerge into the even more extensive post 2015 "sustainable development goals"— and in the United Nations Development Programme's *Human Development Report 2013*), there are still massive gaps in the needed finances, trained workers, technical support, organizational commitment, infrastructure, accountability, and political will to help make good practice a reality.

5. Think critically and act competently. Crossing sectors is something to be done critically. Our learning and actions must be tempered by the legitimate concerns and dissent from both inside and outside the sectors. Just a few of the many examples of the areas to consider for good (ethical/competent) practice are: the involvement of the private sector (commercial/business) as it combines for-profit motives with humanitarian pursuits, the World Health Organization's major influence on global health in view of the People's Health Movement *Global Health Watch* reports and the growing calls by civil society to "democratize" health, global mental health from indigenous perspectives in addition to Western "indigenous" categories of thinking, the ongoing disparity in the equitable flow of resources between the Global South(s) and the Global North(s) in spite of calls to eradicate poverty, human "development" with due regard for sustainable environmental development, and various critiques about humanitarian aid in view of the ongoing status quo of the world's "bottom billion."

Final Thoughts

We believe that crossing sectors represents the next crucial phase for the member care field. It is a strategic practice of the enormous and diverse group of people in government and civil society who seek to work as forces for good. It is also part of the commitment to lifelong learning and for some (including the current and upcoming cohorts of students) will take them into areas of study related to international relations, public health, human rights, etc. As a field we encourage maintaining the *core focus* of member care (i.e., well-being and effectiveness of mission/aid workers) while expanding the *corps function* of member care (i.e., involvement in other sectors by member care workers).

Crossing Sectors points us to the *raison de être* for our efforts in mission/aid and other sectors: improving the lives of fellow humans, many who are impoverished, devoid of basic human rights, and living in places beset with protracted calamities, intractable conflicts, injustice, and inequities. We sincerely hope that this core sampler of solid materials will both inspire and instruct our colleagues around the world in their member care work and service to humanity.

References

Active Learning Network for Accountability and Performance in Humanitarian Action (ALNAP). 2012. *The state of the humanitarian system*. London: Overseas Development Institute.

Johnson, T. and P. Crossing. 2013. Christianity 2013. *International Bulletin of Mission Research* 37 (1): 32–33.

O'Donnell, K., ed. 2002. *Doing member care well: Perspectives and practices from around the world*. Pasadena: William Carey Library.

———. 2011. *Global member care: The pearls and perils of good practice*. Pasadena: William Carey Library.

United Nations Development Programme. 2013. *Human development report 2013: The rise of the South—Human progress in a diverse world*. New York: Author.

Note

Most of the URLs at the end of the chapters (References, Notes, Sources, and Related Resources) are located on the Global MCA website; for easier access: https://sites.google.com/site/globalmca/.

PART ONE

Overview

CROSSING SECTORS
FOR SERVING HUMANITY

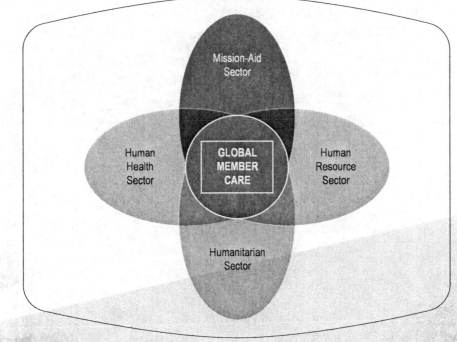

APPLICATIONS FOR
PART ONE

Keep in mind these five goals for crossing sectors as you go through the material.

In what ways could you connect and contribute?

- To support mission/aid workers in their well-being and effectiveness
- To support colleagues in other sectors via materials in the member care field
- To equip mission/aid workers with tools and opportunities for their work with others
- To equip member caregivers who directly work with vulnerable populations and others
- To stay informed as global citizens about current and crucial issues facing humanity

CHAPTER 1

Crossing Well

David Mazel

THERE WAS SO LITTLE OF ME
THAT I JUST COULDN'T COUNT
ON BEING TAKEN THAT SERIOUSLY.

I was standing on the curb, looking right and left, waiting for the cars to go by so that I could cross the street in the crosswalk. I was only six years old, and quite little, so I was afraid to venture across unless the coast was clear on both sides. It was true I had seen people more ample in size and years step out into the striped path and bring traffic to a grumbling halt, almost as if they possessed magical powers. But there was so little of me that I just couldn't count on being taken that seriously.

Finally the traffic cleared to the point where there was only one car coming from my right. It was a very old car, a rusty gray station wagon, with all sorts of household belongings piled in the back. Its tires were bald and so crushed under the weight of their load that they looked almost flat.

The car was chugging up the slight incline so slowly that I could easily have dashed across the street before it reached the crosswalk. But, taking no chances, I waited for it to chug by.

To my amazement, the old car stopped just short of the crosswalk, its brakes squeaking so loudly I almost plugged my ears. A middle-aged man at the wheel, with a face worn and homely as the moon, motioned for me to go ahead and cross, and he smiled encouragement.

This was the first car that had ever stopped to let me cross the street in the crosswalk, and I couldn't move for a few moments. It was crazy, I thought. When I needed cars to stop, so I wouldn't have to wait forever to cross, they zoomed on by. But when all I needed was for one old car to chug by, it stopped.

Finally I headed across, not merely walking but skipping. This was a bit of bravado, but I didn't want the man to think it was my first crossing, solo, while a car waited for me. And besides, I wanted to repay his patience with speediness.

As I passed in front of his car, I turned and gave him a shy smile. His smile in return rooted me on, but there was something in his eyes that confused me. I could have sworn I saw two brightnesses there that looked like tears. How could he be smiling and crying at the same time?

I reached the other side of the street; I at a skip and the car at a chug kept pace with each other for several moments. I was about to break into a run and show the man how I could tear around the corner ahead when he pulled up alongside a mailbox. I went over and tapped on his window. He rolled it down, and I held out my hand to take his letters and mail them for him.

This offer simply sprang out of the goodness of my heart, though it was not without a desire to show the man that I could operate a mailbox as well as use a crosswalk.

"You want to mail my letters for me?" he asked.

I was too shy to speak, but I nodded.

"You are very kind," he said, handing me the letters. "Thank you."

Just for a moment he looked as if he might cry. I was too young then to know that there are people who have taken such a beating in life that when someone is nice to them, good to them, they feel like crying. But instead he held back the brightnesses in his eyes and smiled at me. "You make me feel very important," he said.

I mailed his letters, and as he drove away we waved good-bye. I was sorry I hadn't told him that that's how he'd made me feel in the crosswalk—important. As if my life, young as it was, was entitled to the same stopping of traffic as anybody else's. But before his car disappeared, I did an absolutely spectacular run round the corner toward home, the run of a somebody; and if he was looking in his rear-view mirror, he saw me.

Source

Mazel, D. 1985. A Crossing. In *My Heart's World*, 15–17. Wild Rose, WI: Phunn Publishers. More stories by David Mazel: http://www.ufollow.com/search/fulltext/mazel/facet/author/david.mazel/. Reprinted by permission. For copies of this book, contact: Phunn Publishers, S5707 US Highway; Viroqua, WI 54665–8606 USA.

CHAPTER 2

Charting Your Course through the Sectors

Kelly O'Donnell, Member Care Associates

Can we really offer justice and freedom from want to a mid-twenty-first-century earth of perhaps nine billion people, one-third of whom may live in squalor and desperation? [Surprises and setbacks] should not deter us from responding as best we can, using our talents to improve this always mixed record of trying "to save generations from the scourge of war," "to reaffirm faith in fundamental human rights," and to promote "social progress and better standards of life in larger freedom." The original Preamble to the Charter of the United Nations had it right. The question is, can we do it? (Kennedy 2006, 279, 289)

This chapter is designed to help orient you to the process of crossing sectors. I discuss the nature of sectors and their relevance for member care in mission/aid. I also present ten lessons that I have learned and three suggestions for crossing sectors. You are encouraged to refer back to the suggestions at the end of this chapter periodically as you make your way through the material in this book. So have a go at charting your course through the sectors, serving humanity with good practice.

WHAT IS A SECTOR?

Sectors are fascinating. But what are they exactly? Mathematically, a sector is the area of a circle bounded by any two radii. (Think of a sector as being a triangular piece of pie cut from a round pie.) From this geometric definition emerges the concept of human sectors, or specialized groupings of *people*. For our purposes a sector is a distinct part of society (analogous to the area between two radii in a circle or a piece of pie) with a special albeit broad purpose. It is a large, amorphous yet recognizable block within the international community that provides different types of services and products to people. Each one is comprised of a wide array of people who are part of different organizations; influenced by various disciplines, practices, and goals; and intertwined with many related networks. A sector fundamentally is a *human* entity.

A prime example is the humanitarian sector, which overlaps with many other sectors, including the Christian mission sector. It would be accurate to refer to this sector as a *macro* sector (or even as the humanitarian *world*), which is comprised of many other sectors and subsectors. Just browse through any of the online issues of the *Humanitarian Exchange* from the Overseas Development Institute, and you will quickly see what we mean about the macrosector nature of the humanitarian world (http://www.odihpn.org). The humanitarian sector includes thousands of nongovernmental organizations, government and intergovernmental agencies, and groups from civil society including faith-based groups. These entities provide a myriad of worthwhile services such as medical care, military and civilian peacekeeping in conflict zones, relief response in natural disasters, human rights advocacy, HIV/ AIDS prevention, childhood education, maternal health care, water purification, and so many other areas. Collectively they represent much of humanity's concerted effort to alleviate human misery and promote human well-being.

SECTOR CONNECTORS

Trying to grasp *sectors* both conceptually and practically can thus be a bit of a challenge. It is akin to trying to grasp the sky. Both are readily observable. Both are highly influential. Yet both are hard to "contain," especially as they are so vast and full of variation. It can also be daunting and confusing entering into a new or even overlapping sector. It can feel very "foreign"—a bit like the proverbial fish out of water—as my wife, Michèle, and I found out in our initial efforts to connect and contribute to the global health (GH) sector.

Being psychologists with international experience helped us to enter into GH, of course. Yet coming from the faith-based mission sector with involvement in the humanitarian sector did not guarantee it would be easy to find our way into the mainstream of GH. Entering into different sectors is a dynamic process, not simply a static concept. It felt like a cross-cultural experience, exhilarating yet at times un-nerving as we were stretched by our encounters with a variety of highly experienced people, challenging ideas, and new areas of learning. This diverse sector though, like learning a new culture or language, started to make more sense over time. We attended conferences, workshops, and webinars; learned about projects and research studies; read materials and watched videos; served on committees and task forces; asked lots of questions; and above all met and talked with people from many NGOs, countries, and disciplines within the sector. We built relationships and saw how much we all had to offer each other, highlighting our mutual emphases and goals.

In short, the global health sector, especially the global *mental* health (GMH) part of it, which lies within the much larger human health sector, gradually became more familiar, less foreign, and even less perplexing. So the moral of this short account is to be encouraged as you cross into sectors and subsectors. Maintain your core values and worldview, but be open to new ideas. With time you will learn to navigate your way around the relevant parts of the sectoral terrain—and the sectoral sky!

Member Care: Going Macro

Crossing sectors fits well with the macro member care model from Doing Member Care Well. This model is used internationally and includes five concentric spheres: master care, self/mutual care, sender care, specialist care, and network care (O'Donnell 2002, p. 16). I am updating it here to include a sixth surrounding sphere, sector care (see fig. 2). This sixth sphere (and its four sectors) is permeable and overlaps with all the other spheres. All spheres thus can potentially influence each other via helpful exchanges of information, resources, people, etc. for mutual support, learning, and collaboration. Bringing all six spheres together in this new way reinforces the global purview and relevance of the member care field.

Each sphere in the member care model is summarized with a one-paragraph "Good Practice Principle" (ibid., ch. 1). Here is the summary for Sphere 6, sector care: People with member care responsibility in mission/aid stay in touch with sectors that are relevant for their work. They are willing to cross into new areas—emphases, projects, disciplines, and fields within related sectors—for mutual learning, exchanging resources, and developing skills. Crossing sectors includes a continuum of involvement which is carefully considered in view of one's primary focus in member care: being informed by, integrating with, and/or immersing in a given sector or part of a sector.

I think that intentionally crossing sectors is the next developmental phase for the member care field. What are some resources/practices and challenges/problems within these sectors? What can we learn from each other? How can our experiences in these sectors help us improve our member care efforts for supporting and managing mission/aid staff? We are entering into some new terrain while at the same time solidly building on the field's foundations and core focus on mission/aid workers. In so doing we seek to broaden and further shape the contours of good practice in member care.

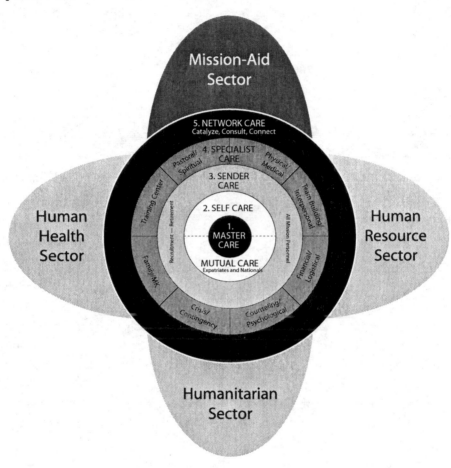

Figure 2
A macro, global model for member care, updated to include the sphere of "sector care"

SECTOR PAIR

Sector care also involves the learning process of "sector pair." Concepts and practices from the different sectors are paired with (related to) similar ones in the member care field. There are just so many helpful points of contact conceptually and practically! For example, thinking of personnel as "human resources having strategic worth" for the humanitarian sector can be compared with the concept of "human beings having intrinsic worth" for member care in the mission/aid sector. Another example is comparing the perspectives on safeguarding international/national staff in unstable settings: how much risk does one take, and what price is one willing to pay regardless of the faith- or non-faith-based motivations for one's service to humanity?

Another application of sector pair involves linking spirituality and core values. For many workers, healthy spirituality, including faith in God, is fundamental to their well-being and work effectiveness. For others, it can involve transcendent principles rather than referencing God per se. Some examples of these principles would be to "do good and do no harm" as derived from the Hippocratic Oath in the health-care fields, the "humanity principle" of the International Red Cross / Red Crescent Movement and similar groups which emphasizes protecting life and health without discrimination, the social responsibility commitment in the business/corporate sector to both "do well" (making money) and to "do good" (helping humans) (e.g., see Crutchfield and Grant 2012), the guiding sociopolitical value of "enlightened self-interest" emphasizing the well-being of others as one seeks his or her own benefit, or other benevolent principles reflected in one's life philosophy. *The point is that there are lots of points—connecting points—when crossing sectors!*

Relating Relevantly

Connecting with other sectors is not new. People, disciplines, fields, and sectors do it all the time! If we simply review how we spend our days—the people, media, and news events we encounter—we quickly realize just how much we actively interact with different sectors. One example with much relevance for member care and highlighted in chapter 3, is Families in Global Transition (http://www.figt.org). This organization brings together people from several sectors to share research and resources and discuss issues and strategies for supporting international, expatriate families. The annual conference, now in its fifteenth year, is a rich source of cross-fertilization and networking with participants from the humanitarian, mission, education, military, arts, human resources, business, and health sectors. The well-being of families, understandably, is a major common concern for all kinds of organizations that send staff and their families to international assignments.

The relevance of crossing sectors is clearly seen in the research by Johnson, Barrett, and Crossing, which advocates for greater interactions between the major religious blocs, especially Christians and non-Christians, in the service of humanity.

What percentage of non-Christians personally know a Christian?

. . . The [research] results are startling in the sense that Christians and non-Christians appear to be living in quite separate worlds. This distance has implications for Christian missions but is also problematic when it comes to dialogue, peace initiatives, environmental and health challenges, and many other areas of human interaction. Our hope is that highlighting the problem will help in planning solutions for the future. (2010, 29)

It is also seen in the need to work together—intergovernmental and civil society—in order to resolutely confront the "problems without passports" that plague humanity. As Shashi Tharoor, the former under-secretary-general of the United Nations, explains in his poignant article "The Good for Something UN":

The United Nations is a 20th-century organization facing a 21st-century challenge as an institution with impressive achievements but also haunting failures, one that mirrors not just the world's hopes but its inequalities and disagreements, and most important, one that has changed but needs to change further . . . The single greatest problem facing the United Nations is that there is no single greatest problem; rather there are a dozen different ones each day clamoring for attention. Some, like the crisis in Lebanon, the Palestinian situation and the nuclear programs in Iran and North Korea, are obvious and trying. Others we call "problems without passports"—issues that cross all frontiers uninvited, like climate change, drug trafficking, human rights, terrorism, epidemic diseases, and refugee movements. Their solutions, too, can recognize no frontiers because no one country or group of countries, however rich or powerful, can tackle them alone. (2006, 15)

And from a theological perspective, the relevance of multisector involvement is seen in the very nature of Christian mission, described here by David Hesselgrave in terms of Ralph Winter's "kingdom mission":

The Christian mission requires that we meet basic human needs for education, food, water, medicine, justice, and peace. As is evident in the Apostle John's assertion that Jesus was sent to "destroy the works of the devil" (1 John 3:8 NASB), our mission is to continue his earthly mission by undertaking the kind of organized research and enterprises that combat evil in all its forms—violence, injustice, poverty, environmental exploitation, drug trafficking, and disease. (2010, 196)

These three quotes suggest that it may in fact (always) be a good time for us as people—as well as for organizations, fields, and sectors—to review the parameters of our involvements, including "comfort zones," and consider how our work can increasingly relate to the plethora of world challenges (see also Stott, 2006).

TRANS-PRACTITIONERS

I want to consider another term that I recently introduced into the member care field: *trans-practitioner*. This term sounds a bit theoretical, but it is actually very practical. Trans-practitioners in member care and other fields are *learners-helpers*. They are skilled, passionate humans who intentionally cross a variety of sectors, usually with others, for mutual learning and good practice. They regularly "stretch" their experiential levels for the sake of benefiting other humans. Some may even be considered "social entrepreneurs": transformative forces who creatively and resolutely initiate and advocate for important causes, changes, and resources to help others (Bornstein 2004).

In addition to crossing sectors, trans-practitioners regularly cross other borders such as disciplines, organizations, networks, and cultures, and are particularly adept at working in "clusters" (groups of people with a diversity of backgrounds and skills focusing on a special topic/problem area). Further, they also willingly cross "deserts" as they sojourn through the refining hardships in life and work. Trans-practitioners in member care and other fields are thus committed to *go broadly* as helpers (connecting and contributing professionally with sectors, disciplines, networks, cultures) and to *grow deeply* as persons (developing personally through difficulties and through their commitment to lifelong learning). Trans-practitioners are *good practitioners* who help pave the way forward in our increasingly globalizing world.

LESSONS LEARNED:
TEN PRACTICAL EXAMPLES FOR GOOD *GLOBAL* PRACTICE

As shared previously, cross-sector experiences are a two-way street. We learn and receive input from other sectors, even as we do from other disciplines and we offer input to other sectors. This section contains ten important lessons (perspectives, principles, and practices) that my wife, Michèle, and I have learned from crossing sectors over the years. Many of the lessons listed in this section are from the humanitarian sector. This makes sense, of course, given the major overlap between member care for mission/aid and human resource management in humanitarian assistance.

One important caveat is that sometimes involvement in the mission/aid sector can be viewed with suspicion. Much of this seems related to a view that faith-based mission/aid is being done by people who proselytize others, inappropriately try to change others' culture and spiritual beliefs, are afraid of diversity, and make assistance contingent on another's religion—all taboos in the humanitarian sector in particular. Likewise, there can be the view (and suspicion) within the faith-based sector that "secular" humanitarian agencies are ignoring or not adequately addressing the spiritual needs of the people with whom they work, that Western commercialism and "relaxed" sexuality will negatively influence and alienate those in need unless other values are modeled, that those who have well-defined moral values are intolerant of others, and that there is a bias against aid workers whose spiritual values motivate them to do good. Misperceptions and genuine concerns are also present when we try to cross sectors and learn from one another. For some helpful perspectives on such contrasting and common views, see chapter 13.

TEN LESSONS FROM CROSSING SECTORS

1. Good management of aid workers is just as important as good support for these workers. Skilled managers and helpful policies are also key resources for worker well-being. Both management and support have become two sides of the "member care coin" for us as we practice member care in mission/aid (People In Aid 2003). See chapter 29.

2. Health hazards including traffic/household accidents and malarial/HIV infections must be included in preassignment training for staff. They are also to be monitored as physical risk factors in various settings. There is thus much more involved in the well-being of workers than approaches to individual stress management (InterHealth and People In Aid 2003). See chapter 30.

3. Sending agencies are not simply accountable to senior leaders or to God. There are recognized codes to follow and standards for good practice and benchmarks to which to aspire. The human resources program must be evaluated regularly in terms of its relevance, and the same is true for any member care program (Management Sciences for Health 2005). See chapters 12 and 26.

4. The collective agreement of humanity, recognized by the vast majority of governments/countries, is that human rights are inalienable, interdependent, and indivisible. These rights are founded upon respect for the dignity and worth of human beings. In particular, religious liberty, via the freedom to have or not have a religion, is a universal right. Human rights are an additional foundation upon which to build the practice of member care (in addition to Judeo-Christian Scripture and good practice/ethics codes) (United Nations General Assembly 1948). See chapters 5 and 15.

5. Aid is not to be used to further a particular religious or political viewpoint. Aid is meant to be neutral, and thus the religious/political beliefs of a recipient person or community do not influence whether they receive aid. The corollary is to be very careful when you share your religious/political beliefs with vulnerable populations (even on request or as "a normal part of talking about life") who are in some important ways dependent upon you (International Federation of Red Cross and Red Crescent Societies 1994). See chapter 7.

6. Mental health and psychosocial support is just as important as physical support when providing relief/development services and primary health-care services. Getting psychological support, for example, to people and communities in disaster settings can help facilitate recovery—to foster *active survivors rather than passive victims* (Inter-Agency Standing Committee 2007; World Federation for Mental Health 2009). See chapters 23 and 24.

7. People in areas of conflict often experience psychological wounds. Yet many also yearn more for social justice than they do for some type of healing for "inner trauma." Do not *de facto* import Western approaches for trauma care into areas where there are conflicts/calamities. People have social memories associated with trauma and not just individual memories. Help faith-based mission workers understand the sociopolitical context and justice yearnings of the people with whom they work (various sources including Summerfield 1998). See chapters 23–25.

8. Corruption is widespread throughout the world, including the humanitarian sector. It is also rampant in the faith-based mission/aid sector. There are plenty of people who will gladly pray for you Sunday and then prey on you Monday. Corruption is not simply limited to financial matters, but rather it is based on the abuse of entrusted power for personal gain. In Christian settings, think of it as "crimianity"—the nefarious substitution of criminal vice for Christian virtue (Bailey 2008). See chapter 10.

9. Transparency and accountability are core practices at all levels of mission/aid. The leaders in the United Nations High Commissioner for Refugees (UNHCR) were committed to assess the quality and influence of the organization's culture on its staff and operations. They also brought in an independent researcher to conduct the assessment. The agency leaders also published a version of the subsequent report online so that the public and its stakeholders could see it. Such transparency/ accountability is a good model for the mission/aid sector and other sectors (Wigley 2005). See chapter 32.

10. Humanitarian journalism is essential to accurately research and inform the public and build global awareness, including informing mission/aid workers, about international events. The humanitarian media is a key part of the humanitarian workforce and should be considered as a viable career/emphasis for mission/ aid workers to undertake as well (Hieber 2001).

The list of lessons goes on and on. And in addition to the humanitarian sector, there are so many opportunities to connect and contribute with various other sectors, such as the international business, education, and diplomatic service sectors.

CHARTING A COURSE:
THREE SUGGESTIONS FOR CROSSING SECTORS

So how do we in fact go about navigating the vast terrain of sectors? Here are three suggestions to further orient us, described in terms of issues, involvements, and influences.

1. Issues: focus on the areas that matter to you. What are you already interested in or involved in? What are you passionate about? What are you naturally motivated to learn a lot more about? Take it further by exploring what is happening in these areas within other sectors. Be prepared to expand your "experiential boundaries," knowing that it can be a bit uncomfortable but also rewarding. It may take time and effort to significantly connect and contribute. Don't go alone but get involved with others. Find compatible colleagues with similar interests and key groups and networks in which you can be part. Need more ideas about an area of focus? Just browse through the articles in this book, including the URLs to the many short video pieces!

2. Involvements: choose your level of activity in crossing sectors. The process of crossing sectors can be understood as a "continuum of involvement." This continuum has three reference points to help identify the degree to which we may want to get involved in a given sector.

←——————————————————————————————→

1. Informed   2. Integrated   3. Immersed

The continuum begins with more minor involvement in a sector, such as reading the quarterly magazines from a human resources organization about things like staff selection and people management (*informed*). It then proceeds to a midpoint and the inclusion of a sector or parts of a sector in one's work such as travel health resources for preventing road traffic accidents and malarial infections (*integrated*). The end of the continuum could involve becoming a recognized part of another sector such as working part time as a human rights advocate in a nongovernmental organization or developing culturally relevant psychosocial support for victims of gender violence (*immersed*). We note that people can also be involved with different sectors informally or formally, occasionally or regularly, conceptually or experientially, and so on.

Crossing sectors might get all of our adrenalin flowing, but as we have learned, it requires clear personal boundaries. If we light a candle at both ends, it gets used up twice as fast. So too much of a good thing is disruptive and can certainly distract us from work priorities. This means we may have to bypass many of the wonderful materials/opportunities that come our way from different conferences, organizations, disciplines, etc., and at times inundate our offices and email boxes. Nonetheless it is still well worth the effort, provided that we draw our parameters and pace ourselves well. Crossing sectors is a practice to intentionally and carefully build into our lifestyle and job description.

3. Influences: get a grid. What has influenced your desire and ability to cross sectors? The grid below can help you to get a better handle on some of the main influences. Use it to track some of the main influences that have personally affected your involvement in crossing sectors. To give you an idea, I have listed some examples from my own life for each of the six categories. As you review your past, you may very well get a better sense of what your future course might look like (the last part of the grid).

CROSSING SECTORS: PERSONAL INFLUENCES

Principles/	1. The "unity of truth" across time and subjects
Beliefs	2. The imago Dei as a basis for loving truth and peace
	3. Moral duty and "blessed to be a blessing"
	4. Resilient virtue is stronger than resilient evil
	5. Human history has a direction and purpose

Documents/	1. Universal Declaration of Human Rights (United Nations, 1948)
Materials	2. *Doing Member Care Well* (2002)
	3. Partnership principles (general)

Organizations/	1. People In Aid (human resources)
Groups	2. Overseas Development Institute (humanitarian assistance)
	3. World Health Organization (global health)
	4. Movement for Global Mental Health
	5. Member Care Associates

People/Models	1. My parents
	2. My wife
	3. The poor in Mexico

Milestones/	1. Spanish classes and Latin America (1970–83)
Gravestones	2. Integration of psychology and theology doctorate (1978–84)
	3. Perspectives on the World Christian Movement course (1981)
	4. "We must develop a macro model for member care" (1990)
	5. Global Member Care Resources affiliation (MemCa, 1998–2006)

Crossing Sectors: Charting A Future Course

1. Greater involvement in global mental health and with mental health as mission
2. Greater involvement in training/consultation within the mission/aid sector
3. Greater involvement in international affairs/international relations

FINAL THOUGHTS

Perseverance and lots of mutual support are needed as we chart our course for crossing sectors. I encourage us all to form a caravan of colleagues and to travel together for the long haul. My conclusion in a recent article about global mental health is also applicable to those of us working with and across sectors.

> Keep in the forefront the need for "selfless moral struggle" in partnering with others (Patel et al. 2011, 90) and the "duty and choice to risk one's own rights and wellbeing" on behalf of vulnerable populations (O'Donnell 2011a, 187). Finally, and in spite of challenges or setbacks, let's celebrate our . . . progress—the "social progress and better standards of life in larger freedom"—as envisioned by the United Nations Charter and as yearned for by humans everywhere. (O'Donnell 2012, 201)

REFERENCES

Bailey, S. 2008. Need and greed: Corruption risks, perceptions, and prevention in humanitarian assistance. Humanitarian Policy Group. http://www.odi.org.uk/resources/details. asp?id=2385&title=corruption-risks-perceptions-prevention-humanitarian-assistance.

Bornstein, D. 2004. *How to change the world: Social entrepreneurs and the power of new ideas.* Oxford: Oxford University Press.

Crutchfield, L., and H. Grant. 2012. *Forces for good: The six practices of high-impact non-profits* (rev. ed.). San Francisco: Jossey-Bass.

Hesselgrave, D. 2010. What happens when apostles disagree. *Evangelical Missions Quarterly* 46: 190–97.

Hieber, L. 2001. *Lifeline media: Reaching populations in crisis; A guide to developing media projects in conflict situations.* Geneva: Media Action International. http://www.preventionweb. net/files/636_10303.pdf.

Inter-Agency Standing Committee. 2007. IASC guidelines on mental health and psychosocial support in emergency settings. Geneva: Inter-Agency Standing Committee. http://www.who.int/ mental_health/emergencies/guidelines_iasc_mental_health_psychosocial_april_2008.pdf.

InterHealth, and People in Aid. 2003. Preventing accidents: Guidelines for the aid sector. London: InterHealth and People in Aid. http://www.eisf.eu/resources/home.asp.

International Federation of Red Cross and Red Crescent Societies. 1994. The code of conduct for the International Red Cross and Red Crescent Movement and NGOs in disaster relief. Geneva: International Federation of Red Cross and Red Crescent Societies. http://www.ifrc. org/en/publications-and-reports/code-of-conduct/.

Johnson, T., D. Barrett, and P. Crossing. 2010. Christianity 2010: A view from the new *Atlas of Global Christianity. International Bulletin of Missionary Research* 34: 29–36. http://www. internationalbulletin.org/archive/all/2010/1.

Kennedy, P. 2006. *The parliament of man: The past, present, and future of the United Nations.* New York: Vintage Books.

Management Sciences for Health. 2005. Human resource management assessment instrument for NGOs and public sector health organizations. Boston: Management Sciences for Health. http://www.msh.org/Documents/HealthManagersToolkit/upload/HRM-Rapid-Assessment-Tool-for-Public-and-Private-Sector-Health-Organizations.pdf.

O'Donnell, K., ed. 2002. *Doing member care well: Perspectives and practices from around the world*. Pasadena: William Carey Library.

———. 2011. *Global member care—volume one: The pearls and perils of good practice*. Pasadena: William Carey Library.

———. 2012. Global mental health: A resource primer for exploring the domain. *International Perspectives in Psychology: Research, Practice, Consultation* 1, no. 3 (July): 191–205.

Patel, V., P. Collins, J. Copeland, R. Kakuma, S. Katontoka, J. Lamichhane, S. Naik, and S. Skeen. 2011. The movement for global mental health. *British Journal of Psychiatry* 198: 88–90.

People In Aid. 2003. Code of good practice in the management and support of aid personnel. London: People In Aid. http://peopleinaid.org/code/.

Stott, J. 2006. *Issues facing Christians today* (4th ed.). Grand Rapids, MI: Zondervan.

Summerfield, D. 1998. The social experience of war and some issues for the humanitarian field. In *Rethinking the trauma of war*, ed. P. Bracken and C. Petty, 9–37. London: Free Association.

Tharoor, S. 2006. The good for something UN. *Newsweek*, September 4. http://tharoor.in/archives/st-for-sg/article-in-newsweek/.

United Nations General Assembly. 1948. Universal declaration of human rights. http://www.ohchr.org/EN/UDHR/Pages/SearchByLang.aspx.

Wigley, B. 2005. The state of the UNHCR's organization culture. Geneva: United Nations High Commissioner for Refugees, Evaluation and Policy Analysis Unit. http://www.unhcr.org/cgi-bin/texis/vtx/home/opendocPDFViewer.html?docid=428db1d62&query=Barb%20Wigley.

World Federation for Mental Health. 2009. Mental health in primary care: Enhancing treatment and promoting mental health. World Federation for Mental Health. http://www.wfmh.org/WMHD%2009%20Languages/ENGLISH%20WMHD09.pdf.

World Health Organization, and World Organization of Family Doctors. 2008. Integrating mental health into primary care: A global perspective. Geneva: World Health Organization. http://www.who.int/mental_health/policy/services/mentalhealthintoprimarycare/en/index.html.

World Health Organization. 2010. Framework for action on interprofessional education and collaborative practice. Geneva: World Health Organization. http://www.who.int/hrh/resources/framework_action/en/index.html.

EDITORS' NOTES

For more information about Member Care Associates: www.membercare.org.

Related Resources

Video: United Nations. "United Nations Year in Review 2012." (United Nations, News and Media [also see other annual reviews]. http://www.epacha.org/Pages/United_Nations_Year_in_Review_2012.aspx.

CONGO. 2012. Compilation of important UN resources, 2012. http://membercareassociates.org/wp-content/uploads/2012/07/Examples-of-important-UN-resources-20121.pdf.

Dorr, D. July–August 2005. Who cares about the Millennium Development Goals? *Mission Frontiers* 27 (4): 14–16.

Dower, N. 2003. *An introduction to global citizenship*. Edinburgh: Edinburgh University Press.

Johnstone, P. 2011. *The future of the global church*. Downers Grove, IL, USA: Intervarsity Press.

O'Donnell, K. 2013. *Global Integration*. http://membercareassociates.org/?page_id=373.

Sciora, R., and A. Stevenson. 2011. *Planet UN: The United Nations confronting the challenges of the twenty-first century*. Geneva: Editions de Tricorne.

Tharoor, S. 2003. Why America still needs the United Nations. *Foreign Affairs*. September–October. http://www.cfr.org/world/why-america-still-needs-united-nations/p7567.

United Nations. 2000. Millennium development goals. http://www.un.org/millenniumgoals/.

World Happiness Report. 2012. John Helliwel, Richard Layard, Jeffery Sachs (Editors). Earth Institute, Columbia University. http://www.earth.columbia.edu/sitefiles/file/Sachs%20Writing/2012/World%20Happiness%20Report.pdf.

CHAPTER 3

Sector Connectors:
Families in Global Transition

Ruth E. Van Reken, Lois Bushong, and Tina Quick

The year was 1998. It was clear that there were now many people working in the growing field of international family transitions, building on the work of pioneers such as the Useems, Dave Pollock, Norma McCaig, and many others. But it took four women with varying international backgrounds sitting around Ruth Van Reken's kitchen table to dream about creating a forum where participants could discuss topics relevant to globally mobile families from many sectors, including international business, foreign service, education, military, mission, and NGO communities. These women wanted not only to help internationally mobile families themselves, but also to increase awareness among those who worked with such families. They believed bringing such diverse groups together for meaningful dialogue would expedite for all the capacity to recognize and navigate the challenges of this lifestyle successfully so the gifts could also be recognized and used well.

This chapter will share how three individuals became involved in this cross-sector dialogue through the organization and annual conference now called Families in Global Transition (FIGT). It will include a discussion of lessons learned in the process of choosing a cross-sector approach and give principles that have kept this cross-sector organization strong. Special resources to help others reach a similar goal are listed at the end.

THE ROOTS OF THE FIGT VISION
THOUGHTS FROM COFOUNDER RUTH E. VAN REKEN

Sometimes it is easy to believe that our experiences in one international community are so different from others' that there is little reason to try and relate to one another. Certainly as a child growing up in a mission community in the 1940s and 1950s, it seemed clear to me that my friends who were children of the British colonialists governing our area of Nigeria lived in a different stratosphere than I did. Their parents bought weekly groceries at Kingsway—the store that imported Golden Syrup and Marmite from Britain. We went to the open air market and battled the flies swarming the freshly cut meat as we bargained with local vendors for our food.

Initially this feeling of separateness continued when I returned to Africa as an adult in 1976. My husband, a pediatrician, had been seconded from our mission organization to work at the Liberian government's public hospital and medical school, where basic supplies were often limited. What did we have in common with the international banker's family who had servants caring for their mansion and a driver taking the children to an expensive private school each day? Once more, it seemed we all lived in separate worlds.

But these feelings began to change when a banker's wife became part of my first extended cross-sector encounter during the early 1980s there in Liberia. A group of women from many sectors—ambassadors' wives, women married to international businessmen, local citizens, NGO and USAID workers, plus another friend and I from the mission community—began to meet weekly for mutual support and spiritual growth. Many in our group were also in cross-cultural marriages. In this close, personal environment, I soon discovered that despite all the external differences in our circumstances, there were countless ways we instantly connected with each other at the emotional and spiritual level.

CROSS-SECTOR MINDSETS

These were the initial days for me to begin seeing beyond the borders of my own mission sector. The real boost towards having a truly cross-sector mindset came in 1987 when I met Norma McCaig, founder of Global Nomads International, at the International Conference on Missionary Kids (ICMK) in Quito, Ecuador. Norma had grown up in the Philippines and India because her American father worked for an international pharmaceutical company. During her years in India, however, she had gone to a school mainly for missionary children. After meeting Dave Pollock at another conference, Norma became convinced that Third Culture Kids (TCKs) of all backgrounds shared many commonalities in their essential experience, despite the differences in their sponsoring organizations or companies (Norma called them "global nomads" because she didn't like being called a kid in her adult years). She attended ICMK Quito as the only nonmission representative to test out her hypothesis. In the end, Norma invited me to present at the first-ever

Global Nomads International (GNI) conference she organized in December 1988 in Washington, DC.

At first I didn't say yes, fearing that I would have nothing to say to this wider community of those who had grown up internationally but in very different worlds than my faith-based, mission sector. But Norma soon convinced me that we all had more things in common than differences, and so I went, and she was right. As we who had grown up globally shared our stories, we laughed and cried together, whether or not we came from the same sector. It was an amazing, life-shaping experience for me to realize that the sometimes "us/them" view of the world in the mission sector could be simplified to "us."

KITCHEN TABLES AS GLOBAL PLATFORMS

Fast forward: by 1998 my husband and I had been living in Indiana for twelve years, and I had become a member of the Association of International Women. Several of us who had lived "overseas" for different reasons began to realize that the issues talked about in conferences such as the three ICMKs (1984, 1986, 1989) or the GNI conferences also applied to our local community of expatriates. However, topics related to global family living seemed almost invisible to the expatriate families living in the heartland of the USA. Such topics were also unrecognized by those working with them such as human resource personnel, local educators, or even therapists. None of the wonderful seminars going on across the ocean or even in Washington, DC, were happening locally.

Three friends—Margie Becker, Christine Dowdeswell, Janet Fischer—and I decided to do something about that. We met for coffee one day around my kitchen table and began to dream of how we could make the issues that concerned internationally mobile families visible to our local community. We decided to have a one-day seminar. Our vision was that if we could bring together those living this global lifestyle with those working with them, we could create a dialogue that would be good for all. And thus Families in Global Transition was born.

We began to strategize on who could help us. After all, we were basically four housewives with a dream and no money! What could we do?

Fortunately I recalled many years ago talking with Jill Briscoe, an author and speaker who came to our community in Liberia for special meetings in 1980. I asked her the secret of her success. She gave me life-changing words: "Ruth, when you don't know how to do everything, ask God what is the one thing you can do and do that one thing. Too many people never do anything because they can't do everything. But if you do the next 'one thing' that you can do, then when you look back, you'll be surprised to see what has grown, one step at a time."

With that advice in mind, we looked at what we could do despite all the seeming setbacks. We called Dave Pollock, an expert in TCKs and expatriate transition. He had begun his work in the mission community but by 1998 had already expanded into other areas, including offering seminars for the United Nations and the Foreign Service Youth in Washington, DC. Amazingly he was free that May 16, 1998, and agreed to come as our plenary speaker. Truly, doing the one-step-at-a-time routine, we found a venue at a local international company (Eli Lilly), devised a program, and managed to get eighty-five people there!

Relational Roots

One great thing about a cross-sector approach is how each of us brings to the table things that may be so "normal" in our backgrounds, yet we don't know that they may not be so for others. I do believe my mission background unknowingly added an important dimension to FIGT. For whatever reason, most conferences among mission workers make it a priority initially to establish relationships with other attendees. We want to know who we are so we can find those of like interest to brainstorm with, to encourage one another, etc. It is part of our collective ethos. Since I didn't realize this might not be a universal value, I proceeded to set things up "mission style" for that first FIGT. I invited all who were attending to come to an open house at my home and meet Dave Pollock the night before. Our living room was jammed full of people who listened intently as Dave stood on the stairs so all could see him while he gave a little preview of the next day's topics. When we met the next day, we were already in the process of becoming friends!

Challenges and Practicalities

But challenges remained. Convincing each sector that they had anything in common with other groups wasn't always an easy sell. Until they came, many remained doubters that, for example, those in the mission sector and those in the corporate sector would have much in common. In addition, as the conference grew, I recognized that while my gifts of enthusiasm and vision were great, doing the practical matters of a conference of this magnitude was beyond me or our committee. We knew we had birthed a baby, but we needed someone to adopt the child! So these are some lessons I would share from learning not only how to birth the baby, but to give it up for adoption.

- You can't do it alone. Find others who share the vision and work together, respecting and using *all* the gifts such as:
  - the visionary—someone who sees the big picture, the end product, even if they don't yet know how to get there;
  - the realist—someone who does, in fact, ask the "How do you plan to do that?" questions; and
  - the organizer—those who can keep track of the details while the visionary keeps soaring with dreams and the realist keeps trying to keep things well-grounded on the earth!
- Be humble. You may have a vision, but you don't know it all yet. Begin to model the idea of learning from other sectors by being willing and eager to do so yourself.
- Recognize it's going to take time for others to catch the vision. Everyone won't instantly get it, but some will. Work with them and just keep doing that next "one thing" that you can do.
- If you, like me, are a visionary and not an organizer, get out of the way when different skill sets are needed. The innovation is not yours to hoard. It is yours to share.

Birthing FIGT happened by exercising the first three principles above. But preserving FIGT meant handing it over to others with different skill sets and experience. Lois Bushong and Tina Quick are two of the people who have carried it forward to places I could never have imagined, so they will tell you what happened next and where FIGT is headed today.

Board Development
Thoughts from former board member Lois Bushong

EXPANDING MY CROSS-SECTOR VISION

As a child growing up in Honduras, I played with local children, the kids of fellow mission workers, and other expat friends whose parents worked for international corporations, embassies, or even the military. Intuitively I grew up knowing I shared many similarities with others from very different backgrounds and worlds. A person's sector rarely played a part in determining who would make a good friend.

Move forward forty years. By then I had served ten years as a mission worker in Latin America, worked in a mission headquarters in the US, gone back to graduate school for a second master's degree, and was now a new marriage and family therapist in Indianapolis, Indiana. I wanted to reach out to a more international clientele, including others who had lived an internationally mobile childhood as I had. At that point, however, I only knew the terms "missionary kid" and "military brat" to describe such an experience.

One day in 1998 a client came into my office and told me he had just spent several hours in a woman's home, and as he listened to her stories of childhood, he was reminded of me. Convinced that I would enjoy her friendship, he gave me the name and phone number of Ruth Van Reken.

When I called Ruth, she invited me to a conference taking place a few days later. Ruth explained her dream that this "first of its kind" conference would bring together people from various international organizations or companies to discuss how to best help families adjust well while moving around the world. Feeling intrigued, I agreed to go to Ruth's house for a preconference open house and the one-day conference at the Lilly Center in Indianapolis and watched firsthand the birth of FIGT. I had no idea that, by attending this conference and learning new concepts as well as meeting new people, my life would change forever.

I definitely wanted to be part of this new happening and eagerly accepted an invitation to become a board member two years later. During that time I had learned a few more lessons while attending the second and third conferences:

- The first was that it will take a little time for most people to be comfortable with those they have previously seen as "other."
- The second lesson involved realizing that, to sustain the dream of what FIGT would be and to carry it forward, there had to be a clear organizational structure around it.
  - No amount of personal enthusiasm or goodwill alone could continue to carry the vision.
  - We would need a team with defined roles so that no matter who held each position the tasks would be clear for them.

Overcoming Initial Hesitancies Regarding the "Other"

The second FIGT conference expanded to two days, and it soon became obvious that participants and presenters from the various sectors weren't quite sure what they should and should not share with those from other sectors. Each sector tended to sit together at mealtime or breaks, not quite convinced that they had much in common with those from other backgrounds, particularly when it came to the idea of mixing up the more traditionally secular communities with the religious groups. How would they all get along?

But the first "aha" moment came for us all during the "Best Practices Panel Discussion," when panelists representing corporate, military, mission, and diplomatic sectors shared how they dealt with specific challenges their communities faced in regard to global transitions of families. As we in the audience watched them get excited via learning from one another, the energy suddenly went from the panel into the audience—and we too got it! We were all members of *one* family. The sector labels were dropped, and the focus became how to deal effectively with the similar challenges before us in all sectors.

Building a Board

By the third conference it had become obvious that although Ruth Van Reken had done a beautiful job of casting the vision, the results were now growing beyond her organizational skills. Many others were becoming excited about the vision and had dreams for even larger places it could go. If that was going to happen, the organizational structure had to change from a few individuals trying to put a program together for a more formal and legally sound organism. Beverly Roman, a woman who had developed her own company to publish and distribute the practical "how-to" books for families on the move both nationally and internationally, became the first official president of the board and asked me to join the board as one of the representatives of the mission community.

A few months later, Beverly asked me to be the chair of the Nominations and Board Development Committee. The committee felt it was imperative to have our board reflect the mission, military, corporate, educational, and diplomatic communities. Because our focus was to help the entire family in their transitions around the world, we also wanted a representation of the Adult Third Culture Kid (ATCK).

The board that formed did amazing work as they wrote up documents and policies on what each part of this new organization would look like. We researched how best to register the organization in the USA and we spent hours on end going over the wording for our bylaws. Each board member invested countless hours in FIGT because they believed so strongly in its mission. Keeping the balance between sectors on the board has been a continual challenge through the years, but we continue to believe it is a key part of our success. Even as the board works together, it is demonstrating to the conference how to drop the sector labels and focus on the overall purpose of FIGT.

In summary: How did we cross sectors effectively? I believe we did it by modeling it on all levels of the organization, from the board of directors to the conference program, and the many conversations that took place on the side.

The Conference and Beyond
Thoughts from board member Tina Quick

THE *FIGT* BOARD OF DIRECTORS

Soon after my first FIGT conference in 2007, then-president of the board Sandy Thomas, USA *Girl Scouts* Overseas Director, invited me to become a member of the FIGT board of directors and shadow Lois, who was by then cochair of the program committee, before Lois transitioned out of her board term. As a military ATCK myself who, as an adult, raised my own TCKs in part of the NGO community, I was deeply honored to be a part of this team of dedicated professionals and was immediately struck at my first board meeting by how there were representatives of each of the sectors. It is also interesting to note how the board has developed from a mostly North American group to a much more international one. At the 2011 meeting we had representatives from the US, Canada, England, and Switzerland. We are seeing that trend continue into 2013 and onward. The following are the statements we have developed and the programs we are trying to implement.

VISION AND MISSION OF *FIGT*

FIGT has been a leader in the worldwide expatriate community to empower families and those who serve them in global transition. FIGT has also served as the premier educational resource for families in global transition and the organizations and service providers who are involved with these families. We build our community by bringing together corporate, diplomatic, academic, education, military, mission, and NGO sectors, and share and develop knowledge, research, and skills in addressing global relocation issues.

We believe:

- Families empowered with the resources to be self-sufficient will thrive while on assignment.
- Employees whose families are well supported will be more fully productive and engaged.
- A global community will thrive when the various relevant sectors are included.

Our passion: laying the foundation for enhanced and transformative global experience.

Our products: leading-edge conferences, workshops, webinars, and educational tools.

THE ANNUAL *FIGT* CONFERENCE

Our archives document that at the first conference in 1998, "of the 85 attendees, over half traveled from outside Indianapolis." By the year 2000 the total attendance grew to "120 people, with representatives from seven countries outside the United States." In 2012 these numbers mushroomed to just over 200 participants.

Another trend that delights us is the number of non–North American proposals that are submitted each year. Since Dr. Copeland took over as program director in 2007, she has seen that number more than double. Of the speakers chosen to present at the 2012 conference, almost all have lived outside their passport country as adults with about one-third currently doing so, about half are TCKs, and about one-fourth are dual citizens. Although we are in the US, about one-third of the participants are non-US citizens from fourteen different countries throughout North and South America, Europe, the Middle East, Asia, and Australia. Half are first-time attendees, and 60 percent are first-time presenters (which we encourage so that there is always fresh blood and ideas in our program). Our attendees bring wonderful diversity in a number of ways other than national culture through their rich and varied experiences in life.

Sector representation has also changed dramatically over the years. In the beginning the number of attendees from faith-based mission organizations was substantial, but now we are seeing the number of attendees from the educational sector steadily expanding. Military presence has been sporadic as their attendance is directly correlated to the US military's international engagements. Since moving the annual conference to Washington, DC, in 2011, the US State Department's presence has grown steadily, and we are beginning to see international human resources and corporate business numbers rising. Recently a growing number of attendees are service providers for expatriate families, including coaches, cross-cultural trainers, language and education specialists, destination service providers, and more. In the last few years, however, some of our numbers from specific sectors have dropped significantly due to the economic crisis and the increased costs to attend the FIGT conference. The FIGT board continues to grapple with how to make the conference cost effective as well as maintain the high quality in order to attract all of the sectors.

From the first conference and onward, we have covered topics particularly related to TCKs and "accompanying partners/spouses." Each year the seminars increase our understanding of these areas and many more aspects of an international lifestyle. Recent topics have included raising bilingual children, repatriation issues, TCKs returning for college, death and divorce while living abroad, and the need for cross-cultural training. Some specific sessions explored areas such as "Understanding How Confucianism Affects the Korean TCK Experience," "Eating Disorders and TCKs," "The Role of Food in the Expat Experience," and "How Repatriation of Asian TCKs Differs from Western TCKs' Repatriation." We have also had some fabulous presentations of artwork and film premieres. Researchers present their findings in both concurrent sessions and posters. Currently we are witnessing a move from the traditional TCK focus to much broader issues that highlight the new concepts and terminology needed to help us keep up with what is happening in our globalizing world. These include such terms as cross-cultural kid (CCK), STARS (Spouses Transitioning and Repatriating Successfully), "lovepats" (people relocating for romantic interests), nationality vs. citizenship, global identity, cultural intelligence, "patchwork families," etc.

Our opening plenary in 2012 had Roy Dunbar—a CCK himself of Jamaican origin who grew up in England—comparing the ways those from Rwanda who were raised outside their country because of war were using the cross-cultural gifts gained from that experience to help rebuild their country now (in a similar way that ATCK leaders of various Fortune 500 companies were using their gifts of a cross-cultural childhood in doing international business). Eva László-Herbert, who grew up in what was then Transylvania, spoke on the forced transitions of her life as she grew up in war-torn Europe. In both sessions it became obvious that the multitude of ways many families experience global transition in our ever-changing world is a topic we must continue to explore. We believe lessons learned in the traditional expat community can be applied to countless other situations as well, and it is part of our commitment for the future. Truly FIGT has become a cutting-edge place where the expanding knowledge regarding globally mobile families is shared and disseminated.

GUIDING PRINCIPLES FOR THE FIGT CONFERENCE

So how has the FIGT conference become such a cutting-edge event? First, of course, the annual conference provides a unique and hospitable forum where networking opportunities are central for all who attend. Networking and knowledge exchange are some of the biggest draws of the conference. Where else can you formally and informally discuss good practices for the same situations you or your organization face with colleagues from your sector or other sectors? In addition, however, the program is shaped with great intentionality from the proposals submitted. Some of the principles or themes that guide us as we seek to maintain both the ethos and the pioneering efforts of FIGT include the following:

- Time for networking is prioritized and encouraged.
- Although we come from different sectors, we find common ground.
- In program selection and development, people speak of their own experiences but endeavor to extend the lessons across the sectors.
- FIGT especially welcomes high-quality, targeted, and practical research studies that offer solutions and tools for understanding the lives of globally mobile individuals and families.
- Presentations by experienced cross-cultural practitioners and entre-preneurs typically make up the bulk of FIGT's value-laden program. These presentations offer resources for colleagues in the field in the form of reviews of good practices, details of successful programs for families, overviews of models, cultural analyses, advice based on professional experience, and the like.
- A strong preference is given to cross-sector topics and presenters, as well as those with non-Western, "understudied," or underrepresented perspectives.

- We strive for equal representation of all sectors when inviting speakers to present.
- Presenters are asked to have tangible take-aways from their sessions that attendees can bring back to their own sector.
- We facilitate people exploring outside their sector but then regrouping within their sectors in order to share lessons learned. An example of this is the "early bird" sessions on the last morning of the conference where sectors meet by tables at breakfast and continue the conversations until the start of the day's program.
- The overall focus of the conference is the family and not the specific sectors.
- The value of personal stories and their relevance across the sectors is emphasized.

RESEARCH COMES TO LIFE

FIGT emphasizes and encourages research on and the practical implications for globally mobile families. For years researchers had been informally meeting together at the annual conference to discuss formulating a network to, among other things:

- build relationships among researchers, and between researchers and those they study,
- increase awareness about emerging research,
- support and guide research using good practices and ethics, and
- promote and share multidisciplinary research and literature.

In 2011 the FIGT Research Network was further developed and launched within the FIGT community. The purpose of the Research Network is "to cultivate, support, and disseminate rigorous research pertinent to families in global transition."

WHERE IS FIGT GOING?

Regional affiliates

The board had long been contemplating a feasible approach for keeping the spark and energy of the annual conference alive throughout the remainder of the year. The idea of regional affiliates was tabled more than a few times until the October 2009 board meeting when Anne Copeland, a researcher into the effects of global transition on accompanying partners, and I, both from the Boston area, agreed to start a charter affiliate for the greater Boston area. The mission of this group is to continue the work of FIGT beyond its annual conference by meeting to support and educate professionals who work to improve the lives of families in global transition.

The first meeting of FIGT Boston was held in January 2010 with fifteen interested persons who were either involved in or pursuing careers and other interests in the intercultural field. Anne and I introduced FIGT as an organization to the group, informed them about the annual conference, and then led a discussion as to how the group preferred to proceed with formatting their future meetings. The group as a whole agreed they wanted to use the affiliate to learn more about what others were doing in their work and to explore networking opportunities.

FIGT Boston has been and continues to be a useful resource and network for those with intercultural connections. Its members come from many backgrounds and interests including educators, relocation experts, those working with refugees and immigrants, students, coaches, trainers, and others. It has served as the stepping stone for other FIGT affiliates such as Korea and Switzerland, which were both launched in 2011, and the UK affiliate launched in 2012. We anticipate that many more affiliates will be set up!

Website and resources

One of the most impactful decisions the board has made in recent years was to create a social media chair to re-create and manage FIGT's website. Tech-savvy Canadian Judy Rickatson truly took the organization global with her expertise in social networking, cyberprograms, and more. The website provides a large inventory of resources for members and nonmembers alike:

- PowerPoint presentations and white papers from the various conferences
- archived webinars and video interviews
- book reviews and an extensive book bibliography
- links to transition and mobility related websites
- press articles, conference reviews, and/or in-house publication comments about FIGT
- articles on education, intercultural challenges, third culture kids, mobile family issues, and more

Access to cross-sector training

With increasing international interest and audience participation, there are discussions about the FIGT conference being set up at international venues once or twice a year. There are also more quality proposals submitted each year than we have slots for presentations at the conference. Consequently we are starting a webinar series to tap these resources and asking potential speakers if they could deliver their session as a webinar at a later date.

FINAL THOUGHTS

Working across sectors is a challenge for sure. We come to our work with different goals, worldviews, political values, financial backgrounds, and organizational cultures. Yet at FIGT, in spite of our differences, we have one unifying mission: to help people who are living outside their passport countries. It doesn't matter if people relocate to make money, offer medical assistance, serve in the military, spread a message of hope, or because of conflicts or calamities. The issues that face the spouses and children, and the personal and emotional issues for everyone, are similar across these sectors. At FIGT, working across sectors allows us to look at our professional challenges from new perspectives and to join our forces to help those in global transition.

EDITORS' NOTES

For more information on vulnerable transitions that affect people around the world, see the brief video from the International Organization for Migration (IOM): "Providing Humane Responses to the Challenges of the 21st Century," http://www.youtube.com/watch?v=WFgphr23938&feature=relmfu.

For more information about Families in Global Transition: http://figt.org/.

For more information about the authors:

- Ruth Van Reken
  - Cross Cultural Kids: http://www.crossculturalkid.org/
  - *Third Culture Kids: Growing Up among Worlds* (2009)
  - *Letters Never Sent* (updated 2012)
- Lois Bushong
  - Quiet Streams Counseling: http://www.quietstreamscounseling.com/

- *Belonging Everywhere and Nowhere: Insights into Counseling the Globally Mobile* (2013)
- Tina Quick
  - International Family Transitions: http://www.internationalfamily-transitions.com/
  - *The Global Nomad's Guide to University Transition* (2010)

RELATED RESOURCES

Video: TCK Academy. "The TCK Story" (film trailer). YouTube. http://www.youtube.com/watch?v=FouOIB_AAfw&feature=related.

Bell-Villada, G., N. Sichel, F. Eidse, and E. Orr, eds. 2011. *Writing out of limbo: International childhoods, global nomads and third culture kids.* Newcastle upon Tyne, UK: Cambridge Scholars Publishing.

CARTUS. 2010. Global mobility policy and practices survey: Navigating a challenging landscape. CARTUS.https://www.cartusmoves.com/docs/6633571334fa8390cc64e7GlobalPolicyandPractices2010.pdf.

Eidse, F., and N. Sichel, eds. 2004. *Unrooted childhoods: Memoirs of growing up global.* Boston: Nicholas Brealey Publishing and Intercultural Press.

Hess, M., and P. Linderman. 2007. *The expert expat: Your guide to successful relocation abroad.* Boston: Nicholas Brealey Publishing.

International Organization for Migration. 2012. World migration report 2011: Communicating effectively about migration. Geneva: International Organization for Migration. http://publications.iom.int/bookstore/index.php?main_page=product_info&cPath=37&products_id=752.

Neither Here nor There. 2011. Documentary film directed by Ema Ryan Yamazaki (an ATCK who explores the issues many bicultural, biracial TCKs face regarding the question of "Where is home?"). http://www.neitherherenorthere-thefilm.com/.

Pascoe, R. 2006. *Raising global nomads: Parenting abroad in an on-demand world.* Vancouver, Canada: Expatriate Press.

The Road Home. 2010. Short film directed by Rahul Gandotra. (an adult CCK who explores the identity for an Indian child caught between his British and Indian worlds; a professional version contains many resources for those working with internationally mobile families and screening rights). http://www.roadhomefilm.com.

CHAPTER 4

Multi-Sector Realities in the Global Response to HIV/AIDS

Sally Smith, UNAIDS

I first became involved with the HIV/AIDS epidemic in the early 1990s while doing health and development work with the United Mission to Nepal, a faith-based development organization. At that time the first reports of this new disease, AIDS, were reaching Nepal and I realized that the small town I lived in was a perfect melting pot for the spread of HIV. Every day a stream of buses and trucks came into the town, disgorged their sweaty passengers and loads to be collected by a waiting army of porters, ready to transport goods and people across the district and up as far as Tibet. In addition, the entire police and army barracks housed in the town were transferred every six months. Since people were coming and going all the time, "market forces" took over, and a small company of sex workers grew up to support all of these mobile people's "needs."

After having set up an HIV/AIDS program for this large organization during the 1990s, I moved with my husband to Geneva, renowned for being an international humanitarian hub. For the last nine years I have worked with UNAIDS in their civil society and community mobilization teams, my major responsibility being to broker and strengthen partnerships with faith-based organizations. My role in UNAIDS is primarily to interact across many sectors: facilitating conversations, partnerships, and working relationships between a very secular and scientific United Nations organization, and a wide range of civil society groups and activists, networks of people living with HIV (PLHIV), women's and youth groups, religious leaders, networks of sex workers, men who have sex with men, people who use drugs, and faith-based organizations. This incredible challenge has taught me the importance of intentionally linking across the sectors in order to tackle some of the great challenges facing our world (such as HIV).

In this chapter I review several of the current, critical issues regarding HIV and in particular the prevention agenda. The HIV epidemic is a multi-sectoral challenge spanning the areas of public health, politics, social justice, human rights, gender and sexuality, and religion and theology. I describe the issues surrounding HIV in each of these six areas and examine how these issues affect the global response to HIV. The faith-based community can play a crucial role as the world community joins efforts to achieve: zero new HIV infections, zero AIDS–related deaths, and zero stigma and discrimination.

HIV IS A PUBLIC HEALTH ISSUE

Public health refers to all organized measures (whether public or private) to prevent disease, promote health, and prolong life among the population as a whole. Its activities aim to provide conditions in which people can be healthy and focus on entire populations, not on individual patients or diseases. Thus, public health is concerned with the total system and not only the eradication of a particular disease. (WHO, 2011b)

HIV is a serious issue in the public health sector since there is no other disease in modern times that has caused such levels of illness and death among working adults. In a relatively short time the epidemic has become one of the greatest public health challenges in history because it does not only affect individuals but whole families, communities, and countries. According to the UN Secretary General Ban Ki Moon:

The year 2011 marks 30 years of AIDS. In that time, AIDS has claimed more than 25 million lives and more than 60 million people have become infected with HIV. Still, each day, more than 7,000 people are newly infected with the virus, including 1,000 children. No country has escaped the devastation of this truly global epidemic…(S. G. UN, 2011: 1)

AS OF DECEMBER 2012 MORE PEOPLE THAN EVER, AN ESTIMATED 34.0 MILLION [31.4 MILLION–35.9 MILLION] ARE LIVING WITH HIV (UNAIDS, 2012A: 8). SUB-SAHARAN AFRICA REMAINS MOST HEAVILY AFFECTED, ACCOUNTING FOR 69 PERCENT OF ALL PEOPLE LIVING WITH HIV AND 71 PERCENT OF ALL PEOPLE NEWLY INFECTED IN 2011. WOMEN MADE UP 50 PERCENT OF ADULTS (AGE 15–49) LIVING WITH HIV GLOBALLY IN 2010 AND 58 PERCENT OF ALL

INFECTIONS IN SUB-SAHARAN AFRICA IN 2011. THE IMPACT ON YOUNG WOMEN (AGE 15–24) IN SUB-SAHARAN AFRICA IS PARTICULARLY ACUTE, WITH 72 PERCENT OF YOUNG PEOPLE INFECTED IN 2010 BEING WOMEN. AS OF DECEMBER 2010, AN ESTIMATED 16.6 MILLION CHILDREN HAD LOST ONE OR BOTH PARENTS TO AIDS — NEARLY 15 MILLION OF THOSE CHILDREN RESIDED IN SUB-SAHARAN AFRICA. FEWER PEOPLE ARE DYING OF AIDS-RELATED CAUSES IN 2011 THAN IN 2005. IN 2011, 1.7 MILLION [1.5 MILLION–1.9 MILLION] PEOPLE DIED FROM AIDS-RELATED CAUSES WORLDWIDE (UNAIDS, 2012A: 12). SINCE 1995, ANTIRETROVIRAL THERAPY HAS SAVED 14 MILLION LIFE-YEARS IN LOW- AND MIDDLE INCOME COUNTRIES, INCLUDING 9 MILLION IN SUB-SAHARAN AFRICA (UNAIDS, 2012A: 12). (S. G. UN, 2012: 3).

AIDS is very different from other diseases in a number of ways: In the first two decades the virus spread rapidly from undetectable levels to 27.5 million persons, roughly equivalent to the population of Malaysia (UNAIDS, 2011a: 15). But HIV is far more than a health issue; most infectious diseases affect the elderly, the young, and the infirm. This disease affects working adults, who constitute society's main human capital, providing stability and security as parents and workforce. Those already marginalized, stigmatized, and those with less power in society—people whose rights are already compromised, for example, women and girls and key populations (men who have sex with men, sex workers, people who use drugs) are more vulnerable to HIV infection and its impact. Thus HIV by association both creates and re-enforces preexisting stigma and discrimination towards vulnerable populations.

FEMALE SEX WORKERS HAVE AN HIV PREVALENCE AROUND 13.5 TIMES GREATER THAN THE GENERAL POPULATION (UNAIDS, 2012A: 23) AND IN 49 COUNTRIES FOR WHICH DATA WAS AVAILABLE PEOPLE WHO INJECT DRUGS HAVE 22 TIMES THE RATE OF HIV INFECTION AS THE REST OF THE POPULATION (UNAIDS, 2012A: 34). HIV PREVALENCE AMONG MEN WHO HAVE SEX WITH MEN IN CAPITAL CITIES SURVEYED IS ON AVERAGE 13 TIMES HIGHER THAN THAT IN THE GENERAL POPULATION OF THOSE COUNTRIES (UNAIDS, 2012A: 25).

Many people do not know their HIV status since the virus can remain in the body for some years before producing symptoms and, because of stigma and discrimination, people are reluctant, or hindered from getting an HIV test or from receiving their results. As a result the disease is more evident in these key populations at higher risk. Some of the hindrances include laws, police practices, stigma, and discrimination in health care settings (S. G. UN, 2012).

The global response to this extraordinary epidemic has also been exceptional. Nonetheless, the global community must strengthen efforts to provide HIV prevention, treatment, care, and support services to all those who need them. UNAIDS has called on countries to know their epidemic and tailor the response accordingly. A combination of methods of HIV prevention are most effective to realize a 'prevention revolution' including: behavior change approaches, consistent and correct condom use, prevention of mother to child transmission of HIV, voluntary male circumcision, the use of antiretroviral treatment as prevention and harm reduction approaches including needle exchange to reduce HIV infection in people who inject drugs (UNAIDS, 2012a).

The global target of ensuring that 15 million people are on antiretroviral therapy by 2015 will require a huge effort from all countries and sectors, including increased efficiency of treatment scale-up, accelerated efforts towards universal voluntary HIV counseling and testing, increased treatment adherence and support to treatment access for key populations and other socially excluded groups. Simpler drug combinations and diagnostics are urgently needed at lower costs and communities must be engaged and mobilized to support the scaling-up of treatment (S. G. UN, 2012: 23).

HIV IS A POLITICAL ISSUE

HIV is a complex issue which cannot be solely managed medically; there is currently no suitable vaccine, nor is there a cure. The political sector must thus be involved because there are risks not only to public health, but also to national economies and security when an epidemic affects large numbers of the population who become ill, who can no longer work, and (particularly in the early days of the epidemic) who die. In addition, the social inequities and human rights issues associated with this epidemic, which often compromise people's ability to make individual choices about sexual behavior to prevent infection, have significant political implications. In order to mount an effective public health response to this epidemic, robust political leadership is needed to address social inequities and human rights abuses through enabling public policy and legislation to protect the human rights of PL-HIV and key populations. Finally, the funding costs of an effective response are significant and require strong political commitment in an increasingly constrained financial environment. HIV prompted the establishment of new ways of funding health through groundbreaking initiatives such as the Global Fund to fight AIDS, Tuberculosis, and Malaria and the Presidents Emergency Plan for AIDS relief. It is critical to ensure that funds are allocated wisely, targeting funding towards the most effective interventions as outlined in the Investment Framework articulated by Schwartländer et al (2011).

The global community has mounted a political response unlike that seen for other diseases. Whilst effective measures to address the HIV epidemic, in particular, structural and social determinants, human rights, and legal and policy frameworks require strong political leadership from governments; this has not always been realized by politicians and leaders. Where leaders have taken a strong political lead, many infections and deaths have been averted and many people provided with treatment, thus enabling them to go back to work. At the same time as the public health process has moved forward, a parallel process of political advocacy, leadership and formal negotiations took place culminating at the High Level Meeting (HLM) in June 2011 in the agreement of the 'Political Declaration on HIV/AIDS: Intensifying our Efforts to Eliminate HIV/AIDS' (UN, 2011). The Political Declaration of 2011 affirms and builds on the Declaration of Commitment (DOC) (UN, 2001), itself a groundbreaking document, the outcome of the first ever UN General Assembly meeting to discuss a health issue, and the Political Declaration of 2006 (UN, 2006). Taken together, these documents provide the most definitive account of how HIV is a political issue.

As life expectancies dropped in countries across Africa in the 1990s, economic, education, health, and agricultural systems struggled to cope or collapsed as workers became sick and died. Some employers, fearful of the disease, discriminated against workers living with HIV. This forced employer's organizations to address issues of the rights of PLHIV in the workplace. In 2001 the International Labour Organization (ILO) issued a Code of Practice on HIV/AIDS in the world of work to provide guidance on policy making and HIV care and practice to employers and employees in organizations (ILO, 2001). This was reinforced in 2010 through the 'Recommendation concerning HIV and AIDS and the World of Work, 2010 (No. 200)', the first international labour standard on HIV and AIDS in the world of work, which was adopted by governments, employers' and workers' representatives from ILO member States at the International Labour Conference in June 2010 (ILO 2010). Member States and international organizations demonstrated political leadership through these steps, calling for stronger legal and policy frameworks to protect PLHIV in the workplace and in situations of humanitarian and political insecurity or crisis.

Political support is also needed for sustainable funding. The advent of Highly Active Antiretroviral Therapy (HAART) for HIV in the mid 1990s was a biomedical triumph, and as a result death rates have dropped dramatically as treatment has been rolled out, resulting in a 24 percent decline since 2005 (UNAIDS, 2012a: 12).

The current levels of global health financing however, are inadequate to provide antiretroviral treatment to all those in medical need, and whilst treatment costs are higher than prevention costs, treatment has also been found to be effective as a form of HIV prevention. Impressive trial results showing HIV infection prevention rates of 96 percent were reported by Cohen et al in 2011 (Cohen M.S. et al 2011). The challenge of scaling up to meet both HIV treatment and prevention needs with the current system and its financial constraints is huge. The Secretary General Report in 2011 notes that:

> Funding for HIV programmes has dramatically increased, helping drive an overall surge in global health financing. Nonetheless, in 2009, international HIV assistance declined for the first time, mirroring reductions in other forms of development aid. (S. G. UN, 2011: 4)

More than ever today political commitment is needed to continue both international and national funding commitments to reach the 2015 targets in order that ground is not lost and crucial scale-up of programmatic activities, enabled by strong social systems, can continue. The Global AIDS response to date, including significant scientific advances, has brought us to a point where it is possible to end AIDS. It is critical that the global community pays now to scale up HIV prevention and treatment services, because if we do not pay now, then we will pay forever.

HIV IS A SOCIAL JUSTICE ISSUE

From the earliest days, the HIV epidemic has been associated with a number of critical social justice issues such as stigma and discrimination, marginalization, gender inequity, legal constraints, and power imbalances. Stigma and discrimination had a profound effect on PLHIV early on in the epidemic, due to the association of HIV infection with sex, blood, death, and morality. PLHIV and the gay rights movement began to demand a place at the decision making table, and access to life saving treatment. In 1983 the Denver Principles were outlined and at the Paris AIDS Summit in 1994 the demands of PLHIV to self-determination, freedom from discrimination and participation in decision making, were recognized in the principle of Greater Involvement of People Living with HIV (GIPA) (UNAIDS, 2011c: 12). This has shifted the way public health engages with people living with disease for HIV and a range of other illnesses, generating a new wave of community activism around health.

Social justice is a critical link between public health, human rights, and theology. Theologian Michael Kelly has developed this argument in his book, *HIV and AIDS: A Social Justice Perspective*. He begins with this quote from Catholic theologian Lisa Sowle Cahill, who expresses this link between AIDS and justice:

> AIDS is a justice issue, not primarily a sex issue. AIDS as a justice issue concerns the social relationships that help spread HIV and fail to alleviate AIDS, relationships of power and vulnerability that are in violation of Catholic norms ...(An) exclusive focus on sexual promiscuity or drug abuse, condoms or needle exchange programs, obscures the fact that the behaviors that transmit HIV are strongly influenced by social conditions. (Kelly, 2010: 13)

Kelly asserts that inequality itself is not equivalent to injustice but that they are often linked. He draws the distinction that inequity becomes injustice when people are denied their inherent right to "human dignity and the full range of rights accorded by the Universal Declaration of Human Rights" (Kelly, 2010: 17). When people are deprived of access to HIV prevention, treatment, care, and support services because they are members of a marginalized key population, their vulnerability to HIV infection and its impact on their lives is increased. Kelly and others have argued that "AIDS exacerbates inequity and injustice: in turn, inequity and injustice increase vulnerability to HIV infection. One cannot be understood without understanding the other" (Kelly, 2010: 17). To illustrate this point, a widow whose husband has died of AIDS, in a country where women are minors in the eyes of the law, cannot inherit the family home. As her property and land are taken from her, she may resort to sex work to support her children. The subsequent advent of AIDS into her life and family as a result of her engaging in sex work exacerbates the gender inequity and social injustice of inheritance law, which increased her vulnerability to HIV infection.

UNAIDS Strategy also makes links between social injustice, stigma and discrimination, human rights abuses, and public health approaches to HIV:

> Stigma and discrimination, homophobia, gender inequality, violence against women and girls and other HIV-related abuses of human rights remain widespread. These injustices discourage

people from seeking the information and services that will protect them from HIV infection, from adopting safe behavior and from accessing HIV treatment and care. Where HIV-related stigma, discrimination, inequality and violence persist, the global response will forever fall short of the transformations required to reach our shared vision. (UNAIDS, 2011b: 19)

HIV IS A HUMAN RIGHTS ISSUE

Dr. Jonathan Mann, the first head of the WHO Global AIDS Programme, pioneered early that it would be critical to protect the human rights of PLHIV (UNAIDS, 2011a: 19). Some countries quickly recognized the inherent connections between human rights and the HIV epidemic and took action to protect the rights of people living with and vulnerable to HIV. Lula de Silva, former president of Brazil, took an exceptionally strong stance and averted many infections and deaths. Not all countries respond in the same way, however. This statement by Jonathan Mann was visionary in 1987, at a time when many were advocating isolation of people living with HIV as the disease was poorly understood and feared.

How societies treat [HIV] and [people living with HIV] will not only test fundamental values but will likely make the difference between success and failure of AIDS strategies at national level. To the extent that we exclude [people with HIV] from society, we *endanger* society, to the extent that we maintain [them] in society, we protect society. This is the message of realism and of tolerance. (Jonathan Mann, Statement at an informal briefing on AIDS of the 42nd Session of the UN General Assembly, 1987; Aidsmap, 2012)

Sadly there is no end to stigma and discrimination and in 2012 both the UN Secretary General and the UNAIDS Global Report rightly highlight the urgent need for intensified action to address HIV-related stigma and discrimination.

Two effects of such punitive laws are to increase the stigma and discrimination towards PLHIV and key populations, and to restrict their access to HIV prevention, treatment and care services. There is no specific evidence, however, that to criminalize HIV transmission is successful either as a criminal justice measure or to reduce HIV transmission; the concern is that such measures undermine both public health and human rights. Most countries have existing criminal laws to deal with the rare instance of intentional transmission of HIV infection. To prosecute someone who has, for example, already disclosed their status to their partner or takes measures to reduce the risks of transmission contradicts the public health efforts to encourage people to seek voluntary testing and access HIV prevention services. Since most HIV transmission takes place soon after infection with the virus, at a time when people are unaware of their status, the risks of miscarriage of justice are significant (UNAIDS, 20120b).

Globally, governments cite stigma as the single greatest impediment to accelerated progress in the response (S. G. UN, 2011: 10). The Global Network of People living with HIV (GNP+) worked with UNAIDS and others to conduct research into stigma and discrimination faced by PLHIV and to document abuses of human rights through two projects, the Stigma Index and Human Rights Count (UNAIDS, 2011c: 8). Reports from interviews with PLHIV include physical violence (33 percent Zambia), verbal abuse, loss of housing or loss of job (65 percent Rwanda), and forced sterilizations (20 percent Namibia) (UNAIDS, 2011a: 36). In response to these abuses the partnership led by GNP+ and UNAIDS has developed the Positive Health Dignity and Prevention Framework (PHDP) (UNAIDS, 2011c). This policy framework provides a structure for countries to put PLHIV at the center of leadership in national HIV responses (UNAIDS, 2012a: 85).

APPROACHING 4 IN 10 COUNTRIES WORLDWIDE STILL HAVE NO SPECIFIC LEGAL PROVISIONS TO PREVENT OR ADDRESS HIV-RELATED DISCRIMINATION (UNAIDS, 2012A: 80). AS OF 2012, ABOUT 60 COUNTRIES HAVE ADOPTED LAWS THAT SPECIFICALLY CRIMINALIZE HIV TRANSMISSION, WITH SOME 600 CONVICTIONS REPORTED ACROSS 24 COUNTRIES (UNAIDS, 2012A: 83). LITTLE PROGRESS HAS BEEN MADE IN REFORMING LAWS THAT DISCRIMINATE AGAINST PEOPLE LIVING WITH HIV AND OTHER KEY POPULATIONS AT HIGHER RISK. IN 2012, NONGOVERNMENTAL INFORMANTS IN 70 PERCENT OF COUNTRIES AND NATIONAL GOVERNMENTS IN 60 PERCENT REPORTED THE EXISTENCE OF LAWS, REGULATIONS OR POLICIES THAT PRESENT OBSTACLES TO EFFECTIVE HIV PREVENTION, TREATMENT, CARE AND SUPPORT FOR KEY POPULATIONS AND VULNERABLE GROUPS (UNAIDS, 2012A: 82). IN 2012, SEVENTY-EIGHT COUNTRIES CRIMINALIZED SAME-SEX SEXUAL RELATIONS BETWEEN CONSENTING ADULTS. MOST COUNTRIES CRIMINALIZE SOME ASPECT OF SEX WORK AND IMPOSE CRIMINAL PENALTIES ON PEOPLE WHO ARE DRUG-DEPENDENT (UNAIDS, 2012A: 83). NOT ONLY DO THESE LAWS MARGINALIZE AND EXPOSE MEMBERS OF KEY POPULATIONS TO VIOLENCE, CRIMINAL SANCTIONS, AND PRISON, THEY ALSO RESULT IN THE EXCLUSION OF THESE GROUPS FROM NATIONAL ECONOMIC, HEALTH, AND SOCIAL SUPPORT PROGRAMMES. (S. G. UN, 2012: 20)

HIV IS A GENDER AND SEXUALITY ISSUE

The issues which put women and young girls at increased risk of HIV infection have been referred to above and extensively documented (UNAIDS, 2010a: 7). The Secretary General's report of 2011 summarizes the issues succinctly:

> This imbalance reflects not only the heightened physiological vulnerability of girls and young women, but also a high prevalence of intergenerational partnerships, lack of woman-initiated prevention methods and broader social and legal inequality that impedes the ability of young women to reduce their sexual risk. Women's odds of living with HIV are inversely correlated with educational attainment, a fact that highlights the role of universal education initiatives in reducing HIV-related vulnerability. Women also bear a disproportionate share of the HIV-related caregiving burden and are often more likely to be the victims of discrimination. (S. G. UN, 2011: 16)

Gender-based violence is both a root cause and a consequence of HIV. Studies have demonstrated that early sexual experience, early marriage, and sexual violence are associated with an increased risk of HIV infection in generalized epidemics. One study in South Africa documented an estimated one in seven of cases where women aged 15–26 years old acquired HIV infection in association with gender power imbalance and intimate partner violence (UNAIDS, 2012b: 70). For example, women in Soweto, South Africa, who had been physically abused by their partners were more likely to be living with HIV. Men who perpetrate gender-based violence are also more likely to be living with HIV, according to similar evidence from both South Africa and India (UNAIDS, 2012b: 72).

Gender inequities do not only apply to women and girls, however. Two of the groups most affected by the HIV epidemic have been men who have sex with men and transgender persons, many of whom are already stigmatized in their communities. Gay activist David Kato set an example that has inspired many others to confront rights violations and inequities that rob them of their health and dignity. He was murdered in 2010, and these are the remarks of Maurice Tomlinson, a legal adviser on marginalized groups for AIDS-Free World, on receiving the inaugural David Kato Vision and Voice Award in London, United Kingdom on 29 January 2012.

I am sure he felt that if his people only knew what tremendous harm intolerance and homophobia were causing to countless of their fellow citizens—including the spread of HIV as a result of vulnerable groups being forced underground away from effective prevention, treatment, care and support interventions—then all Ugandans would, in one voice, call for an end to such acts of cruel inhumanity. (UNAIDS: 2012: 66)

It is estimated that there are about 15 million transgender people in the world and that they are at an increased risk for HIV infection, with up to 68 percent living with HIV and many being vulnerable to gender-based violence. Transgender identity is an expression of gender that differs from their designated sex at birth. Transgender people face significant stigma and discrimination and lack access to information, services, and employment opportunities. Transgendered people as a result may rely on sex work for income and survival, with up to 44 percent of transgendered people involved in some form of sex work (UNAIDS, 2012a: 76).

So how do we go from 'rhetoric to reality' regarding HIV, gender, and human rights? First, countries must undertake a comprehensive review of national policy and laws to revise or remove any which present obstacles to effective and rights-based AIDS responses. Laws should be put in place in all countries, along with support for their implementation, that include specific mechanisms and services to enable people at risk to access justice. Second, community-based programs to address HIV-related stigma, and generate new norms around gender equality and sexual violence must be funded. Finally, building bridges between the broader disciplines/sector of health and the areas of social justice, human rights action, the women's movement, and the energy of youth activism is key for the promotion of human rights and gender equality (S. G. UN, 2012: 23).

HIV IS A RELIGIOUS AND THEOLOGICAL ISSUE

Peter Piot, former executive director of UNAIDS, identifies five reasons why faith communities have a role to play in the HIV epidemic. His remarks are summarized well by Beverly Haddad.

> Religion, he argues, continues to play a pivotal role in society and when there are crisis events such as the HIV epidemic, people look to religious leaders to 'explain what is happening, and to provide a framework for dealing with it.' Second, religious institutions have played an important educative role through centuries of history, meeting their constituencies once a week, 'a feat rarely attained by activists, academics, or politicians.' Third, suggests Piot, the HIV and AIDS epidemic raises issues related to disease as divine retribution or grace, sin, sexuality and taboos. Therefore, theologians 'need to ask what this means for their traditions, and what their traditions mean for AIDS.' Fourth, Piot asserts that 'forty percent of all AIDS care is provided by religious groups.' Last, many PLHIV have strong religious beliefs and look to God and their faith community for support and comfort. Piot's assertions are certainly true for the African continent. (Haddad, 2011: 2)

I believe that the discipline of practical theology, which is interdisciplinary, provides a very useful way to analyze and interact with the HIV epidemic. Swinton and Mowat (Swinton & Mowat, 2006) describe practical theology as "reflecting critically and theologically on the practices of the Church as they interact with the practices of the world. Practical theology seeks to reveal and reflect on the intricate, diverse but complementary meanings of Christian practices and to enable faithful presence and action" (Swinton & Mowat, 2006: 10). Practical theology can also provide a framework to reflect critically and theologically on HIV, its complexity, and how the church can respond with faithful Christian presence and appropriate action. This thinking underpins the following three areas highlighted by the World Council of Churches in 1997 (WCC, 1997).

1. Pastoral Care and the Church as a Healing Community

Pastoral care is central to the ministry of the church. Secular and religious authors highlight the importance of the church's pastoral ministry to PLHIV and those dying from AIDS related illness. Church-run hospital, clinic, and home-based care services have been strong; Vitillo likens this to Christians simply doing what Jesus did, feeding the hungry, visiting the sick, educating, praying for healing, comforting the bereaved and dying (Vitillo, 2007: 187). This strength has been recognized by the international community (UNAIDS, 2009: 11, 14); (UNICEF, 2011: 23); (CIFA, 2010). The church as a healing community has the potential to provide the kinds of non-judgmental environments that are crucial for PLHIV to find both emotional and practical support (Kelly, 2009: 39). Counseling and prayer ministries have been an integral part of the HIV ministries of many churches.

However, the church is not always a safe and healing community, especially when PLHIV receive a judgmental or critical response. Issues described above, such as gender, sexuality, drug use, sex work, contraception, and HIV prevention raise huge pastoral and theological questions and have posed significant challenges to theology and the church. Questions of choice and agency, people who have decision making power and the consequences of those decisions as well as the powerlessness and consequences of powerlessness in their lives have been explored in Christian responses to HIV. The work of Olivier, J.R., & B. (2006) as well as Dube Shomanah (2009) and others in the Circle of Concerned African Women Theologians has reviewed in depth literature exploring some of these challenges to the church and to theology and lamented in their conclusions the lack of adequate theological preparation for clergy to deal with the pastoral and theological enormity of this crisis (Dube Shomanah, 2009).

2. Theology and Ethics

HIV has undergone a great deal of theological reflection. The notion of AIDS being a punishment from God is just one of many examples. Some recent literature argues convincingly that there is no justification whatsoever for this assertion (Chitando, 2009; Gill, 2007). Olivier et al. note that despite the depth of theological reflection on this and other issues, the practical responses of many churches are not always grounded in strong theological frameworks (Olivier, et al., 2006: 60). Second, the theology of sexuality is another vast area of study in its own right; theologies around gender inequity and sexuality have been widely explored in the context of HIV (Dube Shomanah, 2009). Third, moral theologians have explored ethical and theological teachings around HIV prevention and treatment as well as sexuality (Olivier, et al., 2006). Fourth, many authors have drawn a theological link between the body of Christ and AIDS. For instance, the theme of "the body of Christ has AIDS" has been central to many theologians' work (Klinken, 2010). Fifth, the areas of prophetic witness, stigma and discrimination, healing, compassion, suffering and lament are all theological themes that have been explored by a range of recent authors (Chitando, 2009; Dube Shomanah, 2009; Messer, 2004; Olivier, et al., 2006). As this list demonstrates, theological reflection on HIV over the last twenty or more years has been wide ranging; it is also rich and provides a solid foundation on which churches can build HIV responses. One major challenge, however, is for this level of depth and analysis found in these theological resources to be transferred into local church responses. Some of the stigmatizing and discriminatory responses of churches and their leaders are based too often on fear and ignorance. Robust theological foundations exist, but are too often disconnected from practice.

3. Justice and Human Rights: Faith and Secular Perspectives

Most of the challenges to the faith-based community lie in this area of justice and human rights. Conversely, some of the positions of the church on issues such as condom use and sexuality present a huge challenge to the secular community. Issues which generate stigma and discrimination in society can also pose a challenge to the theology and teachings of faith communities.

Both faith and secular communities thus tend to view one another with suspicion. On the one hand they recognize the value and importance that the other worldview has to bring, whilst on the other they are unable to stomach the downsides of the alternative worldview in its more extreme form. As a result, engagement between the secular public health HIV community and faith community swings back and forth like a pendulum. In turn, this can have negative effects on the HIV response, in particular on stigma and discrimination, HIV prevention, and public policy. In recent years these tensions have been visibly played out in the debates around condoms, sexuality education, sexual and reproductive health and rights, gender and men who have sex with men, including same sex marriage, and in the global policy making arenas including the General Assembly, the Commission on the Status of Women, the UNAIDS Programme Coordinating Board, and the Human Rights Council. These public conflicts can reinforce the inherent tendency towards secularization within the public health community, fuel general suspicions of faith-based actors and have a direct knock-on effect of decreasing the visibility of and trust in the faith-based HIV service delivery sector in the global, regional, and national HIV responses.

It is encouraging to note, however, that religious and political figures and international organizations are engaging in respectful public and private dialogue about these tensions and the issues. The Ecumenical Advocacy Alliance (EAA) has worked in partnership with UNAIDS, the Global Network of people living with HIV (GNP+) and the international network of religious leaders living with and affected by HIV (INERELA+) on a number of initiatives over recent years to help foster this kind of respectful dialogue grappling with really difficult issues in a safe environment. The first activity brought together senior global religious and political leaders with people living with HIV and representatives from the networks of key populations for dialogue in a closed environment for a High Level Religious Leaders Summit in 2010. The resulting personal commitment signed by the leaders has led to many taking individual action to bring together similar gatherings at a national level. As a follow up, this same group of partners is developing a tool to facilitate such dialogue at a national level.

Another encouraging example is the We Will Speak Out coalition.

> [This coalition] is one of the initiatives advocating zero toler-
> ance for gender-based violence. Prompted by the findings of a
> report on churches' responses to sexual violence in three African
> countries, Rowan Williams, the Archbishop of Canterbury, and
> Michel Sidibé, UNAIDS Executive Director, supported the launch
> of the coalition in March 2011. The partnership is active in four
> countries in Africa, encouraging believers of all faiths to speak out
> against sexual violence and lead their communities in providing
> counseling and support to survivors, whether men, women or
> children. (UNAIDS, 2012b: 74)

The partnership is being extended to other countries in order to underline the message that gender-based violence is a global phenomenon.

JOINING TOGETHER ACROSS SECTORS

I have explored some of the complexities of the HIV epidemic; several issues in the public, political, social justice, human rights, sexuality/gender, and religious/theological arenas; and the need for a global, multi-sectoral response. By drawing out some of the linkages across the sectors we can set the scene for further discussion, research, and informed action. For example, there is tension between the faith and secular HIV communities around human rights, in which human rights are perceived by the faith community as 'Western impositions,' which promote the individual over community. In such situations, social justice can provide a critical conceptual link between human rights, public health, and theology. Dialogue around issues of social justice can help depolarize the debate and provide a way forward. Using public health concepts as an entry point for this kind of dialogue, in order to demonstrate the importance of people at risk of HIV being able to access HIV prevention services, can be helpful to unlock tension and provide the foundation for more collaborative action. The faith community has long experience of public health work on leprosy, cancer and TB, diseases which are similarly associated with stigma, exclusion, fear and contagion. Comparisons can be drawn between churches' responses to these diseases and important lessons learned which may usefully be applied to HIV.

In some situations of tension and conflict, as mentioned earlier, the conflict is based on fear and often demonstrates a lack of understanding of the rich heritage of theological reflection that exists around the HIV epidemic or a lack of understanding of the role of the faith community in issues of social injustice. Initiatives highlighted above such as the 'We will speak out coalition' and the framework for dialogue being developed by EAA, GNP+, INERELA+ and UNAIDS can go a long way to help both churches and secular AIDS practitioners to challenge together simplistic and judgmental assumptions about agency and individual choice when it comes to sexual behavior. These initiatives create environments for dialogue where the voices of people living with HIV can be heard, some of whom have been subject to gender-based violence, social inequity, and human rights abuses and have found their ability to make choices compromised. These structured personal encounters between religious leaders, PLHIV, public health practitioners, and human rights activists can break down unhelpful stereotypes and build trust, respect, and strong coalitions of actors empowered to challenge injustice together.

Some of the most important actions that churches can take include advocacy for stronger public health responses, sustainable funding and political commitment to create environments free from stigma, and work towards legal and policy environments that protect the rights of the most marginalized and vulnerable in society, be that in the HIV field or another.

Together we can make a difference! My passion is to join with others in order to achieve: *zero new HIV infections, zero AIDS–related deaths, and zero stigma and discrimination.*

REFERENCES

Aidsmap (NAM). 2012. The role of human rights in the global response to HIV. Retrieved from http://www.aidsmap.com/The-role-of-human-rights-in-the-global-response-to-HIV/page/1441834/.

Chitando, E. 2009. *Troubled but not destroyed*. Geneva, Switzerland: World Council of Churches.

Center for Interfaith Action on Global Poverty. 2010. Many faiths, common action: Increasing the impact of the faith sector on health and development. Retrieved from http://www.africachap.org/x5/images/stories/strategic-framework-report%20by%20cifa.pdf.

Cohen, M. S., Chen, Y. Q., McCauley, M., Gamble, T., Hosseinipour, M. C., Kumarasamy, N., . . . null. 2011. Prevention of HIV-1 infection with early antiretroviral therapy. *The New England journal of medicine*, 365(6), 493–505.

Dube Shomanah, M. 2009. HIV and AIDS research and writing in the Circle of African women theologians (2002–2006). In: E. Chitando, ed., *Compassionate circles,* 173–196. Geneva, Switzerland: World Council of Churches.

Dube Shomanah, M., & World Council of Churches, eds. 2003. *HIV/AIDS and the curriculum: Methods of integrating HIV/AIDS in theological programme*. Geneva, Switzerland: World Council of Churches.

Gill, R., ed. 2007. *Reflecting theologically on AIDS: A global challenge*. London, UK: SCM Press.

Haddad, B. 2011. *Religion and HIV and AIDS: Charting the terrain*. Pietermaritzburg, RSA: University of Kwazulu-Natal Press.

International Labour Organization. 2001. The ILO code of practice on HIV/AIDS and the world of work. Geneva, Switzerland: Author. Retrieved from http://www.ilo.org/global/publications/KD00015/lang--en/index.htm.

ILO. 2010. Recommendation concerning HIV and AIDS and the World of Work, 2010 (No. 200) Retrieved from http://www.ilo.org/wcmsp5/groups/public/---ed_protect/---protrav/---ilo_aids/documents/normativeinstrument/wcms_194088.pdf.

Kelly, A. 2009. The body of Christ has AIDS: The Catholic Church responding faithfully to HIV and AIDS in Papua New Guinea. *Journal of Religion and Health*, 48, 16–28.

Kelly, M. 2010. *HIV and AIDS. A Social Justice perspective*. Nairobi, Kenya: Paulines Publications Africa. Retrieved from http://books.google.fr/books/about/HIV_and_AIDS.html?id=owe-XwAACAAJ&redir_esc=y.

Klinken, A. 2010. When the body of Christ has AIDS: A theological metaphor for global solidarity in light of HIV and AIDS. *International Journal of Public Theology*, 4, 446–465.

Messer, D. 2004. *Breaking the conspiracy of silence: Christian churches and the global AIDS crisis*. Minneaplolis, MN: Fortress Press.

Olivier, J., et al. 2006. Literature review: Working in a bounded field of unknowing. Retrieved from: http://www.arhap.uct.ac.za/downloads/arhaplitreview_oct2006.pdf.

Schwartländer, B., Stover, J., Hallett, T., Atun, R., Avila, C., Gouws, E., . . . Padian, N. 2011. Towards an improved investment approach for an effective response to HIV/AIDS. *The Lancet*, 377(9782), 2031–2041.

Swinton, J., & Mowat, H. 2006. *Practical theology and qualitative research.* London, UK: SCM Press.

United Nations. 2001. Declaration of commitment on HIV/AIDS. United Nations General Assembly Special Session on HIV/AIDS. Retrieved from http://data.unaids.org/publications/irc-pub03/aidsdeclaration_en.pdf.

United Nations. 2006. Political declaration on HIV/AIDS. Resolution adopted by the General Assembly 60/262. Retrieved from http://data.unaids.org/pub/report/2006/20060615_hlm_politicaldeclaration_ares60262_en.pdf.

United Nations. 2011a. Political declaration on HIV/AIDS: Intensifying our efforts to eliminate HIV/AIDS. A/65/L.77. Retrieved from http://www.unaids.org/en/media/unaids/contentassets/documents/document/2011/06/20110610_un_a-res-65-277_en.pdf.

United Nations. 2011b. Uniting for universal access: Towards zero new HIV infections, zero discrimination and zero AIDS-related deaths. Report of the Secretary-General. United Nations General Assembly. Retrieved from http://www.unaids.org/en/media/unaids/contentassets/documents/document/2011/20110331_SG_report_en.pdf.

United Nations. 2012. United to end AIDS: Achieving the targets of the 2011 political declaration. New York, USA: Author. Retrieved from http://www.unaids.org/en/media/unaids/contentassets/documents/document/2012/20120402_UNGA_A-66-757_en.pdf.

UNAIDS. 2009. Partnership with faith-based organizations UNAIDS strategic framework. Geneva, Switzerland: Author. Retrieved from http://data.unaids.org/pub/Report/2010/jc1786_fbo_en.pdf.

UNAIDS. 2010a. Agenda for accelerated country action for women, girls, gender equality, and HIV. Geneva, Switzerland: Author. Retrieved from http://www.unaids.org/en/media/unaids/contentassets/documents/unaidspublication/2010/20100226_jc1794_agenda_for_accelerated_country_action_en.pdf.

UNAIDS. 2010b. UNAIDS policy brief. Criminalization of HIV transmission. Geneva, Switzerland: Author. Retrieved from http://data.unaids.org/pub/basedocument/2008/20080731_jc1513_policy_criminalization_en.pdf.

UNAIDS. 2011a. AIDS at 30: Nations at the crossroads. Geneva, Switzerland: World Health Organization. Geneva, Switzerland: Author. Retrieved from http://www.unaids.org/unaids_resources/aidsat30/aids-at-30.pdf.

UNAIDS. 2011b. Getting to zero 2011–2015 strategy. Geneva, Switzerland: Author. Retrieved from http://www.unaids.org/en/media/unaids/contentassets/documents/unaidspublication/2010/jc2034_unaids_strategy_en.pdf.

UNAIDS. 2011c. Positive health, dignity, and prevention; A policy framework. Geneva, Switzerland: Author. Retrieved from http://www.unaids.org/en/media/unaids/contentassets/documents/unaidspublication/2011/20110701_phdp.pdf.

UNAIDS. 2012a. Global report: UNAIDS report on the global AIDS epidemic 2012. Geneva, Switzerland. Retrieved from http://www.unaids.org/en/media/unaids/contentassets/documents/epidemiology/2012/gr2012/20121120_UNAIDS_Global_Report_2012_en.pdf.

UNAIDS. 2012b. Together we will end AIDS. Geneva, Switzerland; Author. Retrieved from http://www.unaids.org/en/media/unaids/contentassets/documents/epidemiology/2012/20120718_togetherwewillendaids_en.pdf.

UNICEF 2011. Partnering with religious communities for children. New York, NY: Retrieved from http://www.unicef.org/eapro/Partnering_with_Religious_Communities_for_Children.pdf.

Vitillo, R. 2007. *Pastoral training for responding to HIV-AIDS.* Nairobi, Kenya: Paulines Publications Africa.

World Council of Churches. 1997. *Facing AIDS The challenge and the churches' response.* Geneva, Swizerland: Author.

World Health Organization. 2011a. Prevention and treatment of HIV and other sexually transmitted infections among men who have sex with men and transgender people. Geneva, Switzerland: Author. Retrieved from http://www.who.int/hiv/pub/guidelines/msm_guidelines2011/en/index.html.

World Health Organization. 2011b. Public Health. Retrieved from http://www.who.int/trade/glossary/story076/en/index.html.

NOTES

For more information about UNAIDS: http://www.unaids.org/en/.

RELATED RESOURCES

Video: Did You Know? UNAIDS. http://www.unaids.org/en/resources/multimediacentre/videos/20121005didyouknowen/.

UNAIDS multimedia video reports and updates: http://www.unaids.org/en/resources/multimediacentre/.

Archbishop of Canterbury. 2012. Human rights and religious faith. Retrieved from http://www.archbishopofcanterbury.org/articles.php/2370/human-rights-and-religious-faith.

Center for Interfaith Action on Global Poverty. 2010. Many faiths, common action: Increasing the impact of the faith sector on health and development. Retrieved from http://www.africachap.org/x5/images/stories/strategic-framework-report%20by%20cifa.pdf.

Messer, D. 2004. *Breaking the conspiracy of silence: Christian churches and the global AIDS crisis.* Minneaplolis, MH: Fortress Press.

United Nations. 2011b. Uniting for universal access: Towards zero new HIV infections, zero discrimination and zero AIDS-related deaths. Report of the Secretary-General. United Nations General Assembly. Retrieved from http://www.unaids.org/en/media/unaids/contentassets/documents/document/2011/20110331_SG_report_en.pdf.

UNAIDS. 2009. Partnership with faith-based organizations UNAIDS strategic framework. Geneva, Switzerland: Author. Retrieved from http://data.unaids.org/pub/Report/2010/jc1786_fbo_en.pdf.

CHAPTER 5

Universal Declaration of Human Rights

United Nations General Assembly

The General Assembly of the United Nations adopted the Universal Declaration of Human Rights on December 10, 1948. The Assembly called upon all member countries to publicize the text of the Declaration and "to cause it to be disseminated, displayed, read, and expounded principally in schools and other educational institutions, without distinction based on the political status of countries or territories." For more information on human rights and to access the Declaration in over 360 languages: http://www.un.org/en/documents/udhr/index.shtml.

PREAMBLE

Whereas recognition of the inherent dignity and of the equal and inalienable rights of all members of the human family is the foundation of freedom, justice, and peace in the world,

Whereas disregard and contempt for human rights have resulted in barbarous acts which have outraged the conscience of mankind, and the advent of a world in which human beings shall enjoy freedom of speech and belief and freedom from fear and want has been proclaimed as the highest aspiration of the common people,

Whereas it is essential, if man is not to be compelled to have recourse, as a last resort, to rebellion against tyranny and oppression, that human rights should be protected by the rule of law,

Whereas it is essential to promote the development of friendly relations between nations,

Whereas the peoples of the United Nations have in the Charter reaffirmed their faith in fundamental human rights, in the dignity and worth of the human person and in the equal rights of men and women and have determined to promote social progress and better standards of life in larger freedom,

Whereas Member States have pledged themselves to achieve, in cooperation with the United Nations, the promotion of universal respect for and observance of human rights and fundamental freedoms,

Whereas a common understanding of these rights and freedoms is of the greatest importance for the full realization of this pledge,

Now, herefore the General Assembly proclaims this Universal Declaration of Human Rights as a common standard of achievement for all peoples and all nations, to the end that every individual and every organ of society, keeping this Declaration constantly in mind, shall strive by teaching and education to promote respect for these rights and freedoms and by progressive measures, national and international, to secure their universal and effective recognition and observance, both among the peoples of Member States themselves and among the peoples of territories under their jurisdiction.

Article 1

All human beings are born free and equal in dignity and rights. They are endowed with reason and conscience and should act towards one another in a spirit of brotherhood.

Article 2

Everyone is entitled to all the rights and freedoms set forth in this Declaration, without distinction of any kind, such as race, colour, sex, language, religion, political, or other opinion, national or social origin, property, birth, or other status. Furthermore, no distinction shall be made on the basis of the political, jurisdictional, or international status of the country or territory to which a person belongs, whether it be independent, trust, non-self-governing, or under any other limitation of sovereignty.

Article 3

Everyone has the right to life, liberty, and security of person.

Article 4

No one shall be held in slavery or servitude; slavery and the slave trade shall be prohibited in all their forms.

Article 5

No one shall be subjected to torture or to cruel, inhuman, or degrading treatment or punishment.

Article 6

Everyone has the right to recognition everywhere as a person before the law.

Article 7

All are equal before the law and are entitled without any discrimination to equal protection of the law. All are entitled to equal protection against any discrimination in violation of this Declaration and against any incitement to such discrimination.

Article 8

Everyone has the right to an effective remedy by the competent national tribunals for acts violating the fundamental rights granted him by the constitution or by law.

Article 9

No one shall be subjected to arbitrary arrest, detention, or exile.

Article 10

Everyone is entitled in full equality to a fair and public hearing by an independent and impartial tribunal, in the determination of his rights and obligations and of any criminal charge against him.

Article 11

(1) Everyone charged with a penal offence has the right to be presumed innocent until proved guilty according to law in a public trial at which he has had all the guarantees necessary for his defense. (2) No one shall be held guilty of any penal offence on account of any act or omission which did not constitute a penal offence, under national or international law, at the time when it was committed. Nor shall a heavier penalty be imposed than the one that was applicable at the time the penal offence was committed.

Article 12

No one shall be subjected to arbitrary interference with his privacy, family, home, or correspondence, nor to attacks upon his honour and reputation. Everyone has the right to the protection of the law against such interference or attacks.

Article 13

(1) Everyone has the right to freedom of movement and residence within the borders of each state. (2) Everyone has the right to leave any country, including his own, and to return to his country.

Article 14

(1) Everyone has the right to seek and to enjoy in other countries asylum from persecution. (2) This right may not be invoked in the case of prosecutions genuinely arising from nonpolitical crimes or from acts contrary to the purposes and principles of the United Nations.

Article 15

(1) Everyone has the right to a nationality. (2) No one shall be arbitrarily deprived of his nationality nor denied the right to change his nationality.

Article 16

(1) Men and women of full age, without any limitation due to race, nationality, or religion, have the right to marry and to found a family. They are entitled to equal rights as to marriage, during marriage and at its dissolution. (2) Marriage shall be entered into only with the free and full consent of the intending spouses. (3) The family is the natural and fundamental group unit of society and is entitled to protection by society and the State.

Article 17

(1) Everyone has the right to own property alone as well as in association with others. (2) No one shall be arbitrarily deprived of his property.

Article 18

Everyone has the right to freedom of thought, conscience, and religion; this right includes freedom to change his religion or belief, and freedom, either alone or in community with others and in public or private, to manifest his religion or belief in teaching, practice, worship, and observance.

Article 19

Everyone has the right to freedom of opinion and expression; this right includes freedom to hold opinions without interference and to seek, receive, and impart information and ideas through any media and regardless of frontiers.

Article 20

(1) Everyone has the right to freedom of peaceful assembly and association. (2) No one may be compelled to belong to an association.

Article 21

(1) Everyone has the right to take part in the government of his country, directly or through freely chosen representatives. (2) Everyone has the right of equal access to public service in his country. (3) The will of the people shall be the basis of the authority of government; this will shall be expressed in periodic and genuine elections which shall be by universal and equal suffrage and shall be held by secret vote or by equivalent free voting procedures.

Article 22

Everyone, as a member of society, has the right to social security and is entitled to realization, through national effort and international cooperation and in accordance with the organization and resources of each State, of the economic, social, and cultural rights indispensable for his dignity and the free development of his personality.

Article 23

(1) Everyone has the right to work, to free choice of employment, to just and favourable conditions of work, and to protection against unemployment. (2) Everyone, without any discrimination, has the right to equal pay for equal work. (3) Everyone who works has the right to just and favourable remuneration ensuring for himself and his family an existence worthy of human dignity, and supplemented, if necessary, by other means of social protection. (4) Everyone has the right to form and to join trade unions for the protection of his interests.

Article 24

Everyone has the right to rest and leisure, including reasonable limitation of working hours and periodic holidays with pay.

Article 25

(1) Everyone has the right to a standard of living adequate for the health and well-being of himself and of his family, including food, clothing, housing, and medical care and necessary social services, and the right to security in the event of unemployment, sickness, disability, widowhood, old age, or other lack of livelihood in circumstances beyond his control. (2) Motherhood and childhood are entitled to special care and assistance. All children, whether born in or out of wedlock, shall enjoy the same social protection.

Article 26

(1) Everyone has the right to education. Education shall be free, at least in the elementary and fundamental stages. Elementary education shall be compulsory. Technical and professional education shall be made generally available and higher education shall be equally accessible to all on the basis of merit. (2) Education shall be directed to the full development of the human personality and to the strengthening of respect for human rights and fundamental freedoms. It shall promote understanding, tolerance, and friendship among all nations, racial, or religious groups, and shall further the activities of the United Nations for the maintenance of peace. (3) Parents have a prior right to choose the kind of education that shall be given to their children.

Article 27

(1) Everyone has the right freely to participate in the cultural life of the community, to enjoy the arts, and to share in scientific advancement and its benefits. (2) Everyone has the right to the protection of the moral and material interests resulting from any scientific, literary, or artistic production of which he is the author.

Article 28

Everyone is entitled to a social and international order in which the rights and freedoms set forth in this Declaration can be fully realized.

Article 29

(1) Everyone has duties to the community in which alone the free and full development of his personality is possible. (2) In the exercise of his rights and freedoms, everyone shall be subject only to such limitations as are determined by law solely for the purpose of securing due recognition and respect for the rights and freedoms of others and of meeting the just requirements of morality, public order, and the general welfare in a democratic society. (3) These rights and freedoms may in no case be exercised contrary to the purposes and principles of the United Nations.

Article 30

Nothing in this Declaration may be interpreted as implying for any State, group, or person any right to engage in any activity or to perform any act aimed at the destruction of any of the rights and freedoms set forth herein.

Editors' Notes

Human rights are also understood in light of human *responsibilities* at all levels of society—persons, families, communities, organizations, nations, and internationally. Rights and responsibilities support both core beliefs about human worth and core practices for human well-being.

For more information about the United Nations and human rights: http://www2.ohchr.org/.
See especially the Fact Sheets on various topics: http://www.ohchr.org/EN/PublicationsResources/Pages/FactSheets.aspx.

Source

United Nations General Assembly. 1948. Universal declaration of human rights. Reprinted by permission. http://www.ohchr.org/EN/UDHR/Pages/SearchByLang.aspx.

Related Resources

Video: Veritas Forum. "Universal Declaration of Human Rights." YouTube. http://www.youtube.com/watch?v=hTlrSYbCbHE&list=PLBA370C50B916BBDD&index=1&feature=plpp_video.

Cairo Declaration on Human Rights in Islam. 1990. http://www.religlaw.org/interdocs/docs/cairohrislam1990.htm.

Faculty of Religious Studies, McGill University et al. 2003. *Universal declaration of human rights by the world's religions.* http://gcwr2011.org/pdf/UDHRWR_en.pdf.

Haas, M. 2008. *International human rights: A comprehensive approach.* Abingdon, UK: Routledge.

Martin, J. P. 2005. *25+ human rights documents.* New York: Columbia University, Institute for the Study of Human Rights.

Nurser, J. 2005. *For all peoples and all nations: Christian churches and human rights.* Geneva: WCC Publications.

United Nations. 1966. International covenants on human rights (International covenant on social, economic, and political rights; International covenant of civil and political rights). United Nations. http://www.ohchr.org/Documents/Publications.

United Nations, Office of the High Commissioner for Human Rights. 2008. Working with the United Nations human rights programme: A handbook for civil society. New York and Geneva: Author. http://www.ohchr.org/EN/AboutUs/CivilSociety/Pages/Handbook.aspx.

PART TWO

Good Practice in the Humanitarian Sector

CONNECTIONS AND CONTRIBUTIONS
FOR SERVING HUMANITY

MISSIO DEI

Mission-Aid
Sector

Human
Health
Sector

GLOBAL
MEMBER
CARE

Human
Resource
Sector

Humanitarian
Sector

MISSIO MUNDI

APPLICATIONS FOR PART TWO

Keep in mind these five goals for crossing sectors as you go through the material.

In what ways could you connect and contribute?

- To support mission/aid workers in their well-being and effectiveness
- To support colleagues in other sectors via materials in the member care field
- To equip mission/aid workers with tools and opportunities for their work with others
- To equip member caregivers who directly work with vulnerable populations and others
- To stay informed as global citizens about current and crucial issues facing humanity

CHAPTER 6

Humanitarian Principles and Themes

Humanitarian Charter and Minimum Standards in Humanitarian Assistance

THE SPHERE PROJECT

The Sphere Project was initiated in 1997 by a group of NGOs and the Red Cross and Red Crescent Movement to develop a set of universal minimum standards in core areas of humanitarian response: the Sphere Handbook. The aim of the Handbook is to improve the quality of humanitarian response in situations of disaster and conflict, and to enhance the accountability of the humanitarian system to disaster-affected people. The Humanitarian Charter and Minimum Standards in Humanitarian Response are the product of the collective experience of many people and agencies. They should therefore not be seen as representing the views of any one agency.

THE HUMANITARIAN CHARTER
OUR BELIEFS

1. The Humanitarian Charter expresses our shared conviction as humanitarian agencies that all people affected by disaster or conflict have a right to receive protection and assistance to ensure the basic conditions for life with dignity. We believe that the principles described in this Humanitarian Charter are universal, applying to all those affected by disaster or conflict wherever they may be, and to all those who seek to assist them or provide for their security. These principles are reflected in international law, but derive their force ultimately from the fundamental moral principle of *humanity*: that all human beings are born free and equal in dignity and rights. Based on this principle, we affirm the primacy of the *humanitarian imperative*:

that action should be taken to prevent or alleviate human suffering arising out of disaster or conflict, and that nothing should override this principle.

As local, national, and international humanitarian agencies, we commit to promoting and adhering to the principles in this Charter and to meeting minimum standards in our efforts to assist and protect those affected. We invite all those who engage in humanitarian activities, including governmental and private sector actors, to endorse the common principles, rights, and duties set out below as a statement of shared humanitarian belief.

OUR ROLE

2. We acknowledge that it is firstly through their own efforts, and through the support of community and local institutions, that the basic needs of people affected by disaster or conflict are met. We recognise the primary role and responsibility of the affected state to provide timely assistance to those affected, to ensure people's protection and security, and to provide support for their recovery. We believe that a combination of official and voluntary action is crucial to effective prevention and response, and in this regard National Societies of the Red Cross and Red Crescent Movement and other civil society actors have an essential role to play in supporting public authorities. Where national capacity is insufficient, we affirm the role of the wider international community, including governmental donors and regional organisations, in assisting states to fulfil their responsibilities. We recognise and support the special roles played by the mandated agencies of the United Nations and the International Committee of the Red Cross.

3. As humanitarian agencies, we interpret our role in relation to the needs and capacities of affected populations and the responsibilities of their governments or controlling powers. Our role in providing assistance reflects the reality that those with primary responsibility are not always fully able to perform this role themselves, or may be unwilling to do so. As far as possible, consistent with meeting the humanitarian imperative and other principles set out in this Charter, we will support the efforts of the relevant authorities to protect and assist those affected. We call upon all state and nonstate actors to respect the impartial, independent, and nonpartisan role of humanitarian agencies and to facilitate their work by removing unnecessary legal and practical barriers, providing for their safety and allowing them timely and consistent access to affected populations.

Common Principles, Rights, and Duties

4. We offer our services as humanitarian agencies on the basis of the principle of humanity and the humanitarian imperative, recognising the rights of all people affected by disaster or conflict—women and men, boys and girls. These include the rights to protection and assistance reflected in the provisions of international humanitarian law, human rights, and refugee law. For the purposes of this Charter, we summarise these rights as follows:

- the right to life with dignity
- the right to receive humanitarian assistance
- the right to protection and security

While these rights are not formulated in such terms in international law, they encapsulate a range of established legal rights and give fuller substance to the humanitarian imperative.

5. The *right to life with dignity* is reflected in the provisions of international law, and specifically the human rights measures concerning the right to life, to an adequate standard of living and to freedom from torture or cruel, inhuman, or degrading treatment or punishment. The right to life entails the duty to preserve life where it is threatened. Implicit in this is the duty not to withhold or frustrate the provision of life-saving assistance. Dignity entails more than physical well-being; it demands respect for the whole person, including the values and beliefs of individuals and affected communities, and respect for their human rights, including liberty, freedom of conscience, and religious observance.

6. The *right to receive humanitarian assistance* is a necessary element of the right to life with dignity. This encompasses the right to an adequate standard of living, including adequate food, water, clothing, shelter, and the requirements for good health, which are expressly guaranteed in international law. The Sphere Core Standards and minimum standards reflect these rights and give practical expression to them, specifically in relation to the provision of assistance to those affected by disaster or conflict. Where the state or nonstate actors are not providing such assistance themselves, we believe they must allow others to help do so. Any such assistance must be provided according to the principle of *impartiality*, which requires that it be provided solely on the basis of need and in proportion to need. This reflects the wider principle of *nondiscrimination*: that no one should be discriminated against on any grounds of

status, including age, gender, race, colour, ethnicity, sexual orientation, language, religion, disability, health status, political or other opinion, national or social origin.

7. The *right to protection and security* is rooted in the provisions of international law, in resolutions of the United Nations and other intergovernmental organisations, and in the sovereign responsibility of states to protect all those within their jurisdiction. The safety and security of people in situations of disaster or conflict are of particular humanitarian concern, including the protection of refugees and internally displaced persons. As the law recognises, some people may be particularly vulnerable to abuse and adverse discrimination due to their status such as age, gender, or race, and may require special measures of protection and assistance. To the extent that a state lacks the capacity to protect people in these circumstances, we believe it must seek international assistance to do so.

The law relating to the protection of civilians and displaced people demands particular attention here:

(i) During *armed conflict* as defined in international humanitarian law, specific legal provision is made for protection and assistance to be given to those not engaged in the conflict. In particular, the 1949 Geneva Conventions and the Additional Protocols of 1977 impose obligations on the parties to both international and noninternational armed conflicts. We stress the general immunity of the civilian population from attack and reprisals, and in particular the importance of the principle of *distinction* between civilians and combatants, and between civilian objects and military objectives; the principles of *proportionality* in the use of force and *precaution* in attack; the duty to refrain from the use of weapons which are indiscriminate or which, by their nature, cause superfluous injury or unnecessary suffering; and the duty to permit impartial relief to be provided. Much of the avoidable suffering caused to civilians in armed conflicts stems from a failure to observe these basic principles.

(ii) The *right to seek asylum or sanctuary* remains vital to the protection of those facing persecution or violence. Those affected by disaster or conflict are often forced to flee their homes in search of security and the means of subsistence. The provisions of the 1951 Convention Relating to the Status of Refugees (as amended) and other international and regional treaties provide fundamental safeguards for those unable to secure protection from the state of their nationality or residence who are forced to seek safety in another country. Chief among these is the principle of *nonrefoulement*: the principle that no one shall be sent back to a country where their life, freedom, or physical security would be threatened or where they are likely to face torture or other cruel, inhuman, or degrading treatment or punishment. The same principle applies by extension to internally displaced persons, as reflected in international human rights law and elaborated in the 1998 Guiding Principles on Internal Displacement and related regional and national law.

Our Commitment

8. We offer our services in the belief that the affected population is at the centre of humanitarian action, and recognise that their active participation is essential to providing assistance in ways that best meet their needs, including those of vulnerable and socially excluded people. We will endeavour to support local efforts to prevent, prepare for and respond to disaster, and to the effects of conflict, and to reinforce the capacities of local actors at all levels.

9. We are aware that attempts to provide humanitarian assistance may sometimes have unintended adverse effects. In collaboration with affected communities and authorities, we aim to minimise any negative effects of humanitarian action on the local community or on the environment. With respect to armed conflict, we recognise that the way in which humanitarian assistance is provided may potentially render civilians more vulnerable to attack, or may on occasion bring unintended advantage to one or more of the parties to the conflict. We are committed to minimising any such adverse effects, in so far as this is consistent with the principles outlined above.

10. We will act in accordance with the principles of humanitarian action set out in this Charter and with the specific guidance in the Code of Conduct for the International Red Cross and Red Crescent Movement and nongovernmental organisations (NGOs) in Disaster Relief (1994).

11. The Sphere Core Standards and minimum standards give practical substance to the common principles in this Charter, based on agencies' understanding of the basic minimum requirements for life with dignity and their experience of providing humanitarian assistance. Though the achievement of the standards depends on a range of factors, many of which may be beyond our control, we commit ourselves to attempting consistently to achieve them, and we expect to be held to account accordingly. We invite all parties, including affected and donor governments, international organisations, private and nonstate actors, to adopt the Sphere Core Standards and minimum standards as accepted norms.

12. By adhering to the Core Standards and minimum standards, we commit to making every effort to ensure that people affected by disasters or conflict have access to at least the minimum requirements for life with dignity and security, including adequate water, sanitation, food, nutrition, shelter, and health care. To this end, we will continue to advocate that states and other parties meet their moral and legal

obligations towards affected populations. For our part, we undertake to make our responses more effective, appropriate and accountable through sound assessment and monitoring of the evolving local context; through transparency of information and decision making; and through more effective coordination and collaboration with other relevant actors at all levels, as detailed in the Core Standards and minimum standards. In particular, we commit to working in partnership with affected populations, emphasising their active participation in the response. We acknowledge that our fundamental accountability must be to those we seek to assist.

OUTLINE OF THE CROSS-CUTTING THEMES

The cross-cutting themes in this Handbook focus on particular areas of concern in disaster response and address individual, group, or general vulnerability issues. In this section, each theme is described in some detail.

Children

Special measures must be taken to ensure all children are protected from harm and given equitable access to basic services. As children often form the larger part of an affected population, it is crucial that their views and experiences are not only elicited during emergency assessments and planning but that they also influence humanitarian service delivery and its monitoring and evaluation. Children and young people are prone to the harmful impact of vulnerability in certain situations, such as malnutrition, exploitation, abduction, and recruitment into armed groups and fighting forces, sexual violence, and lack of opportunity to participate in decision making. The Convention on the Rights of the Child states that a child is considered to be an individual below the age of 18 years. This definition can differ depending on cultural and social contexts. A thorough analysis of how an affected population defines children must be undertaken, to ensure that no child or young person is excluded from humanitarian assistance.

Disaster risk reduction

This is defined as the concept and practice of reducing disaster risks through systematic efforts to analyse and manage the causal factors of disasters, including through reduced exposure to hazards, lessened vulnerability of people and property, wise management of land and the environment, and improved preparedness for adverse events. Such adverse events include natural disasters like storms, floods, droughts, and sea-level rise. As they appear to become increasingly variable and severe, these phenomena are increasingly attributed to global climate change.

Environment

The environment is understood as the physical, chemical, and biological elements and processes that affect disaster-affected and local populations' lives and livelihoods. It provides the natural resources that sustain individuals and contributes to quality of life. It needs protection and management if essential functions are to be maintained. The minimum standards address the need to prevent overexploitation, pollution, and degradation of environmental conditions and aim to secure the life-supporting functions of the environment, reduce risk and vulnerability, and seek to introduce mechanisms that foster adaptability of natural systems for self-recovery.

Gender

Gender refers to the fact that people experience a situation differently according to their gender. Sex refers to biological attributes of women and men. It is natural, determined by birth and, therefore, generally unchanging and universal.

The equal rights of women and men are explicit in the human rights documents that form the basis of the Humanitarian Charter. Women and men have the same entitlement to humanitarian assistance and protection, to respect for their human dignity, to acknowledgment of their equal human capacities including the capacity to make choices, to the same opportunities to act on those choices, and to the same level of power to shape the outcome of their actions. Humanitarian responses are more effective when they are based on an understanding of the different needs, vulnerabilities, interests, capacities, and coping strategies of women and men, girls and boys of all ages and the differing impacts of disaster or conflict upon them. The understanding of these differences, as well as inequalities in women's and men's roles and workloads, access to and control over resources, decision-making power, and opportunities for skills development, is achieved through gender analysis. Gender cuts across other cross-cutting themes. The humanitarian aims of proportionality and impartiality mean that attention must be paid to achieving fairness between women and men and ensuring equality of outcome. Historically, attention to gender relations has been driven by the need to address women's and girls' needs and circumstances, as women and girls are typically more disadvantaged than men and boys. However, increasingly, the humanitarian community recognises the need to understand what men and boys face in crisis situations.

HIV and AIDS

Knowing the HIV prevalence in a specific humanitarian context is important to understand vulnerabilities and risks and to plan an effective response. In addition to the most at-risk populations (i.e., men who have sex with men, intravenous drug users, and sex workers), who often need to receive specific measures to protect themselves against neglect, discrimination, and violence, some contexts may have other vulnerable groups such as refugees, migrants, youth, and single mothers. Mass displacement may lead to increased HIV vulnerabilities and risks due to separation of family members and breakdown of community cohesion and of social and sexual norms regulating behaviour. Women and children may be exploited by armed groups and be particularly vulnerable to HIV due to sexual violence and exploitation. During humanitarian emergencies, people may no longer have access to HIV interventions such as prevention programmes, and the disruption of antiretroviral therapy (ART), tuberculosis (TB) treatment and prevention, and treatment for other opportunistic infections may occur.

People living with HIV (PLHIV) often suffer from discrimination and stigma and, therefore, confidentiality must be strictly adhered to and protection made available when needed. The sector activities in this Handbook should provide appropriate HIV interventions according to prevalence and context, and not increase people's vulnerabilities and risks to HIV.

Older People

Older men and women are those aged over 60 years, according to the UN, but a definition of "older" can vary in different contexts. Older people are often among the poorest in developing countries and comprise a large and growing proportion of the most vulnerable in disaster- or conflict-affected populations (for example, the over-80s are the fastest-growing age group in the world) and yet they are often neglected in disaster or conflict management. Isolation and physical weakness are significant factors exacerbating vulnerability in older people in disasters or conflict, along with disruption to livelihood strategies and to family and community support structures, chronic health and mobility problems, and declining mental health. Special efforts must be made to identify and reach housebound older people and households headed by older people. Older people also have key contributions to make in survival and rehabilitation. They play vital roles as carers of children, resource managers, and income generators, have knowledge and experience of community coping strategies and help to preserve cultural and social identities.

Persons with Disabilities

The World Health Organization (WHO) estimates that between 7 and 10 percent of the world's population—including children and older people—live with disabilities. Disasters and conflict can cause increased incidence of impairment and subsequent disability. The UN Convention on the Rights of Persons with Disabilities (CRPD) defines disability as an evolving concept that results from the interaction between persons with impairments (which may be physical, sensory, intellectual, or psychosocial) and the attitudinal and environmental barriers that hinder their full and effective participation in society on an equal basis with others. It is, therefore, the presence of these barriers that prevent persons with disabilities from fully and meaningfully participating in, or benefiting from, mainstream humanitarian assistance programmes. The new CRPD makes specific reference to the safety and protection of persons with disabilities in conflict and emergency situations (Article 11).

Persons with disabilities face disproportionate risks in disaster situations and are often excluded from relief and rehabilitation processes. Such exclusion makes it more difficult to effectively use and participate in standard disaster support services. Importantly, persons with disabilities are a diverse population including children and older people, whose needs cannot be addressed in a "one size fits all" approach. Humanitarian responses, therefore, must take into consideration the particular abilities, skills, resources, and knowledge of individuals with different types and degrees of impairments. It is also important to remember that persons with disabilities have the same basic needs as everyone else in their communities. In addition, some may also have specific needs, such as replacement of aids or appliances, and access to rehabilitation services. Furthermore, any measures targeting persons with disabilities must not lead to their separation from their family and community networks. Finally, if the rights of persons with disabilities are not taken into consideration in humanitarian responses, a huge opportunity is lost to rebuild communities for all people. It is essential, therefore, to include persons with disabilities in all aspects of relief and recovery. This requires both mainstreamed and targeted responses.

Psychosocial Support

Some of the greatest sources of vulnerability and suffering in disasters arise from the complex emotional, social, physical, and spiritual effects of disasters. Many of these reactions are normal and can be overcome with time. It is essential to organise locally appropriate mental health and psychosocial supports that promote self-help, coping, and resilience among affected people. Humanitarian action is strengthened if at the earliest appropriate moment, affected people are engaged in guiding and implementing the disaster response. In each humanitarian sector, the manner in which aid is administered has a psychosocial impact that may either support or cause harm to affected people. Aid should be delivered in a compassionate manner that promotes dignity, enables self-efficacy through meaningful participation, respects the importance of religious and cultural practices and strengthens the ability of affected people to support holistic well-being.

REFERENCES

United Nations. 1989. Convention on the rights of the child. http://www2.ohchr.org/english/law/crc.htm.

United Nations General Assembly. 2006. Convention on the rights of persons with disabilities. http://www.un.org/disabilities/convention/news.shtml.

World Health Organization. 2011. Disabilities and rehabilitation. World Health Organization. http://www.who.int/disabilities/en/.

EDITORS' NOTES

For more information about the Sphere Project: http://www.sphereproject.org/.

SOURCE

The Sphere Project. 2011. Humanitarian charter and minimum standards in humanitarian response. Geneva: The Sphere Project, pp. ii, 14–17, 20–24. http://www.sphereproject.org/handbook/. Reprinted by permission.

RELATED RESOURCES

Video: The Sphere Project. "Introducing the Sphere Handbook 2011." The Sphere Project. http://www.sphereproject.org/handbook/.

Cornwall, A., and D. Eade, eds. 2010. *Deconstructing development discourse: Buzzwords and fuzzwords*. Bourton on Dunsmore, UK: Practical Action Publishing.

Gray, I. 2008. Fragile states and neglected emergencies. *Global Future* 2: 22–23. http://www.wvi.org/wvi/wviweb.nsf/0/77C7AFAA5B293ACF882576E900701916?opendocument.

International Federation of Red Cross and Red Crescent Societies. 2012. World disaster report 2011 Editor: Focus on hunger and malnutrition. http://www.ifrc.org/publications-and-reports/world-disasters-report/.

Janz, M., and J. Slead, eds. 2000. *Complex humanitarian emergencies: Lessons from practitioners*. Monrovia, CA: World Vision International.

Klugman, J. 2011. Human development report 2011: Sustainability and equity; A better future for all. New York: United Nations Development Programme. http://hdr.undp.org/en/reports/global/hdr2011/.

Nading, A. 2012. The Sphere Project: Taking stock. *Humanitarian Exchange* 53: 30–32. http://www.odihpn.org/humanitarian-exchange-magazine/issue-53/the-sphere-project-taking-stock.

United Nations. 2012. World humanitarian day (August 19). United Nations. http://www.un.org/en/events/humanitarianday/.

United Nations Office for the Coordination of Humanitarian Affairs (OCHA) (website with resources). http://www.unocha.org/.

CHAPTER 7

Code of Conduct in Disaster Relief

THE CODE OF CONDUCT FOR THE INTERNATIONAL RED CROSS AND RED CRESCENT MOVEMENT AND NON-GOVERNMENTAL ORGANISATIONS (NGOS) IN DISASTER RELIEF

International Federation of Red Cross and Red Crescent Societies and the ICRC[1]

This Code of Conduct seeks to guard our standards of behaviour. It is not about operational details, such as how one should calculate food rations or set up a refugee camp. Rather, it seeks to maintain the high standards of independence, effectiveness and impact to which disaster response NGOs and the International Red Cross and Red Crescent Movement aspires. It is a voluntary code, enforced by the will of the organisation accepting it to maintain the standards laid down in the Code. In the event of armed conflict, the present Code of Conduct will be interpreted and applied in conformity with international humanitarian law. The Code of Conduct is presented first. Attached to it are three annexes, describing the working environment that we would like to see created by Host Governments, Donor Governments and Inter-Governmental Organisations in order to facilitate the effective delivery of humanitarian assistance.

DEFINITIONS

NGOs: (Non-Governmental Organisations) refers here to organisations, both national and international, which are constituted separately from the government of the country in which they are founded.

NGHAs: For the purposes of this text, the term Non-Governmental Humanitarian Agencies (NGHAs) has been coined to encompass the components of the International Red Cross and Red Crescent Movement—The International Committee of the Red Cross, The International Federation of Red Cross and Red Crescent Societies and its member National Societies—and the NGOs as defined above. This code refers specifically to those NGHAs who are involved in disaster response.

IGOs: (Inter-Governmental Organisations) refers to organisations constituted by two or more governments. It thus includes all United Nations Agencies and regional organisations.

Disasters: A disaster is a calamitous event resulting in loss of life, great human suffering and distress, and large-scale material damage.

THE CODE OF CONDUCT: TEN PRINCIPLES

1. The humanitarian imperative comes first.

The right to receive humanitarian assistance, and to offer it, is a fundamental humanitarian principle which should be enjoyed by all citizens of all countries. As members of the international community, we recognise our obligation to provide humanitarian assistance wherever it is needed. Hence the need for unimpeded access to affected populations is of fundamental importance in exercising that responsibility. The prime motivation of our response to disaster is to alleviate human suffering amongst those least able to withstand the stress caused by disaster. When we give humanitarian aid it is not a partisan or political act and should not be viewed as such.

2. Aid is given regardless of the race, creed, or nationality of the recipients and without adverse distinction of any kind. Aid priorities are calculated on the basis of need alone.

Wherever possible, we will base the provision of relief aid upon a thorough assessment of the needs of the disaster victims and the local capacities already in place to meet those needs. Within the entirety of our programmes, we will reflect considerations of proportionality. Human suffering must be alleviated whenever it is found; life is as precious in one part of a country as another. Thus, our provision of aid will reflect the degree of suffering it seeks to alleviate. In implementing this approach, we recognise the crucial role played by women in disaster-prone communities and will ensure that this role is supported, not diminished, by our aid programmes. The implementation of such a universal, impartial and independent policy can only be effective if we and our partners have access to the necessary resources to provide for such equitable relief, and have equal access to all disaster victims.

3. Aid will not be used to further a particular political or religious standpoint.

Humanitarian aid will be given according to the need of individuals, families and communities. Notwithstanding the right of NGHAs to espouse particular political or religious opinions, we affirm that assistance will not be dependent on the adherence of the recipients to those opinions. We will not tie the promise, delivery, or distribution of assistance to the embracing or acceptance of a particular political or religious creed.

4. We shall endeavour not to act as instruments of government foreign policy.

NGHAs are agencies which act independently from governments. We therefore formulate our own policies and implementation strategies and do not seek to implement the policy of any government, except in so far as it coincides with our own independent policy. We will never knowingly—or through negligence—allow ourselves or our employees to be used to gather information of a political, military, or economically sensitive nature for governments or other bodies that may serve purposes other than those which are strictly humanitarian, nor will we act as instruments of foreign policy of donor governments. We will use the assistance we receive to respond to needs and this assistance should not be driven by the need to dispose of donor commodity surpluses, nor by the political interest of any particular donor. We value and promote the voluntary giving of labour and finances by concerned individuals to support our work and recognise the independence of action promoted by such voluntary motivation. In order to protect our independence we will seek to avoid dependence upon a single funding source.

5. We shall respect culture and custom.

We will endeavour to respect the culture, structures and customs of the communities and countries we are working in.

6. We shall attempt to build disaster response on local capacities.

All people and communities—even in disaster—possess capacities as well as vulnerabilities. Where possible, we will strengthen these capacities by employing local staff, purchasing local materials and trading with local companies. Where possible, we will work through local NGHAs as partners in planning and implementation, and cooperate with local government structures where appropriate. We will place a high priority on the proper coordination of our emergency responses. This is best done within the countries concerned by those most directly involved in the relief operations, and should include representatives of the relevant UN bodies.

7. Ways shall be found to involve programme beneficiaries in the management of relief aid.

Disaster response assistance should never be imposed upon the beneficiaries. Effective relief and lasting rehabilitation can best be achieved where the intended beneficiaries are involved in the design, management and implementation of the assistance programme. We will strive to achieve full community participation in our relief and rehabilitation programmes.

8. Relief aid must strive to reduce future vulnerabilities to disaster as well as meeting basic needs.

All relief actions affect the prospects for long-term development, either in a positive or a negative fashion. Recognising this, we will strive to implement relief programmes which actively reduce the beneficiaries' vulnerability to future disasters and help create sustainable lifestyles. We will pay particular attention to environmental concerns in the design and management of relief programmes. We will also endeavour to minimise the negative impact of humanitarian assistance, seeking to avoid long-term beneficiary dependence upon external aid.

9. We hold ourselves accountable to both those we seek to assist and those from whom we accept resources.

We often act as an institutional link in the partnership between those who wish to assist and those who need assistance during disasters. We therefore hold ourselves accountable to both constituencies. All our dealings with donors and beneficiaries shall reflect an attitude of openness and transparency. We recognise the need to report on our activities, both from a financial perspective and the perspective of effectiveness. We recognise the obligation to ensure appropriate monitoring of aid distributions and to carry out regular assessments of the impact of disaster assistance. We will also seek to report, in an open fashion, upon the impact of our work, and the factors limiting or enhancing that impact. Our programmes will be based upon high standards of professionalism and expertise in order to minimise the wasting of valuable resources.

10. In our information, publicity and advertising activities, we shall recognise disaster victims as dignified humans, not hopeless objects.

Respect for the disaster victim as an equal partner in action should never be lost. In our public information we shall portray an objective image of the disaster situation where the capacities and aspirations of disaster victims are highlighted, and not just their vulnerabilities and fears. While we will cooperate with the media in order to enhance public response, we will not allow external or internal demands for publicity to take precedence over the principle of maximising overall relief assistance. We will avoid competing with other disaster response agencies for media coverage in situations where such coverage may be to the detriment of the service provided to the beneficiaries or to the security of our staff or the beneficiaries.

THE WORKING ENVIRONMENT

Having agreed unilaterally to strive to abide by the Code laid out above, we present below some indicative guidelines which describe the working environment we would like to see created by donor governments, host governments and the intergovernmental organisations—principally the agencies of the United Nations—in order to facilitate the effective participation of NGHAs in disaster response.

These guidelines are presented for guidance. They are not legally binding, nor do we expect governments and IGOs to indicate their acceptance of the guidelines through the signature of any document, although this may be a goal to work to in the future. They are presented in a spirit of openness and cooperation so that our partners will become aware of the ideal relationship we would seek with them.

ANNEX I:
RECOMMENDATIONS TO THE GOVERNMENTS
OF DISASTER-AFFECTED COUNTRIES

1. **Governments should recognise and respect the independent, humanitarian and impartial actions of NGHAs.** NGHAs are independent bodies. This independence and impartiality should be respected by host governments.

2. **Host governments should facilitate rapid access to disaster victims for NGHAs.** If NGHAs are to act in full compliance with their humanitarian principles,

they should be granted rapid and impartial access to disaster victims, for the purpose of delivering humanitarian assistance. It is the duty of the host government, as part of the exercising of sovereign responsibility, not to block such assistance, and to accept the impartial and apolitical action of NGHAs. Host governments should facilitate the rapid entry of relief staff, particularly by waiving requirements for transit, entry and exit visas, or arranging that these are rapidly granted. Governments should grant overflight permission and landing rights for aircraft transporting international relief supplies and personnel, for the duration of the emergency relief phase.

3. **Governments should facilitate the timely flow of relief goods and information during disasters.** Relief supplies and equipment are brought into a country solely for the purpose of alleviating human suffering, not for commercial benefit or gain. Such supplies should normally be allowed free and unrestricted passage and should not be subject to requirements for consular certificates of origin or invoices, import and/or export licences, or other restrictions, or to importation taxation, landing fees, or port charges.

The temporary importation of necessary relief equipment, including vehicles, light aircraft and telecommunications equipment, should be facilitated by the receiving host government through the temporary waiving of licence or registration restrictions. Equally, governments should not restrict the reexportation of relief equipment at the end of a relief operation.

To facilitate disaster communications, host governments are encouraged to designate certain radio frequencies, which relief organisations may use in-country and for international communications for the purpose of disaster communications, and to make such frequencies known to the disaster response community prior to the disaster. They should authorise relief personnel to utilise all means of communication required for their relief operations.

4. **Governments should seek to provide a coordinated disaster information and planning service.** The overall planning and coordination of relief efforts is ultimately the responsibility of the host government. Planning and coordination can be greatly enhanced if NGHAs are provided with information on relief needs and government systems for planning and implementing relief efforts as well as information on potential security risks they may encounter. Governments are urged to provide such information to NGHAs.

To facilitate effective coordination and the efficient utilisation of relief efforts, host governments are urged to designate, prior to disaster, a single point-of-contact for incoming NGHAs to liaise with the national authorities.

5. Disaster relief in the event of armed conflict. In the event of armed conflict, relief actions are governed by the relevant provisions of international humanitarian law.

ANNEX II:
RECOMMENDATIONS TO DONOR GOVERNMENTS

1. Donor governments should recognise and respect the independent, humanitarian and impartial actions of NGHAs. NGHAs are independent bodies whose independence and impartiality should be respected by donor governments. Donor governments should not use NGHAs to further any political or ideological aim.

2. Donor governments should provide funding with a guarantee of operational independence. NGHAs accept funding and material assistance from donor governments in the same spirit as they render it to disaster victims; one of humanity and independence of action. The implementation of relief actions is ultimately the responsibility of the NGHA and will be carried out according to the policies of that NGHA.

3. Donor governments should use their good offices to assist NGHAs in obtaining access to disaster victims. Donor governments should recognise the importance of accepting a level of responsibility for the security and freedom of access of NGHA staff to disaster sites. They should be prepared to exercise diplomacy with host governments on such issues if necessary.

ANNEX III:
RECOMMENDATIONS TO INTER-GOVERNMENTAL
ORGANISATIONS

1. IGOs should recognise NGHAs, local and foreign, as valuable partners. NGHAs are willing to work with UN and other inter-governmental agencies to effect better disaster response. They do so in a spirit of partnership which respects the integrity and independence of all partners. Inter-governmental agencies must respect the independence and impartiality of the NGHAs. NGHAs should be consulted by UN agencies in the preparation of relief plans.

2. IGOs should assist host governments in providing an overall coordinating framework for international and local disaster relief. NGHAs do not usually have the mandate to provide the overall coordinating framework for disasters which require an international response. This responsibility falls to the host government and the relevant United Nations authorities. They are urged to provide this service in a timely and effective manner to serve the affected state and the national and international disaster response community. In any case, NGHAs should make all efforts to ensure the effective coordination of their own services. In the event of armed conflict, relief actions are governed by the relevant provisions of international humanitarian law.

3. IGOs should extend security protection provided for UN organisations to NGHAs. Where security services are provided for inter-governmental organisations, this service should be extended to their operational NGHA partners where it is so requested.

4. IGOs should provide NGHAs with the same access to relevant information as is granted to UN organisations. IGOs are urged to share all information, pertinent to the implementation of effective disaster response, with their operational NGHA partners.

NOTES

1. Sponsored by Caritas Internationalis*, Catholic Relief Services*, The International Federation of Red Cross and Red Crescent Societies*, International Save the Children Alliance*, Lutheran World Federation*, Oxfam*, The World Council of Churches*, The International Committee of the Red Cross (* members of the Steering Committee for Humanitarian Response).

For more information about the International Red Cross and Red Crescent Movement: http://www.icrc.org/eng/who-we-are/movement/index.jsp.

SOURCE

International Federation of Red Cross and Red Crescent Societies and the ICRC. 1994. The code of conduct for the International Red Cross and Red Crescent Movement and non-governmental organisations (NGOs) in disaster relief. Geneva: International Federation of Red Cross and Red Crescent Societies and the ICRC. Reprinted by permission. http://www.ifrc.org/en/publications-and-reports/code-of-conduct/.

RELATED RESOURCES

Videos: ICRC Video Newsroom (various topics and current events). http://www.icrc.org/eng/resources/12-video-newsroom/index.jsp.

International Committee of the Red Cross. n.d. *The fundamental principles of the Red Cross and Red Crescent*. Geneva: Author. http://www.icrc.org/eng/resources/documents/publication/p0513.htm.

————. 1988. Basic rules of the Geneva Conventions and their additional protocols: Understanding humanitarian law. http://www.icrc.org/eng/assets/files/other/icrc_002_0365.pdf.

————. 1999. People on war report: ICRC worldwide consultation on the rules of war. Geneva: International Committee of the Red Cross. http://www.icrc.org/eng/assets/files/other/icrc_002_0758.pdf.

————. 2011. International humanitarian law and the challenges of contemporary armed conflict. (31st International Conference of the Red Cross and Red Crescent, Geneva, 28 November to 1 December 2011). http://www.icrc.org/eng/resources/documents/report/31-international-conference-ihl-challenges-report-2011–10–31.htm.

NGO conference on The Code of Conduct of the Red Cross and Red Crescent Movement and NGOs in Disaster Relief. 2004. Ten years code of conduct: Principles in practice. The Hague, the Netherlands: Conference on The Code of Conduct of the Red Cross and Red Crescent Movement and NGOs in Disaster Relief. https://icvanetwork.org/system/files/versions/doc00004271.pdf.

CHAPTER 8

Spirituality and Mental Health in Humanitarian Contexts

AN EXPLORATION BASED ON WORLD VISION'S HAITI EARTHQUAKE RESPONSE

Alison Schafer, World Vision Australia

FOR THE INTERNATIONAL NONGOVERNEMENTAL ORGANISATION WORLD VISION INTERNATIONAL, THE HAITI EARTHQUAKE RESPONSE REVEALED A SIGNIFICANT GAP IN MATERIALS AND INTERVENTIONS THAT COMBINED SPIRITUAL NEEDS WITH THE MENTAL HEALTH AND PSYCHOSOCIAL SUPPORT NEEDS OF AFFECTED COMMUNITIES. DESPITE GROWING SCIENTIFIC EVIDENCE THAT SPIRITUALITY CAN HAVE BENEFICIAL EFFECTS ON MENTAL HEALTH AND PSYCHOSOCIAL WELLBEING, THERE IS LITTLE GUIDANCE AND CONSENSUS ABOUT PSYCHO-SPIRITUAL APPROACHES IN HUMANITARIAN CONTEXTS. THIS IS ESPECIALLY PERTINENT FOR THE EMERGENCY RESPONSE IN HAITI WHERE RELIGIOUS PRACTICE AND FAITH UNDERPINS LOCAL CULTURE. THIS CAN LEAD TO PRACTICAL AND ETHICAL DILEMMAS. CHURCHES, THE CLERGY AND PEOPLES' SPIRITUALITY ARE AN IMPORTANT AREA FOR HUMANITARIAN PRACTICE TO EXPLORE, PARTICULARLY WITHIN THE MENTAL HEALTH AND PSYCHOSOCIAL SUPPORT DOMAIN.

INTRODUCTION

In response to the devastating earthquake that struck the tiny nation of Haiti on 12 January 2010, World Vision International (WVI) engaged the full partnership of relief teams in deployment. The response of the organisation included food aid, water and sanitation, emergency health and nutrition, child protection and provisions of other non-food items including temporary shelter. For the first time in WVI's emergency response history a focal point person for mental health and psychosocial support (MHPSS) was also deployed. Although reporting to the health team, this person worked across sectors and in collaboration with the broader MHPSS Working Group that was established through the UN Cluster System.

As a faith-based, nongovernmental organisation (NGO), WVI considered ways to engage in the '*spiritual nurture*' of people affected by the Haiti earthquake as part of our overall response. This was based on the mission of the organisation to overtly recognise and support the spiritual needs of people affected by emergencies, and was considered appropriate to the Haitian context. For WVI, spiritual needs and subsequent support may include faith-based counselling, spiritual guidance, peer support, or opportunities to explore issues related to faith or religious practice. WVI recognised that spiritual support may be helpful or sought by individuals, families or communities, and also considered spiritual support for staff and local clergy through partnerships with churches. Through this strategy clear links and opportunities between the spiritual nurture activities and MHPSS activities became apparent. However, it also became apparent that combining spiritual nurture and MHPSS was a new approach for the organisation and it lacked personnel, materials and programmatic resources that would serve both the spiritual nurture and MHPSS as part of the church engagement of the organisation. It raised questions about whether more spiritual approaches, or technical MHPSS interventions, were appropriate within WVI: there were concerns over whether these combined approaches for spiritual nurture and MHPSS complied with the *Code of Conduct for the International Red Cross and Red Crescent Movement and NGOs in Disaster Relief* (IFRC/ICRC, 1994), where it states that aid should not be used to promote a particular religious standpoint. WVI also questioned whether combined spiritual nurture and MHPSS approaches would be consistent with the *IASC Guidelines on Mental Health and Psychosocial Support in Emergency Settings* (IASC, 2007). It is unlikely these concerns are specific to WVI given there is a lack of guidance on spirituality and MHPSS in the overall humanitarian sector. Elicited from WVI's experience in Haiti and our organisational need to explore the links between spirituality and mental health, this paper reviews some literature on the topic. It also analyses psycho-spiritual approaches to health and wellbeing and considers some rudimentary recommendations for a way forward for humanitarian agencies.

SPIRITUALITY AND MENTAL HEALTH AND WELLBEING

The psychological literature has begun to use the terms "religion" and "spirituality" synonymously; although there is recognition that religion usually refers to beliefs, practices and rituals related to a specific sacred being, while spirituality is a diverse construct referring to existential concerns such as life and death, personal life direction, general wellbeing, comfort and inner peace (Koenig, 2009). For the purposes of this paper, the terms "spirituality" and "religion" will also be used synonymously as they appropriately represent both the formalised religions of Haiti, namely Catholicism and Protestant traditions, as well as other spiritual dimensions of Haitians, such as widely held beliefs in Vodou (WHO, 2010).

Throughout history the religious clergy and churches of various denominations have cared for people with psychosocial concerns and mental illness. With the advances of medical and social science, the conventions of psychiatry and psychology have tended to disconnect from the church and functioned as separate service providers, at least in the more developed north (Boehnlein, 2006). However, worldwide it is estimated that approximately 40 percent of people who experience mental health concerns still turn to their clergy or church for firstline assistance (Openshaw & Harr, 2009). Accounting for religious practice and faith as a prominent feature of culture in underdeveloped nations, up to 90 percent of the world's population remain active in some form of religious or spiritual custom (Koenig, 2009).

As with the current humanitarian context in Haiti, religion and spiritual practice is foundational to local culture and coping (WHO, 2010). It is expected that future humanitarian emergencies will face similar needs to account for, and work with, local religious influences as coping mechanisms for affected communities. This is an important consideration to mental health and wellbeing given that spiritual beliefs and practice directly contribute to a community's frame of reference and their finding meaning in a crisis and, ultimately, their access to resources and capacities for coping (Tankink, 2007; Wortmann & Park, 2009). Studies directly exploring the associations between spirituality and mental health generally find that spirituality contributes to improved quality of life, reduced incidences of affective disorders, including depression and anxiety, lowered rates of suicide and abstinence from alcohol or other substance abuse (Koenig & Larson, 2001; Sawatzky, Ratner & Chiu, 2005). Baetz & Toews (2009) reported that the positive effects of typical spiritual messages, such as promotion of altruism and thoughts of gratitude and forgiveness, have also shown significant and positive relationships to an improved sense of wellbeing, stress reduction, and increases in life satisfaction. While the majority of research into spirituality and mental health has been conducted in developed contexts, the theories and suggested processes for its causal influences may be germane to all contexts, even if the nuanced practice of religion and spirituality differs.

Three main processes appear to generate mental health gains through spiritual and religious practice (Koenig & Larson, 2001). First, that spiritual beliefs and practices encourage more optimistic worldviews that offer people a sense of meaning and purpose in their lives, even in light of turmoil or intensely stressful events. This has been consistently supported in other research including those around issues of bereavement and loss (Wortmann & Park, 2009), the atrocities of war (Tankink, 2007), and natural disasters (Henderson, Roberto & Kamo, 2009), as well as trauma (Peres, Moreira-Almeida, Nasallo & Koenig, 2007; Vis & Boynton, 2008). Hill & Pargament (2003) have further suggested that a perceived closeness to God may be likened to a positive attachment, such as those that children form with parents, which offers a sense of being cared for and protected in times of fear or adversity, including ill health, major life stressors or post disaster. Second, most religious practice promotes the support and care of others, which subsequently then promotes greater psychosocial interaction, realises the benefits of altruism and, along with faith itself, promotes a sense of human agency (Tankink, 2007). Third, religious and spiritual practice has been shown to consistently correlate with increased social support (Hill & Pargament, 2003). Koenig & Larson (2001) noted that such enhanced social supports for practising religious people also ensured the presence of assistance at times of stress, greater coping options and a protector against emotional disorder. Koenig (2009) theorised that social support may help to prevent suicide by ensuring people at risk are surrounded by others in a caring environment.

By and large, evidence points towards a positive correlation between spirituality and mental health, but some negative impacts have also been documented. Wortmann & Park (2009) found in their study on bereavement and loss that 40 percent of participants found comfort, meaning and acceptance of their losses through religious experiences and practices. However, they also found that an equivalent number of people in their study perceived their losses to contribute to significant religious struggles, including questioning their faith and worldviews, which subsequently led to higher stress, anxiety and distress. In post war Uganda, Tankink's (2007) study on born-again Christians showed that while the majority benefited from renewed faith, prayer and worship, others viewed the church commitment to be too intense with overwhelming expectations for participating in a gamut of church activities. As a consequence, some people in Tankink's study withdrew from their church communities and felt less connected with others.

Approaches to spiritual practice have also been shown to moderate the possible benefits of mental health. Masters & Spielmans (2007) found that frequency of prayer correlated with improved mental health, but the content and processes of prayer affected the outcomes. They reported that when people felt subjectively close to God, their wellbeing increased, but the more ritualistic and prescribed prayers became, greater loneliness, depression and tension was experienced, along with subjective feelings of being distant from God. In a similar vein, Rosmarin, Pirutinsky & Pargament (2009) reported that Orthodox Jews who tended to practice more conservative spiritual activities encountered greater anxiety and depression. Braam, Sonnenberg, Beekman, Deeg & VanTilburg (2000) revealed that religious practice and denomination was influential in the presentation and severity of symptoms for depression. Braam's study indicated that amongst clinically depressed elderly people in Europe, traditional Calvinist followers showed more feelings of worthlessness and guilt than their Roman Catholic counterparts; but the practising Catholics in the sample showed significantly higher and more severe depression symptoms than non-practising Roman Catholics.

'Toto' (name changed for privacy) survived the January 12 earthquake in Haiti. When it occurred he was at his local church where he worshipped every Tuesday. Many people viewed Toto to be 'blessed' because he survived without injury, along with his immediate family members and others of his church community. However, Toto's losses were still significant. For more than twenty years Toto had been a retailer for cosmetics and beauty products, which he used to sell in downtown Port-au-Prince. Following the earthquake, all his supplies were crushed or lost in the rubble, along with his prospects for future business. Approximately two months after the earthquake Toto started feeling low. He lost his appetite, began withdrawing from his family, friends, and church community, and was seen to be crying a lot. People heard Toto say things like 'no one wants me.' Somehow Toto became stripped of all purpose and meaning in his life. Where faith had once supported his worldview, it seemed to be unfathomable to understand in the new environment.

Toto attended hospital for treatment as his lack of food intake became more serious, and his blood pressure and sugar levels fluctuated. Toto's church paid for his hospital costs but they were uncertain about what else they could offer him. Toto's family and church friends attempted to support Toto by encouraging him to look towards the future and the makeshift home they were preparing for him. They also attempted to access psychological assistance for Toto, but this was too difficult and unavailable in the chaos of other medical needs being attended to in post earthquake Haiti. Three months after the earthquake in Haiti, Toto was still unable to eat and he had not had mental health assistance for his depression. He eventually passed away. His family and church community believe that Toto will enjoy a peaceful afterlife with God, but wished they had been able to do more for him, both spiritually and mentally, before he died.

SPIRITUALITY AND MENTAL HEALTH AND WELLBEING IN HUMANITARIAN SETTINGS

For humanitarian actors bound by the *Do No Harm* framework in conflict settings and aid interventions (Inter-Agency Standing Committee (IASC), 2007) the findings that the relationship between spirituality and mental health has the potential to elicit both positive and negative impacts indicate the necessity for caution and care when implementing programmes aimed at meeting the two needs. A logical question might be whether or not spiritual nurture activities should continue to be separated from MHPSS interventions and vice versa. This has been a challenging debate for WVI's response in Haiti. While the ideal has been to source materials promoting spiritual nurture and practice, as well as support people in coping with their distress, losses, and stressful life circumstances, WVI has not been able to identify culturally validated materials that have confirmed 'no harm' nor even to access resources that provided an appropriate balance between spiritual nurture and MHPSS. On the one hand, some materials have been more biblical in nature and suggestive that faith, fundamental acceptance of the tenets of Christianity and a cathartic approach to 'trauma recovery' will assist to promote mental health and wellbeing. The approaches that directly encourage people to recount traumatic experiences without trained counsellors or professional follow-up, even in writing or prayer, do not comply with the *IASC Guidelines on Mental Health and Psychosocial Support in Emergency Settings* (IASC, 2007) or the *IASC Guidance Notes for MHPSS in Haiti* (IASC, 2010). Some of these materials have also been quite evangelistic (i.e., intended to lead people to make a confession of faith in Jesus Christ). The use of such materials could be viewed as a form of proselytising, and thus be in contravention of WVI policy and humanitarian codes of conduct. On the other hand, MHPSS resources have tended to either completely ignore spiritual aspects of wellbeing or, at best, address spirituality as a nebulous construct where it is unlikely to adequately address meaningful spiritual connection, which is a fundamental aspect of peoples' lives in Haiti.

Adding to the complexity, there are no international guidelines to offer clear direction for how psycho-spiritual interventions can or should be utilised. International consensus agrees that Western methodologies, interventions and materials should not be merely 'translated' to local language and people, they should be encouraged to participate in traditional religious and cultural activities (IASC, 2010). The *Humanitarian Charter and Minimum Standards in Disaster* (The Sphere Project, 2004) and other codes of conduct (IFRC/ICRC, 1994) all indicate the need to respect spiritual and religious beliefs, but they do not provide recommendations for leveraging those practices by faith-based and/or secular humanitarian agencies. While it is important that agencies do not conceptualise peoples' spiritual beliefs or practices as a medium for realising humanitarian goals, guidance would better assist the humanitarian sector to identify ethical approaches to supporting peoples' spiritual needs and engagement.

For example, WVI is a Christian humanitarian organisation and is well positioned to provide spiritual nurture programmes associated with Christian aspects of faith. However, our capacity to provide or develop programmes for the spiritual nurture and support to other faiths is relatively limited. If WVI were to neglect other faiths or religious traditions and only offer psychospiritual approaches to Christian groups, this may be seen as discrimination or advancing the organisation's own religious framework. In addition, current guidelines and codes do not provide adequate recommendations for how secular NGOs may also contribute to the emerging link between spiritual practice and MHPSS. Another central aspect to this debate is the uncertainty about what specifically constitutes a psycho-spiritual approach, how it is implemented and whether such approaches are effective for protecting or promoting mental health and wellbeing.

In the aftermath of the Haiti earthquake, WVI, as a faith-based NGO, was approached by many Western-based church groups and publishing organisations. They submitted materials that they believed would be helpful to support the spiritual and mental wellbeing of congregations and other communities in Haiti to WVI. There was also a suggestion that materials could be used in nonchurch-based programs, such as child friendly spaces. While some aspects of the materials were potentially beneficial, such as encouraging children to talk with others about their feelings, or to use mediums such drawing or diarising their unhappy thoughts, many also suggested simplistic approaches to complex issues. For example, some materials suggested that if children prayed to God, or confessed their sins and followed Jesus Christ, they would feel cared for and listened to. Other materials suggested that based on group discussion topics alone, church communities may be able to lead and support people affected by loss and grief, domestic violence, or rape. Most materials also promoted traditional Christian values or practices, like confession and forgiveness. One of the primary concerns for WVI has been to carefully screen materials for overt or covert evangelical messages (which breach organisational policy), but it has also been to explore how such materials can or should be utilised. This has brought us to explore appropriate psycho-spiritual interventions, but the main learning has been an awareness of how rare such approaches are and how challenging they may be in humanitarian contexts; even in emergency responses like Haiti where faith and spirituality is a cultural foundation.

PSYCHO-SPIRITUAL APPROACHES

Guidance around psycho-spiritual interventions through churches or MHPSS programmes may still be problematic and take time to evolve. Even in developed countries and Western psychology, the psycho-spiritual approach is a relatively new area. Effective interventions are still largely unknown, and minimal research has indicated evidence-based practice (Blazer, 2009).

Elsass & Phuntsok (2008) researched the coping mechanisms of Tibetan torture survivors living in refugee settlements in India. Participants reported that despite their strong religious and political beliefs forming an important aspect of their coping, they still benefited from psychosocial support and counselling, even though interventions did not specifically focus on their spiritual frameworks. A meta-analysis by Smith, Bartz & Richards (2007) regarding spiritual-based psychological interventions found that spiritual adaptations to psychotherapy benefited the vast majority of clients, but six-month follow-ups revealed those benefits to be equal to therapeutic interventions that had not addressed spiritual issues. The mental health benefits of both groups were sustained.

Baskin & Enright (2004) studied one specific ideology of spirituality-forgiveness. Their study analysed three models of forgiveness including: encouragement to forgive in individual therapy, encouragement to forgive in group therapy, and a brief decision-to-forgive cognitive-based model. Individual therapy was found to be more effective than group therapy, and both were found to be more effective than a decision-based model. In support of further research (Baetz & Toews, 2009), forgiveness correlated significantly with lowered symptoms of mental illness and higher overall wellbeing. It indicated that spiritual ideals cannot be forced or promoted simply at a rational level, but that it requires considerable psychotherapeutic process and consideration to ensure meaningful change.

Another question these psycho-spiritual approaches evoke is whether or not spiritually adapted MHPSS interventions should be recommended if the client has not specifically requested it, or a client has not been assessed for being willing to engage in spiritual aspects of their care. The commentary about spirituality and mental health has now begun to focus on the importance of more thorough assessment of clients' needs, spiritual engagements and ensuing treatment formulation (Baetz & Toews, 2009; Koenig & Larson, 2001). This also corresponds with the need to ensure basic spiritual and religious tenets are respected during mental health interventions. For example, Western psychology may emphasise knowledge and understanding to elicit changes in perception, but in Islam, knowledge is often perceived as pointless unless it can be translated into practical action (Basit, 2007). Whereas Buddhists may perceive catastrophe as part of their karma, and believe they require spiritual endurance to faithfully cope during difficult times (Chhean, 2007). The need to base MHPSS, spiritual or psycho-spiritual support and interventions must always be based on sound assessment and expression of mental illness and spirituality in any context. This is not unlike standard humanitarian practice where needs of communities and individuals must be assessed in accordance with all of their other cultural traditions (IASC, 2007).

Recommendations

In the Haiti context, and in future emergencies, spiritual assessment should be a part of the overall MHPSS assessments. Assessments should not simply determine 'faith' or 'church engagement' but other aspects of spirituality, such as whether or not people desire psycho-spiritual approaches to care, or direct spiritual nurturing activities. Similarly, agencies wishing to partner with local churches and spiritual nurturing activities need to assess the MHPSS needs in those communities and congregations. For faith-based organisations, there is a need to recognise the diversity of spiritual practices active in Haiti that include the Catholic, Protestant and Vodou beliefs (WHO, 2010). This will not only ensure compliance with the IFRC/ ICRC Code of Conduct (Principle 3: 'Aid will not be used to further a particular political or religious standpoint'), but it ensures people of all faiths will have the opportunity to participate in MHPSS programmes, especially if churches are going to form part of the MHPSS services and networks.

Also, based on this code of conduct, and in the current absence of guidelines for faith-based organisations and spiritual care activities, agencies should not be offering psycho-spiritual approaches and services to only one faith group and not to others. Understanding how psycho-spiritual approaches care for each spiritual tradition may need to be explored and developed in Haiti, as well as other specific contexts for existing or new emergency settings. Additionally, the humanitarian sector needs to engage more fully in developing guidance for humanitarian agencies about what is appropriate for spiritual nurture and psycho-spiritual programming. Disaster response standards, such as The Sphere Project (2004), may also benefit from developing minimum standards around spiritual and/or psycho-spirituality in emergencies.

Future assessments conducted in Haiti should include church leadership and the capacity of the clergy or church members to provide MHPSS interventions. NGOs, the local clergy, and MHPSS programmes may share a common goal to support holistic healing of people in distress, but religious functionaries (clergy), even in the USA, often feel inadequate to deal with mass disaster and are likely to need training on basic counselling skills, spiritual support, and how to manage referrals to other MHPSS service providers (Openshaw & Harr, 2009). This is also likely to provide better assessment data on both the MHPSS and spirituality needs of affected communities.

In accordance with the *IASC MHPSS Guidelines* (IASC, 2007), it will also be important for faith-based NGOs, partnering with local religious groups such as churches, to ascertain where in the recommended intervention pyramid they wish to focus (p.12). This ensures that churches are working within an MHPSS framework that appropriately matches their levels of expertise and resources. It further encourages greater coordination with other agencies working in the MHPSS sector.

Based on the evidence, churches may be one of the most opportune ways to increase community and family support. This is a critical emergency response activity that churches have a long history of implementing. A focus on raising community supports cannot be underestimated, particularly given the evidence that social support, including church and spiritual engagement, have positive impacts on mental health and wellbeing.

For more focused non-specialised supports that aim to provide targeted interventions for people experiencing considerable distress or trauma, research demonstrates the need for a slow and carefully planned approach. Adapting mental health interventions to psycho-spiritual approaches has been shown to have the potential to cause harm, and therefore needs to be undertaken or overseen by trained care providers. Also, in the absence of existing materials, or research into psycho-spiritual approaches to mental health care, it seems more appropriate for targeted pilot studies to be developed and validated, particularly within the Haiti context and its various spiritual traditions. This may prevent possible harm from a '*roll-out*' of materials that have not been adequately assessed or evaluated.

RESEARCH AND POLICY OPPORTUNITIES FOR THE HUMANITARIAN SECTOR

This paper demonstrates that there are clear links between spirituality and mental health. It has identified a significant gap in the humanitarian literature, as well as humanitarian and organisational policy regarding the topic. Despite evidence indicating that *on balance* spirituality has positive mental health impacts on the general population and those experiencing distress (Koenig, 2009), there is little or no guidance on how organisations may optimise that association. Furthermore, the humanitarian MHPSS sector needs to also analyse how spiritual messages and support could be fostered through MHPSS programmes. Given the context-specific nature of spiritual practice, such approaches will inevitably need to be re-explored in each particular emergency.

Deliberately or not, humanitarian response seems to have shifted away from serving the spiritual needs of people in emergency settings. Spirituality continues to be a difficult topic to discuss, research and put into operation in policies or guidelines. It is a challenging issue for the sector, and its stakeholders, because it can provoke strong personal feelings. Additionally, people will inevitably approach the topic with their own beliefs and the priorities of the organisations they represent. However, based on the evidence, it is important to continue assessing and exploring spirituality.

Within the present humanitarian environment, secular organisations and faith-based NGOs may find it difficult to balance complying with guidelines and codes of conduct, while at the same time embracing the proven benefits of spiritual practice and engagement. Even in the most challenging of crises, spirituality can enhance the mental health and psychosocial wellbeing of people through offering them personal life meaning, a framework for understanding their circumstances, and facilitate building localised support networks. Although spirituality and MHPSS may be viewed as contentious and difficult to address, we should not only continue exploring the topic throughout the long-term Haiti recovery phases, but also in preparation for future emergencies.

REFERENCES

Baetz, M., & Toews, J. (2009). Clinical implications of research on religion, spirituality and mental health. *The Canadian Journal of Psychiatry* 54 (5), 292–301.

Baskin, T. W., & Enright, R. D. (2004). Intervention studies on forgiveness: A meta analysis. *Journal of Counselling Development* 82, 79–90.

Basit, A. (2007). An Islamic perspective on coping with catastrophe. *Southern Medical Journal* 100 (9), 950–951.

Blazer, D. G. (2009). Religion, spirituality, and mental health: What we know and why this is a tough topic to research. *The Canadian Journal of Psychiatry* 54 (5), 281–282.

Boehnlein, J. K. (2006). Religion and spirituality in psychiatric care: Looking back, looking ahead. *Transcultural Psychiatry* 43, 634–651.

Braam, A. W., Sonnenberg, C. M., Beekman, A. T. F., Deeg, D. J. H., & VanTilburg,W. (2000). Religious denomination as a symptom-formation factor of depression on older Dutch Citizens. *International Journal of Geriatric Psychiatry* 15, 458–466.

Chhean, K. (2007). A Buddhist perspective on coping with catastrophe. *Southern Medical Journal* 100 (9), 952–953.

Elsass, P., & Phuntsok, K. (2009). Tibetans' coping mechanisms following torture: An interview study of Tibetan torture survivors' use of coping mechanisms and how these were supported by Western counselling. *Traumatology* 15, 3–10.

Henderson, T. L., Roberto, K. A., & Kamo, Y. (2009). Older adults' responses to Hurricane Katrina: Daily hassles and coping strategies. *Journal of Applied Gerontology* 29, 48–69.

Hill, P. C. & Pargament, K. I. (2003). Advances in the conceptualization and measurement of religion and spirituality. Implications for physical and mental health research. *American Psychologist* 58 (1), 64–74.

International Federation of the Red Cross and Red Crescent Movement. (1994). Code of conduct for the International Red Cross and Red Crescent Movement and NGOs in Disaster Relief. Downloaded on 3 May 2010 from http://www.ifrc.org/publicat/conduct/code.asp.

Inter-Agency Standing Committee (IASC) (2007), IASC guidelines on mental health and psychosocial support in emergency settings. Geneva: IASC.

Inter-Agency Standing Committee (IASC). (2010). Guidance note for mental health and psychosocial support: Haiti earthquake emergency response. Geneva: IASC. Downloaded on 3 May from http://psychosocialnetwork.net/regions/153/upload/guidance_note_mhpss_in_haiti_fnal/view_resource/.

Koenig, H. G., & Larson, D. B. (2001). Religion and mental health: Evidence for an association. *International Journal of Psychiatry* 13, 67–78.

Koenig, HG (2009). Research on religion, spirituality, and mental health: A review. *The Canadian Journal of Psychiatry* 54 (5), 283–291.

Masters, K. S., & Spielmans, G. I. (2007). Prayer and health: Review, meta-analysis, and research agenda. *Journal of Behavioural Medicine* 30, 329–338.

Openshaw, L., & Harr, C. (2009). Exploring the relationship between clergy and mental health professionals. *Social Work and Christianity* 36 (3), 301–325.

Peres, J. F. P., Moreira-Almeida, A., Nasello, A. G., & Koenig, H. G. (2007). Spirituality and resilience in trauma victims. *Journal of Religion and Health* 46, 343–350.

Rosmarin, D. H., Pirutinsky, S. & Pargament, K. I. (2009). Are religious beliefs relevant to mental health among Jews? *Psychology of Religion and Spirituality* 1 (3), 180–190.

Sawatzky, R., Ratner, P. A., & Chiu, L. (2005). A meta-analysis of the relationship between spirituality and quality of life. *Social Indicators Research* 72, 153–188.

Smith, T. B., Bartz, J., & Richards, P. S. (2007). Outcomes of religious and spiritual adaptations to psychotherapy: A meta-analytic review. *Psychotherapy Research* 17 (6), 643–655.

The Sphere Project. (2004). Humanitarian charter and minimum standards in disaster response. Downloaded on 3 May 2010 from http://www.sphereproject.org/component/option.com_docman/Itemid,203/lang,english/.

Tankink, M. (2007).The moment I became born again the pain disappeared: The healing of devastating war memories in born-again Churches in Mbarara district, southwest Uganda. *Transcultural Psychiatry* 44, 203–231.

Vis, J. & Boynton, H. M. (2008). Spirituality and transcendent meaning making: Possibilities for enhancing posttraumatic growth. *Journal of Religion and Spirituality in Social Work* 27 (1^2), 69–86.

World Health Organization. (2010). *Mental health in Haiti: A literature review*. Geneva: WHO.

Wortmann, J. H., & Park, C. L. (2009). Religion/spirituality and change in meaning after bereavement: Qualitative evidence for the meaning making model. *Journal of Loss and Trauma* 14, 17–34.

Editors' Notes

To read some responses to this article:

Onyango, G., M. Parathayail, S. van den Berg, R. Reiffers, L. Snider, and C. Eriksson. 2011. Spirituality and psychosocial work in emergencies: Four commentaries and a response. *Intervention* 9 (1), 61–73. http://www.ourmediaourselves.com/archives/91pdf/Onyango,%20Paratharayil,%20vdBerg%20et%20al.pdf.

Source

RELATED RESOURCES

Video: Trip the Light. Matt Harding and Melissa Nixon. http://www.youtube.com/watch?v=Pwe-pA6TaZk.

Aid Workers Network. Aid Blogs [issues and insights from aid workers, including personal reflections on adjustment/growth]. Retrieved from http://www.aidworkers.net/?q=blogs.

Member Care Associates, Inc. 2011. Master care. *Resources for Good Practice* [Christian spirituality]. Retrieved from http://membercareassociates.org/?page_id=125.

Member Care Associates, Inc. 2012. Member care tools. *CORE Member Care Blog*. Retrieved from http://corememberesare.blogspot.fr/search/label/MC%20tools.

Professional Quality of Life [online tool for people in helping roles assessing their compassion satisfaction, compassion fatigue, and burnout]. Available from http://www.proqol.org/.

Schwiebert, P., & DeKlyen, C. (1999). *Tear soup: A recipe for healing after loss*. Portland, OR: Grief Watch. Available from http://www.griefwatch.com/.

CHAPTER 9

Strategies for Security Management

OPERATIONAL SECURITY MANAGEMENT IN VIOLENT ENVIRONMENTS

GOOD PRACTICE REVIEW 8

Humanitarian Practice Network, Overseas Development Institute

[The] global security environment has changed significantly over the past decade. Increasing violence against aid workers, including more kidnappings and lethal attacks against humanitarian aid workers and their operations, has had serious implications for international humanitarian assistance. Attacks have been both politically motivated and an expression of rising levels of banditry and criminality. This growing violence has generated a deeper awareness of the security challenges faced by operational agencies, giving rise to new adaptations and strategies in security management and growing professionalism and sophistication in humanitarian security practices and interagency coordination . . .

This [Good Practice Review (GPR)] is written primarily for senior operational managers who directly oversee and support operations in violent environments. This includes not only field security advisers but also senior representatives in a given operating environment, including programme managers and coordinators. A wide range of others, from local staff to senior policy managers, may also make use of it. Although the content is oriented particularly to nongovernmental organisations (NGOs), both international and national, other organisations may also find it useful.

This GPR focuses on security defined as relating to acts of politically and economically motivated violence and crime. Insecurity, however, is not the only type of risk to the life and well-being of aid workers. Health and safety risks—including illness and accidents, fires and environmental hazards—are also serious threats, but these are covered in other guidelines. Local communities receiving assistance and other civilians may be at equal or greater risk of violence and in need of major assistance and protection. This GPR does not address these protection challenges, not least because the strategies used to protect civilians are often quite different from those used to protect aid workers . . .

Finally, good practice means integrating security management across the organisation. It is not an add-on or a luxury. Lack of time is often given as a reason for not devoting enough attention to lots of things, including security management. This must be challenged. It should not be acceptable for someone to be seriously injured or killed because their agency has failed to take the time to implement good practice. Organisations without exception take the time to implement financial checks and controls. Why should protecting the lives of agency staff not merit similar attention? And is time really that scarce and are workloads really that heavy, or is this simply a reflection of an organisational culture that encourages staff to see themselves as forever under pressure, rushing from crisis to crisis with no time to pause and draw breath? Ultimately, security management in high-risk areas is both a moral and a legal obligation, and agencies must make the time to see that it is done properly and well.

More importantly, good practice in security management is closely linked with, builds on, and reinforces good practice in programme and personnel management more broadly. These are not separate tasks and workloads; there is an important, positive multiplier effect. Good programme management requires an understanding of the operating environment and the impact of your agency's presence and its work, building good relationships, managing international and national staff well, and collaborating effectively with other agencies.

KEY CONCEPTS AND PRINCIPLES
OF SECURITY MANAGEMENT

Why Manage Security Risks?

Managing security is not an end in itself. The primary concern is to be able to deliver humanitarian assistance in an impartial manner, which may require establishing and maintaining a presence in highly insecure contexts. High insecurity jeopardises or impedes the achievement of that goal. Security management is therefore a means to an operational end. At the same time, security management is about protecting and preserving the lives and well-being of agency staff (and possibly partners)—and about protecting the organisation's assets, as well as its programmes and reputation. This point holds true from two perspectives:

- Pragmatically speaking, the temporary or permanent loss of assets or injury of a staff member reduces operational capacity and may even lead the agency to suspend its programme or withdraw.
- Morally, agencies have a duty of care towards their employees and colleagues. While aid work implies a certain level of risk, agencies need to be sure that all reasonable measures are taken to mitigate this risk.

The legal requirement of duty of care of the employer is becoming increasingly important. Many countries have labour laws that impose obligations on employers to ensure safety in the workplace. Although such obligations have rarely been considered in the context of international aid work, aid organisations are open to growing legal challenges if they fail to properly inform staff about the risks associated with a particular assignment, or fail to take all necessary measures to reduce those risks.

Effectively managing security risks is therefore essential from an operational, moral, and legal point of view. The aim is to protect staff and assets, while enabling assistance to reach some of the world's neediest people.

Combining Security Risks with Other Risks

Not all risk management concerns security risks; organisations and individuals take other factors into account when they consider risks. There may be financial incentives for an organisation to decide to go into or stay in an environment with very significant security risks. Reputational considerations often also come into play. In some cases organisations have strong reputational and financial reasons to be present in a high-profile crisis, even if it is a very dangerous one.

Individual staff, particularly national staff, may agree to work in very dangerous environments because of the economic incentives that might not otherwise be available to them. A different type of consideration, which merits greater attention, concerns the need that agencies are trying to address. What would the consequences be for people in need if a programme is discontinued? How effective can a programme be under these conditions? How many people can realistically be reached? How severe are their material and protection needs? These issues are discussed in detail in the following chapters.

A Basic Framework for Security Risk Management

Figure 1 [not reproduced here] shows the basic framework for security risk management. Its fundamental logic is the same as that of the project management cycle: assess, plan, implement (and adjust if needed), review, and reassess. Note that built into the model is the possibility of not implementing a programme should the risks be deemed too high, radically altering it should risks change, or discontinuing it.

The main steps of the security management process are:

- Identify a potential programme: a need exists and the organisation has the mission or mandate and the capacities to respond to that need.
- Thoroughly assess the security risks and the organisation's capacities (human, financial, time resources) to manage those risks. (The risk assessment process is covered in detail in chapter 2 [of this source].)
- Determine the threshold of acceptable risk. This may differ depending on the potential benefits of having a presence and a programme, and on the mandate of the organisation.
- Ask whether the risks are beyond the organisation's ability to manage; if so, do not proceed with the programme (or alternatively "transfer" the risk to another actor that can manage it). If there is sufficient security management capacity that the risk can be reduced to an acceptable level, initiate the programme.
- Develop a context- and situation-specific operational security strategy (the concepts of acceptance, protection, and deterrence are explained in chapter 3 [of this source]).
- Responsible security management requires not only taking preventive measures to avoid an incident, but also investing in the capacity to manage an actual crisis situation and the consequences of a critical incident. This also requires ongoing assessment of security conditions to determine whether the security strategy remains appropriate to the threats in that environment, and whether the risks remain acceptable.
- Establish critical incident procedures. Even with the best preventive approach and measures, an incident may happen. Those caught up in the incident will have to do their best to survive it (in which their preparedness—or lack thereof—will be a significant factor), while the organisation will mobilise an immediate critical incident response.

- Provide postincident support. Support will be required by the survivors of a critical incident, and possibly also by other staff and/or the families of affected staff.
- Perform postincident reviews ("after action reviews"). Objectively and honestly analyse how the incident came to happen, how the risks were assessed, and how appropriate and effective the security measures were. Evaluate the quality of the critical incident response and overall preparedness. These reviews and evaluations may result in adjustments to the operational security management strategy, or they may lead to the conclusion that the risks have become unmanageable and that more significant programme changes need to be made, or activities suspended.

Main Actors in Security Management

National authorities are responsible for the security of all civilians in their territory. In practice, however, many governments are unable to meet this responsibility. That does not mean that the authorities should be ignored. It does mean that additional measures will be needed to manage security effectively.

As noted, organisations have a formal responsibility as employers towards all their staff. A key concept in that regard is "duty of care." An organisation's duty of care towards its employees should be defined in its security policy. It is also the responsibility of the organisation to proactively inform employees, potential employees, and associated personnel such as consultants about security risks. This allows individuals to exercise "informed consent"; i.e., to accept a degree of risk after having been made fully aware of the extent of the risk. The organisation is also responsible for ensuring that risks are reduced to a reasonable level.

Managers within an organisation also have a responsibility towards their staff. If the organisation is accused of negligence with regard to security, as a result of which a staff member has been hurt or killed, senior managers or field-level representatives can in some cases be individually pursued for legal redress. An "accountability framework," which may cover issues beyond security, is one means to make these responsibilities and accountabilities clear to managers at all levels. It should also be made very clear to all staff, from guards and drivers to senior programme managers, that each individual has a responsibility for their own security—and for the security of the team as a whole, as well as the organisation's assets. All staff should be involved in regular security-related discussions and activities, including training. An organisation may also have to exercise responsibility on behalf of those other than its staff. Dependents are one such category, certainly for international staff. Define responsibilities carefully and clearly, and make sure that people understand the extent of their responsibility and the security procedures they must follow. For international staff, home country embassies may have a role to play in alerting their citizens to possible risks. As a general rule, embassies maintain a very low risk threshold for visitors and those who do not operate under any security framework. While the embassy's guidance should be sought, an organisation may still be able to operate securely outside of this guidance if it has an effective security management system. Organisations also have a responsibility to communicate vital security-related information to other agencies operating in the same location. Failure to alert others that a staff member has narrowly escaped an ambush attempt on a particular road, for example, may mean that others unnecessarily become the victims of a violent incident.

Many international organisations employ global security advisers to provide support to field offices. Some also have regional security advisers, who oversee a specific high-risk operational area and provide surge capacity to the country programme. In other organisations, security management is integrated into line management, and no separate security advisers exist. In-country it is the responsibility of the senior representative (i.e., the country director) to ensure that organisational policies and procedures are implemented and adhered to, though in practice many security management tasks may be delegated to a security adviser or security focal point (given the sensitivities around the word "security," in some countries the title "safety adviser" is used instead). The decision to appoint a security adviser (either full-time or, where the security focal point has other responsibilities, on a part-time basis) should be based on a range of considerations, including the risk rating for the location, the scope of work, and the resources available.

Many organisations devolve decision-making authority to the country director or his or her field staff, rather than maintaining responsibility in a regional office or international HQ. Ultimate responsibility, however, lies with the executive director, or in some cases the board of trustees. These responsibilities must be clearly articulated in job descriptions. Specific decisions may also need formal approval from a higher authority than the senior field representative. These include:

- to downgrade the risk rating of a country or an area in a country,
- to return to an area from which staff have been relocated because of security risks,

- to adopt a "low-visibility" approach and remove logos and flags from offices and vehicles,
- to use armed protection, and
- to use a private security provider.

Major incidents, such as a kidnapping or hostage taking, also usually require the ongoing involvement of the organisation's senior leadership. Official donors may have imposed contractual obligations regarding the visibility ("branding") of assistance they fund, in which case the organisation may have to seek their formal approval to forego this requirement.

ORGANISATIONAL SECURITY MANAGEMENT

While most organisations delegate decisions as closely as possible to the field, the operational management of security is intricately linked to wider organisational practices and decision making. This includes:

- The development of an organisation-wide safety and security policy and practical guidance on security management.
- Organisational skills and responsibilities for certain serious incidents, including the establishment of a critical-incident management team in the regional office and/or global headquarters (for international organisations).
- The establishment and maintenance of a centralised reporting system so that all security incidents and near-misses are gathered together in a central point, to enable a global analysis of security incidents affecting the organisation.

Decisions about whether to initiate operations in a certain country, and what type of programme to undertake, are usually the responsibility of headquarters. The organisation may also require that senior headquarters staff make decisions on certain major security issues, as outlined above. In addition, much of the media and communications as well as fundraising for field programmes may be done at headquarters, and other human resource issues such as the establishment of insurance policies are also often handled organisation-wide, rather than at the individual operational level.

An aid agency that deploys people to high-risk areas should have the policies, procedures, and capacities to manage such operations. The following is a list of documents in which these policies could be spelled out. These documents have an organisation-wide remit, are developed at and by HQ, and constitute general reference resources.

- Agency mandate, general mission statement, or statement of values and principles.
- General agency-wide security policy and, where relevant, policy statements on specific security-related issues, such as the use of armed protection, private security providers, and information protection.
- Management accountability structure, spelling out where responsibilities for security management and critical-incident management and decision making lie (differentiating between HQ and the field).
- General reference guides and handbooks; for instance, on radio use.

Security Planning and Preparedness

At the field level the cornerstone of security management is the security plan. The quality of a good operational security plan is dependent on the quality of the planning process. Team planning—with national and international staff—is preferable to individual planning, as it brings to bear collective knowledge and experience and facilitates ownership of the final product. A good planning process needs to be followed up with periodic reviews; as the environment changes, there is a need to adapt the plan.

Different organisations produce different security plans to reflect their organisational needs, the context, and their organisational policies and procedures. A good security plan might include the following major components:

1. A synopsis of the country context, including conflict, if relevant.
2. Specific mission objectives in the country.
3. A security risk assessment (see chapter 2 [of this source]).
4. A threshold of acceptable risk. Such a statement should include a commentary on how that threshold was arrived at (see chapter 2 [of this source]).
5. A statement of responsibilities in terms of security management.
6. Preventative measures. Some measures will be covered in standard operating procedures (SOPs), as they will involve issues such as site

security, movement, and communications. Some of these SOPs can translate into checklists. Other preventive measures do not exist as SOPs or checklists; for example, efforts to increase acceptance among local actors.

7. A clarification of the roles and responsibilities for incident response and crisis management. In some cases, involvement by a regional office or HQ may be required or mandatory (see chapter 5 [of this source]).

8. Procedures for incident reporting, as well as incident-response analysis.

9. Retreat plans (hibernation, relocation, evacuation).

10. A statement of principles or policy regarding collaboration on security with others operating in the same environment, such as acknowledging the interdependencies between aid providers and the resulting minimum responsibilities, including communicating "alerts" to others and possibly collaborating in areas such as risk analysis and assessment, pooling or sharing of resources, or logistics in case of a withdrawal.

11. A statement on when the plan was produced or last reviewed, how it was produced (the planning process and who was involved), who signed off on it, and when it will be reviewed again.

12. Maps of the operating environment, including office locations.

There are a number of issues to bear in mind with regard to security plans:

- A plan is a piece of paper. Paper does not reduce any risks. Plans need to be shared, explained, and implemented.
- A good plan today may no longer be appropriate six months from now. If the situation evolves, review the analysis and plans.
- People not familiar with security plans and procedures cannot adhere to them. All staff and visitors need to be briefed as soon as they arrive and after any important changes are made.
- Good implementation depends on competencies. The best possible plan falls apart without the knowledge and skills to implement it. Some aspects of security management require specialised knowledge or skills.

- Effective security management depends to a degree on practice. Practicing—through simulations and training—is vital.

Reviewing Security Plans

Even in a quiet and secure environment, security plans should be reviewed annually. In higher-risk environments, they should be reviewed more frequently to ensure that they reflect prevailing risks, and that the information they contain is up to date.

When to review

- When there are significant changes in the external context, especially as a result of the actions of the major protagonists.
- When another agency has been affected by an incident, especially in or near the same operational zone.
- When someone else is affected by an incident that in its nature or intensity appears to introduce a new element into the original risk assessment.

What to review

Virtually everything can be a potential candidate for review:

- the wider context and situational analysis
- the threat assessment
- the risk assessment
- the security strategy
- the preventive/risk-controlling standard operating procedures
- programme choices and/or implementation strategy
- staffing policy and recruitment criteria
- vehicle and transport choices
- interagency security information-sharing arrangements/practices
- the contacts and connections used to maintain acceptance

If the review suggests a significant deterioration in security, staff may be assembled and briefed on the new assessment of the situation and what realistically can be done to mitigate the risks. Staff need to be able to reassess the situation in light of their own personal threshold of acceptable risk, and reconfirm their "informed consent"—or not.

Developing a Security Culture

Much of the focus in security management tends to be on specific operational needs, such as security policies and plans, but there is also a need to take a step back and look at how to develop a culture of security within the organisation, including developing capacity. One of the most important priorities is to make sure that all staff know the organisation and its mission in any given context. It is not uncommon for many staff, including national staff, not to know much about the agency that they represent. Staff need to be told what the organisation is about. Key questions include:

- Why is this organisation here?
- What is it doing here?
- Where does it get its money from? What does it use that money for?
- Who directs its activities?
- Is it serving foreign political interests?
- What is its political agenda?
- Does it want to change local society, culture, values, or religion?
- Is it on the side of the government (or another political actor in that environment)?

Consider providing staff with some written material in their own language(s), and go through it with them in an interactive way, periodically bringing staff together to hear from them what sort of questions and comments they most regularly get from those in the community and how they answer them. In addition, treat security as a staffwide priority, not a sensitive management issue to be discussed only by a few staff members behind closed doors. Specifically:

- Make sure that all staff are familiar with the context, the risks, and the commitments of the organisation in terms of risk reduction and security management.
- Make sure that all staff are clear about their individual responsibilities with regard to security, teamwork, and discipline.
- Advise and assist staff to address their medical, financial, and personal insurance matters prior to deployment in a high-risk environment.
- Be clear about the expectations of managers and management styles under normal and high-stress circumstances.

- Make security a standing item (preferably the first item) on the agenda of every management and regular staff meeting.
- Stipulate reviews and, if needed, updates of basic safety and security advice, as well as countrywide and area-specific security plans, as described above.
- Invest in competency development. It is not uncommon for aid agencies to scramble to do security training when a situation deteriorates. Investment should be made in staff development, including security mitigation competences, in periods of calm and stability.
- Ensure that security is a key consideration in all programme planning.
- Perform periodic inspections of equipment by a qualified individual, including radios, first-aid kits, smoke alarms, fire extinguishers, intruder alarms, and body armour.
- Carry out after-action reviews (AARs). The focus is on assessing what happened and how the team acted in a given situation, not on individual responsibilities. It is a collective learning exercise.

Mainstreaming a security culture, both at the level of individual staff members and as an organisation, means considering the security implications involved in everything the organisation does (or chooses not to do), from discussions about programme design and public messages to funding decisions and the hiring of external contractors. People "think security," and act accordingly because they understand the importance of it and are respected for doing so. The importance of security is continually reinforced, not just in written policies but also in actions. Senior staff are held accountable for decisions that impact positively or negatively on overall staff security. Organisations have also started to undertake annual security audits of their field offices against a series of benchmarks. This is usually announced in advance but may not be. Audits can take place after a critical incident, in times or places of heightened risk, or periodically in any dangerous environment.

EDITORS' NOTES

For more information about the Humanitarian Practice Network: http://www.odihpn.org/.

SOURCE

Humanitarian Practice Network. 2010. *Operational security management in violent environments*, rev. ed. London: Overseas Development Institute, 1–24. Reprinted by permission. http://www.odihpn.org/report.asp?id=3159.

RELATED RESOURCES

Video: Humanitarian Policy. "The Price of Anything." YouTube. http://www.humanitarian-policy.org/. Four parts: http://www.youtube.com/watch?v=INkqw02iqB4&feature=relmfu.

Bickley, S. 2010. Safety first: A safety and security handbook for workers. London: Save the Children. http://www.eisf.eu/resources/library/SafetyFirst2010.pdf.

Brugger, P. 2009. ICRC operational security: Staff safety in armed conflict and in ternal violence. *International Review of the Red Cross* 91, no. 874: 431–45. doi:10.1017/S1816383109990075.

Humanitarian Practice Network. 2010. Humanitarian security management. Special issue, *Humanitarian Exchange* 47 (June). http://www.odihpn.org/humanitarian-exchange-magazine/issue-47/humanitarian-security-management.

Inter-Agency Standing Committee. 2013. *IASC Non-Binding Guidelines on the Use of Armed Escorts for Humanitarian Convoys*. Geneva, Author. https://docs.unocha.org/sites/dms/Documents/2013%2002%2027%20Guidelines%20on%20the%20Use%20of%20Armed%20Escorts%20-%20Final.pdf.

International Committee of the Red Cross. 2011. Health care in danger: Making the case. Geneva: Author. http://www.icrc.org/eng/resources/documents/publication/p4072.htm.

Jackson, A. 2012. Talking to the other side: Humanitarian engagement with armed non-state actors (June). *HPG Policy Brief 47*. http://www.odi.org.uk/sites/odi.org.uk/files/odi-assets/publications-opinion-files/7711.pdf.

Lilly, D. 2010. Peacekeeping and the protection of civilians: An issue for humanitarians? *Humanitarian Exchange* 48. http://www.odihpn.org/humanitarian-exchange-magazine/issue-48/peacekeeping-and-the-protection-of-civilians-an-issue-for-humanitarians.

United Nations General Assembly. 1994. *Convention on the protection of United Nations and associated personnel*. New York: Author. http://untreaty.un.org/cod/avl/ha/csunap/csunap.html.

United Nations General Assembly. 2005. *Optional protocol to the convention on the protection of United Nations and associated personnel,* New York: Author. http://untreaty.un.org/cod/avl/ha/csunap/csunap.html.

United Nations High Commissioner for Refugees. 2000. Too high a price? *Refugee* 4, no. 121. http://www.unhcr.org/3b69138b2.html.

United Nations Office for the Coordination of Humanitarian Affairs. *Humanitarian Civil-Military Coordination* (various documents online). http://www.unocha.org/what-we-do/coordination-tools/UN-CMCoord/publications.

CHAPTER 10

Preventing Corruption in Humanitarian Work

NEED AND GREED:
CORRUPTION RISKS, PERCEPTIONS, AND PREVENTION IN HUMANITARIAN ASSISTANCE

Sarah Bailey, Humanitarian Policy Group

KEY MESSAGES

- Humanitarian assistance injects valuable resources into resource-poor and often insecure contexts with high levels of need. The complexity of humanitarian operations and their rapidly increasing budgets make addressing corruption—and the taboos surrounding it—absolutely essential for aid agencies.
- Despite recent efforts by humanitarian agencies to increase participation, accountability, and transparency, humanitarian assistance remains an opaque process to those impacted by crisis. Investing in appropriate and effective accountability systems is imperative to demystify the process and prevent, detect, and respond to corruption.
- Practices and policies to tackle corruption risks go hand in hand with promoting programme quality, particularly monitoring. Donors should permit and encourage flexibility in allocating funds to these functions, while not unduly pressuring agencies to accelerate spending.
- Although there is no clear consensus on the trade-offs between speed and control, above all in the critical phases of an emergency, we argue that the humanitarian imperative of saving lives and alleviating suffer-

ing is compatible with using time and resources to minimise corruption risks.

Emergency environments present unique corruption risks for agencies operating within them. Relief is delivered amidst weak or absent rule of law, endemic corruption, and immense need. The capacities of governments and humanitarian agencies to assist affected people are stretched to the limit, and agencies are under pressure to intervene rapidly. Assistance is injected into resource-poor settings where powerful people have disproportionate control over resources. In the case of armed conflicts, predatory economies often develop when influential groups attempt to direct these resources for their own ends.

The high level of needs of crisis-affected populations means that they can ill afford corruption that compromises their access to assistance. While humanitarian agencies have taken steps to increase accountability and the quality of assistance through the development of standards such as Sphere, the Humanitarian Accountability Partnership, and codes of conduct, there remains limited shared analysis about the extent and impact of corruption in humanitarian assistance. Aid agencies, many of which rely on donations to support their operations, are sensitive to how their image and funding could be affected by the negative attention that might result from a corruption scandal, and are therefore often reluctant to talk about corruption openly.

The scale of corruption, corruption risks in specific programming areas, and how corruption impacts people affected by emergencies all need to be more fully explored. The following findings are based on research that has begun this process: mapping risks of corruption in humanitarian assistance; extensive interviews with staff from seven international nongovernmental organisations about corruption risks; and case studies on perceptions of corruption among crisis-affected populations in Afghanistan, Liberia, Northern Uganda, and Sri Lanka.[1]

---

1   This HPG Policy Brief draws primarily from Maxwell et al. (2008). The examples referring to Afghanistan, Liberia, Northern Uganda, and Sri Lanka are taken from Savage et al. (2007); Savage (2007); Bailey (2008); and Elhawary (2008).

Box 1.
CORRUPTION AND THE HUMANITARIAN IMPERATIVE

Saving lives in an emergency is a fundamental humanitarian principle. Preventing people from abusing the aid process and ensuring that lifesaving resources end up in the hands of those who need them are hardly incompatible aims. However, the complex environment of humanitarian operations, particularly in the early phases of an acute crisis, presents aid workers with potential conflicts between corruption and access. In areas with endemic corruption, the payment of unofficial fees to move commodities through ports, borders, and checkpoints may be undesirable options on a short list of problematic alternatives to transport aid. Concerns that aid can fuel conflict through diversion or misappropriation has been a rich source of research and debate. There is no clear consensus on the trade-offs between effective response and corruption control, which is part of a larger discussion of programming quality, accountability, and efficiency.

CORRUPTION IN HUMANITARIAN ASSISTANCE: DEFINITION AND SIGNIFICANCE

Transparency International (TI)'s definition of corruption is: "the abuse of entrusted power for private gain," including financial corruption such as fraud, bribery, and kickbacks. It also encompasses nonfinancial forms of corruption, such as the manipulation or diversion of humanitarian assistance to benefit nontarget groups; the allocation of relief resources in exchange for sexual favours; preferential treatment in the assistance or hiring processes for family members or friends; and the coercion and intimidation of staff or beneficiaries to turn a blind eye to or participate in corruption.

Corruption is notoriously hard to quantify. Indices rely on perceptions of how much corruption occurs, rather than data on losses. There is also ambiguity between corruption and wastage, mismanagement and gross inefficiency; a report on the Hurricane Katrina response, for example, noted that contracts worth an estimated $8.75 billion were plagued by the mutually reinforcing problems of "waste, fraud, abuse and mismanagement." The narrow focus on financial forms of corruption and limited inter- and intra-agency dialogue on corruption "cases" add to the difficulty of describing its scale. Because those affected by crisis have limited information to determine whether corruption is hindering their access to assistance, and because of few channels to report such problems, agencies may not grasp the scope of corruption related to assistance in these communities.

Box 2.
PERCEPTIONS OF CORRUPTION AMONG CRISIS-AFFECTED POPULATIONS

People affected by conflict and natural disaster lack power within the assistance process and influence over the agencies that assist them. The assistance system is opaque: lodging complaints is difficult, and few have even a basic understanding of the process. In displacement camps in Northern Uganda, for instance, people left off beneficiary lists were told time and time again that "the computer deleted their names"—despite their having no knowledge of what a computer was and that computer error was not the likely cause of their exclusion.

The ability of crisis-affected populations to distinguish corruption from inefficiency, limited resources, effective targeting, or other issues depends in part on availability and access to information about the assistance process. In its simplest form this means knowing what they are supposed to receive, who is supposed to receive it, and how to access it. Lack of information about the relief system may lead beneficiaries to jump to the conclusion that corruption is behind acts that are in fact part of standard aid agency practices, such as reducing assistance because of decreased needs or lack of funding.

Crisis-affected populations also have access to different types of information than aid agencies, including knowledge about others in their community and direct experience of abuses, such as being asked or forced to pay a bribe, share their assistance, or exchange sexual favours for access to assistance. Aid agencies by and large only have secondhand knowledge, if any at all, of these acts. The perceptions of crisis-affected populations derive from official information about the assistance process; observation; personal experience; the experiences of friends, family and others; and discussions, theories, and rumours.

Identifying the Risks

Types of corruption risks and high-risk areas are better understood than issues of scale. From community leaders subverting the targeting process, to logisticians accepting bribes to award contracts, the list of areas where corruption can occur is long.

Interpretations of what acts constitute corruption differ according to contexts, cultures, and individuals. Perceived corruption may or may not fall under a standard interpretation of "abuse of entrusted power for private gain." For example, kinship and social networks may play a greater role in business interactions than in Western cultures, whereby "kickbacks" and hiring or making purchases through relatives is considered normal practice—even one that ensures the quality of goods and services. For aid recipients, leaders benefiting disproportionately from assistance may be seen as an acceptable privilege, while aid agencies transporting undistributed relief supplies back to their warehouses may be perceived as the theft or diversion of relief commodities "belonging" to those affected by the crisis. There is also the ethical question of whether the exaggeration of needs by crisis-affected populations is "corruption" or a survival strategy when access to critical resources has been lost. Despite these issues, certain processes, sectors, programme support areas, and methods of engagement in humanitarian assistance are considered by aid agency staff and aid recipients alike as particularly vulnerable.

Food aid, construction, and other highly valued assistance are perceived as at highest risk of corruption. Bountiful and highly prized in humanitarian contexts, food aid can be diverted physically during transport and storage, or indirectly through the manipulation of assessments, targeting, registration, and distributions to favour certain groups or individuals. In construction and shelter, the copious opportunities for diversion and profit through substandard workmanship, kickbacks for contracts, and favouritism in the delivery of valuable shelter material make it a high-risk sector. Other commodities, such as expensive and scarce drugs, fishing boats, and tents, are a target for diversion because of their value. In Sri Lanka following the tsunami, corruption was perceived in the allotment of newly constructed houses according to political support and affiliation rather than need. In Northern Uganda, payment for inclusion on recipient lists was associated with highly valued tents and nonfood items. In Liberia, diversion was chiefly related to food aid and medicines.

The assessment, targeting, and registration of recipients determines "who gets what" in humanitarian assistance. Efforts by aid agencies to reach the "right" people are challenged by attempts to distort information, direct assistance to certain groups, or solicit bribes for inclusion in assistance.

Whereas aid agencies are most concerned about "inclusion errors," because this diverts their resources, recipients themselves are most concerned about *exclusion*. For people affected by crisis, being registered as a camp resident—for a food ration card, home reconstruction, or other assistance—is the primary entry point to accessing aid. Perceived corruption includes the deliberate inclusion of noneligible households and the exclusion of eligible ones, multiple registration, and bribes or sexual favours for inclusion on beneficiary lists. Refusing to submit to extortion can affect access to assistance, as in Liberia, where women have reported not receiving food aid because they would not have sex with camp leaders. Corruption in registration can also take the form of manipulating household statistics (e.g., family size) to increase or decrease assistance packages, the trafficking of fake ration cards, and the sale of ration cards by those responsible for distributing them. The perceived "gains" to those responsible include helping friends and family, rewarding supporters, punishing enemies, or obtaining money, sex, and increased assistance that can be gifted, used, or sold.

Corruption in the distribution of material assistance occurs when those in charge of doling it out control the amounts or have the discretion to give it to people who are not registered for it. The distribution of prepackaged food (rather than using scoops, which can be filled to varying amounts), using beneficiary lists in addition to beneficiary/ration cards (rather than only using cards), and direct oversight by aid agencies all reduce this discretion.

Announcing the type and quantity of assistance enables recipients to determine if they received the correct amount. Even if people receive the correct amount, local elites can impose "taxes" once the distribution is over and the aid agency has left. In Afghanistan, one bus driver reported that camp leaders would hire his truck once a week to take relief commodities to the local market—items that were either never distributed or were taken from people by force.

Among programme support areas, procurement and financial management provide numerous possibilities for fraud and collusion, compelling aid agencies to develop detailed procedures and regulations for these functions. The greatest risk in human resources is the favouring of certain groups in hiring, and the pressure to engage staff rapidly in emergencies may lead to procedural shortcuts that increase risks of corruption, such as skipping or delaying background checks and inductions.

Logistics, particularly the transport of goods, storage in secondary warehouses, and vehicle and fleet management, presents opportunities such as corruptly diverting goods and fuel by the staff involved. One scam involves removing relief items from prepackaged kits that are normally not weighed, such as household nonfood item kits, which are then resealed so as to appear unmolested.

The relationships and structures through which aid agencies implement their programmes create their own risks. Working through local partners builds local capacity to respond to emergencies, can increase local accountability, and might provide greater knowledge of local power relations, but partnerships may also decrease oversight in comparison to the direct implementation of programmes. Partners could engage in any of the risk areas mentioned above; aid agencies often lack clear and predefined response strategies should corruption occur in partnership arrangements.

Box 3.

CAMP GOVERNANCE AND ASSISTANCE COMMITTEES: CATALYST OF CORRUPTION, OR CURE?

Aid agencies and governments typically create a governance model in displacement camps intended to facilitate the management of the camp and the delivery of humanitarian assistance. The system divides camps into blocks with "block leaders," who perform tasks related to these subdivisions, and a camp commander (usually elected by camp residents) oversees the management of the camp and liaises with aid agencies. Aid agencies may also minimise the involvement of or completely circumvent government structures by using elected committees in noncamp settings to assist with or conduct targeting, registration, and distribution. Alternatively, aid can be entirely channeled through the government.

An implicit assumption in electing new representation structures to liaise in the assistance process is that preexisting leadership structures may not impartially allocate assistance because they are entrenched in local power systems. However, elected structures can also be involved in extortion or other corruption. Aid agencies need to ensure that the representation systems they create or use are accountable and transparent, rather than assuming that this is an inevitable result of an election or the formation of a committee.

Engaging through committees elected by crisis-affected populations opens these groups to potential control by local elites, while local leaders, often an asset in reaching people in need because of their influence and intimate knowledge of their communities, can use this power to divert assistance to unintended recipients. Corruption poses a threat in any process that passes through gatekeepers—people or groups who control access to information and assistance. The "best" way for an agency to engage depends not on an isolated focus on corruption risks but on a variety of factors. However, many agencies shy away from analysing the risks inherent in these methods of engagement.

ADDRESSING CORRUPTION RISKS: POLICIES AND PRACTICES OF AID AGENCIES

Aid agencies' policies, procedures, and ethical standards are seldom specific to corruption or emergency settings; rather, they are measures with the intent or effect of preventing fraud and abuse, commingled with other procedures in finance, procurement, logistics, human resources, and programming guidelines: codes of conduct, sexual exploitation policies, audits, spending and approval limits, adaptation of procedures to emergency settings, deployment of special surge-capacity staff, segregation of duties, rotation of key staff, complaints mechanisms, communication of information on entitlements, training on organisational values, and the use of committees in hiring, contracting, and procurement.

Agencies have also developed measures that directly address corruption risks in emergencies. "Whistle-blower" policies are confidential mechanisms designed to encourage aid agency staff to report corruption. The effectiveness of these relatively new procedures is an open question, but many staff are simply not aware of their existence and perceive disincentives to reporting corruption, such as reduced job security or creating grudges. They are generally not accessible to local partners or aid recipients.

"Zero tolerance" policies can reduce corruption by conveying to local actors that the agency does not engage in corrupt actions, but can also discourage open discussion of corruption pressures by reinforcing taboos. One humanitarian worker described such a policy as a "dreamer's opinion," while others understand "zero tolerance" as meaning that corruption must be addressed openly by the agency. In areas with endemic corruption, agencies may avoid direct involvement but end up "outsourcing" corruption to intermediaries, transporters, or even partners and lower-level staff, implicitly using a "don't ask, don't tell policy" to accomplish tasks requiring bribery.

Actions taken by aid agencies in preparing for and undertaking emergency responses directly and indirectly address certain high-risk corruption areas. Interagency coordination offers a forum for sharing blacklists of contractors and discussing consolidated approaches for dealing with corrupt authorities. Developing a surge capacity of trained staff, including finance and procurement staff, who can deploy quickly to establish or support humanitarian operations reduces the risks inherent in the rapid scale-up of programmes. Establishing policies specific to emergency humanitarian programming (e.g., to permit rapid hiring and procurement) reduces the likelihood that standard procedures will be ineffective or unofficially short-circuited. Emergency preparedness should take into account corruption risks, as time pressures in the early stages of response leave little space for this analysis; however, this is rarely done by aid agencies.

Policies alone are inadequate to address corruption risks. There is a clear gap between policy development in agency headquarters and implementation in the field. Project monitoring—key in verifying the effectiveness of systems, detecting corruption, and more generally a standard good practice part of programme quality, learning, and accountability—continues to be hampered by underinvestment. Aid agencies are increasingly committed to enhancing accountability through complaints mechanisms and community participation in assessments, registration, and targeting, but time, staff, and training are still too limited. Even the basic act of communicating information about aid entitlements is not always undertaken.

When channels for aid recipients to file complaints do exist, fear of losing access to assistance discourages the reporting of corruption against those who control it. Yet complaints are often routed through the very aid governance systems responsible for the two high-risk areas of targeting and registration. Complaint mechanisms that require literacy or amount to symbolic gestures that do not result in action or resolution are likewise discouraging and ineffective. Aid recipients distinguish—and can identify by name—agencies that address their complaints and ones that do not. In Northern Uganda, whether or not these agencies had official complaint mechanisms was of little consequence in their ability to address complaints, evidenced by the fact that the one agency that actually had a complaint desk was considered the least responsive by aid recipients.

No system is foolproof; it ultimately boils down to the individuals who operate it. However, human resources in emergencies has not received nearly as much emphasis as finance and procurement functions, even though successfully implementing programmes and addressing corruption risks depend on the quality and commitment of staff. Aid agency staff believe that organisational values, when communicated and reinforced through training, opportunities for advancement, appraisals, and examples set by senior managers, promote honesty and loyalty to the agency. Finding the balance between trusting and empowering staff and partners on the one hand, and control and effective verification on the other, is complicated by the power imbalances between international aid agencies and local partners, and between expatriate and national staff.

The practices of individual aid agencies that address corruption risks have not been accompanied by systemwide analysis and action in the humanitarian community to promote information sharing and joint action. In particular, coordination forums could be used to develop common strategies dealing with specific emergency environments where corruption is endemic.

	HIGH RISK AREAS	CORRUPTION RISK EXAMPLES
Assistance process	**Assessment**	Incorrect information provided to direct assistance to certain households, groups, or regions, or to inflate needs
	Registration	Names added to beneficiary lists in exchange for payment or sexual favours; bribes demanded; multiple registrations
	Targeting	Leaders/staff/committees provide false information about which households meet targeting criteria
	Distribution	Distributors modify ration amounts or composition, or knowingly distribute commodities to "ghost" beneficiaries or nonbeneficiaries

Sector	**Food aid**	Manipulation or bribery in assessments, registration, and targeting; diversion and sale during transport or storage; skimming rations
	High-value items (e.g., medicines)	Manipulation or bribery in assessments, registration, and targeting; diversion during transport or storage; substandard goods
	Construction	Intentional use of substandard materials, manipulation of land titles
Programme support	**Procurement**	Collusion, kickbacks, multiple submissions of same invoices, conflicts of interest
	Human resources	"Ghost" staff, nepotism
	Finance	Falsified or inflated invoices or receipts, manipulation of exchange rates, abuse of bank accounts, embezzlement
	Fleet management	Unauthorised private use of vehicles, siphoning off fuel, collusion with fuel/ service providers, falsified records
	Logistics	Falsification of warehouse documents, diversion during transport

Engagement modality	**Partnership arrangements**	Partners can engage in any of the above corruption areas
	Scaling up local offices for direct delivery	HR recruitment and other programme support risks, bribes required for permits or access to public services
	Working through committees	Diversion of assistance to their own networks, acceptance of bribes for inclusion on lists
	Working through local leadership structures/ local government	Diversion of assistance to their own networks and political supporters, acceptance of bribes for inclusion on lists

Table 1
Corruption risk areas and examples in humanitarian assistance

HIGHER RISK	**LOWER RISK**
War	Peace
High levels of precrisis corruption	Low levels of precrisis corruption
Limited transparency and accountability	Transparent and accountable aid
Weak rule of law	Strong rule of law
Limited familiarity with context	Considerable familiarity with context
Rapid scale-up of operations	Gradual or limited scale-up of operations
Pressure to spend funds rapidly	Flexible spending timelines

Table 2
Variables affecting corruption risks (Adapted from Ewins et al. 2006.)

CONCLUSION

Corruption poses a serious threat in the complex endeavour of humanitarian assistance—to the people trying to access lifesaving resources, to the ability of agencies to programme assistance in exploitative and corrupt settings, and to the reputations of all actors involved in saving lives and alleviating suffering in the wake of crisis.

The extent to which agency practices that mitigate corruption risks do or do not slow down responses in the early stages of a crisis needs to be further explored, but there are clear steps that agencies can take. Reports, evaluations, guidelines, and good practice reviews recommend investment in programme quality and accountability to aid recipients; preventing corruption is yet one more reason why these measures are essential. Humanitarian agencies can benefit from examining anticorruption tools and strategies developed by institutions outside of the humanitarian world, and a handbook focusing on preventing corruption in humanitarian assistance is being developed by Transparency International. Donors can help by providing more resources for audits and monitoring, increasing the flexibility with which funds are allocated to programme support and quality enhancement functions, and refraining from pressuring agencies to unnecessarily accelerate spending. The humanitarian enterprise is inherently risky, and aid agencies and donors need to have realistic expectations about delivering relief in contexts where corruption and diversion are all but inevitable. Addressing corruption risks might not itself make headlines, but it may prevent attention-grabbing scandals about greed, abuse, and wastage. More importantly, it supports the fundamental objective of humanitarian assistance: to provide assistance wherever it is needed, to the people who need it.

Key Recommendations for Aid Agencies

General

- Ensure that policies that mitigate or prevent corruption are implemented in the field and that resources are available for this.
- Proactively and openly discuss corruption with staff and explain agency policies and systems related to corruption, reducing the "taboo" around the subject.
- Strengthen downwards accountability mechanisms to prevent and detect corruption.

Programming

- Focus on and invest in programme quality, and ensure increased vigilance when engaging in high-risk areas (construction/shelter, food aid, and highly valued commodities).
- Improve analysis of corruption risks, the operating environment, and the local political economy; incorporate this analysis into emergency preparedness planning.

- Allocate greater resources to programme monitoring, particularly in the field.

Programme Support

- Give greater attention to setting up good support systems at the beginning of a response and to human resources, particularly recruitment, induction, and performance monitoring.
- Establish mechanisms to guard against "burn rates" and other pressures to spend rapidly.
- Continue to invest in audit capacity, emphasising that audits go beyond paper trails.

New Strategies

- Pilot innovative ideas like drama groups, hiring anthropologists, engaging the local media and civil society groups to act as watchdogs, and using citizen report cards.
- Put in place—individually or collectively—independent, external, or peer-group evaluation mechanisms.
- Verify anticorruption systems; for example, by seeing if they catch "fake" documents.

Addressing Corruption Perceived by Crisis-affected Populations

- Establish and verify the effectiveness of complaints mechanisms; make sure that they incorporate awareness of local power structures, security, and cultural factors hindering complaints; avoid channeling them though "gatekeepers" or those involved in targeting and registration.
- During targeting and registrations, clearly explain the processes and make clear that people should not make payments to be included; photocopy and read aloud any lists prepared by leaders or committees.
- Explain how assistance distributions work, including the process of transporting leftover commodities back to agency warehouses for future distributions; investigate any complaints related to the sale of goods in transit.

References and Further Reading

Bailey, S. 2008. Perceptions of corruption in humanitarian assistance among internally displaced persons in northern Uganda. London: Humanitarian Policy Group.

Elhawary, S. 2008. Beneficiary perceptions of corruption in humanitarian assistance: Sri Lanka case study. With M. M. M. Aheeyar. London: Humanitarian Policy Group.

Ewins, P., P. Harvey, H. Savage, and A. Jacobs. 2006. Mapping the risks of corruption in humanitarian action. London: Overseas Development Institute.

Maxwell, D., P. Walker, C. Church, P. Harvey, K. Savage, S. Bailey, R. Hees, and M. Ahlendorf. 2008. Preventing corruption in humanitarian assistance: Final research report. Berlin: Transparency International. http://www.odi.org.uk/resources/docs/1836.pdf.

Savage, K. et al. 2007. Corruption perceptions and risks in humanitarian assistance: A Liberia case study. With M. S. Jackollie, D. M. Kumeh, and E. Dorbor. London: Overseas Development Institute.

Savage, K. et. Al. 2007. Corruption perceptions and risks in humanitarian assistance: An Afghanistan case study. With M. S. Jackollie, D. M. Kumeh, and E. Dorbor. London: Overseas Development Institute.

US House of Representatives, Committee on Government Reform—Minority Staff, Special Investigations Division. 2006. Waste, fraud, and abuse in Hurricane Katrina contracts.

Willitts-King, B. and P. Harvey. 2005. Managing the risk of corruption in humanitarian relief operations. London: Humanitarian Practice Group.

Notes

For more information about the Humanitarian Policy Group: http://www.odihpn.org/.

Source

Bailey, S. 2008. Need and greed: Corruption risks, perceptions, and prevention in humanitarian assistance. *HPG Policy Briefs* 32 (September). Reprinted by permission. http://www.odi.org.uk/resources/details.asp?id=2385&title=corruption-risks-perceptions-prevention-humanitarian-assistance.

Related Resources

Video: Zimbardo, Phil. "The Lucifer Effect (The Psychology of Evil)." TED Talks. http://www.ted.com/talks/philip_zimbardo_on_the_psychology_of_evil.html.

Batchelor, P., and S. Osei-Mensah. 2011. Salt and light: Christians' role in combating corruption. The Lausanne Global Conversation. October 31. http://conversation.lausanne.org/en/conversations/detail/12129.

Member Care Associates. 2012. Confronting corruption: Safeguards for staff and senders. *Resources for Good Practice* (April). http://membercareassociates.org/?page_id=125.

Memon, K. 2008. Employee fraud in humanitarian organizations: Taking from the givers. *Fraud Magazine*, March–April, 20–23.

O'Donnell, K. & Lewis O'Donnell, M. 2013. Loving truth and peace: A case study of family resilience in dealing with mission/aid corruption. In J. Bonk (Ed.). *Family accountability in missions: Korean and Western case studies*. New Haven, CT: OMSC Publications.

United Nations Office on Drugs and Crime. 2004. United Nations convention against corruption. New York: United Nations. http://www.unodc.org/unodc/en/treaties/CAC/index. html.

Mukesh Kapila, 2013. Against a Tide of Evil: How One Man Became the Whistleblower to the First Mass Murder of the 21st Century. Edinburgh, UK: Mainstream Publishing. http:// www.mukeshkapila.org/book/about-book.html

Vian, T., W. Savedoff, and H. Mathisen, eds. 2010. *Anticorruption in the health sector: Strategies for transparency and accountability*. Herndon, VA: Kumarian Press. http://www.bu.edu/ actforhealth/pdf/Flyer%20-%20Anticorruption.pdf.

CHAPTER 11

Partnerships in Emergency Assistance

Building the Future of Humanitarian Aid: Local Capacity and Partnerships in Emergency Assistance

Katherine Nightingale, Christian Aid[2]

A significant common message from the East Africa food crisis, Pakistan floods, Haiti earthquake, and the 2004 tsunami—and almost every emergency in recent years—is that investment in building resilience, reducing disaster risk, and strengthening local capacity to respond saves lives and speeds recovery.

Executive Summary

In any emergency the first people to respond and give lifesaving help are those affected by it. "Friends and neighbours search through the rubble for loved ones after earthquakes; local hospitals work through the night to care for the injured."[3] In Kenya, for example, the church and national organisations have played a key role in managing drought risks and providing emergency relief in the face of the 2011 food crisis.

In some countries frequently affected by natural hazards, governments and local organisations have become adept at disaster prevention and response. Whether through local government, neighbourhood organisations, faith networks, or NGOs, the reality is that a significant amount of humanitarian assistance is ultimately delivered by the citizens of disaster-affected countries themselves. But local

---

2   For more information about Christian Aid: http://www.christianaid.org.uk/.

3   Humanitarian Emergency Response Review (HERR), 2011, p13, dfid.gov. uk/Documents/publications1/HERR.pdf.

capacity, national government, and civil society institutions can be undermined by humanitarian actors in the urgency to respond and the tight-spending timeframes for humanitarian funds. Independent evaluations in 2007 of the tsunami response criticised the humanitarian sector for sidelining local capacity and organisations. "The way in which the humanitarian sector is funded, by sudden inputs following public appeals, encourages an emphasis on rapid service delivery, exaggeration of the agencies' own importance and understatement of the role of local people."[4]

National governments have primary responsibility for protecting citizens from preventable disasters and leading emergency response efforts. But while some are leading the way in preparedness and emergency response, others lack the necessary capacity or use their efforts in a partisan way.

Partnerships between international humanitarian agencies and local organisations—as part of government-led response plans—are an important way to reinforce local leadership and deliver effective response in line with humanitarian principles. Where partnerships bring local knowledge and experience together with humanitarian expertise in a working relationship that is collaborative, risk sharing, and inclusive, they can deliver better emergency aid and more resilient development in the long term.

But working through partnerships can only build on and benefit from local capacity when there is a genuine commitment to cooperation and shared responsibility. Learning from recent humanitarian responses suggests that partnerships between international aid agencies and southern organisations can often fall short of genuine supportive collaboration. Partnerships can be in name only, and Southern organisations can be treated simply as a pipeline for delivery, with little say in their work and little sense of sustainability or of shared learning and mutual accountability. Where investment in supporting partners is not sufficient, then their ability to deliver responses on time and to the desired standard can be impaired.

Other challenges include how to make the partnership approach to emergency response help local organisations deliver to scale, proportionally balance risk and responsibility and, crucially, how partnership approaches to response can be recognised and funded in a humanitarian sector that has historically favoured top-down operational working models.

This report looks at Christian Aid's own experience of working with local partners in disaster risk reduction (DRR), preparedness, emergency response, and recovery.

---

4   Arjuna Parakrama, 'Impact of the tsunami response on local and national capacities,' Forced Migration Review 28, July 2007, p. 7, fmreview.org/FMRpdfs/FMR28/full.pdf.

It draws on direct experience of partnership approaches to emergency work and its challenges, with examples from a range of emergency contexts, including India, the Philippines, Kenya, Burkina Faso, Malawi, and Burma, and a detailed case study on Haiti. The report then builds on Christian Aid's experience of influencing progressive thinking on DRR and resilience and supporting local and national advocacy on disaster prevention and response to ask what these lessons mean for the wider humanitarian sector.

Ultimately it is the changing external context that may be the greatest driver for the system to get its act together. With disasters increasing in scale and number, the international system is under ever-growing strain to mount effective and timely responses. The role of national civil society and governments will become more important. This will require changes in the way international humanitarian actors work that are far from trivial. These changes include "adapting the ways in which international humanitarian action is appealed for, financed, coordinated, staffed, assessed and delivered."[5] The need for greater partnerships and local capacities is slowly moving to the centre of the humanitarian policy debate. As the Ashdown review found in 2011: "If the world is going to get better at the challenges [faced], then [international agencies] have to work with governments, and with affected people . . . They have to support local institutions rather than weaken them."[6]

Delivering this fundamental reorientation of the humanitarian sector towards "supporting and facilitating communities' own relief and recovery priorities"[7] requires action on three levels:

- **Change in practice:** the humanitarian agencies should develop best practice on collaborative partnership approaches for disaster prevention and response that builds local capacity.
- **Change in global perspective:** the importance of DRR and emergency response to building resilience and development makes it central to global development and aid debates; the UN secretary-general should appoint a high-level panel to lead a global review of disaster prevention and response to feed into the post–Millenium Development Goals (MDGs) agenda.

---

5   ALNAP meeting paper: The role of national governments in international humanitarian response, p. 4, alnap.org/pool/files/meeting-paper-2011.pdf.

6   See note 1.

7   Tsunami Evaluation Coalition: Joint evaluation of the international response to the Indian Ocean tsunami, January 2007, p. 22, alnap.org/pool/files/Syn_Report_Sum.pdf.

- **Change in funding, coordination, and attitude:** donors, UN coordination mechanisms, and national governments should fund, coordinate, and deliver emergency responses as if local capacity mattered. They must develop structures that reinforce and fund best practice for working with local capacity in emergency response.

THE IMPORTANCE OF LOCAL CAPACITY AND PARTNERSHIPS IN EMERGENCY RESPONSE

1. Local capacities are key in building resilience to disasters and delivering rapid, effective emergency response—but their neglect continues.

The importance of local capacity and the role of local organisations in emergency response are becoming well recognised. Successive studies and evaluations have found that local capacities can make a critical difference to humanitarian responses. Partnerships between international humanitarian actors (whether donors, UN, or aid agencies) and the government and local and national organisations of affected countries are emerging as a key way to work with local capacity as part of a coordinated response.

But this approach requires a change in attitude in the humanitarian sector that is not happening fast enough. The real-time evaluation of the Haiti emergency in 2010 identified the failure to adequately involve local actors as a key challenge even a year after the earthquake hit.[8] The Humanitarian Emergency Response Review published in 2011 recognised that, despite the policy commitments and growing evidence base of the importance of local and national organisations in the humanitarian sector, "all too often the international response arrives as though this were not the case, sweeping aside local responders and adding to the chaos rather than alleviating it."[9]

The call by aid agencies in January this year to invest in early action and channel funds to prevention in the wake of the East Africa food crisis is an important one. But there is also a deeper point that needs to be addressed. Releasing money earlier, while essential for saving lives and preserving livelihoods, should be accompanied by a more fundamental change: "[a] fundamental reorientation from supplying aid

---

8   For example, Evaluation of the OCHA Response to the Haiti Earthquake, January 2011, see pp. 31–32, ochanet.unocha.org/p/Documents/Evaluation%20of%20OCHA%20Response%20to%20the%20Haiti%20Earthquake.pdf.

9   See note 1.

to supporting and facilitating communities' own relief and recovery priorities," as called for by the Tsunami Evaluation Coalition in 2007.[10]

Box 1 gives some examples of the kinds of statements found in policy documents and evaluations.

Box 1.

STATEMENTS ON LOCAL CAPACITY AND PARTNERSHIP IN KEY HUMANITARIAN POLICIES AND REPORTS

"Local capacity is one of the main assets to enhance and on which to build. Whenever possible, humanitarian organizations should strive to make it an integral part in emergency response." (Global Humanitarian Platform 2007)

"[Donors should] strengthen the capacity of affected countries and local communities to prevent, prepare for, mitigate and respond to humanitarian crises, with the goal of ensuring that governments and local communities are better able to meet their responsibilities and coordinate effectively with humanitarian partners." (Good Humanitarian Donorship Principles 2003)

"The international humanitarian community needs a fundamental reorientation from supplying aid to supporting and facilitating communities' own relief and recovery priorities." (Tsunami Evaluation Coalition 2007)

"The paradigm is still viewing the affected population too much as what economist Julian Le Grand has called 'pawns' (passive individuals) and the international community as 'knights' (extreme altruists). This approach costs. Local capacities are not utilised, the beneficiary is not involved enough and the quality of delivery is lower than it should be." (Humanitarian Emergency Response Review 2011, 26)

"Local actors are usually the first responders in a crisis . . . Local community capacity building is a crucial element in a transitional context (post-crisis situation) and necessary to ensure the sustainability of DRR efforts." (DG ECHO Guidelines on Strengthening Humanitarian Responses through Global Capacity Building and Grant Facility 2011, 6)

---

10   See note 5.

"Particularly in sudden onset crises, immediate humanitarian assistance such as search and rescue and the provision of water, food and
shelter are undertaken by neighbouring communities on a voluntary basis.
In these communities, religious groups often play a very important role.
It may take some days for organised national or international assistance
to arrive in the affected areas. Local capacities save lives in the first vital
hours and days." (Irish Aid 2009, 8)

"Immediate family, neighbours and members of the local community
are the first to help those around them when disaster strikes. The UK
will help strengthen these local actors' ability to respond." (Department
for International Development 2011, 9)[11]

2. Disasters are increasing in scale, frequency, and complexity, which makes the importance of local capacity more acute, with some contexts still remaining very difficult

In 2010 the Centre for Research on the Epidemiology of Disasters recorded 373
natural disaster events that killed more than 296,800 people, affected the lives of
208 million, and cost nearly US$110 billion.[12]

Statistics such as these are alarming but are set to worsen. Year on year, risk
drivers such as rapid, unplanned urbanisation, population growth, environmental
degradation, and climate change are increasing the exposure to and impact of
hazards such as earthquakes, cyclones, floods, and droughts. These risk drivers are
also resulting in disasters of greater complexity. For example, massive urban centres,
such as earthquake-hit Port-au-Prince or Metro Manila after Typhoon Ketsana,
required new and innovative approaches to delivering humanitarian assistance.
Political factors also add to the complexity, with examples including conflict in
Somalia and authoritarian states such as Burma also impacting on the access or
nature of an international emergency response in those contexts.

---

11   Saving lives, presenting suffering and building resilience: the UK Government's Humanitarian Policy, DFID, 2011, p. 9, dfid.gov.uk.

12   Centre for Research on the Epidemiology of Disasters (CRED), February 2011, relief-
web.int/sites/reliefweb.int/ files/resources/F7E6E30438715736C125784C004D2F49-Full_Re-
port.pdf.

The increasing numbers and complex nature of emergencies means it is even more important that the humanitarian sector incorporates local emergency capacity at its heart and builds that capacity as part of resilient development plans. Partnerships between international development and humanitarian organisations and their donors with local and national organisations is an important way to do this.

3. Changing attitudes to partnership in the humanitarian system.

Partnership is a core part of humanitarian response structures. In July 2007, UN and non-UN humanitarian agencies agreed to five Principles of Partnership, at the Global Humanitarian Platform:[13]

- equality
- transparency
- result-oriented approach
- responsibility
- complementarity

The principle of complementarity firmly recognised the importance of local capacity and committed agencies to putting it at the heart of their humanitarian partnerships.

> The diversity of the humanitarian community is an asset if we build on our comparative advantages and complement each other's contributions. Local capacity is one of the main assets to enhance and on which to build. Whenever possible, humanitarian organizations should strive to make it an integral part in emergency response. Language and cultural barriers must be overcome.[14]

Box 2 provides examples of some of the findings of evaluations and policy statements that emphasise the importance of partnerships and capacities.

---

13   Global Humanitarian Platform, July 2007, globalhumanitarianplatform.org/pop. html#pop.

14   Ibid.

Box 2.

EVALUATION FINDINGS ON IMPORTANCE OF PARTNER-
SHIPS WITH LOCAL ACTORS TO REINFORCE OR USE THE
LOCAL CAPACITY IN EMERGENCY RESPONSE

"What is clear is that new models of partnership and preparedness will be
required to respond to the crises of the next decade, with a focus on the
frontline capacities of communities, authorities and civil society." (Knudsen
2011, 8)[15]

"The partnership approach allows for a more locally relevant response
and greatly facilitates the transition process from relief to recovery, and wider
social development." (Christian Aid Tsunami Evaluation 2007)[16]

"Partnerships with local NGOs are the best means for external aid
agencies to scale up." (Gujarat DEC Evaluation 2001)[17]

"The TEC studies found that international agencies experienced major
problems in scaling up their own responses. Those agencies that had invested
(before the disaster) in developing their emergency response capacity had
the potential to be more effective. Preexisting links, and mutual respect,
between international agencies and local partners also led to better use of both
international and local capacities." (Tsunami Evaluation Coalition 2007, 4)[18]

"The reflections from Haiti show that collaboration with local partners
can be a highly effective way of ensuring that humanitarian action opens
doors to innovative programming." (Allen 2011, 40)[19]

---

15   Knudsen, C. 2011. Partnership in principle, partnership in practice. *Humanitarian
Exchange* 50 (April): 5–8. http://www.odihpn.org/humanitarian-exchange-magazine/issue-50.

16   Christian Aid Tsunami Evaluation, 2007.

17   Gujarat DEC Evaluation, 2001, alnap.org/pool/files/erd-3432-full.pdf.

18   See note 5.

19   Allen, R. Partnerships in rapid-onset emergencies: Insights from Pakistan and Haiti. *Humanitarian Exchange* 50 (April): 38–40. http://www.odihpn.org/
humanitarian-exchange-magazine/issue-50.

"In its relationship with local partners, this INGO has demonstrated a strong commitment to the principles of partnership . . . The partner has been included in all aspects of programme design, implementation and monitoring and evaluation. The close relationship and strong partnership trust that has developed between [the organisations] . . . has been facilitated by their shared values and programme scope. The investment made in partnership has not only contributed to the successful achievement of the Programme objectives to date, but has resulted in a strengthened local partner . . . better able to contribute to [the country's] long-term development." (Tearfund 2008)[20]

It should be recognised that in contexts where the local capacity is extremely weak and emergency needs are overwhelming, the humanitarian imperative requires a response that meets those needs. There will always be some local capacity to collaborate with, but, where displaced or refugee communities number in the tens or hundreds of thousands, an international operational response and implementing method may be the most appropriate. Similarly, in the midst of an internal conflict, operational responses to meet the needs of vulnerable or affected populations by international agencies or INGOs [international nongovernmental organisations] may be a preferred mechanism to deliver a scaled response.

But partnership approaches that deliver emergency responses through local organisations have the flexibility to play a central role in a large variety of contexts. Parts of the humanitarian system already recognise this by working in a partnership, capacity-enhancing mode by default, albeit with varying degrees of success.

There are a number of faith-based organisations such as Christian Aid and CAFOD that are part of wider networks—Christian Aid is part of Action by Churches Together (ACT) and CAFOD is part of the Caritas network. These work through networks of national and local organisations in order to deliver assistance. Some NGOs such as Action Aid also work through local capacities, while others, such as Oxfam and World Vision, have both operational and partnership approaches and are strengthening their ability to work through partnerships. For example, World Vision has established a partnership unit to strengthen its partnership approach as a core part of its next three- to five-year plan.

20   Tearfund, Liberia Evaluation, 2008, tilz.tearfund.org/webdocs/Tilz/Topics/DMT/
DMt%20Liberia%20Evaluation %20%28Final%20Impact%2005–08%29.pdf.

Another key partnership network is the International Red Cross and Red Crescent Movement, which is built on the idea of an international federation for humanitarian response, in which national members play a central role in disaster preparedness, response, recovery, and risk reduction, often supported by the northern members.

Learning on what makes effective partnerships is emerging from networks such as the Humanitarian Practice Network (HPN) and the Active Learning Network for Accountability and Performance in Humanitarian Action (ALNAP), and operational agencies are also tackling questions of partnership, with many building local capacity through initiatives such as the Emergency Capacity Building project (ECB).[21]

There is also growing recognition in UN coordination processes of the need to strengthen access and involvement of local actors. The IASC [Inter-Agency Standing Committee] Cluster leadership training highlights the importance of local actors in their training guide on partnerships and recommends: "Engage local NGOs, seek their input on strategies and priorities, and find ways to transfer and build their capacity. Local NGOs often have, among other things, a comparative advantage in early response and operational planning due to their links with local communities and authorities."[22] These efforts are being complemented by INGOs that support partners' engagement in humanitarian coordination through initiatives such as the Humanitarian Reform Project consortium.[23]

Despite this recognition of the importance of local capacity and for partnerships as a way of delivering locally led humanitarian aid, there is still a long way to go before the changes are made to deliver this, and even longer to see a humanitarian system built on local and national structures. As Oxfam's report *Crises in a New World Order* states: "It will take years, in places decades, to build genuinely global humanitarian action, rooted in crisis-affected countries."[24]

---

21   Emergency Capacity Building Project, ecbproject.org.

22   IASC Cluster/Sector Leadership Training (CSLT), 2007, allindiary.org/pool/resources/partnership-in-clusters.pdf.

23   NGOs and humanitarian reform project (CAFOD, Action Aid, CARE, IRC, Oxfam and Save the Children), icva.ch/ngosandhumanitarianreform.html.

24   Crises in a New World Order, Oxfam 2012, p. 3.

4. Partnership approaches for emergency response must be collaborative and based on principles of transparency and mutual accountability.

When one becomes aware of the moves towards more local partnerships or locally led humanitarian agencies, there is some cause for optimism. But pressure to deliver at speed and scale in complex emergencies and report on an agency's own impact to donors and the northern public can distort partnerships in practice.

The reality is that despite the policy commitments and growing evidence base of the importance of local capacity and the need to work in genuine partnerships, there are some repeated and disheartening lessons that emerge from many humanitarian responses.

In brief summary, these indicate that:

- local capacities are frequently undermined or excluded, often systematically so.
- southern partnerships are sometimes in name only, and partners are treated as a pipeline for delivery, with little sense of sustainability of work.

Box 3 illustrates some examples of the poor performance of the system with regard to partnerships and local capacity.

Box 3.

THE REALITY OF PARTNERSHIPS AND LOCAL CAPACITY WORK

"They would bring a team of people to a management meeting and then put several detailed strategies on the table, saying that this was the draft strategy and if there were any comments, they were needed within a few days. It didn't make us feel like we were a real part of the process." (International NGO Partnerships Evaluation, 2007)

"We are seldom recognised for the work we do in propping up the international system—we are the unseen workhorses." (Southern NGO director, speaking at AHA Symposium in Addis Ababa, 2004)

"They [Southern partner] have to be really special to turn around to us [Northern partner] and say we want to do things another way." (International NGO manager, ALNAP research, 2009)

"Although we talk about partnerships and capacities, the underlying principle seems to be to make 'them' work more like 'us.'" (International NGO manager, talking at ALNAP workshop, 2009)

"The weak link of partnership is relations between international organisations and their national and local counterparts, especially as national and local organisations are sometimes the only means to deliver protection and other forms of assistance to displaced persons in the type of environments we face today." (NGOs and Humanitarian Reform Project, Report on Strengthening Partnerships for Effective Humanitarian Response, 2010)

This Christian Aid report starts from the position that local capacity (national civil society and government institutions) should be central to emergency response and that efforts to adapt "the way international humanitarian action is appealed for, financed, coordinated, staffed, assessed and delivered"[25] must be prioritised to accelerate this.

As part of this adaptation of humanitarian action, partnerships with local organisations need to be at the heart of an inclusive and empowering approach to disaster prevention, emergency response, and recovery.

Failure to deliver in practice on policy commitments and rhetoric supporting local partnerships must be challenged.

Practical support and guidance should be developed to strengthen best practice for working through partnerships in emergencies.

In this report Christian Aid has drawn on its experience in order to contribute to the work that is needed. Five key areas have emerged from this research that will be explored in the following chapter [of this source]:

1. Knowledge and understanding of the partnership model and its principles
2. Partnerships for disaster risk reduction (DRR) and resilience
3. Partnerships for response

---

25 See note 3.

4. Partnerships for advocacy
5. The risks and responsibilities of the partnership model

In the subsequent chapters [of this source] we then look at the case of Haiti and draw out the lessons from Christian Aid's experience in these key areas.

SOURCE

Nightingale, K. 2012. Building the future of humanitarian aid: Local capacity and partnerships in emergency assistance. *Christian Aid*, 2–8. Reprinted by permission. http://www. christianaid.org.uk/images/building-the-future-of-humanitarian-aid.pdf.

RELATED RESOURCES

Video: Humanitarian Innovation Fund. "Innovation Film Clips." Humanitarian Innovation Fund. http://www.humanitarianinnovation.org/innovation-resource-centre/films.

Davey, E. 2012. New players through old lenses: Why history matters in engaging with Southern actors. *HPG Policy Briefs* 48 (July). http://www.odi.org.uk/resources/details. asp?id=6692&title=history-humanitarian-action-aid-ngos.

Enhancing Learning and Research for Humanitarian Assistance. 2012. ELRHA guide to constructing effective partnerships. ELRHA. http://www.elrha.org/uploads/effective-partnerships-report.pdf.

Global Humanitarian Platform. 2007. Principles of partnership: A statement of commitment. Global Humanitarian Platform. http://www.globalhumanitarianplatform.org/pop.html.

Global Social Observatory. 2012. Overview of best practices for multi-stakeholder engagement. Geneva: Global Social Observatory. https://sites.google.com/site/gmhmap/home/affiliations-and-partnerships.

O'Donnell, K. 2002. Developing member care affiliations. GMH-Map. https://sites.google.com/site/gmhmap/home/affiliations-and-partnerships.

World Association of Non-Governmental Organizations. 2007. Code of ethics and conduct for NGOs. WANGO. http://www.wango.org/codeofethics.aspx.

CHAPTER 12

Accountability Standards

THE 2010 HAP STANDARD IN ACCOUNTABILITY AND QUALITY MANAGEMENT

Humanitarian Accountability Partnership

The *2010 HAP Standard in Accountability and Quality Management* helps organisations that assist or act on behalf of people affected by or prone to disasters, conflict, poverty, or other crises to design, implement, assess, improve, and recognise accountable programmes. It represents broad consensus on what matters most when organisations engage in humanitarian action. The 2010 edition of the *Standard* was developed through an extensive process of reviewing the 2007 edition. Over 1,900 crisis-affected people, aid workers, and donor representatives contributed to this review, bringing to the process authentic experiences from the perspective of different groups.

ACCOUNTABILITY AND THE *HAP STANDARD*

Accountability has many meanings. Traditionally it was understood as the way in which those who authorised others to act on their behalf made sure that authority was being used as agreed. Accountability is now more often understood to *also* be a right of anyone affected by the use of authority. This recent meaning of accountability is the foundation for the *HAP Standard*. For the purpose of the *HAP Standard*, *accountability is the means through which power is used responsibly.*

It is a process of taking into account the views of, and being held accountable by, different stakeholders, and primarily the people affected by authority or power. Accountability is particularly necessary for organisations that assist or act on behalf of people affected by or prone to disasters, conflict, poverty, or other crises. Such organisations exercise significant power in their work to save lives and reduce suffering. In contrast, crisis-affected people have no formal control, and often little influence, over these organisations. As a result it is difficult for those people to hold organisations to account for actions taken on their behalf.

Being accountable to crisis-affected people helps organisations to develop quality programmes that meet those people's needs and reduces the possibility of mistakes, abuse, and corruption. Accountability processes that are managed effectively make the organisations perform better. In this context the *HAP Standard* helps organisations to assess, improve, and recognise the quality and accountability of their work, and benefits both the organisations and the people affected by crises.

THE *HAP STANDARD* COMMITMENT

Recognising that the essence of accountability is to respect the needs, concerns, capacities, and situation of the people they aim to assist, and to be answerable for their actions and decisions to these people and other stakeholders;

Respecting international humanitarian law, international refugee law, human rights law, and other relevant international treaties and national laws;

Reaffirming the primary responsibility of states for all persons on their territories and their duty to provide assistance and protection to people in need;

Upholding the right of people in need to receive assistance and protection on the basis of their informed consent, and everyone's right to offer assistance appropriate to people's needs;

Acknowledging the duty of care shared by all those involved in humanitarian action for the well-being of the people they aim to assist; and

Recognising also that the responses to the humanitarian imperative can take different forms, and may be affected by external constraints;

Organisations that meet the *HAP Standard* make a commitment to the *HAP Standard* Principles and to being held accountable according to the requirements of the *HAP Standard*.

THE *HAP STANDARD* PRINCIPLES[26]

Humanity: concern for human welfare and respect for the individual.

Impartiality: providing humanitarian assistance in proportion to need, and giving priority to the most urgent needs, without discrimination (including that

---

26   The first four principles are derived from the Fundamental Principles of the Red Cross. The next six are specifically relevant to accountability, with some derived from the HAP Principles of Accountability.

based upon gender, age, race, disability, ethnic background, nationality, or political, religious, cultural, or organisational affiliation).

Neutrality: aiming only to meet human needs and refraining from taking sides in hostilities or giving material or political support to parties to an armed conflict.

Independence: acting only under the authority of the organisation's governing body and in line with the organisation's purpose.

Participation and informed consent: listening and responding to feedback from crisis-affected people when planning, implementing, monitoring, and evaluating programmes, and making sure that crisis-affected people understand and agree with the proposed humanitarian action and are aware of its implications.

Duty of care: meeting recognised minimum standards for the well-being of crisis-affected people, and paying proper attention to their safety and the safety of staff.

Witness: reporting when the actions of others have a negative effect on the well-being of people in need of humanitarian assistance or protection.

Offer redress: enabling crisis-affected people and staff to raise complaints, and responding with appropriate action.

Transparency: being honest and open in communications and sharing relevant information, in an appropriate form, with crisis-affected people and other stakeholders.

Complementarity: working as a responsible member of the aid community, coordinating with others to promote accountability to, and coherence for, crisis-affected people.

The *HAP Standard* Requirements

There are six benchmarks in the *HAP Standard*. Each has related requirements, indicated by the word "shall," and means of verification, which specify the source of information that allows assessment as to whether the requirements are met. The first requirement of each benchmark covers organisational policy or corporate statements, and subsequent requirements cover an organisation's practice. Sources of information are a combination of documents, interviews with a cross-section of the relevant stakeholders, and observation of practice.

The benchmarks are set out below, followed by tables relating to each benchmark, its requirements, and their means of verification: [Editors' note: These tables are not included in this chapter. We strongly encourage readers to download the online document to review them.]

1. Establishing and delivering on commitments. The organisation sets out the commitments that it will be held accountable for, and how they will be delivered.

2. Staff competency. The organisation ensures that staff have competencies that enable them to meet the organisation's commitments.

3. Sharing information. The organisation ensures that the people it aims to assist and other stakeholders have access to timely, relevant, and clear information about the organisation and its activities.

4. Participation. The organisation listens to the people it aims to assist, incorporating their views and analysis in programme decisions.

5. Handling complaints. The organisation enables the people it aims to assist and other stakeholders to raise complaints and receive a response through an effective, accessible, and safe process.

6. Learning and **continual improvement.** The organisation learns from experience to continually improve its performance.

THE HAP PRINCIPLES OF ACCOUNTABILITY

1. Commitment to humanitarian standards and rights

- Members state their commitment to respect and foster humanitarian standards and the rights of beneficiaries.

2. Setting standards and building capacity

- Members set a framework of accountability to their stakeholders.[27]
- Members set and periodically review their standards and performance indicators, and revise them if necessary.
- Members provide appropriate training in the use and implementation of standards.

---

27   Framework of accountability includes standards, quality standards, principles, policies, guidelines, training, and other capacity-building work, etc. The framework must include measurable performance indicators. Standards may be internal to the organisation or they may be collective (e.g., Sphere or People In Aid).

3. Communication

- Members inform and consult with stakeholders, particularly beneficiaries and staff, about the standards adopted, programmes to be undertaken, and mechanisms available for addressing concerns.

4. Participation in programmes

- Members involve beneficiaries in the planning, implementation, monitoring, and evaluation of programmes and report to them on progress, subject only to serious operational constraints.

5. Monitoring and reporting on compliance

- Members involve beneficiaries and staff when they monitor and revise standards.
- Members regularly monitor and evaluate compliance with standards, using robust processes.
- Members report at least annually to stakeholders, including beneficiaries, on compliance with standards. Reporting may take a variety of forms.

6. Addressing complaints

- Members enable beneficiaries and staff to report complaints and seek redress safely.

7. Implementing partners

- Members are committed to the implementation of these principles if and when working through implementation partners.

EDITORS' NOTES

For more information on the Humanitarian Accountability Partnership: http://www.hapinternational.org/.

SOURCE

Humanitarian Accountability Partnership. 2010. *The 2010 HAP standard in accountability and quality management.* Geneva: HAP International. http://www.hapinternational.org/pool/files/2010-hap-standard-in-accountability.pdf. Reprinted by permission.

RELATED RESOURCES

Video: Wickrama, Katharina Samara. "Accountable Aid." YouTube. http://www.youtube.com/watch?v=ep7RWMI0YbE.

Bon, J., ed. 2011. *Accountability in missions: Korean and Western case studies.* Eugene, OR: Wipf & Stock.

Humanitarian Practice Network. 2011. Humanitarian accountability. Special issue, *Humanitarian Exchange* 52 (October). http://www.odihpn.org/humanitarian-exchange-magazine/issue-52/humanitarian-accountability.

Joint Standards Initiative. Humanitarian standards for aid workers. http://www.jointstandards.org/.

Taylor, G., A. Stoddard, A. Harmer, K. Haver, and P. Harvey. 2012. The state of the humanitarian system. With K. Barber, L. Schreter, and C. Wilhelm. London: Overseas Development Institute. http://www.alnap.org/pool/files/alnap-sohs-2012-lo-res.pdf.

World Humanitarian Day. http://www.whd-iwashere.org/.

World Vision International. 2011. Accountability report. Monrovia, CA: World Vision International. http://www.wvi.org/wvi/wviweb.nsf/0DA5D0279F5038378825764F006DA5CE/$file/ACCOUNTABILITYREPORT_FY10web.pdf.

CHAPTER 13

Faith-based Humanitarians

SOME MYTHS ABOUT FAITH-BASED HUMANITARIAN AID

Wilfred Mlay, World Vision International

Since the terrorist attacks of 11 September 2001, many commentators have devoted attention to an apparent clash between the values of the West and those of Islam. The humanitarian sector has not escaped this debate. Unfortunately the discussion is impoverished by persistent myths and an inappropriate focus on the values of the humanitarians, rather than on the value of those being assisted.

A familiar story is being repeated along the following lines: humanitarianism is a Western-driven, neocolonial enterprise. In particular, the story goes, the threats to international aid workers and the assets of Western aid organisations in Afghanistan and Iraq are simply the manifestation of a growing clash between Islam and the West. Samuel Huntington's well-known work, *The Clash of Civilizations*, supposedly exposes the causes of this confrontation, while David Rieff's book *A Bed for the Night: Humanitarianism in Crisis* pronounces the near death of a humanitarianism allegedly beholden to Western governments and their interests. Even the UN under-secretary-general for humanitarian affairs, Jan Egeland, has mused privately that aid organisations in Afghanistan are "too Western."

This search to find cultural underpinnings for the travails of humanitarianism is remarkable in its neglect of any serious exploration of its religious aspects. Thin attempts to do this often create caricatures of religious humanitarianism and thus perpetuate misunderstanding. Humanitarianism is best served not by a navel-gazing examination of the many values of its large cast, but by a dedication to greater accountability and transparency to those for whom faith-based humanitarian agencies claim to act. However, caricatures and generalisations lead to commonly held assumptions about the role of faith in humanitarian assistance that are false and inhibit the effectiveness of the ensemble. Three prevalent myths about Christian humanitarian organisations are worth our attention.

Myth no. 1: Christian humanitarian organisations embody the West's clash with Islam.

Adherents of the "culture-clash" theory often make the uncharitable claim that today's Western aid organisations are simply last century's white European missionaries in new clothing. Furthermore, they contend that Christian humanitarians are particularly pernicious in carrying out a "civilising mission" that unwittingly or deliberately promotes the values of the world's major Western powers. According to this theory, a web-page image of a Christian aid worker kneeling next to a burqa-clad Afghan woman is just a modern version of the lithograph of the pith-helmeted missionary standing next to a Masai warrior in battle dress. While such caricatures distort both past and present, they are hurled broadly at Western-based aid agencies, but particularly at Christian organisations.

Such conflation falsely presents Christianity as a "Western" religion and Islam as an "Eastern" religion. In fact both faiths are global religions whose adherents live predominantly in developing countries of the South. Christianity, like Islam, began in the Middle East, and now has 1.1 billion followers in Latin America, Africa, and Asia, compared with 800 million in North America and Europe. In demographic terms, the average Anglican is African, female, under the age of 30, a mother of three, walks four kilometres a day to fetch water, lives on less than $1.50 a day, and is related to someone with HIV/AIDS.[28]

To conflate Christianity with the West is delusion. As Philip Jenkins notes in his book *The Next Christendom*, Christianity has been in China about as long as it has been in England, and the Ethiopian church prospered for centuries before the first Anglo-Saxon was converted.

It is equally misleading to treat Islam as if it were synonymous with the Middle East or with speaking Arabic. More Muslims speak non-Arabic languages than Arabic. Indonesia accounts for more Muslims than any other single country. Throughout the West—in North America and Europe in particular—mosques are almost as easy to find as churches.

Just as Christianity and Islam are global, so are most of the large, international humanitarian organisations. Far from being Western enterprises, the composition of the staff and governance structures of many aid organisations reflects a true global

---

28   Anglican Communion News Service. 2004. Anglican telecommunications: An instrument of community. Anglican Communion Office. 9 February. http://www.anglicancommunion.org/acns/news.cfm/2004/2/9/ACNS3775.

diversity. This is a global diversity usually lacking from the boardrooms of the largest multinational corporations and even the senior management level of UN agencies.

World Vision International is one example of this diversity. Its twenty-four-strong board includes members from nineteen different countries, with an equal balance from the North and South. Of the organisation's forty-nine member offices, twenty-seven are full-fledged indigenous entities with staff and governing boards composed almost entirely of nationals. Another twenty-two are guided by indigenous advisory councils that are expected to become self-governing. Most of the agency's staff embrace one of three Christian expressions: Catholicism, Protestantism, or Eastern Orthodoxy. However, despite the organisation's Christian character, many non-Christians seek employment and are employed by World Vision in countries where Christians are a minority. In the Middle East and Asia, many staff members are Muslim. In Southeast Asia many are Buddhist.

What is true for its staff and organisation is also true for World Vision's private donors. In the West, Christians provide the majority of private contributions to World Vision's relief and development work. But World Vision also raises substantial funds in developing countries, some of which have very modest Christian populations. For example, in Taiwan, Japan, Thailand, and elsewhere, the overwhelming majority of contributors to World Vision are non-Christians. World Vision's appeal to assist those afflicted by poverty, HIV/AIDS, or disaster presumably touches their compassion and common humanity, not their religious affiliation.

World Vision is not unique among Christian NGOs. Other Christian humanitarian organisations are equally diverse in staffing, governance, and funding sources. Such global diversity suggests that the blanket charge against them of Western cultural imperialism is mislaid.

Myth no. 2: Religious approaches create conflicts rather than solve them.

The argument here is threefold:

1. Religions define themselves by competing truth claims.
2. This competition inevitably provokes violent conflicts for which religion is inescapably culpable (the Balkans, the Horn of Africa, South Asia, and so on).
3. Therefore religious organisations or persons have nothing to offer societies wracked by religious conflicts, even when those societies are in need of humanitarian assistance.

R. Scott Appleby's *Ambivalence of the Sacred: Religion, Violence and Reconciliation* explodes this myth. Appleby does not shy away from examining "religion's violent accomplices," namely religious zealots who invoke faith to justify violent acts. But he distinguishes between militants for violence and "militants for peace," namely religious zealots who sacrifice their lives for reconciliation, for the poor, or for the common good. Positive examples of "zealots for peace" include the Buddhist Dhammayietra in Cambodia, the Catholic Community of Sant'Egidio in Mozambique, and the Inter-Religious Council of Sierra Leone. Appleby notes two things about such groups: (1) explicitly religious approaches to humanitarianism succeeded in the midst of religiously "loaded" conflicts; and (2) religious approaches succeeded where nonreligious ones had failed.

The character of a religious organisation often opens up conversations that are not available to secular humanitarian organisations. An NGO case study by the Conflict Transformation Working Group in 2002 demonstrated that religious leaders are often viewed within a conflict as nonpartisan actors. Thus they are able to mobilise large constituencies in peace-building efforts. All major conflicts have a complex, multifaceted, political economy that goes far beyond any single issue, such as faith; but, in conflicts that are openly defined by religious differences, having an ear for religion is preferable to being religiously tone deaf.

For example, in Indonesia, World Vision has been able to work effectively with Muslim communities, including in areas suffering ongoing Muslim–Christian violence. In the North Maluku region of Indonesia, World Vision recruited Muslim and Christian staff members, then paired them together to work in communities divided along religious lines. The strategy helped to build bridges between Muslims and Christians.

In 1999, in Mitrovica, the Kosovo city bitterly divided ethnically (between Albanians and Serbs) and religiously (between Muslim, Orthodox, and Catholic), World Vision facilitated the formation of a multiethnic and multireligious Community Council on Peace and Tolerance. The council, which drew together representatives of five ethnic groups and three faiths, established a dialogue that reduced violence, eased tensions, and created community-building initiatives. Council participants said that the faith-based nature of World Vision was important in establishing trust and mutual respect.

Myth no. 3: Faith-based organisations cannot carry out neutral or impartial humanitarian assistance because their real intent, whether overt or covert, is religious conversion.

Several codes of conduct govern the humanitarian sector. These normative principles, which cover the provision of humanitarian assistance, are the result of wide interagency consultation, predominantly, though not exclusively, among Western humanitarian organisations.

Almost all of these codes of conduct explicitly eliminate religious "transactions" from the humanitarian equation. Most importantly, they establish that human need alone should determine humanitarian assistance. Moreover, they stipulate that recipients should evaluate the effectiveness of that assistance.

Two principles in the Code of Conduct for the International Red Cross and Red Crescent Movement and Non-Governmental Organisations in Disaster Relief speak clearly to the question of religious humanitarianism:

Principle 2: Aid is given regardless of the race, creed, or nationality of the recipients and without adverse distinction of any kind.

Principle 3: Aid will not be used to further a particular political or religious standpoint.

While Principle 3 explicitly prohibits "the promise, delivery or distribution of assistance to the embracing or acceptance of a particular political or religious creed," it adds an important nuance. It emphasises that humanitarian NGOs can espouse "particular political or religious opinions" and still adhere to the letter and spirit of the Code.

It is important to distinguish between the erroneous belief that being motivated by faith to assist people fundamentally undermines principles of impartiality and neutrality and the real examples of the partial delivery of assistance that have led to the development of these codified principles. Any organisation, whether overtly faith-based or firmly rooted in secular humanism, is capable of taking advantage of its position of power to promote an organisational agenda. Similarly, individuals within organisations may do the same to promote an individual agenda. Examples abound of secular and faith-based agencies, or members of agencies, that have used aid to advance their cause, have directed aid to those of their own creed, or have delivered aid only to the side of the conflict that adheres to the same political ideology as they do, at the expense of others. This is precisely what gave rise to initiatives such as the Code of Conduct, the Humanitarian Accountability Partnership International, and the Sphere standards. These self-regulation efforts add to the legitimacy of humanitarian action and provide a gauge by which to measure specific actions and avoid generalised stereotypes. Not only do World Vision and many other faith-based organisations adhere to these codes, but they belong to the organisations that safeguard them; World Vision helps to fund the Humanitarian Accountability Partnership and is represented on its board of directors.

Jesus articulated the humanitarian imperative codified in the ICRC [International Committee of the Red Cross] / NGO Code. He taught that the most important task in doing God's will is to respond to people's needs as if every person is God: "For I was hungry and you gave me something to eat, I was thirsty and you gave me something to drink, I was a stranger and you invited me in, I needed clothes and you clothed me, I was sick and you looked after me, I was in prison and you came to visit me" (Matt 25:35,36).

Far from being at odds with humanitarianism, this spiritual vision common to many faiths establishes the principle that "aid priorities are calculated on the basis of need alone." Faith-based organisations marry their spiritual vision to the neutral and impartial humanitarian imperative when they heed their own religious texts. Loving one's neighbour is a Jewish and Christian commandment. Assisting the poor is one of the five pillars of Islam. It is a sacred task for Buddhism and a holy injunction for other religions. Humanitarianism is a task that unites religions rather than divides them.

REFERENCES AND FURTHER READING

Appleby, R. Scott. 1999. *The ambivalence of the sacred.* Lanham, MD: Rowman & Littlefield.

Conflict Transformation Working Group. 2002. Building peace from the ground up: A call to the UN for stronger collaboration with civil society. New York: Conflict Transformation Working Group.

Galama, Anneke, and Paul van Tongeren, eds. 2002. *Towards better peacebuilding practice: On lessons learned, evaluation practices and aid and conflict.* Utrecht, the Netherlands: European Centre for Conflict Prevention.

Helmick, Raymond G., and Rodney L. Peterson, eds. 2001. *Forgiveness and reconciliation: Religion, public policy and conflict transformation.* Radnor, PA: Temple Foundation Press.

Huntington, Samuel P. 1996. *The clash of civilizations and the remaking of world order.* New York: Simon & Schuster.

Jenkins, Philip. 2002. *The next Christendom: The coming of global Christianity.* New York: Oxford University Press.

Johnston, Douglas, and Cynthia Sampson, eds. 1995. *Religion: The missing dimension of statecraft.* Oxford: Oxford University Press.

Rieff, David. 2002. *A bed for the night: Humanitarianism in crisis*. New York: Simon & Schuster.

Scholaert, Rudy. 2002. United and committed to building peace: Mitrovica's Community Council for Peace and Tolerance. Ed. Lowrey. World Vision. http://www.justice-and-peace.org/PolicyAdvocacy/pahome2.5.nsf/crresourceTrain/FC7A33CA3C936C6E88256E46008360DD/$file/CCPT.pdf.

Editors' Notes

"The extensive literature on Western humanitarianism seldom does justice to its religious traditions. Western humanitarianism was moulded by Catholic monastic orders, by the Geneva Calvinist founders of the Red Cross, by the Salvation Army, by the Leprosy Mission and by the Oxford Quakers who helped to found Oxfam. Church organisations dominated international aid until the Nigerian civil war of the late 1960s, with the founding of the secular agency Médecins Sans Frontières (MSF). Even today, strands of Christian humanitarianism are strongly represented by Caritas, World Vision, the Order of Malta, Christian Aid and the Nordic churches . . . Although it is likely that practising Christians are in a minority among the personnel who work for Western humanitarian agencies, the West is widely perceived as Christian, and the liberal humanism underpinning Western humanitarianism, even in its 'secular' form, is arguably itself underpinned by a heritage of Judeo-Christian values" (Jonathan Benthal, "Humanitarianism, Islam, and 11 September." *Humanitarian Policy Group Briefing* 11, July 2003, 1, 2. http://www.odi.org.uk/resources/docs/351.pdf).

For more information about World Vision International: http://www.wvi.org/.

Source

Mlay, W. 2004. Some myths about faith-based humanitarian aid. *Humanitarian Exchange* 27 (July): 48–51. Reprinted by permission. http://www.odihpn.org/humanitarian-exchange-magazine/issue-27/some-myths-about-faith-based-humanitarian-aid.

Related Resources

Video: Warren, Rick. 2006. "Rick Warren: A Life of Purpose." TED Talks video, 21:48. http://www.youtube.com/watch?v=640BQNxB5mc.

Podcast: BBC World Service. "Dangerous Mission." 26:30. BBC, Heart and Soul (radio documentary/interviews about mission workers in "hostile" settings). http://www.bbc.co.uk/iplayer/episode/p007l92y/Heart_And_Soul_Dangerous_Mission/.

Kristof, N. D. 2008a. Evangelicals a liberal can love. *New York Times*, 3 February. http://www.nytimes.com/2008/02/03/opinion/03kristof.html?ex=1202274000&en=1886d30c178f2ba3&ei=5087%0A&_r=1&.

———. 2008b. My responses to your responses. *On the Ground* (blog). *New York Times*, 4 February. http://kristof.blogs.nytimes.com/2008/02/04/my-responses-to-your-responses/.

MABDA. 2012. *A common word: Between us and you.* English Monograph Series 20. Amman, Jordan: Royal Aal Al-Bayt Institute for Islamic Thought. http://www.acommonword.com/category/new-fruits/publications/.

Member Care Associates, Resource Update, May 2013. Faith-Based Perspectives. http://www.membercare.org/.

Micah Network. 2007. Proselytism. Micah Network. http://www.micahnetwork.org/sites/default/files/doc/library/proselytism_policy_statement.pdf.

Mlay, W. Africa is not for fixing. 2012. *Faith and Leadership*, Duke University. Retrieved from http://www.faithandleadership.com/qa/wilfred-mlay-africa-not-for-fixing.

O'Donnell, K., ed. 2002. *Doing member care well: Perspectives and practices from around the world.* Pasadena: William Carey Library.

OnlineClasses.org. 2010. 100 best books for humanitarians. OnlineClasses.org. http://www.onlineclasses.org/2010/06/17/100-best-books-for-humanitarians/.

Rice, C., ed. 2005. Reconciliation as the mission of God: Christian witness in a world of destructive conflicts and divisions. *Lausanne Occasional Paper* 51. http://www.lausanne.org/docs/2004forum/LOP51_IG22.pdf.

CHAPTER 14

Sexual Violence and Armed Conflict

MENTAL HEALTH AND PSYCHOSOCIAL SUPPORT FOR CONFLICT-RELATED SEXUAL VIOLENCE: PRINCIPLES AND INTERVENTIONS

World Health Organization, United Nations Population Fund, United Nations Children's Fund et al.

Sexual violence is an important problem associated with armed conflict (see box 1 for definition). There are great variations in the extent, scale, type, targeting, intent, profile of perpetrator, and population impact of conflict-related sexual violence.

Box 1.
DEFINITION OF CONFLICT-RELATED SEXUAL VIOLENCE

Conflict-related sexual violence includes "rape, sexual slavery, forced prostitution, forced pregnancy, enforced sterilization, or any other form of sexual violence . . . against women, men, girls or boys. Such incidents or patterns occur in conflict or post-conflict settings or other situations of concern (e.g., political strife). They also have a direct or indirect nexus with the conflict or political strife itself, i.e., a temporal, geographical and/or causal link" (UN Action against Sexual Violence in Conflict, 3).

Sexual violence is perpetrated in the context of men's power over women. Sexual violence is perpetrated primarily by men against women and girls. In conflict, however, boys and men are also targeted. Sexual violence may be commanded or condoned as a tactic of war.

Health and Social Consequences

- Sexual violence can have multiple physical, psychological, and social effects on survivors, their social networks, and their communities.
- Sexual and reproductive health consequences include sexually transmitted infections, including HIV, unwanted pregnancies, unsafe abortions, gynaecological problems, and physical injuries.
- Psychological/mental health consequences include nonpathological distress (such as fear, sadness, anger, self-blame, shame, sadness, or guilt), anxiety disorders (including post-traumatic stress disorder—PTSD), depression, medically unexplained somatic complaints, and alcohol and other substance use disorders, as well as suicidal ideation and self-harm.
- Social consequences include stigma and its sequelae—including social exclusion, discrimination, rejection by family and community, and further poverty.

General Principles of Humanitarian Programming

- Mental health and psychosocial supports are essential components of the comprehensive package of care and aim to protect or promote psychosocial well-being and/or prevent or treat mental disorders among survivors of sexual violence.
- Interventions must be conducted in accordance with existing humanitarian guidance. All interventions and supports should be based on participatory principles and implemented together with communities. They should be based on assessment of capacities and needs, and build and strengthen existing resources and helpful practices. They should promote human rights and protect affected populations from violations of human rights; humanitarian actors should promote equity and nondiscrimination.
- Mental health and psychosocial support planners should ensure that programmes do no harm. This requires alertness to possible adverse effects during programme planning, and measuring and recording unintended negative consequences through monitoring and evaluation. Unintended consequences of programmes include cultural, economic,

political, psychological, security, and social aspects. Some avoidable causes of harmful outcomes of particular relevance to sexual violence programming are presented in box 2.

Box 2.
POTENTIAL HARMFUL HUMANITARIAN PRACTICES RELEVANT TO SEXUAL VIOLENCE PROGRAMMING (WESSELLS 2009)

- Poor coordination
- Discrimination and excessive targeting
- Too much or too little attention to severe problems
- Undermining of existing supports
- Services that heighten vulnerability or revictimize
- Stigmatizing labeling
- Emphasis on pathology and deficits
- Medicalization of complex problems
- Aggressive questioning
- Fragmentation of systems
- Poor-quality counseling, with little training and supervision

---

General Principles of Conflict-related Sexual Violence Programming

- A range of supports for improved mental health and psychosocial well-being should be inclusive of—and not exclusively target—survivors of sexual violence. While the needs of survivors of sexual violence must be addressed by programmes, specific targeting of survivors of sexual violence should be avoided as it risks a range of further problems such as stigma, discrimination, and violence.
- Mental health and psychosocial support programming for survivors of conflict-related sexual violence should, as far as possible, be integrated into general health services, as well as a range of other services and community supports, including reproductive health, antenatal care, infant and young-child nutrition, gender-based violence prevention

and response, child protection, microfinance initiatives, and existing community-support mechanisms.

- Interventions should be rights based and contextualize violence against women and girls. The interest of the survivor and respect for his or her decisions is of primary importance; all actions must always be guided by a survivor-centred approach and the principles of confidentiality, safety and security, respect, and nondiscrimination.

Box 3.
KEY PRINCIPLES FOR CONFLICT-RELATED SEXUAL VIOLENCE PROGRAMMING

- Avoid specific targeting of survivors of sexual violence
- Integrate supports into wider systems (e.g., general health services, existing community support mechanisms)
- Adhere to the principles of confidentiality, safety and security, respect, and nondiscrimination

---

Multilevel Supports for Conflict-related Sexual Violence

- Supports should be multilevel; in other words, they should target both persons and communities (or segments thereof). Community-focused psychosocial interventions generally seek to enhance survivor well-being by improving the overall recovery environment. Person-focused interventions concentrate on the individual survivor and the survivor's immediate family and social network. They include psychological first aid and linking survivors with other services, psychological interventions (such as talking therapies) and, where indicated, specialist mental health care. Types of interventions by level are shown in figure 1.

Community-focused Interventions

- Community-focused psychosocial supports seek to respond to identified needs, as well as to potentially play a role in protecting dignity, promoting psychosocial well-being, and preventing mental health problems associated with sexual violence (see box 4).

- Interventions should aim to be socially inclusive and address stigma and its negative consequences; members of the stigmatized group must be involved in design, delivery, and evaluation. Antistigma actions include educational interventions to address misconceptions. Care must be taken when designing interventions to ensure that harmful outcomes such as increased stigma do not arise.
- Safe social spaces can be organized around a physical space such as a community centre or a women's centre, or can be an ad hoc social space. Safe spaces are places where women, adolescent girls, and (other) child survivors can go to receive compassionate, caring, appropriate, and confidential assistance. Examples include women's activity groups, wellness centres, support groups, drop-in centres, and child-friendly spaces. They are not limited to women's shelters, which may increase risks for women.
- Relevant community-mobilization activities include women's and men's support groups, dialogue groups, and community education and advocacy. Supports should be socially inclusive and engage local leadership (women, men, and young people). Possible aspects of psychosocial support for survivors of sexual violence include building a protective environment, addressing stigma, changing norms around gender-based violence, and promoting existing protective norms. Community mobilization may initially not be concerned explicitly with sexual violence by armed groups.
- Socioeconomic-empowerment initiatives can be implemented in all postacute emergency phases of humanitarian response and, if present prior to the crisis, can be supported to continue during the emergency phase. Examples include village savings and loans associations that rely on collective pooling and sharing of financial resources, which may support the mental health and psychosocial well-being of survivors of sexual violence and potentially reduce stigma.

Box 4.
COMMUNITY-FOCUSED INTERVENTIONS

- Community-based psychosocial programming is an important element of the mental health and psychosocial response to sexual violence in most conflict-affected settings.
- Community-focused interventions in the acute emergency can include community-mobilization activities and establishment of safe social spaces for women and children.
- As the situation stabilizes, these interventions need to be expanded, and socioeconomic-empowerment activities for women, such as village savings and loans associations, may be introduced.

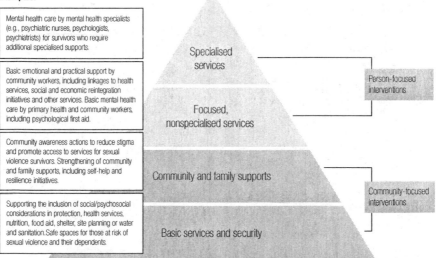

Examples:

Mental health care by mental health specialists (e.g., psychiatric nurses, psychologists, psychiatrists) for survivors who require additional specialised supports.

Basic emotional and practical support by community workers, including linkages to health services, social and economic reintegration initiatives and other services. Basic mental health care by primary health and community workers, including psychological first aid.

Community awareness actions to reduce stigma and promote access to services for sexual violence survivors. Strengthening of community and family supports, including self-help and resilience initiatives.

Supporting the inclusion of social/psychosocial considerations in protection, health services, nutrition, food aid, shelter, site planning or water and sanitation. Safe spaces for those at risk of sexual violence and their dependents.

Specialised services

Focused, nonspecialised services

Community and family supports

Basic services and security

Person-focused interventions

Community-focused interventions

Figure 1
Different levels of psychosocial and mental health intervention for survivors of conflict-related sexual violence (adapted from Inter-Agency Standing Committee 2007).

Person-focused Interventions

- There should be an emphasis on building the capacity of local staff (such as primary health-care workers or social workers), lay workers, and other professionals who can sustainably carry this on in subsequent phases. Clear guidance needs to be provided on minimum skills, training, supervision, and resources, as well as the type of interventions that can be delivered by workers with no professional experience (such as psychological first aid and basic referral).
- Training should be participatory and based on active learning principles; it should be well designed and focus on sexual abuse and sexuality, as well as skills in self-care and stress management for help providers. Training should also incorporate communications skills, and self-reflection on the provider's own experiences and attitudes (particularly towards gender-based violence and women's empowerment). Training needs to be modified to the level of education and skills of trainees and the operational context. Ongoing structured supervision, including technical and emotional support, should be provided by skilled mental health workers. Linkages between mental health, primary health, social services, protection, and gender-based violence services should be developed and strengthened.
- A phased approach to delivering person-focused interventions is recommended, so that, as a minimum, all survivors of sexual violence have access to psychological first aid, even in the initial phase of response. In addition, some may require further psychological and specialized mental health care (depending on the time since the event, the severity of symptoms, and degree of functioning). As the situation stabilizes and the response matures, more complex interventions can be delivered. These interventions are shown in table 1.

Monitoring, Evaluation, Research, and Collaborative Learning

- Because the evidence base regarding the effectiveness and sustainability of diverse interventions is weak, it is a priority to strengthen intervention research, evaluation, and collaborative learning that can improve practice in this important area.
- It is important to determine the benefits and possible harms of interventions. Participatory processes should be used to evaluate programming.

Outcome indicators should be developed, including locally defined measures of acceptance at individual, family, and community levels.

- All data-collection efforts must follow existing WHO (2007) safety and ethical standards for researching, documenting, and monitoring sexual violence in emergencies.

ACTIVITY	PROPOSED SUPPORTS FOR CONFLICT-RELATED SEXUAL VIOLENCE	
	Acute-phase response	Postacute-phase response
Psychosocial care with help-seeking survivors.	Incorporate psychological first aid into a standard package of post-rape care offered by (locally determined) first point of contact.	Continue to implement and strengthen delivery of psychological first aid and linkages with services and supports.
	Provide in-depth training on psychological first aid to a selected group of focal points (as points of first contact).	Strengthen social networks.
	Train care coordinators in established protocols for help-seeking survivors of sexual violence to link to relevant services and supports, including provision of survivor-centred information (including what to expect from a medical examination and step-by-step guide to seeking legal assistance).	
	Provide linkages to available community supports, social services, general health services, and mental health care, according to identified need and referral.	

Psychological intervention with help-seeking survivors, integrated into wider systems, such as health, educational, or nutrition care.	Research potential benefits and harms of adding a psychological intervention (such as supportive brief counseling or cognitive-behavioural techniques) to case management (which is coordination of care for individual persons). Research the potential value of single-session psychological care, including psychoeducation, building coping skills, and safety planning.	Safely implement manualized psychological talking therapies for people who are not functioning well because of their symptoms. The current evidence base favours culturally validated adaptation of: • cognitive-behavioural approaches for PTSD and depression and alcohol dependence • interpersonal therapy for moderate–severe depression (which is depression affecting daily functioning) • brief intervention for harmful or hazardous substance use Research into interventions without an evidence base, such as supportive counseling as a stand-alone form of support, and traditional, spiritual, and religious healing practices.
Clinical management of mental disorders in survivors of sexual violence by general health-care providers (e.g., general nurses, health officers, and doctors in primary health centres, postsurgery wards, women's wellness centres).	Provide clinical care with follow-up for severe mental disorders (adapted to the local context and monitored for adverse effects, and accessible to all who require care).	Provide clinical care with follow-up for both severe and common mental disorders. Safely implement manualized psychological talking therapies (as above).

Clinical management of mental disorders in survivors of sexual violence by specialized mental health-care providers (e.g., psychiatrists, psychiatric nurses, and psychologists).	Provide clinical care with follow-up for both severe and common mental disorders (by mental health-care providers with advanced knowledge in mental health care of survivors of sexual violence). Safely implement manualized psychological talking therapies (as above).

Table 1
Programme response (and research) matrix for person-focused interventions

REFERENCES

Inter-Agency Standing Committee. 2007. Guidelines on mental health and psychosocial support in emergency settings. Geneva: Inter-Agency Standing Committee.

Wessels M. 2009. Do no harm: Toward contextually appropriate psychosocial support in international emergencies. *American Psychologist* 64, no. 8: 842–54.

World Health Organization. 2007. Ethical and safety recommendations for researching, documenting and monitoring sexual violence in emergencies. Geneva: World Health Organization.

KEY RESOURCES

Batniji, R., M. van Ommeren, and B. Saraceno. 2006. Mental and social health in disasters: Relating qualitative social science research and the Sphere standard. *Social Science and Medicine* 62, no. 8: 1853–64.

Chen, L. et al. 2010. Sexual abuse and lifetime diagnosis of psychiatric disorders: Systematic review and meta-analysis. *Mayo Clinic Proceedings* 85, no. 7: 618–29.

Dua, T., C. Barbui, N. Clark, A. Fleischmann, V. Poznyak, M. van Ommeren, M. T. Yasamy, J. L. Ayuso-Mateos, G. L. Birbeck, C. Drummond, M. Freeman, P. Giannakopoulos, I. Levav, I. S. Obot, O. Omigbodun, V. Patel, M. Phillips, M. Prince, A. Rahimi-Movaghar, A. Rahman, J. W. Sander, J. B. Saunders, C. Servili, T. Rangaswamy, J. Unützer, P. Ventevogel, L. Vijayakumar, G. Thornicroft, and S. Saxena. 2011. Evidence-based guidelines for mental, neurological, and substance use disorders in low- and middle-income countries: Summary of WHO recommendations. *PLoS Medicine* 8, no. 11: e1001122. doi:10.1371/journal.pmed.1001122.

Inter-Agency Standing Committee. 2005. Guidelines on gender based violence interventions in humanitarian settings. Geneva: Inter-Agency Standing Committee.

Jewkes, R., P. Sen, and C. Garcia-Moreno. 2002. Sexual violence. In *World report on violence and health*, ed. E. Krug, L. Dahlberg, J. Mercy, A. Zwi, and R. Lozano, 147–82. Geneva: World Health Organization.

Patel, V., N. Chowdharry, R. Rahman, and H. Verdeli. 2011. Improving access to psychological treatments: Lessons from developing countries. *Behaviour Research and Therapy* 49 (9): 523–28.

Stark L., and A. Ager. 2011. A systematic review of prevalence studies of gender-based violence in complex emergencies. *Trauma, Violence and Abuse* 12, no. 3: 127–34.

The Sphere Project. 2011. *Humanitarian charter and minimum standards in disaster response*. Geneva: The Sphere Project. http://www.sphereproject.org/handbook/.

Tol W. A., C. Barbui, A. Galappatti, D. Silove, T. S. Betancourt, R. Souza, A. Golaz, and M. van Ommeren. 2011. Mental health and psychosocial support in humanitarian settings: Linking practice and research. *Lancet* 378, no. 9802 (29 October): 1581–91. doi:10.1016/S0140-6736(11)61094-5.

Tol W. A., V. Patel, M. Tomlinson, F. Baingana, A. Galappatti, C. Panter-Brick, D. Silove, E. Sondorp, M. Wessells, and M. van Ommeren. 2011. Research priorities for mental health and psychosocial support in humanitarian settings. *PLoS Medicine* 8, no. 9 (20 September): e1001096. doi:10.1371/journal.pmed.1001096.

World Health Organization. 2010. mhGAP Intervention guide for mental, neurological and substance use disorders in non-specialized health settings. Geneva: World Health Organization.

NOTES

This is a summary of the report from a meeting on Responding to the Psychosocial and Mental Health Needs of Sexual Violence Survivors in Conflict-affected Settings, organized by the World Health Organization (WHO), with United Nations Population Fund (UNFPA), and United Nations Children's Fund (UNICEF), on behalf of United Nations Action against Sexual Violence in Conflict (UNAction), on 28–30 November 2011 in Ferney-Voltaire, France.

For more information about the World Health Organization: http://www.who.int/.

SOURCE

World Health Organization, United Nations Population Fund, United Nations Children's Fund, et al. 2012. Mental health and psychosocial support for conflict-related sexual violence: Principles and interventions. Geneva: World Health Organization. Reprinted by permission. http://apps.who.int/iris/bitstream/10665/75179/1/WHO_RHR_HRP_12.18_eng.pdf.

RELATED RESOURCES

Video: Missmahl, Inge. "Bringing Peace and Healing in Afghanistan." TED Talks. http://www.ted.com/talks/inge_missmahl_brings_peace_to_the_minds_of_afghanistan.html.

Christie, D. J., B. S. Tint, R. V. Wagner, and D. D. Winter. 2008. Peace psychology for a peaceful world. *American Psychologist* 63, no. 6 (September): 540–52. doi:10.1037/0003-066X.63.6.540.

Hieber, L. 2001. Lifeline media: Reaching populations in crisis; A guide to developing media projects in conflict situations. Geneva: Media Action International. http://www.preventionweb.net/files/636_10303.pdf.

Keeping Children Safe Coalition. 2006. Keeping children safe toolkit: A toolkit for child protection. London: Keeping Children Safe. http://www.keepingchildrensafe.org.uk/toolkit.

Lutheran World Federation. 2010. A faith reflection on gender and power. Geneva: Lutheran World Federation. http://www.lutheranworld.org/lwf/wp-content/uploads/2009/04/DMD-Gender_Power-EN-low.pdf.

United Nations High Commissioner for Refugees. 2008. UNHCR manual for the protection of women and girls. Geneva: United Nations High Commissioner for Refugees. http://www.unhcr.org/refworld/pdfid/47cfc2962.pdf.

CHAPTER 15

Human Rights and Religious Freedom

DECLARATION ON THE ELIMINATION OF ALL FORMS OF INTOLERANCE AND OF DISCRIMINATION BASED ON RELIGION OR BELIEF

United Nations General Assembly

THE GENERAL ASSEMBLY,

Considering that one of the basic principles of the Charter of the United Nations is that of the dignity and equality inherent in all human beings, and that all Member States have pledged themselves to take joint and separate action in cooperation with the Organization to promote and encourage universal respect for and observance of human rights and fundamental freedoms for all, without distinction as to race, sex, language, or religion,

Considering that the Universal Declaration of Human Rights and the International Covenants on Human Rights proclaim the principles of nondiscrimination and equality before the law and the right to freedom of thought, conscience, religion, and belief,

Considering that the disregard and infringement of human rights and fundamental freedoms, in particular of the right to freedom of thought, conscience, religion, or whatever belief, have brought, directly or indirectly, wars and great suffering to mankind, especially where they serve as a means of foreign interference in the internal affairs of other States and amount to kindling hatred between peoples and nations,

Considering that religion or belief, for anyone who professes either, is one of the fundamental elements in his conception of life and that freedom of religion or belief should be fully respected and guaranteed,

Considering that it is essential to promote understanding, tolerance, and respect in matters relating to freedom of religion and belief and to ensure that the use of religion or belief for ends inconsistent with the Charter of the United Nations, other relevant instruments of the United Nations, and the purposes and principles of the present Declaration is inadmissible,

Convinced that freedom of religion and belief should also contribute to the attainment of the goals of world peace, social justice, and friendship among peoples and to the elimination of ideologies or practices of colonialism and racial discrimination,

Noting with satisfaction the adoption of several, and the coming into force of some, conventions, under the aegis of the United Nations and of the specialized agencies, for the elimination of various forms of discrimination,

Concerned by manifestations of intolerance and by the existence of discrimination in matters of religion or belief still in evidence in some areas of the world,

Resolved to adopt all necessary measures for the speedy elimination of such intolerance in all its forms and manifestations and to prevent and combat discrimination on the ground of religion or belief,

Proclaims this Declaration on the Elimination of All Forms of Intolerance and of Discrimination Based on Religion or Belief:

Article 1

- Everyone shall have the right to freedom of thought, conscience, and religion. This right shall include freedom to have a religion or whatever belief of his choice, and freedom, either individually or in community with others and in public or private, to manifest his religion or belief in worship, observance, practice, and teaching.
- No one shall be subject to coercion which would impair his freedom to have a religion or belief of his choice.
- Freedom to manifest one's religion or belief may be subject only to such limitations as are prescribed by law and are necessary to protect public safety, order, health, or morals or the fundamental rights and freedoms of others.

Article 2

- No one shall be subject to discrimination by any State, institution, group of persons, or person on the grounds of religion or other belief.
- For the purposes of the present Declaration, the expression "intolerance and discrimination based on religion or belief" means any distinction, exclusion, restriction, or preference based on religion or belief and having as its purpose or as its effect nullification or impairment of the recognition, enjoyment, or exercise of human rights and fundamental freedoms on an equal basis.

Article 3

- Discrimination between human beings on the grounds of religion or belief constitutes an affront to human dignity and a disavowal of the principles of the Charter of the United Nations, and shall be condemned as a violation of the human rights and fundamental freedoms proclaimed in the Universal Declaration of Human Rights and enunciated in detail in the International Covenants on Human Rights, and as an obstacle to friendly and peaceful relations between nations.

Article 4

- All States shall take effective measures to prevent and eliminate discrimination on the grounds of religion or belief in the recognition, exercise, and enjoyment of human rights and fundamental freedoms in all fields of civil, economic, political, social, and cultural life.
- All States shall make all efforts to enact or rescind legislation where necessary to prohibit any such discrimination, and to take all appropriate measures to combat intolerance on the grounds of religion or other beliefs in this matter.

Article 5

- The parents or, as the case may be, the legal guardians of the child have the right to organize the life within the family in accordance with their religion or belief and bearing in mind the moral education in which they believe the child should be brought up.
- Every child shall enjoy the right to have access to education in the matter of religion or belief in accordance with the wishes of his parents or, as the case may be, legal guardians, and shall not be compelled to

receive teaching on religion or belief against the wishes of his parents or legal guardians, the best interests of the child being the guiding principle.

- The child shall be protected from any form of discrimination on the ground of religion or belief. He shall be brought up in a spirit of understanding, tolerance, friendship among peoples, peace, and universal brotherhood, respect for freedom of religion or belief of others, and in full consciousness that his energy and talents should be devoted to the service of his fellow men.

- In the case of a child who is not under the care either of his parents or of legal guardians, due account shall be taken of their expressed wishes or of any other proof of their wishes in the matter of religion or belief, the best interests of the child being the guiding principle.

- Practices of a religion or belief in which a child is brought up must not be injurious to his physical or mental health or to his full development, taking into account article 1, paragraph 3, of the present Declaration.

Article 6

In accordance with article 1 of the present Declaration, and subject to the provisions of article 1, paragraph 3, the right to freedom of thought, conscience, religion, or belief shall include, inter alia, the following freedoms:

(a)   to worship or assemble in connection with a religion or belief, and to establish and maintain places for these purposes;

(b)   to establish and maintain appropriate charitable or humanitarian institutions;

(c)   to make, acquire, and use to an adequate extent the necessary articles and materials related to the rites or customs of a religion or belief;

(d)   to write, issue, and disseminate relevant publications in these areas;

(e)   to teach a religion or belief in places suitable for these purposes;

(f)   to solicit and receive voluntary financial and other contributions from individuals and institutions;

(g)   to train, appoint, elect, or designate by succession appropriate leaders called for by the requirements and standards of any religion or belief;

(h)   to observe days of rest and to celebrate holidays and ceremonies in accordance with the precepts of one's religion or belief; and

(i) to establish and maintain communications with individuals and communities in matters of religion and belief at the national and international levels.

Article 7

The rights and freedoms set forth in the present Declaration shall be accorded in national legislation in such a manner that everyone shall be able to avail himself of such rights and freedoms in practice.

Article 8

Nothing in the present Declaration shall be construed as restricting or derogating from any right defined in the Universal Declaration of Human Rights and the International Covenants on Human Rights.

Editors' Notes

For more information about the United Nations and human rights: http://www2.ohchr.org/.

Source

United Nations General Assembly. 1981. Resolution 36/55. Declaration on the elimination of all forms of intolerance and of discrimination based on religion or belief. 25 November. http://www2.ohchr.org/english/law/religion.htm. Reprinted by permission.

Related Resources

Video: Veritas.Forum. "History of Human Rights: What Are Human Rights?" Veritas. Forum. http://www.youtube.com/watch?v=nCQWwkERit4&feature=BFa&list=PLBA370C50B 916BBDD.

Banchor, T., and R. Wuthnow, eds. 2011. *Religion and the global politics of human rights.* Oxford: Oxford University Press.

Charter of Conscience. 2012. The global charter of conscience: A global covenant concerning faiths and freedom of conscience. http://charterofconscience.org/.

Darcy, J. 1997. Human rights and international legal standards: What do relief workers need to know? *Relief and Rehabilitation Network Paper* 19. London: Overseas Development Institute. http://www.odi.org.uk/resources/docs/2325.pdf.

Thames, H., C. Seiple, and A. Rowe. 2009. *International religious freedom advocacy: A guide to organizations, law, and NGOs.* Waco, TX: Baylor University Press.

United Nations, Office of the High Commissioner for Human Rights. http://www.ohchr.org.

WEA Religious Liberty Commission. http://www.worldevangelicals.org/commissions/rlc/.

White, J., and M. Green, eds. 2012. *Religion and human rights: An introduction.* Oxford: Oxford University Press.

Wong, W. 2002. Human rights advocacy in missions. In *Doing member care well: Perspectives and practices from around the world,* ed. K. O'Donnell, 477–88. Pasadena: William Carey Library.

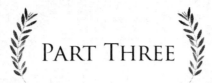

PART THREE

Good Practice in the Human Health Sector

CONNECTIONS AND CONTRIBUTIONS FOR SERVING HUMANITY

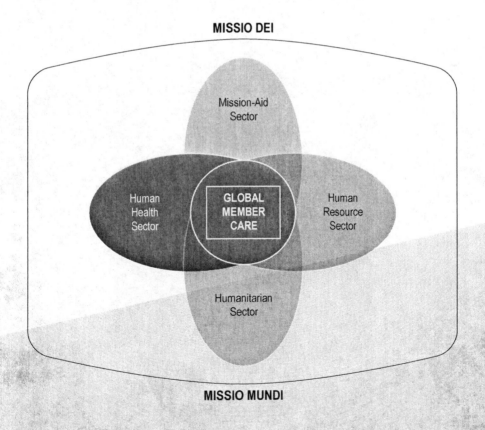

MISSIO DEI

Mission-Aid Sector

Human Health Sector

GLOBAL MEMBER CARE

Human Resource Sector

Humanitarian Sector

MISSIO MUNDI

APPLICATIONS FOR PART THREE

Keep in mind these five goals for crossing sectors as you go through the material.

- To support mission/aid workers in their well-being and effectiveness
- To support colleagues in other sectors via materials in the member care field
- To equip mission/aid workers with tools and opportunities for their work with others
- To equip member caregivers who directly work with vulnerable populations and others
- To stay informed as global citizens about current and crucial issues facing humanity

CHAPTER 16

Health and Human Rights

THE RIGHT TO HEALTH

*Office of the United Nations High Commissioner for
Human Rights and the World Health Organization*

As human beings, our health and the health of those we care about is a matter of daily
concern. Regardless of our age, gender, socioeconomic, or ethnic background, we
consider our health to be our most basic and essential asset. Ill health, on the other
hand, can keep us from going to school or to work, from attending to our family
responsibilities, or from participating fully in the activities of our community. By the
same token, we are willing to make many sacrifices if only that would guarantee us
and our families a longer and healthier life. In short, when we talk about well-being,
health is often what we have in mind.

The right to health is a fundamental part of our human rights and of our understanding of a life in dignity. *The right to the enjoyment of the highest attainable standard
of physical and mental health*, to give it its full name, is not new. Internationally, it
was first articulated in the 1946 Constitution of the World Health Organization
(WHO), whose preamble defines health as "a state of complete physical, mental and
social well-being and not merely the absence of disease or infirmity." The preamble
further states that "the enjoyment of the highest attainable standard of health is one
of the fundamental rights of every human being without distinction of race, religion,
political belief, economic or social condition."

The 1948 Universal Declaration of Human Rights also mentioned health as
part of the right to an adequate standard of living (art. 25). The right to health was
again recognized as a human right in the 1966 International Covenant on Economic,
Social and Cultural Rights. Since then, other international human rights treaties have
recognized or referred to the right to health or to elements of it, such as the right to

medical care. The right to health is relevant to all States: every State has ratified at least one international human rights treaty recognizing the right to health. Moreover, States have committed themselves to protecting this right through international declarations, domestic legislation and policies, and at international conferences.

In recent years, increasing attention has been paid to the right to the highest attainable standard of health, for instance by human rights treaty monitoring bodies, by WHO, and by the Commission on Human Rights (now replaced by the Human Rights Council), which in 2002 created the mandate of Special Rapporteur on the right of everyone to the highest attainable standard of physical and mental health. These initiatives have helped clarify the nature of the right to health and how it can be achieved.

This fact sheet aims to shed light on the right to health in international human rights law as it currently stands, amidst the plethora of initiatives and proposals as to what the right to health *may* or *should be*. Consequently, it does not purport to provide an exhaustive list of relevant issues or to identify specific standards in relation to them.

The fact sheet starts by explaining what the right to health is and illustrating its implications for specific individuals and groups, and then elaborates upon States' obligations with respect to the right. It ends with an overview of national, regional, and international accountability and monitoring mechanisms.

What Is the Right to Health?
Key Aspects of the Right to Health[29]

The right to health is an inclusive right. We frequently associate the right to health with access to health care and the building of hospitals. This is correct, but the right to health extends further. It includes a wide range of factors that can help us lead a healthy life. The Committee on Economic, Social and Cultural Rights, the body responsible for monitoring the International Covenant on Economic, Social and Cultural Rights,[30] calls these the "underlying determinants of health." They include:

---

29   Many of these and other important characteristics of the right to health are clarified in general comment N° 14 (2000) on the right to health, adopted by the Committee on Economic, Social and Cultural Rights.

30   The Covenant was adopted by the United Nations General Assembly in its resolution 2200A (XXI) of 16 December 1966. It entered into force in 1976 and by 1 December 2007 had been ratified by 157 States.

- safe drinking water and adequate sanitation
- safe food
- adequate nutrition and housing
- healthy working and environmental conditions
- health-related education and information
- gender equality

The right to health contains freedoms. These *freedoms* include the right to be free from nonconsensual medical treatment, such as medical experiments and research or forced sterilization, and to be free from torture and other cruel, inhuman, or degrading treatment or punishment.

The right to health contains entitlements. These *entitlements* include:

- the right to a system of health protection providing equality of opportunity for everyone to enjoy the highest attainable level of health
- the right to prevention, treatment, and control of diseases
- access to essential medicines
- maternal, child, and reproductive health
- equal and timely access to basic health services
- the provision of health-related education and information
- participation of the population in health-related decision making at the national and community levels

Health services, goods, and facilities must be provided to all without any discrimination. Nondiscrimination is a key principle in human rights and is crucial to the enjoyment of the right to the highest attainable standard of health (see section on nondiscrimination below).

All services, goods, and facilities must be available, accessible, acceptable, and of good quality.

- Functioning public health and health-care facilities, goods, and services must be *available* in sufficient quantity within a State.
- They must be *accessible* physically (in safe reach for all sections of the population, including children, adolescents, older persons, persons with disabilities, and other vulnerable groups) as well as financially and on the basis of nondiscrimination. *Accessibility* also implies the right to seek, receive, and impart health-related information in an

accessible format (for all, including persons with disabilities), but does not impair the right to have personal health data treated confidentially.

- The facilities, goods, and services should also respect medical ethics, and be gender-sensitive and culturally appropriate. In other words, they should be medically and culturally *acceptable*.
- Finally, they must be scientifically and medically appropriate and of *good quality*. This requires, in particular, trained health professionals, scientifically approved and unexpired drugs and hospital equipment, adequate sanitation, and safe drinking water.

COMMON MISCONCEPTIONS ABOUT THE RIGHT TO HEALTH

The right to health is not the same as the right to be healthy. A common misconception is that the State has to guarantee us good health. However, good health is influenced by several factors that are outside the direct control of States, such as an individual's biological make-up and socioeconomic conditions.

Rather, the right to health refers to the right to the enjoyment of a variety of goods, facilities, services, and conditions necessary for its realization. This is why it is more accurate to describe it as the right to the *highest attainable standard* of physical and mental health, rather than an unconditional right to be healthy.

The right to health is not only a programmatic goal to be attained in the long term. The fact that the right to health should be a tangible, programmatic goal does not mean that no immediate obligations on States arise from it. In fact, States must make every possible effort, within available resources, to realize the right to health and to take steps in that direction without delay.

Notwithstanding resource constraints, some obligations have an immediate effect, such as the undertaking to guarantee the right to health in a nondiscriminatory manner, to develop specific legislation and plans of action, or other similar steps towards the full realization of this right, as is the case with any other human right. States also have to ensure a minimum level of access to the essential material components of the right to health, such as the provision of essential drugs and maternal and child health services.

A country's difficult financial situation does not absolve it from having to take action to realize the right to health. It is often argued that States that cannot afford it are not obliged to take steps to realize this right or may delay their obligations indefinitely. When considering the level of implementation of this right in a particular State, the availability of resources at that time and the development context are taken into account. Nonetheless, no State can justify a failure to respect its obligations because of a lack of resources. States must guarantee the right to health to the maximum of their available resources, even if these are tight.

While steps may depend on the specific context, all States must move towards meeting their obligations to respect, protect, and fulfil.

THE LINK BETWEEN THE RIGHT TO HEALTH AND OTHER HUMAN RIGHTS

Human rights are interdependent, indivisible, and interrelated.[31] This means that violating the right to health may often impair the enjoyment of other human rights, such as the rights to education or work, and vice versa.

The importance given to the "underlying determinants of health"—that is, the factors and conditions which protect and promote the right to health beyond health services, goods, and facilities—shows that the right to health is dependent on, and contributes to, the realization of many other human rights. These include the rights to food, to water, to an adequate standard of living, to adequate housing, to freedom from discrimination, to privacy, to access to information, to participation, and the right to benefit from scientific progress and its applications.

It is easy to see interdependence of rights in the context of poverty. For people living in poverty, their health may be the only asset on which they can draw for the exercise of other economic and social rights, such as the right to work or the right to education. Physical health and mental health enable adults to work and children to learn, whereas ill health is a liability to the individuals themselves and to those who must care for them.

Conversely, individuals' right to health cannot be realized without realizing their other rights, the violations of which are at the root of poverty, such as the rights to work, food, housing, and education, and the principle of nondiscrimination.

---

31   See Vienna Declaration and Programme of Action (A/CONF.157/23), adopted by the World Conference on Human Rights, held in Vienna, 14–25 June 1993.

LINKS BETWEEN THE RIGHT TO HEALTH
AND THE RIGHT TO WATER

Ill health is associated with the ingestion of or contact with unsafe water, lack of clean water (linked to inadequate hygiene), lack of sanitation, and poor management of water resources and systems, including in agriculture. Most diarrhoeal disease in the world is attributable to unsafe water, sanitation, and hygiene. In 2002, diarrhoea attributable to these three factors caused approximately 2.7 percent of deaths (1.5 million) worldwide.[32]

HOW DOES THE PRINCIPLE OF NONDISCRIMINATION
APPLY TO THE RIGHT TO HEALTH?

Discrimination means any distinction, exclusion, or restriction made on the basis of various grounds which has the effect or purpose of impairing or nullifying the recognition, enjoyment, or exercise of human rights and fundamental freedoms. It is linked to the marginalization of specific population groups and is generally at the root of fundamental structural inequalities in society. This, in turn, may make these groups more vulnerable to poverty and ill health. Not surprisingly, traditionally discriminated and marginalized groups often bear a disproportionate share of health problems. For example, studies have shown that, in some societies, ethnic minority groups and indigenous peoples enjoy fewer health services, receive less health information, and are less likely to have adequate housing and safe drinking water, and their children have a higher mortality rate and suffer more severe malnutrition than the general population.

The impact of discrimination is compounded when an individual suffers double or multiple discrimination, such as discrimination on the basis of sex *and* race or national origin or age. For example, in many places indigenous women receive fewer health and reproductive services and information, and are more vulnerable to physical and sexual violence than the general population.

Nondiscrimination and equality are fundamental human rights principles and critical components of the right to health. The International Covenant on Economic, Social and Cultural Rights (art. 2 (2)) and the Convention on the Rights of the Child (art. 2 (1)) identify the following nonexhaustive grounds of discrimination:

---

32   World Health Organization, *Water, sanitation and hygiene: Quantifying the health impact at national and local levels in countries with incomplete water supply and sanitation coverage*, Environmental Burden of Disease Series, No. 15 (Geneva, 2007).

race, colour, sex, language, religion, political or other opinion, national or social origin, property, disability, birth, or other status. According to the Committee on Economic, Social and Cultural Rights, "other status" may include health status (e.g., HIV/AIDS) or sexual orientation. States have an obligation to prohibit and eliminate discrimination on all grounds and ensure equality to all in relation to access to health care and the underlying determinants of health. The International Convention on the Elimination of All Forms of Racial Discrimination (art. 5) also stresses that States must prohibit and eliminate racial discrimination and guarantee the right of everyone to public health and medical care.

Nondiscrimination and equality further imply that States must recognize and provide for the differences and specific needs of groups that generally face particular health challenges, such as higher mortality rates or vulnerability to specific diseases. The obligation to ensure nondiscrimination requires specific health standards to be applied to particular population groups, such as women, children, or persons with disabilities. Positive measures of protection are particularly necessary when certain groups of persons have continuously been discriminated against in the practice of States parties or by private actors.

Along the same lines, the Committee on Economic, Social and Cultural Rights has made it clear that there is no justification for the lack of protection of vulnerable members of society from health-related discrimination, be it in law or in fact. So even if times are hard, vulnerable members of society must be protected, for instance through the adoption of relatively low-cost, targeted programmes.[33]

NEGLECTED DISEASES:
A RIGHT-TO-HEALTH ISSUE WITH MANY FACES

Neglected diseases are those seriously disabling or life-threatening diseases for which treatment options are inadequate or nonexistent. They include leishmaniasis (kala-azar), onchocerciasis (river blindness), Chagas' disease, leprosy, schistosomiasis (bilharzia), lymphatic filariasis, African trypanosomiasis (sleeping sickness), and dengue fever. Malaria and tuberculosis are also often considered to be neglected diseases.[34]

There are clear links between neglected diseases and human rights:

33 General comment N° 14, para. 18.

34 However, they occur in both wealthy and low-income countries, and international attention and treatment options for them have dramatically increased in recent years (see, e.g., the Roll Back Malaria Partnership, http://www.rbm.who.int).

- Neglected diseases almost exclusively affect poor and marginalized populations in low-income countries, in rural areas and settings where poverty is widespread. Guaranteeing the *underlying determinants of the right to health* is therefore key to reducing the incidence of neglected diseases.
- *Discrimination* is both a cause and a consequence of neglected diseases. For example, discrimination may prevent persons affected by neglected diseases from seeking help and treatment in the first place.
- *Essential drugs* against neglected diseases are often unavailable or inadequate. (Where they are available, they may be toxic.)
- *Health interventions and research and development* have long been inadequate and underfunded (although the picture has changed in recent years, with more drug development projects under way).[35]

The obligation is on States to promote the development of new drugs, vaccines, and diagnostic tools through research and development and through international cooperation.

THE RIGHT TO HEALTH
IN INTERNATIONAL HUMAN RIGHTS LAW

The right to the highest attainable standard of health is a human right recognized in international human rights law. The International Covenant on Economic, Social and Cultural Rights, widely considered as the central instrument of protection for the right to health, recognizes "the right of everyone to the enjoyment of the highest attainable standard of physical and mental health." It is important to note that the Covenant gives both mental health, which has often been neglected, and physical health equal consideration.

INTERNATIONAL COVENANT ON ECONOMIC,
SOCIAL AND CULTURAL RIGHTS, ART. 12

1. The States Parties to the present Covenant recognize the right of everyone to the enjoyment of the highest attainable standard of physical and mental health.

---

35 Mary Moran and others, *The new landscape of neglected disease drug development* (London School of Economics and Political Science and The Wellcome Trust, 2005).

2. The steps to be taken by the States Parties to the present Covenant to achieve the full realization of this right shall include those necessary for:

    (a) the provision for the reduction of the stillbirth rate and of infant mortality and for the healthy development of the child;

    (b) the improvement of all aspects of environmental and industrial hygiene;

    (c) the prevention, treatment, and control of epidemic, endemic, occupational, and other diseases; and

    (d) the creation of conditions which would assure to all medical service and medical attention in the event of sickness.

Subsequent international and regional human rights instruments address the right to health in various ways. Some are of general application while others address the human rights of specific groups, such as women or children.

INTERNATIONAL HUMAN RIGHTS TREATIES RECOGNIZING THE RIGHT TO HEALTH

- The 1965 International Convention on the Elimination of All Forms of Racial Discrimination: art. 5 (e) (iv)
- The 1966 International Covenant on Economic, Social and Cultural Rights: art. 12
- The 1979 Convention on the Elimination of All Forms of Discrimination against Women: arts. 11 (1) (f), 12 and 14 (2) (b)
- The 1989 Convention on the Rights of the Child: art. 24
- The 1990 International Convention on the Protection of the Rights of All Migrant Workers and Members of Their Families: arts. 28, 43 (e) and 45 (c)
- The 2006 Convention on the Rights of Persons with Disabilities: art. 25. 10

In addition, the treaty bodies that monitor the International Covenant on Economic, Social and Cultural Rights, the Convention on the Elimination of All Forms of Discrimination against Women, and the Convention on the Rights of the Child have adopted general comments or general recommendations on the right to health and health-related issues. These provide an authoritative and detailed interpretation of the provisions found in the treaties.[36] Numerous conferences and declarations, such as the International Conference on Primary Health Care (resulting in the Declaration of Alma-Ata[37]), the United Nations Millennium Declaration and Millennium Development Goals,[38] and the Declaration of Commitment on HIV/ AIDS,[39] have also helped clarify various aspects of public health relevant to the right to health and have reaffirmed commitments to its realization.

DECLARATION OF ALMA-ATA, 1978

The Declaration affirms the crucial role of primary health care, which addresses the main health problems in the community, providing promotive, preventive, curative, and rehabilitative services accordingly (art. VII). It stresses that access to primary health care is the key to attaining a level of health that will permit all individuals to lead a socially and economically productive life (art. V) and to contributing to the realization of the highest attainable standard of health.

The right to health is also recognized in several regional instruments, such as the African Charter on Human and Peoples' Rights (1981), the Additional Protocol to the American Convention on Human Rights in the Area of Economic, Social and Cultural Rights, known as the Protocol of San Salvador (1988), and the European Social Charter (1961, revised in 1996). The American Convention on Human Rights (1969) and the European Convention for the Promotion of Human Rights and Fundamental Freedoms (1950) contain provisions related to health, such as the right to life, the prohibition on torture and other cruel, inhuman, and degrading treatment, and the right to family and private life.

Finally, the right to health or the right to health care is recognized in at least 115 constitutions. At least six other constitutions set out duties in relation to health, such as the duty on the State to develop health services or to allocate a specific budget to them.

---

36   For more details on these treaty bodies, see Fact Sheet N° 30.

37   Declaration of Alma-Ata, International Conference on Primary Health Care, Alma-Ata, USSR, September 1978.

38   See http://www.un.org/millenniumgoals/.

39   General Assembly resolution S-26/2 of 27 July 2001.

Editors' Notes

For more information about the United Nations and human rights: http://www2.ohchr.org/. See especially the *Fact Sheets* on various topics at http://www.ohchr.org/EN/PublicationsResources/Pages/FactSheets.aspx.

Source

Office of the United Nations High Commissioner for Human Rights, and World Health Organization. 2008. *The right to health.* Fact Sheet 31. Geneva: Office of the United Nations High Commissioner for Human Rights and World Health Organization, 1–11. Reprinted by permission. http://www.ohchr.org/Documents/Publications/Factsheet31.pdf.

Related Resources

Videos: Global Health TV (short overviews and examples of health development around the world). http://www.globalhealthtv.com/.

Lawrence Gostin, *Journal of the American Medical Association* 307, no 19 (May 16, 2012): 2087-2091., A Framework Convention on Global Health: Health for All, Justice for All.

People's Health Movement. 2000. People's charter for health. People's Health Movement. http://www.phmovement.org/en/resources/charters/peopleshealth.

———, Medact, Health Action International, Medicos International, and Third World Network. 2011. *Global health watch 3: An alternative world health report.* London: Zed Books. http://www.ghwatch.org/sites/www.ghwatch.org/files/global%20health%20watch%203.pdf.

United Nations General Assembly. 1991. Resolution 46/119. Principles for the protection of persons with mental illness and the improvement of mental health care. 17 December. http://www2.ohchr.org/english/law/principles.htm.

Gostin, L. 2012. A framework convention on global health: Health for all, justice for all. *Journal of the American Medical Association*, 307(19), 2087-2092. http://papers.ssrn.com/sol3/papers.cfm?abstract_id=2072457

World Health Organization. 2009. 2008–2013 Action plan for the global strategy for the prevention and control of noncommunicable diseases. Geneva: World Health Organization. http://www.who.int/nmh/publications/9789241597418/en/.

———. 2010. The world health report: Health systems financing; The path to universal coverage. Geneva: World Health Organization. http://www.who.int/whr/2010/en/index.html.

———. 2012. WHO quality rights tool kit: Assessing and improving quality and human rights in mental health and social care facilities. Geneva: World Health Organization. http://www.who.int/mental_health/policy/quality_rights/en/.

The Grand Decade for Global Health: 1998-2008. London: The Royal Institute for International Affairs. http://www.chathamhouse.org/sites/default/files/public/Research/Global%20Health/0413_who.pdf.

CHAPTER 17

Primary Health Care and Faith-based Organizations

BUILDING FROM COMMON FOUNDATIONS: THE WORLD HEALTH ORGANIZATION AND FAITH-BASED ORGANIZATIONS IN PRIMARY HEALTH CARE

Geneva Global and World Health Organization

EXECUTIVE SUMMARY

The World Health Organization (WHO) worked with faith-based organizations (FBOs) in preparing for the Alma-Ata Declaration of 1978. Together they gained a clearer picture of health care in the developing world and then established the concept of primary health care. This report is intended to assist in the process of rejuvenating dialogue and partnership with FBOs in the face of widespread health challenges in communities around the world, not least of which is HIV/AIDS. The revival of the primary health-care model within WHO underscores that if this framework is to be promoted as a more sustainable system of health servicing and delivery, then the inclusion of FBOs will add greater potential for breadth and effectiveness.

KEY FINDINGS

- FBOs are major health providers in developing countries, providing an average of about 40 percent of services in sub-Saharan Africa. Despite being closely aligned with community needs, FBOs often go unrecognized because they usually operate outside government planning processes.
- FBOs' core values lead them to offer compassionate care to people in need. Commitment to individual dignity and worth is consistent with

best practices in providing decent care. Engaging with FBOs entails challenges, but with careful alignment much can be gained from partnership.

- Evidence from studies of FBO responses to HIV/AIDS demonstrates that they have delivered a range of treatment, care, and prevention activities in accordance with WHO strategic priorities and primary health-care principles.
- With attention to accountability and monitoring, governments can work with FBOs on the basis that such partnerships will deliver public value and narrow gaps in national health planning systems.
- Local interest in participative planning is strong, according to exercises in community mapping. Engineering a network of FBO and other community assets could open new possibilities for comprehensive health systems.

KEY OBSERVATIONS

- In partnership with FBOs, WHO can develop the concept of primary health care to provide guidance for the engagement of religious health assets.
- WHO can engage in dialogue with faith institutions to consider the interplay between their respective values of compassion and decent care, and to ascertain the relative roles and contributions of FBOs in developing health-care systems.
- WHO can encourage national governments to consider public values created by FBOs and engage FBOs when developing national health plans.
- WHO has an opportunity to spearhead pilot programs of health system reengineering so potentially successful models can be evaluated for widespread adoption.
- WHO can promote interaction among FBOs, governments, and donors to forge constructive relationships and advocate for inclusion of civil society actors in the contexts of broader health policy, global health partnerships, and financing mechanisms.
- WHO can develop relationships with faith-based development agencies (FBDAs) to identify roles that will allow them to facilitate development of religious entities in health systems.

- As a matter of urgency, FBOs and FBDAs (as part of broader civil society) and their national umbrella organizations (such as [Christian health associations]) could be supported in developing proposals on behalf of member agencies to submit to financing mechanisms such as [Global Fund to Fight AIDS, Tuberculosis, and Malaria]; and ensure on a broader scale the recruitment and retention of staff to support accelerated scale-up of primary health care and HIV/AIDS prevention, treatment, and care.
- Monitoring and accountability frameworks that are fit for purpose for use with a variety of FBOs could be developed by WHO and its Member States.

PRIMARY HEALTH CARE: MOBILIZING CIVIL SOCIETY TO MEET NATIONAL HEALTH TARGETS (CHAPTER 1)

The 1975 introduction of the concept of primary health care to the WHO executive board was a departure from the organization's previous approaches to developing and strengthening health systems. A global search for evidence for alternative approaches to improving health services was conducted through an alliance with the Christian Medical Commission (CMC) of the World Council of Churches (WCC). Data was collected from countries where innovative health systems approaches were tested through church agencies associated with WCC in partnership with governments and communities. These innovative approaches reflected the refocusing of Christian medical mission on preventive and comprehensive services, with the assessment that curative efforts in more than 1,200 hospitals operated by WCC-associated organizations were not changing basic patterns of preventable disease in the communities where they were located.[40] Evidence collected from these countries reinforced developing momentum in WHO leadership for the case for primary health care and enabled support at the 1978 International Conference on Primary Health Care held in Alma-Ata (now Almaty, Kazakhstan) by nongovernmental organizations (NGOs), including religious communities, concerned with community health.[41]

---

40 Litsios, S., "The Christian Medical Commission and the Development of WHO's Primary Health Care Approach," *American Journal of Public Health*, November 2004, 94(11) 1884–93.

41 Alma-Ata: Primary Health Care, HFA Sr. No. 1, WHO, 1978.

The 1978 Alma-Ata declaration outlined essential components of primary health care, which were characterized as "essential health care based on practical, scientifically sound and socially acceptable methods and technology made universally accessible to individuals and families in the community through their full participation and at a cost that the community and the country can afford to maintain at every stage of their development in the spirit of self-determination."

The Alma-Ata conference was described as a watershed event.[42] Supported by the international donor and NGO communities, many countries adopted the primary health-care model. Those countries that implemented adequately resourced primary health-care approaches were able to demonstrate reductions in infant mortality rates,[43] improvements in immunization coverage levels,[44] and reductions in measles mortality.[45] Some observers, however, have noted the equivocal impact of primary health-care approaches on the health outcomes of marginalized populations after more than two decades of implementation.[46]

Changes in economic and political views in the 1990s saw a shift from emphasizing primary health care to a more private-sector-focused health reform agenda. Principles of primary health care, such as community control, participation, and multisectoral involvement, were replaced by concepts of user pays, cost recovery, private health insurance, and public–private partnerships. Primary health-care goals of universal access to services were replaced by more rational economic objectives framed around the benefit that improved health could deliver, and stated in terms of improvement of human capital for development.[47]

---

42   Banerji, D., "Reflections on the 25th Anniversary of the Alma-Ata Declaration," *International Journal of Health Services*, 2003, 33(4): 813–18.

43   Hill, A. et al., "Decline of Mortality in Children in Rural Gambia: the Influence of Village-Level Primary Health Care," *Tropical Medicine and International Health*, 2000, 5: 107–18.

44   *Global Measles Vaccine Coverage and Reported Cases, 1980– 1999*, WHO, 2000, http://www.who.int/vaccines-surveillance/graphics/htmls/measlescascov.htm, accessed Nov. 12, 2007.

45   Rutstein, S., "Factors Associated With Trends in Infant and Child Mortality in Developing Countries During the 1990s," *Bulletin of the WHO*, 2000, 78 1256–1270.

46   Allotey, P., Does Primary Health Care Still Have Currency in Improving Sexual and Reproductive Health of Women? 2005, EGM/WPD-EE/2005/EP.7.

47   Hall, J. and Taylor, R., "Health for All Beyond 2000: the Demise of the Alma-Ata Declaration and Primary Healthcare in Developing Countries," *Medical Journal of Australia*, 2007, 178(1):17–20.

But in the early 2000s, WHO regional offices,[48] learning from the lessons of health-sector reform and following the release of the reports of the second consultation of the Commission for Macroeconomics and Health,[49] began to advocate for a reinvigorated primary health-care model.

The new approach would bring to primary health care the gains delivered by the health-sector reform process, including more sustainable financing models, workforce development strategies, and a comprehensive, multisectoral approach encompassing civil society (including FBOs) and private sector actors. It was argued that this approach would allow countries to "address new challenges such as epidemiological and demographic changes, new sociocultural and economic scenarios, emerging infections and/or pandemics, the impacts of globalization on health and the increasing healthcare costs within the particular characteristics of national health systems."[50]

An additional element to the rising popularity of rejuvenated primary health care arose from the 2005 evaluation of the implementation of a "three by five" initiative to accelerate the uptake of antiretroviral therapy for HIV. The evaluation report[51] noted that the global response to HIV/AIDS was shifting focus, even during the initiative, toward the ambitious goal of universal access to HIV prevention, treatment, and care services. The report noted that for WHO, "supporting national governments to get public health approach (PHA) guidelines into practice will become increasingly important as countries scale up coverage by decentralizing their HIV treatment services (which requires direct support to primary care providers in first-level facilities)."[52]

---

48   *Primary Health Care: 25 Years After Alma-Ata,* WHO Regional Committee for the Eastern Mediterranean, 2003, gis.emro.who.int/HealthSystemObservatory/PDF/Technicaland-DiscussionPapers/PRIMARY%20HEALTH%20CARE%2025%20YEARS%20AFTER%20ALMAATA.pdf, accessed Oct. 10, 2007; *Declaration of the Americas on the Renewal of Primary Healthcare,* PAHO, 2004:25, http://www.paho.org/english/ad/ths/os/PHC-orientation.htm, accessed Oct. 10, 2007; Consultation Report: the Second Consultation on Macroeconomics and Health Increasing Investments in Health for the Poor, WHO, 2003, http://www.who.int/macrohealth/events/health_for_poor/en/E_REPORT.pdf, accessed Oct. 10, 2007.

49   Evaluation of WHO's Contribution to "Three by Five," Main Report, WHO, Geneva, 2006:24.

50   *Declaration of the Americas on the Renewal of Primary Healthcare,* PAHO, 2004:25, http://www.paho.org/english/ad/ths/os/PHC-orientation.htm, accessed Oct. 10, 2007.

51   Evaluation of WHO's Contribution to "Three by Five," Main Report, WHO, Geneva, 2006:24.

52   Ibid.

The report added that "WHO has missed opportunities for expanding both the coverage and quality of HIV-related PHA interventions through the nonstate (private) sector in a number of these settings and has not offered technical support to national governments to exercise more effective stewardship over private providers."[53]

The report strongly recommended that WHO "urgently establish the effectiveness and feasibility of sustaining integrated service delivery approaches as the 'common platform' for strengthening primary healthcare services through which a broader public health approach package of essential disease control interventions can also be delivered."[54]

Although the mention of nongovernment actors in this context appears to be limited to private, forprofit providers, WHO has a clear opportunity to support countries in their engagement with civil society entities, including FBOs, as health service providers in achieving the universal access goal of prevention, treatment, and care for people with HIV/AIDS. Attention to nongovernment health-sector civil society is necessary when it provides a critically large segment of health care in a nation. Given the previous seminal role of the CMC in the initial development of Alma-Ata primary health-care models, there is a precedent for engaging with multiple FBOs in the articulation of new primary care paradigms. The current scale of FBOs' involvement in health care in sub-Saharan Africa makes a compelling case that religious entities could become significant players in the new primary health-care approach to strengthening health systems, especially related to achieving the goal of universal access.

FAITH AND HEALTH CARE CONNECTIONS (CHAPTER 3)

One reason FBOs are ignored by some national agencies and intergovernmental organizations appears to go beyond the traditional governmental agency / NGO gap. It is related to the secular nature of most governments and intergovernmental forums that tend to keep their distance from professed religious values, even if their values overlap. But in health care, religious entities may have value that outweighs their perceived disadvantages. These added values are composed of

- values they convey in terms of a holistic conception of health and health care,[55]

---

53 Ibid.

54 Ibid.

55 Bok, S., *Rethinking the WHO Definition of Health,* Harvard Health Center for Population and Development Studies, October 2004, Working Paper Series Vol.14, No.7, http://www.

- quality of their roots in the communities they serve, and
- potential for further primary health-care outreach.

COMPASSION: THE UNIVERSAL ATTRIBUTE OF FAITH

Compassion is the primary value underlying major religious systems. This is often summarized in the ethic of reciprocity:[56] do unto others as you would wish them to do unto you. For a person of faith to reflect on how they would feel if they were in a position of another is to elicit the compassion that drives them to act on the other's behalf. Belief in the divine origin of compassion compels believers to offer compassion to others.[57]

Many complex layers of religious practice and tradition overlie the basic principle of treating others as one would want to be treated, but each recognizes the call toward the care of others as a divine calling. Most religious belief systems underscore the value of the individual, but with an emphasis that he or she has a firm grounding within their community. For instance, foundational to the Jewish faith are the Ten Commandments and the Torah, which express a commitment to a system of social justice that aspires to a harmonious community in which each person is valued. Christians follow Jesus' summary of this law, which further establishes the duty to "love your neighbor as yourself." Muslims recognizing Allah as fundamentally compassionate and merciful accept this version of the Golden Rule. Buddhists seek to alleviate the realities of suffering; to offer help and assistance so they can live out the four sublime states of loving-kindness, compassion, sympathetic joy, and equanimity. Hinduism has a similar basis in compassion.[58]

Before the establishment of secular health systems in the 1800s, religious communities, motivated by their calling for compassion, offered remedies for sickness and care for suffering people. This was the case in many temples, mosques, monasteries, or churches. This continues to express itself today in a range of health

globalhealth.harvard.edu/hcpds/wpweb/Bok_wp1407_3.pdf, accessed Nov. 12, 2007.

56   For "Ethic of reciprocity" and further discussions on religious adaptations of it, see Wikipedia article, en.wikipedia.org/wiki/Ethic_of_reciprocity, accessed Nov. 12, 2007.

57   Armstrong, K., *The Great Transformation,* London, Atlantic, 2006.

58   Bano, M. and Nair, P., Faith-based Organizations in South Asia: Historical Evolution, Current Status and Nature of Interaction with the State, University of Birmingham, 2007, Religion and Development Working Paper 12, www.rad.bham.ac.uk/files/resourcesmodule/@ random45c8b732cd96d/1194256405_Faith_Based_Organisations_South_Asia.pdf, accessed Nov. 12, 2007.

activities. Some resemble the ancient practice of refuge and care within a traditional religious community. Others have developed a level of professionalism consistent with modern medicine and include the most advanced medical facilities. The degree of explicit religious intent apparent in these activities varies considerably, but each has been inspired by the religious call to compassion for the sick, and each has its origins in the action of committed religious adherents.

In caring for others, religious communities not only act out of compassion, but also act out of an ethic of decency. This ethic of decency prescribes values and principles about how to treat others in accordance with their humanity and establishes an imperative to abolish conditions that would damage or degrade people's inherent dignity. This ethic demands that care is provided that meets people's individual needs and respects their dignity and self-worth. Out of respect for the individual's dignity and agency, it is imperative that health-care systems and FBOs in particular provide individuals with decent care (comprehensive or holistic care services that address the individual's medical, physical, mental, social, and spiritual well-being) and place the individual at the center of these services. While this understanding and practice of decent care is not new—it has been a critical component of nursing and provision of care to people in community, hospital, hospice, and assisted-living settings—it is critical related to HIV/AIDS. Built on the foundation of the primary health-care movement, reinforced in Alma-Ata, and subscribed to by WHO,[59] decent care includes treatment literacy, patient advocacy, and person-centered care. Decent care focuses not only on the quality of care, which is crucial, but also carefully considers the input of those receiving care. In this process, care recipients help define and manage the care they need and receive in collaboration with health-care providers and those providing supportive services. This is of particular importance in faith communities and FBOs that provide HIV caregiving and support services and in those that, because of the enormous losses to HIV/AIDS, are just now entering this critical arena. To successfully provide decent care, however, health-care providers and recipients must overcome the damaging stigma and discrimination often associated with particular behaviors and diagnoses.

DILEMMAS IN FAITH-BASED HEALTH CARE

Much attention has been given to the difficulties expressed by FBOs related to HIV spread predominantly through sexual contact. The epidemiological concern for

---

59   Report on the Global Consultation on Decent Care, WHO, Geneva, August 2006.

nonjudgmental protection has come into tension with religious values that discourage risky behavior. Moreover, the tension has impacted not only local strategies for distributing condoms, but has also influenced policy debates and strategic actions in the global environment. In an era when debate focuses on the growing influence of fundamentalist religions,[60] secular public-policy institutions are generally cautious, though this was less clear in studies keying on Asia, where there seems to be a greater degree of interdependence between faith and health. Lack of clarity on the degree to which some religious organizations seek power to reshape predominantly liberal societies according to their particular values is of concern to the secular public health policy institutions, as is the perceived proselytizing ambitions of some religious groups.

In general, public institutions cannot harness only the secular elements of faith-based health care.[61] Religious values have deeper and indivisible purposes. They seek to promote a more humane and spiritual environment under the terms of their ethical construct with a service philosophy that encompasses a more holistic set of practices. In addition, religious values suggest a greater range of human assets than might be expressed in a secular economic development model.[62] In an attempt to fulfill the physical needs of the global population, religious tradition critiques the materialist basis upon which development models are built. FBOs relieve poverty and bring health gains to vulnerable communities, but they also offer less tangible means for self-fulfillment and communal well-being.

The five ways FBOs use or deploy faith, drawn up by G. Clarke in "Faith Matters: Development and the Complex World of Faith-based Organizations,"[63] can be used to describe the range of FBO mandates and agendas:

60   "In God's Name—a Special Report on Religion and Public Life," *The Economist*, November 3–9, 2007.

61   Tomalin, E., *Sociology, Religion and Development—Literature Review*, University of Birmingham, 2007, Religion and Development Working Paper 4, http://www.rad.bham.ac.uk/files/resourcesmodule/@random45c8b732cd96d/1186738002_WP4.pdf, accessed Nov. 12, 2007.

62   Rakodi, C., *Understanding the Roles of Religion in Development*, University of Birmingham, 2007, Religions and Development Working paper 9, www.rad.bham.ac.uk/files/resourcesmodule/@random45c8b732cd96d/1191926371 _RolesReligionDevelopmentRaDApproach.pdf, accessed Nov. 12, 2007.

63   Clarke, G., *Faith Matters: Development and the Complex World of Faith-based Organisations*, paper presented at the annual conference of the Development Studies Association, the Open University, Milton Keynes, Sept. 7–9, 2005, http://www.devstud.org.uk/Conference05/papers/clarke.doc, accessed Oct. 20, 2007.

- peak body representation [i.e., an organization that represents a sector, industry, or community to a government]
- charitable or developmental work
- sociopolitical action
- missionary endeavor
- radicalized or militant action

Drawing on analyses from other authors,[64] Clark also proposed a four-term gradation in the style of a Likert scale to describe the degree to which faith influences relationships with beneficiaries:

Passive. Faith is subsidiary to broader humanitarian principles as a motivation for action and in mobilizing staff and supporters. Faith plays a secondary role in identifying, helping, or working with beneficiaries and partners.

Active. Faith provides an important and explicit motive for working with beneficiaries and partners, although there is no discrimination against nonbelievers and the organization supports multifaith cooperation.

Persuasive. Faith provides an important and explicit motivation for action and in mobilizing staff and supporters. It plays a significant role in identifying, helping, or working with beneficiaries and partners and provides the dominant basis for engagement. It also aims to bring new converts to the faith or to advance the faith at the expense of others.

Exclusive. Faith provides the principal or overriding motivation for action and in mobilizing staff and supporters. It provides the principal or sole consideration in identifying beneficiaries. Social and political engagement is rooted in the faith and is often militant or violent and directed against one or more rival faiths.

Analyses incorporating the different uses of faith and the character of the faith-beneficiary relationship can provide an approach to defining the challenges in working with particular types of FBOs, and for assessing the opportunities to include FBOs in multisectoral health development enterprises and partnerships.

---

64   Green, J. and Sherman, A., Fruitful Collaborations: a Survey of Government Funded Faith-based Programs, Washington, D.C., Hudson Institute, 2002, downloads.weblogger.com/gems/cpj/NPCBriefingTranscript020904.pdf, accessed Oct. 10, 2007.

HEALTH, HEALING, AND THE EMERGENCE
OF PRIMARY HEALTH CARE

Many religious traditions are characterized by a focus on healing: "A primary focus of religious expectations in the 21st century is the multidimensional longing for healing of body and mind, of soul and spirit, of personal and social relations, of political and ecological dimensions in this broken world."[65]

African Religious Health Assets Programme studies have identified a range of expressions of this approach to healing that characterize the wider values and purposes of religious entities. Their hospitals, clinics, care groups, and educational activities encompass this broad notion of healing the individual, community, and society. Within this spectrum is a commitment to a holistic approach to primary care.[66]

Some religious leaders may articulate the full range of these aspirations; others may focus on more limited aspects.[67] Evidence for wider interest and enthusiasm for holistic primary care is evident in church reports.[68] The concept of healing within religious entities is a patchwork of activities ranging from the purely spiritual to scientific biomedical.

It is noteworthy that the CMC, established in 1968 by the WCC, reassessed the theological basis and the manner in which church mission organizations engaged in health-related activities. Based on the outcomes of two related consultations (Tübingen I in May 1964 and Tübingen II in September 1967), CMC deliberations resulted in a reappraisal of the use of church resources for health. That work proved to be a major influence in the development of the primary health-care model in collaboration with WHO that would later receive global endorsement through the 1978 Alma-Ata conference.

In summary, engagement of secular health-care authorities with FBOs raises questions of power and influence on individuals and policies. But it also opens the biomedical environment to a more holistic perspective on the nature of people in communities. Religious compassionate and communal values suggest a strong public service mentality. Religious ideas also challenge materialist approaches to health and

---

65   Jesudasan, U. and Rüppell, G., *Healing as Empowerment*, World Council of Churches, Geneva, 35.

66   Let Us Embrace: Masangane Case Study—A Comprehensive, Integrated Response to HIV and AIDS, African Religious Health Assets Programme, Cape Town, 2006.

67   Jesudasan, *Healing*, 88.

68   Ibid., 62.

well-being and offer more holistic perspectives, bringing a qualitative contribution through religious faith for individuals and communities.

EDITORS' NOTES

For more information about Geneva Global and the World Health Organization: http://www.genevaglobal.com/ and http://www.who.int/.

SOURCE

Geneva Global, and World Health Organization. 2008. Building from common foundations: The World Health Organization and faith-based organizations in primary healthcare. Geneva: World Health Organization. Reprinted by permission. http://www.ccih.org/bulletin/0608files/BuildingFromCommonFoundations_WHO_and_FBOs.pdf.

RELATED RESOURCES

Videos: Global Health TV (short overviews and examples of health development around the world). http://www.globalhealthtv.com/.

Christian Connections for International Health (CCIH). Retrieved from http://www.ccih.org/.

James, R. 2009. What is distinctive about FBOs? How European FBOs define and operationalise their faith. *Praxis Paper* 22. International NGO Training and Research Centre. http://www.intrac.org/data/files/resources/482/Praxis-Paper-22-What-is-Distinctive-About-FBOs.pdf.

Teaching-aids at Low-Cost. http://www.talcuk.org/.

World Federation for Mental Health. 2009. Mental health in primary care: Enhancing treatment and promoting mental health. World Federation for Mental Health. http://www.wfmh.org/WMHD%2009%20Languages/ENGLISH%20WMHD09.pdf.

World Health Organization. 2008. The world health report 2008: Primary health care—Now more than ever. Geneva: World Health Organization. http://www.who.int/whr/2008/en/.

———, and World Organization of Family Doctors. 2008. Integrating mental health into primary care: A global perspective. Geneva: World Health Organization. http://www.who.int/mental_health/policy/services/mentalhealthintoprimarycare/en/index.html.

CHAPTER 18

Social Determinants of Health

RIO POLITICAL DECLARATION ON THE SOCIAL DETERMINANTS OF HEALTH

World Conference on Social Determinants of Health

1. Invited by the World Health Organization, we, Heads of Government, Ministers, and government representatives came together on the twenty-first day of October 2011 in Rio de Janeiro to express our determination to achieve social and health equity through action on social determinants of health and well-being by a comprehensive intersectoral approach.

2. We understand that health equity is a shared responsibility and requires the engagement of all sectors of government, of all segments of society, and of all members of the international community, in an "all for equity" and "health for all" global action.

We underscore the principles and provisions set out in the World Health Organization Constitution and in the 1978 Declaration of Alma-Ata as well as in the 1986 Ottawa Charter and in the series of international health promotion conferences, which reaffirmed the essential value of equity in health and recognized that "the enjoyment of the highest attainable standard of health is one of the fundamental rights of every human being without distinction of race, religion, political belief, economic, or social condition." We recognize that governments have a responsibility for the health of their peoples, which can be fulfilled only by the provision of adequate health and social measures and that national efforts need to be supported by an enabling international environment.

We reaffirm that health inequities within and between countries are politically, socially, and economically unacceptable, as well as unfair and largely avoidable, and that the promotion of health equity is essential to sustainable development and to a better quality of life and well-being for all, which in turn can contribute to peace and security.

We reiterate our determination to take action on social determinants of health as collectively agreed by the World Health Assembly and reflected in resolution WHA62.14 ("Reducing health inequities through action on the social determinants of health"), which notes the three overarching recommendations of the Commission on Social Determinants of Health: to improve daily living conditions; to tackle the inequitable distribution of power, money, and resources; and to measure and understand the problem and assess the impact of action.

Health inequities arise from the societal conditions in which people are born, grow, live, work, and age, referred to as social determinants of health. These include early years' experiences, education, economic status, employment and decent work, housing and environment, and effective systems of preventing and treating ill health. We are convinced that action on these determinants, both for vulnerable groups and the entire population, is essential to create inclusive, equitable, economically productive, and healthy societies. Positioning human health and well-being as one of the key features of what constitutes a successful, inclusive, and fair society in the twenty-first century is consistent with our commitment to human rights at national and international levels.

Good health requires a universal, comprehensive, equitable, effective, responsive, and accessible quality health system. But it is also dependent on the involvement of and dialogue with other sectors and actors, as their performance has significant health impacts. Collaboration in coordinated and intersectoral policy actions has proven to be effective. Health in All Policies, together with intersectoral cooperation and action, is one promising approach to enhance accountability in other sectors for health, as well as the promotion of health equity and more inclusive and productive societies. As collective goals, good health and well-being for all should be given high priority at local, national, regional, and international levels.

We recognize that we need to do more to accelerate progress in addressing the unequal distribution of health resources as well as conditions damaging to health at all levels. Based on the experiences shared at this Conference, we express our political will to make health equity a national, regional, and global goal and to address current challenges, such as eradicating hunger and poverty, ensuring food and nutritional security, access to safe drinking water and sanitation, employment and decent work, and social protection, protecting environments, and delivering equitable economic growth, through resolute action on social determinants of health across all sectors and at all levels. We also acknowledge that by addressing social determinants we can contribute to the achievement of the Millennium Development Goals.

The current global economic and financial crisis urgently requires the adoption of actions to reduce increasing health inequities and prevent worsening of living conditions and the deterioration of universal health-care and social protection systems.

We acknowledge that action on social determinants of health is called for both within countries and at the global level. We underscore that increasing the ability of global actors, through better global governance, promotion of international cooperation and development, participation in policy-making and monitoring progress, is essential to contribute to national and local efforts on social determinants of health. Action on social determinants of health should be adapted to the national and subnational contexts of individual countries and regions to take into account different social, cultural, and economic systems. Evidence from research and experiences in implementing policies on social determinants of health, however, shows common features of successful action. There are five key action areas critical to addressing health inequities: (i) to adopt better governance for health and development; (ii) to promote participation in policy-making and implementation; (iii) to further reorient the health sector towards reducing health inequities; (iv) to strengthen global governance and collaboration; and (v) to monitor progress and increase accountability. Action on social determinants of health therefore means that we, the representatives of governments, will strive individually and collectively to develop and support policies, strategies, programmes, and action plans, which address social determinants of health, with the support of the international community, that include:

11. To adopt better governance for health and development

11.1 Acknowledging that governance to address social determinants involves transparent and inclusive decision-making processes that give voice to all groups and sectors involved, and develop policies that perform effectively and reach clear and measurable outcomes, build accountability and, most crucially, are fair in both policy development processes and results;

11.2 We pledge to:

(i) Work across different sectors and levels of government, including through, as appropriate, national development strategies, taking into account their contribution to health and health equity and recognizing the leading role of health ministries for advocacy in this regard;

(ii) Develop policies that are inclusive and take account of the needs of the entire population with specific attention to vulnerable groups and high-risk areas;

(iii) Support comprehensive programmes of research and surveys to inform policy and action;

(iv) Promote awareness, consideration, and increased accountability of policy makers for impacts of all policies on health;

(v) Develop approaches, including effective partnerships, to engage other sectors in order to identify individual and joint roles for improvements in health and reduction of health inequities;

(vi) Support all sectors in the development of tools and capacities to address social determinants of health at national and international levels;

(vii) Foster collaboration with the private sector, safeguarding against conflict of interests, to contribute to achieving health through policies and actions on social determinants of health;

(viii) Implement resolution WHA62.14, which takes note of the recommendations of the final report of the Commission on Social Determinants of Health;

(ix) Strengthen occupational health safety and health protection and their oversight and encourage the public and private sectors to offer healthy working conditions so as to contribute to promoting health for all;

(x) Promote and strengthen universal access to social services and social protection floors;

(xi) Give special attention to gender-related aspects as well as early child development in public policies and social and health services;

(xii) Promote access to affordable, safe, efficacious, and quality medicines, including through the full implementation of the WHO Global Strategy and Plan of Action on Public Health, Innovation and Intellectual Property;

(xiii) Strengthen international cooperation with a view to promoting health equity in all countries through facilitating transfer on mutually agreed terms of expertise, technologies, and scientific data in the field of social determinants of health, as well as exchange of good practices for managing intersectoral policy development.

12. To promote participation in policy-making and implementation

12.1 Acknowledging the importance of participatory processes in policy-making and implementation for effective governance to act on social determinants of health;

12.2 We pledge to:

(i) Promote and enhance inclusive and transparent decision making, implementation, and accountability for health and health governance at all levels, including through enhancing access to information, access to justice, and public participation;

(ii) Empower the role of communities and strengthen civil society contribution to policy-making and implementation by adopting measures to enable their effective participation for the public interest in decision making;

(iii) Promote inclusive and transparent governance approaches, which engage early with affected sectors at all levels of governments, as well as support social participation and involve civil society and the private sector, safeguarding against conflict of interests;

(iv) Consider the particular social determinants resulting in persistent health inequities for indigenous people, in the spirit of the United Nations Declaration on the Rights of Indigenous Peoples, and their specific needs and promote meaningful collaboration with them in the development and delivery of related policies and programmes;

(v) Consider the contributions and capacities of civil society to take action in advocacy, social mobilization, and implementation on social determinants of health;

(vi) Promote health equity in all countries particularly through the exchange of good practices regarding increased participation in policy development and implementation;

(vii) Promote the full and effective participation of developed and developing countries in the formulation and implementation of policies and measures to address social determinants of health at the international level.

13. To further reorient the health sector towards reducing health inequities

13.1 Acknowledging that accessibility, availability, acceptability, affordability, and quality of health care and public health services are essential to the enjoyment of the highest attainable standard of health, one of the fundamental rights of every human being, and that the health sector should firmly act to reduce health inequities;

13.2 We pledge to:

(i) Maintain and develop effective public health policies which address the social, economic, environmental, and behavioural determinants of health with a particular focus on reducing health inequities;

(ii) Strengthen health systems towards the provision of equitable universal coverage and promote access to high-quality, promotive, preventive, curative, and rehabilitative health services throughout the life cycle, with a particular focus on comprehensive and integrated primary health care;

(iii) Build, strengthen, and maintain public health capacity, including capacity for intersectoral action, on social determinants of health;

(iv) Build, strengthen, and maintain health-financing and risk-pooling systems that prevent people from becoming impoverished when they seek medical treatment;

(v) Promote mechanisms for supporting and strengthening community initiatives for health-financing and risk-pooling systems;

(vi) Promote changes within the health sector, as appropriate, to provide the capacities and tools to act to reduce health inequities, including through collaborative action;

(vii) Integrate equity, as a priority within health systems, as well as in the design and delivery of health services and public health programmes;

(viii) Reach out and work across and within all levels and sectors of government by promoting mechanisms for dialogue, problem-solving, and health impact assessment with an equity focus to identify and promote policies, programmes, practices, and legislative measures that may be instrumental for the goal pursued by this Political Declaration and to adapt or reform those harmful to health and health equity;

(ix) Exchange good practices and successful experiences with regard to policies, strategies, and measures to further reorient the health sector towards reducing health inequities.

14. To strengthen global governance and collaboration

14.1 Acknowledging the importance of international cooperation and solidarity for the equitable benefit of all people and the important role the multilateral organizations have in articulating norms and guidelines and identifying good practices for supporting actions on social determinants, and in facilitating access to financial resources and technical cooperation, as well as in reviewing and, where appropriate, strategically modifying policies and practices that have a negative impact on people's health and well-being;

14.2 We pledge to:

(i) Adopt coherent policy approaches that are based on the right to the enjoyment of the highest attainable standard of health, taking into account the right to development as referred to, inter alia, by the 1993 Vienna Declaration and Programme of Action, that will strengthen the focus on social determinants of health towards achieving the Millennium Development Goals;

(ii) Support social protection floors as defined by countries to address their specific needs and the ongoing work on social protection within the United Nations system, including the work of the International Labour Organization;

(iii) Support national governments, international organizations, nongovernmental entities, and others to tackle social determinants of health as well as to strive to ensure that efforts to advance international development goals and objectives to improve health equity are mutually supportive;

(iv) Accelerate the implementation by the State Parties of the WHO Framework Convention on Tobacco Control (FCTC), recognizing the full range of measures including measures to reduce consumption and availability, and encourage countries that have not yet done so to consider acceding to the FCTC as we recognize that substantially reducing tobacco consumption is an important contribution to addressing social determinants of health and vice versa;

(v) Take forward the actions set out in the political declaration of the United Nations General Assembly High-Level Meeting on the Prevention and Control of Noncommunicable Diseases at local, national, and international levels—ensuring a focus on reducing health inequities;

(vi) Support the leading role of the World Health Organization in global health governance, and in promoting alignment in policies, plans, and activities on social determinants of health with its partner United Nations agencies, development banks, and other key international organizations, including in joint advocacy, and in facilitating access to the provision of financial and technical assistance to countries and regions;

(vii) Support the efforts of governments to promote capacity and establish incentives to create a sustainable workforce in health and in other fields, especially in areas of greatest need;

(viii) Build capacity of national governments to address social determinants of health by facilitating expertise and access to resources through appropriate United Nations agencies' support, particularly the World Health Organization;

(ix) Foster North-South and South-South cooperation in showcasing initiatives, building capacity, and facilitating the transfer of technology on mutually agreed terms for integrated action on health inequities, in line with national priorities and needs, including on health services and pharmaceutical production, as appropriate.

15. To monitor progress and increase accountability

15.1 Acknowledging that monitoring of trends in health inequities and of impacts of actions to tackle them is critical to achieving meaningful progress, that information systems should facilitate the establishment of relationships between health outcomes and social stratification variables, and that accountability mechanisms to guide policy-making in all sectors are essential, taking into account different national contexts;

15.2 We pledge to:

(i) Establish, strengthen, and maintain monitoring systems that provide disaggregated data to assess inequities in health outcomes as well as in allocations and use of resources;

(ii) Develop and implement robust, evidence-based, reliable measures of societal well-being, building where possible on existing indicators, standards, and programmes, and across the social gradient, that go beyond economic growth;

(iii) To promote research on the relationships between social determinants and health equity outcomes with a particular focus on evaluation of effectiveness of interventions;

(iv) Systematically share relevant evidence and trends among different sectors to inform policy and action;

(v) Improve access to the results of monitoring and research for all sectors in society;

(vi) Assess the impacts of policies on health and other societal goals, and take these into account in policy-making;

(vii) Use intersectoral mechanisms such as a Health in All Policies approach for addressing inequities and social determinants of health; enhance access to justice and ensure accountability, which can be followed up;

(viii) Support the leading role of the World Health Organization in its collaboration with other United Nations agencies in strengthening the monitoring of progress in the field of social determinants of health and in providing guidance and support to Member States in implementing a Health in All Policies approach to tackling inequities in health;

(ix) Support the World Health Organization on the follow-up to the recommendations of the Commission on Information and Accountability for Women's and Children's Health;

(x) Promote appropriate monitoring systems that take into consideration the role of all relevant stakeholders including civil society, nongovernmental organizations, as well as the private sector, with appropriate safeguard against conflict of interests, in the monitoring and evaluation process;

(xi) Promote health equity in and among countries, monitoring progress at the international level and increasing collective accountability in the field of social determinants of health, particularly through the exchange of good practices in this field;

(xii) Improve universal access to and use of inclusive information technologies and innovation in key social determinants of health.

16. Call for global action

16.1 We, Heads of Government, Ministers, and government representatives, solemnly reaffirm our resolve to take action on social determinants of health to create vibrant, inclusive, equitable, economically productive, and healthy societies, and to overcome national, regional, and global challenges to sustainable development. We offer our solid support for these common objectives and our determination to achieve them.

16.2 We call upon the World Health Organization, United Nations agencies, and other international organizations to advocate for, coordinate, and collaborate with us in the implementation of these actions. We recognize that global action on social determinants will need increased capacity and knowledge within the World Health Organization and other multilateral organizations for the development and sharing of norms, standards, and good practices. Our common values and responsibilities towards humanity move us to fulfil our pledge to act on social determinants of health. We firmly believe that doing so is not only a moral and a human rights imperative but also indispensable to promote human well-being, peace, prosperity, and sustainable development. We call upon the international community to support developing countries in the implementation of these actions through the exchange of best practices, the provision of technical assistance, and in facilitating access to financial resources, while reaffirming the provisions of the United Nations Millennium Declaration as well as the Monterrey Consensus of the International Conference on Financing for Development.

16.3 We urge those developed countries which have pledged to achieve the target of 0.7 percent of GNP for official development assistance by 2015, and those developed countries that have not yet done so, to make additional concrete efforts to fulfil their commitments in this regard. We also urge developing countries to build on progress achieved in ensuring that official development assistance is used effectively to help achieve development goals and targets.

16.4 World leaders will soon gather again here in Rio de Janeiro to consider how to meet the challenge of sustainable development laid down twenty years ago. This Political Declaration recognizes the important policies needed to achieve both sustainable development and health equity through acting on social determinants.

16.5 We recommend that the social determinants approach is duly considered in the ongoing reform process of the World Health Organization. We also recommend that the 65th World Health Assembly adopts a resolution endorsing this Political Declaration.

EDITORS' NOTES

For more information about the World Health Organization: http://www.who.int/.

SOURCE

World Conference on Social Determinants of Health. 2011. Rio Political Declaration on the Social Determinants of Health. Rio de Janeiro: World Health Organization. Reprinted by permission. http://www.who.int/sdhconference/declaration/en/index.html.

RELATED RESOURCES

Video: "The Girl Who Changed the World for Five Minutes." http://www.youtube.com/watch?v=TQmz6Rbpnu0.

Collier, P. 2007. *The bottom billion: Why the poorest countries are failing and what can be done about it*. Oxford: Oxford University Press. [See this author's related TED Talk: http://www.ted.com/talks/paul_collier_shares_4_ways_to_help_the_bottom_billion.html.]

Gostin, L. O. 2012. A framework convention on global health: Health for all, justice for all. *Journal of the American Medical Association* 307, no. 19: 2087–92. doi:10.1001/jama.2012.4395.

People's Health Movement. 2011. *Global health watch 3: An alternative world health report*. London; Zed books. http://www.ghwatch.org/sites/www.ghwatch.org/files/global%20health%20watch%203.pdf.

Pantuliano, S., ed. 2009. *Uncharted territory: Land, conflict, and humanitarian action*. Burton on Dunsmore, UK: Practical Action Publishing.

United Nations. 2000. Millennium development goals. http://www.un.org/millenniumgoals/.

———. 2012. The future we want. Rio de Janeiro: United Nations. http://www.earthsummit2012.org/resources/useful-resources/1157-the-future-we-want-rio20-outcome-document.

World Health Organization & Commission on Social Determinants of Health. 2008. *Closing the gap in a generation: Health equity through action on social determinants of health*. Geneva: Author. http://www.who.int/social_determinants/thecommission/finalreport/en/index.html.

World Health Organization. 2011. *Social determinants approaches to public health: From concept to practice*. Geneva: Author. http://www.who.int/sdhconference/background/news/socialdeterminantsapproachestopublichealth/en/.

CHAPTER 19

Disabilities: Overview and Action

WORLD REPORT ON DISABILITY

World Health Organization and the World Bank

MAIN MESSAGES AND RECOMMENDATIONS

The *World Report on Disability* is the first of its kind, providing global guidance on implementing the United Nations Convention on the Rights of Persons with Disabilities (CRPD) and giving an extensive picture of the situation of people with disabilities, their needs and unmet needs, and the barriers they face to participating fully in their societies. Successive chapters document data, health, rehabilitation, assistance and support, enabling environments, education, and employment. For each area, the report highlights a range of good practice examples which governments and civil society can emulate, to help establish an inclusive and enabling society in which people with disabilities can flourish.

THE MAIN MESSAGES OF THE REPORT ARE AS FOLLOWS:

There has been a paradigm shift in approaches to disability. In recent decades the move has been away from a medical understanding towards a social understanding. Disability arises from the interaction between people with a health condition and their environment. The CRPD reflects this emphasis on removing environmental barriers which prevent inclusion.

Disability prevalence is high and growing. There are over 1 billion people with disabilities in the world, of whom between 110 and 190 million experience very significant difficulties. This corresponds to about 15 percent of the world's population and is higher than previous World Health Organization (WHO) estimates, which date from the 1970s and suggested a figure of around 10 percent. The prevalence of disability is growing due to population ageing and the global increase in chronic health conditions. Patterns of disability in a particular country are influenced by trends in health conditions and trends in environmental and other factors, such as road traffic crashes, natural disasters, conflict, diet, and substance abuse.

Disability disproportionately affects vulnerable populations. Disability is more common among women, older people, and households that are poor. Lower income countries have a higher prevalence of disability than higher income countries.

Disability is very diverse. Stereotypical views of disability emphasize wheelchair users and a few other "classic" groups such as blind people and deaf people. However, the disability experience varies greatly. While disability correlates with disadvantage, not all people with disabilities are equally disadvantaged. School enrolment rates differ, with children with physical impairments generally faring better than those with intellectual or sensory impairments. Those most excluded from the labour market are often those with mental health difficulties or intellectual impairments. People with more severe impairments often experience greater disadvantage.

People with disabilities face widespread barriers in accessing services (health, education, employment, transport, as well as information). These include inadequate policies and standards, negative attitudes, lack of service provision, inadequate funding, lack of accessibility, inadequate information and communication, and lack of participation in decisions that directly affect their lives.

People with disabilities have worse health and socioeconomic outcomes. Across the world, people with disabilities have poorer health, lower education achievements, less economic participation, and higher rates of poverty than people without disabilities.

Many of the barriers people with disabilities face are avoidable, and the disadvantage associated with disability can be overcome.

THE CROSS-CUTTING RECOMMENDATIONS OF THE REPORT, BASED ON THE MAIN FINDINGS, ARE AS FOLLOWS:

1. Enable access to all mainstream systems and services. People with disabilities have ordinary needs, which can and should be met through mainstream programmes and services. Mainstreaming is the process by which governments and other stakeholders address the barriers that exclude persons with disabilities from participating equally in any service intended for the general public, such as education, health, employment, and social services. This requires changes to laws, policies, institutions, and environments. Mainstreaming not only fulfils the human rights of persons with disabilities, it can also be more cost effective.

2. Invest in programmes and services for people with disabilities. Some people with disabilities may require access to specific measures, such as rehabilitation, support services, or vocational training, which can improve functioning and independence and foster participation in society.

3. Adopt a national disability strategy and plan of action. All sectors and stakeholders should collaborate on a strategy to improve the well-being of people with disabilities. This will help improve coordination between sectors and services. Progress should be monitored closely.

4. Involve people with disabilities. In formulating and implementing policies, laws, and services, people with disabilities should be consulted and actively involved. At an individual level, persons with disabilities are entitled to have control over their lives and therefore need to be consulted on issues that concern them directly.

5. Improve human resource capacity. Human resource capacity can be improved through effective education, training, and recruitment. For example, training of health professionals, architects, and designers should include relevant content on disability and be based on human rights principles.

6. Provide adequate funding and improve affordability. Adequate and sustainable funding of publicly provided services is needed to remove financial barriers to access and ensure that good quality services are provided.

7. Increase public awareness and understanding about disability. Mutual respect and understanding contribute to an inclusive society. It is vital to improve public understanding of disability, confront negative perceptions, and represent disability fairly.

8. Improve the availability and quality of data on disability. Data need to be standardized and internationally comparable to benchmark and monitor progress on disability policies and on the implementation of the CRPD nationally and internationally. At the national level, disability should be included in data collection. Dedicated disability surveys can also be carried out to gain more comprehensive information.

9. Strengthen and support research on disability. Research is essential for increasing public understanding about disability, informing disability policy and programmes, and efficiently allocating resources. More research is needed, not just about the lives of people with disabilities, but also about social barriers and how these can be overcome.

EDITORS' NOTES

For more information about the World Health Organization and the World Bank: http://www.who.int/ and http://www.worldbank.org/.

SOURCE

World Health Organization, and the World Bank. 2011. *World report on disability* (fact sheet). Geneva: World Health Organization and the World Bank. http://www.who.int/disabilities/world_report/2011/factsheet.pdf. Full report: http://www.who.int/disabilities/world_report/2011/en/index.html.

© 2011 World Health Organization and the World Bank. Reprinted by permission.

RELATED RESOURCES

Videos: World Health Organization and the World Bank. "What's Disability to Me?" World Health Organization (short video clips about people around the world with different disabilities). http://www.who.int/disabilities/world_report/2011/videos/en/index.html.

Lausanne Movement. 2012. Disability ministry. *Connecting Point*. 24 May. http://www.lausanne.org/en/blog/1786-friendship-respect-love-and-justice-for-people-with-disabilities.html.

Pan African Network of People with Psychosocial Disabilities. 2011. Cape Town declaration of 16 October 2011. Pan African Network of People with Psychosocial Disabilities. http://www.panusp.org/.

United Nations. International Day of Persons with Disabilities. http://www.un.org/disabilities/default.asp?id=1597.

World Health Organization. 2001. International classification of functioning, disability, and health. World Health Organization. http://www.who.int/classifications/icf/en.

———. 2010. Community-based rehabilitation guidelines. Geneva: World Health Organization. http://www.who.int/disabilities/cbr/guidelines/en/index.html.

CHAPTER 20

Healthy Women, Healthy World

WOMEN AND HEALTH:
TODAY'S EVIDENCE, TOMORROW'S AGENDA
(EXECUTIVE SUMMARY)

World Health Organization

This is a report on women and health—both women's health needs and their contribution to the health of societies. Women's health has long been a concern for WHO, but today it has become an urgent priority. This report explains why. Using current data, it takes stock of what we know *now* about the health of women throughout their lives and across the different regions of the world.

Highlighting key issues—some of which are familiar, others that merit far greater attention—the report identifies opportunities for making more rapid progress. It points to areas in which better information—plus policy dialogue at national, regional, and international levels—could lead to more effective approaches. The report shows the relevance of the primary health-care reforms set out in *The World Health Report 2008: Primary Health Care—Now More than Ever*, laying particular emphasis on the urgent need for more coherent political and institutional leadership, visibility, and resources for women's health, to enable us to make progress in saving the lives and improving the health of girls and women in the coming years. Finally, it sets out what the implications are in terms of data collection, analysis, and dissemination.

The life-course approach taken in this report fosters a deeper understanding of how interventions in childhood, through adolescence, during the reproductive years, and beyond, affect health later in life and across the generations. It also highlights the interplay of biological and social determinants of women's health and draws attention to the role of gender inequality in increasing exposure and vulnerability to risk, limiting access to health care and information, and impacting on health outcomes. While the report calls for greater attention to health problems that affect only women—such as cervical cancer and the health risks associated with pregnancy and childbirth—it also shows that women's health needs go beyond sexual and reproductive concerns.

The report draws attention to the consequences and costs of failing to address health issues at the appropriate points of women's lives. In a world with an ageing population, the challenge is to prevent and manage the risk factors of today to ensure that they do not lead to the chronic health problems of tomorrow.

The life-course approach reveals the importance of women's multiple contributions to society—in both their productive and reproductive roles, as consumers and, just as importantly, as providers of health care. It is in recognition of this fact that the report calls for reforms to ensure that women become key agents in health-care provision—centrally involved in the design, management, and delivery of health services.

KEY FINDINGS

1. Widespread and Persistent Inequities

Disparities between women and men. While women and men share many similar health challenges, the differences are such that the health of women deserves particular attention. Women generally live longer than men because of both biological and behavioural advantages. But in some settings, notably in parts of Asia, these advantages are overridden by gender-based discrimination so that female life expectancy at birth is lower than or equal to that of males.

Moreover, women's longer lives are not necessarily healthy lives. There are conditions that only women experience and whose potentially negative impact only they suffer. Some of these—such as pregnancy and childbirth—are not diseases, but biological and social processes that carry health risks and require health care. Some health challenges affect both women and men but have a greater or different impact on women and so require responses that are tailored specifically to women's needs. Other conditions affect women and men more or less equally, but women face greater difficulties in getting the health care they need. Furthermore, gender-based inequalities—for example in education, income, and employment—limit the ability of girls and women to protect their health.

Differences between high- and low-income countries. While there are many commonalities in the health challenges facing women around the world, there are also striking differences due to the varied conditions in which they live. At every age, women in high-income countries live longer and are less likely to suffer from ill health and premature mortality than those in low-income countries. In richer countries, death rates for children and young women are very low, and most deaths occur after sixty years of age. In poorer countries, the picture is quite different: the population is on average younger, death rates among children are higher, and most female deaths occur among girls, adolescents, and younger adult women. The most striking difference between rich and poor countries is in maternal mortality—99 percent of the more than half a million maternal deaths every year happen in developing countries. Not surprisingly, the highest burden of morbidity and mortality—particularly in the reproductive years—is concentrated in the poorest and often the institutionally weakest countries, particularly those facing humanitarian crises.

Inequalities within countries. Within countries, the health of girls and women is critically affected by social and economic factors, such as access to education, household wealth, and place of residence. In almost all countries, girls and women living in wealthier households have lower levels of mortality and higher use of health-care services than those living in the poorest households. Such differences are not confined to developing countries but are found in the developed world.

2. Sexuality and Reproduction are Central to Women's Health

Women's health during the reproductive or fertile years (between the ages of fifteen and forty-nine years) is relevant not only to women themselves, but also has an impact on the health and development of the next generation. Many of the health challenges during this period are ones that only young girls and women face. For example, complications of pregnancy and childbirth are the leading cause of death in young women aged between fifteen and nineteen years old in developing countries. Globally, the leading cause of death among women of reproductive age is HIV/AIDS. Girls and women are particularly vulnerable to HIV infection due to a combination of biological factors and gender-based inequalities, particularly in cultures that limit women's knowledge about HIV and their ability to protect themselves and negotiate safer sex. The most important risk factors for death and disability in this age group in low- and middle-income countries are lack of contraception and unsafe sex. These result in unwanted pregnancies, unsafe abortions, complications of pregnancy and childbirth, and sexually transmitted infections including HIV. Violence is an additional significant risk to women's sexual and reproductive health and can also result in mental ill-health and other chronic health problems.

3. The Toll of Chronic Diseases, Injuries, and Mental Ill-health

While the sexual and reproductive health needs of women are generally well known, they also face other important health challenges.

Road traffic injuries are among the five leading causes of death for adolescent girls and women of reproductive age in all WHO regions—except for Southeast Asia, where burns are the third leading cause of death. While many are the result of cooking accidents, some are homicides or suicides, often associated with violence by an intimate partner. More research is needed to better understand the underlying causes of these deaths and to identify effective prevention strategies.

Suicide is among the leading causes of death for women between the ages of twenty and fifty-nine years globally and the second leading cause of death in the low- and middle-income countries of the WHO Western Pacific Region. Suicidal behaviour is a significant public health problem for girls and women worldwide. Mental health problems, particularly depression, are major causes of disability for women of all ages. While the causes of mental ill-health may vary from one individual to another, women's low status in society, their burden of work, and the violence they experience are all contributing factors.

For women over sixty years of age in low-, middle- and high-income countries, cardiovascular disease and stroke are major killers and causes of chronic health problems. Another significant cause of death and disability is chronic obstructive pulmonary disease, which has been linked to women's exposure to smoke and indoor air pollution, largely as a result of their household roles. For many women, ageing is accompanied by loss of vision—every year more than 2.5 million older women go blind. Much of this burden of disability could be avoided if they had access to the necessary care, particularly surgery for cataracts. In low-income countries, trachoma is a significant but preventable cause of blindness that affects women in particular.

4. A Fair Start for All Girls Is Critical for the Health of Women

Many of the health problems faced by adult women have their origins in childhood. Proper nutrition is a key determinant of health, both in childhood and beyond. The nutritional status of girls is particularly important due to their future potential reproductive role and the intergenerational repercussions of poor female nutrition. Preventing child abuse and neglect and ensuring a supportive environment in early childhood will help children to achieve optimal physical, social, and emotional development. These will also help avoid risky behaviours and a significant burden of disease, including mental health disorders and substance use later in life.

Changing behaviour now brings major health benefits later. It is essential to address the health and development needs of adolescents if they are to make a healthy transition to adulthood. Societies must tackle the factors that promote potentially harmful behaviours in relation to sex, tobacco and alcohol use, diet, and physical activity, as well as provide adolescents with the support they need to avoid these harmful behaviours. In many high-income countries, adolescent girls are increasingly using alcohol and tobacco, and obesity is on the rise. Supporting adolescents to establish healthy habits in adolescence will bring major health benefits later in life, including reduced mortality and disability due to cardiovascular diseases, stroke, and cancers.

Addressing the needs of older women will be a major challenge to health systems. Because they tend to live longer than men, women represent a growing proportion of all older people. Societies need to prepare now to prevent and manage the chronic health problems often associated with old age. Establishing healthy habits at younger ages can help women to live active and healthy lives until well into old age. Societies must also prepare for the costs associated with the care of older women. Many high-income countries currently direct large proportions of their social and health budgets to care for the elderly. In low-income settings, such care is often the responsibility of the family, usually of its female members. Policies are needed in relation to health financing, pension and tax reform, access to formal employment and associated pension and social protection, and to the provision of residential and community care.

5. Societies and Their Health Systems Are Failing Women

Health system shortfalls deprive women of health care. The reasons why health systems fail women are often complex and related to the biases they face in society. However, these shortfalls can be understood, and they can and should be challenged and changed. For example, women face higher health costs than men due to their greater use of health care, yet they are more likely than their male counterparts to be poor, unemployed, or else engaged in part-time work or work in the informal sector that offers no health benefits. One of the keys to improving women's health, therefore, is the removal of financial barriers to health care. For instance, where there are user fees for maternal health services, households pay a substantial proportion of the cost of facility-based services, and the expense of complicated deliveries is often catastrophic. Evidence from several countries shows that removing user fees for maternal health care, especially for deliveries, can both stimulate demand and lead to increased uptake of essential services. Removing financial barriers to care must be accompanied by efforts to ensure that health services are appropriate, acceptable, of high quality, and responsive to the needs of girls and women.

Health systems depend on women as providers of health care. Paradoxically, health systems are often unresponsive to the needs of women despite the fact that women themselves are major contributors to health through their roles as primary caregivers in the family and also as health-care providers in both the formal and informal health sectors. The backbone of the health system, women are nevertheless rarely represented in executive or management-level positions, tending to be concentrated in lower-paid jobs and exposed to greater occupational health risks. In their roles as informal health-care providers at home or the community, women are often unsupported, unrecognized, and unremunerated.

Societal failings damage women's health. Women's health is profoundly affected by the ways in which they are treated and the status they are given by society as a whole. Where women continue to be discriminated against or subjected to violence, their health suffers. Where they are excluded by law from the ownership of land or property or from the right to divorce, their social and physical vulnerability is increased. At its most extreme, social or cultural gender bias can lead to violent death or female infanticide. Even where progress is being made, there are reasons to keep pushing for more. While there has been much progress in girls' access to education for example, there is still a male–female gap when it comes to secondary education, access to employment, and equal pay. Meanwhile, the greater economic independence enjoyed by some women as a result of more widespread female employment may have benefits for health, but globally, women are less well protected in the workplace, both in terms of security and working conditions.

DEVELOPING A SHARED AGENDA FOR WOMEN'S HEALTH

In publishing this report WHO seeks to identify key areas for reform, both within the health sector and beyond. Primary health care, with its focus on equity, solidarity, and social justice, offers an opportunity to make a difference through policy action in the following four areas.

1. Building Strong Leadership and a Coherent Institutional Response

National and international responses to women's health issues tend to be fragmented and limited in scope. Identifying mechanisms to foster bold, participatory leadership around a clear and coherent agenda for action will be critical to making progress. The involvement and full participation of women and women's organizations is essential. The significant advances in women's health achieved in some countries indicate that it can be done. The interventions are known and the resources are attainable.

The Millennium Development Goals (MDGs) have been vitally important in maintaining a focus on development and in setting benchmarks in the face of many competing claims on the world's attention. The existence of a separate goal on maternal health draws attention to the lack of progress in this area, and has attracted both political and financial support for accelerating change. The addition of the target on universal access to reproductive health has helped broaden the scope of the goal. There is now a need to extend attention to the many other challenges to and determinants of women's health described in this report. In doing so, attention should be paid to ensuring gender equality and women's empowerment (MDG 3). The situation is complex due to the way women's issues are handled both within and between governments and international organizations, with multiple initiatives competing for resources. More collaboration is needed to develop supportive structures, incentives, and accountability mechanisms for improving women's health.

2. Making Health Systems Work for Women

The report highlights the need to strengthen health systems so that they are better geared to meet women's needs—in terms of access, comprehensiveness, and responsiveness. This is not just an issue in relation to sexual and reproductive health; it is relevant throughout the life-course. Progress in increasing access to the services that could make a difference to women's health is patchy and uneven. Some services, such as antenatal care, are more likely to be in place than others, such as those related to mental health, sexual violence, and cervical cancer screening and care. Abysmally low levels of coverage with basic interventions, such as immunization and skilled birth attendance, are found in several countries, and not only in those with humanitarian crises. Exclusion from health care of those in need, particularly the poor and vulnerable, is common, and the equity gap is increasing in many countries. Approaches to extending coverage must deal with the content of benefit packages and must include a greater range of services for girls and women of all ages. They must also address the issue of financial protection by moving away from user charges and promoting prepayment and pooling schemes.

3. Healthier Societies: Leveraging Changes in Public Policy

The report shows how social and economic determinants of health impact on women. Many of the main causes of women's morbidity and mortality—in both rich and poor countries—have their origins in societies' attitudes to women, which are reflected in the structures and systems that set policies, determine services, and create opportunities. While technical solutions can mitigate immediate consequences, sustainable progress will depend on more fundamental change. Public policies have the potential to influence exposure to risks, access to care, and the consequences of ill health in women and girls. The report provides examples of such policies—from targeted action to encourage girls to enrol in school and pursue their education (by ensuring a safe school environment and promoting later marriage), to measures to build "age-friendly" environments and increase opportunities for older women to contribute productively to society. Intersectoral collaboration is required to identify and promote actions outside the health sector that can enhance health outcomes for women. Broader strategies, such as poverty reduction, increased access to literacy, training, and education, and increased opportunities for women to participate in economic activities, will also contribute to making sustainable progress in women's health. Experience suggests that this requires a gender equality and rights-based approach that harnesses the energy of civil society and recognizes the need for political engagement.

4. Building the Knowledge Base and Monitoring Progress

The report highlights major gaps in knowledge that seriously limit what we can say with real authority about the health of women in different parts of the world. While much is known about women's health, many gaps remain in our understanding of the dimensions and nature of the special challenges they face and how these can be effectively addressed. We must also be able to measure progress—and we must do it now. The foundations of better information about women and health need to be strengthened, starting with civil registration systems that generate vital statistics—including cause of death by age and by sex—and collection and use of age- and sex-disaggregated data on common problems. These data are essential for programme planning and management, and without such systems, efforts to monitor changes in, for example, maternal mortality will remain thwarted. Research must systematically incorporate attention to sex and gender in design, analysis, and interpretation of findings. We must focus more attention on assessing progress in increasing coverage with key interventions, together with the tracking of relevant policies, health system performance measures, and equity patterns.

CONCLUSION

In reviewing the evidence and setting an agenda for the future, this report points the way towards the actions needed to better the health of girls and women around the world. The report aims to inform policy dialogue and stimulate action by countries, agencies, and development partners.

While this report highlights differences between women and men, it is not a report just about women and not a report just for women. Addressing women's health is a necessary and effective approach to strengthening health systems overall—action that will benefit everyone. Improving women's health matters to women, to their families, communities, and societies at large.

Improve women's health—improve the world.

Editors' Notes

The health, human rights, and protection of all humans is crucial. As stated in the physician's oath of the original Geneva Declaration by the World Medical Association (1948): "I will maintain the utmost respect for human life from the time of conception, even under threat, I will not use my medical knowledge contrary to the laws of humanity." This section of the Declaration, as currently amended, reads, "I will maintain the utmost respect for human life" (http://en.wikipedia.org/wiki/Declaration_of_Geneva).

Note also the need to safeguard all human life emphasized in the preambles of the Declaration of the Rights of the Child (1959) and and the Convention on the Rights of the Child (1989): "The child, by reason of his physical an mental immaturity, needs special safeguards and care, including appropriate legal protection, before as well as after birth." http://www.un.org/cyberschoolbus/humanrights/resources/child.asp http://www.ohchr.org/EN/ProfessionalInterest/Pages/CRC.aspx

For more information about the World Health Organization: http://www.who.int/.

Source

World Health Organization. 2009. *Women and health: Today's evidence, tomorrow's agenda.* Geneva: World Health Organization. Reprinted by permission. http://www.who.int/gender/women_health_report/en/.

Related Resources

Video: World Vision. "Strong Women, Strong World." World Vision. http://www.worldvision.org/m/display/remarketing/strongWomenStrongWorld.html?campaign=1134180.

ACT Alliance. 2012. Clapping with both hands: Promoting gender equality; 15 studies of good practice. ACT Alliance. http://www.actalliance.org/stories/resources/publications/AC_Gender_Good-Practice_Report_2012_A3.pdf/.

Kristof, N. and S. WuDunn. 2008. *Half the sky: Turning oppression into opportunity for women worldwide.* New York: Knopf Doubleday Publishing Group. http://www.halftheskymovement.org/.

United Nations. 2000. Millennium development goals. http://www.un.org/millenniumgoals/ (e.g., Improve maternal health (fact sheet), http://www.un.org/millenniumgoals/pdf/MDG_FS_5_EN_new.pdf).

United Nations Department of Economic and Social Affairs. 2009. 2009 world survey on the role of women in development: Women's control over economic resources and access to financial resources, including microfinance. New York: United Nations. http://www.un.org/womenwatch/daw/public/WorldSurvey2009.pdf.

United Nations Population Fund. 2010. Sexual and reproductive health for all: Reducing poverty, advancing development and protecting human rights. New York: Author. http://www.unfpa.org/webdav/site/global/shared/documents/publications/2010/uarh_report_2010.pdf.

UN Women. Commission on the Status of Women. http://www.un.org/womenwatch/daw/csw/.

World Vision. 2012. Strong women, strong world. World Vision. http://www.worldvision.org/resources.nsf/main/press-statements/$file/SWSW.pdf.

CHAPTER 21

Exploring Global Mental Health

A Global Map for a Global Movement

Kelly O'Donnell, Member Care Associates

> But the world is not so happy a place . . . Can we really offer justice
> and freedom from want to a mid-twenty-first-century earth of
> perhaps nine billion people, one-third of whom may live in squalor
> and desperation? . . . The only answer, as I can see it, is by trying
> . . . and not giving up. (Kennedy 2006, 289)

When was the last time you were lost—professionally? For me it was a few years ago. I was trying to better understand a vast, amorphous entity that has recently blossomed into a major social movement: the multisectoral and multidisciplinary field of *global mental health* (GMH). I wanted to explore this strategic health domain and its priority of improving and achieving equality in mental health for all people worldwide (Patel and Prince 2010).

I thought sorting out GMH would be pretty easy going, having lived and worked internationally as a consulting psychologist for nearly twenty-five years. But it reminded me of trying to grasp the multilayered reality in movies like *The Matrix*, *Syriana*, or *Inception*. It was as intriguing as it was daunting. And I was not alone in this mixed experience.

So I read, researched, attended conferences, listened to lectures, and met with some of GMH's remarkable movers and shakers. I figured that if I could at least identify *some* recent hallmarks and *some* major precursors, then I could begin to create a map of GMH. Eventually I developed this definition of GMH:

GMH is an international, interdisciplinary, and multisectoral domain which promotes human well-being, the right to health, and equity in health for all. It encourages healthy behaviors and lifestyles; is committed to preventing and treating mental, neurological, and substance use conditions; and seeks to improve policies and programs, professional practices and research, advocacy and awareness, and social and environmental factors that affect health and well-being.

RESOURCES FOR CONNECTING AND CONTRIBUTING

My GMH mapping project clearly revealed both encouraging progress and enormous challenges. One cannot help but be fascinated by the advances made by the World Health Organization (e.g., Inter-Agency Standing Committee 2007; World Health Organization 2008, 2010a, 2011). Also intriguing are the landmark human rights documents from the United Nations protecting those with mental disabilities (United Nations General Assembly 1991; United Nations General Assembly 2006); special journal issues on the status of GMH in the 2007 and 2011 *Lancet* series; conferences replete with GMH topics including the 2011 American Psychological Association Convention in Washington, DC (for example, see Office of International Affairs 2011), and both the World Mental Health Congress in 2011 and the International Congress of Psychology in 2012 convened in South Africa respectively by the World Federation for Mental Health and the International Union of Psychological Science; and influential events like the annual celebration of World Mental Health Day beginning in 1992, the annual mhGAP Forums beginning in 2009 in Geneva, and the 2009 and 2011 Movement for Global Mental Health Summits (Athens and Cape Town).

Nonetheless, one can quickly become overwhelmed by the enormity of mental health needs: 450 million humans having some type of mental, neurological, or substance use disorder (MNS), accounting for about 13 percent of the global burden of disease; an estimated 1.71 million additional mental health workers needed in the 144 low- to middle-income countries by 2015; and the ongoing disparities of resources, priorities, and policies regarding mental health (World Health Organization 2008, 2011; Collins et al. 2011). Permeating the disconcerting data is the need to bolster mental health globally in three areas: human and financial resources; informed political will and evidence-based action; and public awareness to prevent stigmatization and discrimination for those with MNS conditions (World Health Organization 2009a, 2010a).

I thus ended up developing and refining with the help of many colleagues a "global resource map" (O'Donnell 2012). It is a core *sampler* of GMH resources, a primer that addresses key historical highlights from the last two decades with emphasis on the past five years. Take careful note though that the map is shaped by its focus on materials in English; organizations in North America and Europe; public health, human rights, and psychology fields; evidence-based approaches; and the World Health Organization. However, the inclusion of cross-cultural and indigenous mental health materials helps provide international perspectives, approaches, and sources to do justice to the "global" realities of GMH.

TOURING THE TERRAIN: THE SIXTY-MINUTE GMHER

This next section launches us into GMH via a quick overview. The ten concise resources—written and multimedia—can be reviewed in about sixty minutes. This overview can also be a tool for group discussion about connecting and contributing to GMH. These ten resources are free and can be accessed via their URLs in the References section.

But one caveat bears repeating: it can be both inspiring and unsettling to journey into the heart of GMH and encounter the plight of millions of people with MNS conditions. Some we know courageously overcome their difficulties and lead productive lives via supportive communities and quality care (World Health Organization 2009a). Many others though live in misery, often marked with social isolation, discrimination, human rights abuses, and increased mortality (World Health Organization 2010a).

Resource 1.

These two quotes on human health and human rights are foundational and worth memorizing.

> Health is a state of complete physical, mental and social well-being and not merely the absence of disease or infirmity. Mental health is a state of well-being in which an individual realizes his or her own abilities, can cope with the normal stresses of life, can work productively and is able to make a contribution to his or her community. (World Health Organization 2010b)

All persons have the right to the best available mental health care, which shall be part of the health and social care system. All persons with a mental illness, or who are being treated as such persons, shall be treated with humanity and respect for the inherent dignity of the human person . . . Every person with a mental illness shall have the right to exercise all civil, political, economic, social and cultural rights. (United Nations General Assembly 1991)

Resource 2.

Take a five-minute tour of GMH by viewing the *WHO: Mental Health* video produced by the World Health Organization (2009b).

Resource 3.

Review the summary statistics about mental health from two fact sheets from the World Health Organization. The first is *Ten Facts on Mental Health* (2010d) and the second is *Mental Health: Strengthening Our Response* (2010b). These statistics are also worth remembering and form a solid epidemiological basis for scaling up GMH interventions. For example, about 20 percent of the world's children are estimated to have some form of mental disorder or problem; depression is the leading cause of disability worldwide; an average of 800,000 people commit suicide each year, with over 85 percent coming from low- and middle-income countries.

Resource 4.

Read the overview article in the *British Journal of Psychiatry*, "The Movement for Global Mental Health" (MGMH), by Patel et al. (2011). This article describes the formation and principles of the MGMH and concludes with a call for a "selfless moral struggle" in order to partner effectively together within the various GMH-related communities.

Resource 5.

Read the brief article in the July 2011 issue of *Nature*, "Grand Challenges in Global Mental Health," by Collins et al. The twenty-five top challenges are identified by over four hundred mental health professionals in sixty countries. The top five challenges (not in order) are: integrating mental health into primary health care, reducing the cost and improving the supply of medications, providing effective and affordable community-based health care and rehabilitation, improving children's access to evidence-based care by trained health providers in low-resource countries, and strengthening mental health training for all health-care personnel.

Resource 6.

Advocacy for scaling up mental health resources along with the rights of people who have MNS conditions is a major part of GMH. See the Joint Statement on Mental Health and the Scope of Noncommunicable Diseases prepared for the United Nations General Assembly's High-level Meeting in New York (19–20 September 2011) by the NGO Forum for Health (2011) in Geneva and the NGO Committee on Mental Health in New York, as well as the Cape Town Declaration (16 October 2011) by the Pan African Network of People with Psychosocial Disabilities (2011).

Resource 7.

There are hundreds of journalistic articles, interviews, and personal accounts of MNS conditions. Here is an encouraging example from Nepal in the *Kathmandu Post*: "An Uncharacteristic Happy Ending" by Jagannath Lamichhane (2011). Other stories and links are in the GMH Voices section at https://sites.google.com/site/gmhmap/.

Resource 8.

Another primary concern in GMH is the relationship between mental health and vulnerable groups in low- and middle-income countries (LMICs). See the Executive Summary (xxiv-xxviii) of the World Health Organization report on *Mental Health and Development: Targeting People with Mental Health Conditions as a Vulnerable Group* (2010a).

Resource 9.

The *mhGAP Intervention Guide for Mental, Neurological and Substance Use Disorders in Non-specialized Health Settings* (World Health Organization 2010c) provides evidence-based guidelines for assessing and treating nine priority conditions (depression, psychosis, epilepsy/seizures, developmental disorders, behavioral disorders, dementia, alcohol use disorders, drug use disorders, and self-harm/suicide). The *Guide* is especially oriented for those working in primary health-care settings, as these settings usually have substantial access to people with MNS conditions. For a quick overview, see the introductory materials on pp. 1–8.

Resource 10.

One of the *many* organizations that have inspired me during my research is the Banyan in Chennai, India (http://www.thebanyan.org/). The five-minute video on their website about their work with homeless women with mental disorders is an aesthetic and encouraging reminder of the reason for our GMH efforts—promoting well-being and improving the lives of fellow humans, many of whom are in dire need.

SUGGESTIONS FOR CONNECTING AND CONTRIBUTING TO GMH

> The capacity to cause change grows in an individual over time as small-scale efforts lead gradually to larger ones. But the process needs a beginning—a story, an example, an early taste of success—something along the way that helps a person form a belief that it is possible to make the world a better place. Those who act on such a belief spread it to others. They are highly contagious. Their stories must be told. (Bornstein 2004, 282)

Would more people consider GMH as a career, or as a significant part of one's career, if the path were clearer? Definitely. Is it possible for people to get a better idea about how to access GMH-related updates and core resources? Definitely. Could GMH perspectives/practices be included more as part of health-related training programs, professional conferences, collegial interactions, and work activities? Definitely. And above all, would the well-being of the most vulnerable people drastically improve, as a result of the greater integration of GMH into the lives and practices of health-care workers, policy makers, and government leaders? Definitely! Here now are five items to help people from a variety of backgrounds and levels of experience to further connect/contribute to GMH.

1. Find your GMH passion(s).

Review GMH via taking the time to explore several of the URLs and materials previously mentioned in this chapter. What are you already interested in or involved in, such as a specific disorder, population, language group, region, organization, network, issue, service, project, or media form? Stay current and focused in your GMH passion(s)—your global niche.

2. Stretch yourself.

Be prepared to expand your personal and professional GMH boundaries. Take some risks and keep growing in your GMH mindset and involvement. Be open to the ongoing exploration of lifestyle choices, values, and barriers in our own minds including fears and prejudices in light of GMH realities. Continue to explore and refine this global map as you connect and contribute to GMH.

3. Get involved.

Identify a few core newsletter updates and information places (websites) to which you want to regularly connect—GMH literacy. Join a GMH-related organization—join the Movement for Global Mental Health. There are GMH-related social networks, blogs, websites, and groups of which you can be part. Be part of World Mental Health Days in October. Introduce GMH-related items/topics into your setting. Conferences—yes! A part of a commitment to lifelong learning can be to take advantage of informal training available online.

4. Stay sane.

Maintain your work/life balance and avoid being overwhelmed with the expansive and almost multi-everything nature of GMH. Consider a GMH involvement continuum, with its two reference points, to help identify the degree (depth) to which you want to connect/contribute to a specific area: *informed* on one end and *immersed* on the other end.

5. Persevere.

It will take time and effort to find your flow in GMH. You may feel lost, unappreciated, or alone at times. This is certainly true of those who do GMH advocacy or pioneer new GMH areas. It's like learning a language—time, effort, and social contexts are needed to learn it well. Don't go alone but find a caravan of colleagues to help you on your journey. Keep going with GMH, in spite of obstacles.

RESOURCES FOR NICHE-WORKING AND NETWORKING

This section offers additional materials (written and multimedia sources) that reflect important aspects of GMH. The materials are organized into ten overlapping "niche-net" areas that can be quickly reviewed. The goal is for colleagues in the health fields to relevantly participate in GMH by identifying and considering opportunities in various GMH niches (niche-working) and networks (networking).

As mentioned earlier, trying to make inroads into GMH can be a challenging and lonely experience. This domain is behemoth, and it is easy to get lost or discouraged in the effort to meaningfully connect and contribute. In addition, not every colleague, organization, or graduate program is oriented towards global issues and global applications of mental health. In spite of our increasingly globalized world, there are many challenges that keep us focused on our own immediate, nearby "worlds." Making a living, paying off school loans, raising a family, keeping abreast of one's own field, or meeting the demands of a rigorous academic program can seriously affect living our lives as "global citizens."

Let me quickly balance the above comments with a far more influential, positive factor in light of having lived and worked internationally for twenty-five years as a consulting psychologist. During this time I have seen the increasing desire of mental health professionals and students around the world to be more meaningfully involved in international issues. Regardless of challenges, they want to use their training, passions, and resources to help make a positive difference in the quality of life for people. To support these growing aspirations, I recently set out on a collaborative project called GMH-Map to further orient people to GMH through publications, presentations, and web-based resources. The materials listed in this article are an example. Have a look at the ten *au courant* areas below to see what interests you. Do so with others! They can help us go further into our GMH "niche-working and networking."

Niche-net 1: Human Rights.

Here are quotes from two foundational instruments that describe the rights of all humans and those with disabilities, including mental conditions. The first is from the Universal Declaration of Human Rights (UDHR) (United Nations General Assembly 1948; currently in over 380 languages). The second is from the Convention on the Rights of Persons with Disabilities (CRPD) (United Nations General Assembly 2006; currently in six languages).

> All human beings are born free and equal in dignity and rights. They are endowed with reason and conscience and should act towards one another in a spirit of brotherhood. (UDHR, article 1)

> The purpose of the present Convention is to promote, protect and ensure the full and equal enjoyment of all human rights and fundamental freedoms by all persons with disabilities, and to promote respect for their inherent dignity. Persons with disabilities include those who have long-term physical, mental, intellectual or sensory impairments which in interaction with various barriers may hinder their full and effective participation in society on an equal basis with others. (CRPD, article 1)

Going further: See the website, United Nations Office of the High Commissioner for Human Rights (http://www.ohchr.org/), as well as the QualityRights Project by the World Health Organization (2012b; e.g., fact sheet and toolkit).

Niche-net 2: GMH Overview.

The World Health Organization has produced several educational videos which overview GMH facts and issues. *Mental Health* (2011) is a seven-minute video presenting general GMH information along with examples of mental health improvements in Jordan (http://www.youtube.com/watch?v=KBihf2R3Yzk&feature=related).

Going further: Watch the six-minute video interview about GMH in 2011 by the Global Health Institute at Duke University. It is an interview with Vikram Patel, who highlights the serious issues in GMH, shares strategies for reducing mental health gaps, and argues for the global prioritization of mental health (http://www.youtube.com/watch?v=ptnP-TWhKgY).

Niche-net 3: Updates.

The Movement for Global Mental Health (MGMH) is a premier network connecting the diversity of GMH colleagues. It was launched in 2008 and currently has nearly one hundred institutional members and over 1,800 individual members. The MGMH compiles regular newsletters with updates and information and offers various resources on its website. Have a look through the listed items/links on the home page to get a feel for what is happening in GMH (http://www.globalmentalhealth.org/).

Going further: Stay in touch via the newsletter updates from the WHO mhGAP Programme (http://www.who.int/mental_health/en/) and the news stories from the World Federation for Mental Health (http://www.wfmh.org/01NewsStories.htm#Global_Mental_Health_Information).

Niche-net 4: GMH Research.

The Lancet's special GMH issue (2011) has six articles summarizing research on mental health and poverty, child and adolescent mental health, mental health in humanitarian settings, scaling-up mental health services, human resources for mental health, and human rights. In addition see the special GMH issues of the *Harvard Review of Psychiatry* (Greenfield 2012) and International Health (March 2013).

Going further: Read the Executive Summary of the World Health Organization *Mental Health Atlas 2011* (2011, 10–11) on how mental health resources internationally continue to be "insufficient, inequitably distributed, and inefficiently utilized." There is also a seven-minute podcast interview/transcript about the findings.

Niche-net 5: Humanitarian and Developmental Assistance.

The *IASC Guidelines on Mental Health and Psychosocial Support in Emergency Settings* by the Inter-Agency Standing Committee (2007) is a landmark collaborative project worth reviewing and disseminating broadly. *Prioritizing Mental Health in Development Aid Programs* by the Global Initiative on Psychiatry (2010) is a six-page overview for "improving psychosocial and mental health care in transitional and developing countries."

Going further: Read the article "The Development and Maturation of Humanitarian Psychology" in the *American Psychologist* (Jacobs 2007). See also the Sphere Project's *Humanitarian Charter and Minimum Standards in Humanitarian Response* that includes mental health assistance in emergency and humanitarian settings (2011, 333–36).

Niche-net 6: Training.

The Centre for Global Mental Health (CGMH) in London has launched a Master of Science program in GMH in association with the London School of Hygiene and Tropical Medicine and the Institute of Psychiatry. Three other master's programs in GMH are at Glasgow University, the New University of Lisbon, and the Massachusetts School of Professional Psychology. See the training section on the GMH-Map website (https://sites.google.com/site/gmhmap).

Going further: More examples of training include the international mental health courses at the University of Melbourne's Centre for International Mental Health (http://cimh.unimelb.edu.au/) and GMH-related presentations at conferences such as the International Congress of Psychology (http://www.icp2012.com/). Noteworthy also are the GMH texts, edited by Eliot Sorel, *21ˢᵗ Century Global Mental Health* (2013), and edited by Richard Mollica, Global *Mental Health: Trauma and Recovery* (2011).

Niche-net 7: GMH Advocacy and Policy.

Two major developments in the global effort to promote mental health and reduce the treatment gap are the resolution on The Global Burden of Mental Disorders and the Need for a Comprehensive Coordinated Response from Health and Social Sectors at the Country Level (World Health Organisation 2012a, 2013), from which has stemmed the Development of a Global Mental Health Action Plan 2013–2020 (World Health Organization 2012a). These documents are especially oriented for member states (governments) yet call upon the active involvement of all stakeholders in civil society.

Going further: To get a better sense of the global issues and power structures that influence human health, see the summary and materials from the 2010 workshop on Democratizing Global Health Governance, organized by Global Health Watch and other international organizations (http://www.ghwatch.org/who-watch/ghg-launch).

Niche-net 8: Personal Stories.

Patient Voices is a special part of the Health section in the online *New York Times* with audio and photos of people discussing their experiences with chronic diseases and mental health conditions. Listen to the short personal accounts (http://www. nytimes.com/interactive/2009/09/10/health/Patient_Voices.html?ref=healthguide).

Going further: Have a look at the stories from around the world in the GMH Voices section of the GMH-Map website (https://sites.google.com/site/gmhmap/home/gmh-voices).

Niche-net 9: Resources for Practitioners and Consumers.

Psychological First Aid: Guide for Field Workers (World Health Organization et al. 2011) is an international effort to provide principles to help people support those affected by distressing events. Reading through the table of contents will give you a good idea of the approaches used, and looking over the three case scenarios at the end provides a good sense of how psychological first aid can be applied in natural disasters, violence, displacement, and accidents. See also the Universal Declaration of Ethical Principles for Psychologists (International Union of Psychological Science and International Association of Applied Psychology 2008), consisting of four broad principles and values related to each principle. The four principles are: respect for the dignity of persons and peoples, competent caring for the well-being of persons and peoples, integrity, and professional and scientific responsibility to society.

Going further: The National Institute of Mental Health is one of many organizations offering materials on mental health for the general public, including their four-minute video on major depression (symptoms, help, neuroscience research; http://www.nimh.nih.gov/health/index.shtml). Other examples based in the USA are Athealth (http://www.athealth.com/), National Empowerment Center (http://www.power2u.org/), and National Alliance on Mental Illness (http://www.nami.org/).

Niche-net 10: Media Matters.

Madness Radio has over 125 archived radio programs online for free. The programs are diverse both in the subject matter and the perspectives shared on mental health. One example: listen to the personal story and comments by Dr. Daniel Fischer, a psychiatrist who recovered from schizophrenia and who has been influential in the development of the consumer/survivor movement (aired 1 August 2011) (http://www.madnessradio.net/).

Going further: To explore the broader context for GMH involvement, watch a promotional video for the International Day of Peace on the homepage for the American Psychological Association's Division of Peace Psychology (http://www.peacepsych.org/) as well as the United Nations Year in Review from the United Nations News and Media (http://www.unmultimedia.org/tv/webcast/2011/12/un-year-in-review-2011.html).

STAYING THE COURSE IN GMH

I want to encourage all of us in the various health fields to take the time to explore the GMH domain. A great way to do this is by reviewing the materials in this chapter: to use the material as a GMH map for connecting and contributing and for niche-working and networking. GMH involvement is not always easy. Persevere as you seek to connect and contribute, knowing that GMH involvement is part of a lifelong journey that many mental health professionals around the world are undertaking together.

Seek to integrate GMH materials into training curriculum, coursework, and research at academic institutions; topical themes, presentations, and interest groups at conferences; your areas of professional practice; and above all, as part of a lifestyle that reflects commitments to equality, justice, and well-being for all.

Ultimately GMH is not about our own fulfilment but about the fulfilment of others. It is about resolutely rallying on behalf of vulnerable people and populations around the world, such as the estimated 450 million people currently struggling with MHS conditions, often exacerbated by stigma and discrimination, poverty and despair, and inadequate resources to help.

Through it all, diligently maintain your work/life balance as you stay the course in GMH. Celebrate life in spite of its hardships.

References

The Banyan. n.d. *The Banyan* (video). http://www.youtube.com/watch?v=THdLdJDc6go.

Bornstein, D. 2004. *How to change the world: Social entrepreneurs and the power of new ideas.* Oxford: Oxford University Press.

Collins, P. Y., V. Patel, S. S. Joestl, D. March, T. R. Insel, A. S. Daaar, I. Boirdin, E. J. Costello, M. Durkin, C. Fairburn, R. I. Glass, W. Hall, Y. Huang, S. E. Hyman, K. Jamison, S. Kaaya, S. Kapur, A. Kleinman, A. Ogunniyi, A. Otero-Ojeda, M. Poo, V. Ravindranath, B. J. Sahakian, S. Saxena, P. A. Singer, D. J. Stein, W. Anderson, M. A. Dhansay, W. Ewart, A. Phillips, S. Shurin, and M. Walport. 2011. Grand challenges in global mental health. *Nature* 475 (07 July): 27–30. doi:10.1038/475027a. Note: See also the additional research articles on the Grand Challenges in Global Mental Health, PLOS Medicine online journal: http://www.plosmedicine.org/article/info%3Adoi%2F10.1371%2Fjournal.pmed.1001434].

Global Initiative on Psychiatry. 2010. Prioritizing mental health in development aid programs: Improving psychosocial and mental health care in transitional and developing countries. Hilversum, the Netherlands: Global Initiative on Psychiatry. http://www.gip-global.org/.

Greenfield, S. F., ed. 2012. Global mental health. Special issue, *Harvard Review of Psychiatry* 20, no. 1 (January–February). http://informahealthcare.com/toc/hrp/20/1.

Inter-Agency Standing Committee. 2007. IASC guidelines on mental health and psychosocial support in emergency settings. Geneva: Inter-Agency Standing Committee. http://www.who.int/mental_health/emergencies/guidelines_iasc_mental_health_psychosocial_april_2008.pdf.

International Union of Psychological Science, and International Association of Applied Psychology. 2008. Universal declaration of ethical principles for psychologists. International Union of Psychological Science. http://www.am.org/iupsys/resources/ethics/univdecl2008.html.

Jacobs, G. A. 2007. The development and maturation of humanitarian psychology. *American Psychologist* 62, no. 8 (November): 932–41. doi:10.1037/0003-066X.62.8.932.

Kennedy, P. 2006. The *parliament of man: The past, present, and future of the United Nations.* New York: Vintage Books.

Lamichhane, J. 2011. An uncharacteristic happy ending. *Kathmandu Post*, 18 May. http://www.ekantipur.com/the-kathmandu-post/2011/05/18/oped/an-uncharacteristic-happy-ending/221860.html.

Lancet. 2007. Global mental health. *Lancet* 370, no. 9590 (08 September). http://www.thelancet.com/series/global-mental-health.

———. 2011. Global mental health. *Lancet* 378, no. 9801 (22 October). http://www.thelancet.com/series/global-mental-health-2011.

Mollica, R. ed. 2011. *Global mental health: Trauma and recovery: A companion guide for field and clinical care or traumatized people worldwide.* Cambridge, MA: Harvard Program in Refugee Trauma. http://www.lulu.com/shop/richard-f-mollica/textbook-of-global-mental-health-trauma-and-recovery-a-companion-guide-for-field-and-clinical-care-of-traumatized-people-worldwide/ebook/product-16599951.html.

NGO Forum for Health, and NGO Committee on Mental Health. 2011. Joint statement on mental health and the scope of noncommunicable diseases. http://www.apa.org/international/united-nations/noncommunicable-disease.pdf.

O'Donnell, K. 2012. Global mental health: A resource primer for exploring the domain. *International Perspectives in Psychology: Research, Practice, Consultation* 1, no. 3 (July): 191–205. doi:10.1037/a0029290.

Office of International Affairs. 2011. International program: Convention programs with an international focus and listing of international convention authors. Washington, DC: American Psychological Association.

Pan African Network of People with Psychosocial Disabilities. 2011. Cape Town declaration. Pan African Network of People with Psychosocial Disabilities. http://www.panusp.org/.

Patel, V., P. Collins, J. Copeland, R. Kakuma, S. Katontoka, J. Lamichanne, S. Naik, and S. Skeen. 2011. The movement for global mental health. *British Journal of Psychiatry* 198: 88–90. doi:10.1192/bjp.bp.109.074518.

Patel, V., and M. Prince. 2010. Global mental health: A new global health field comes of age. *Journal of the American Medical Association* 303, no. 19: 1976–77. doi:10.1001/jama.2010.616.

Sorel, E., ed. 2013. *21st century global mental health.* Burlington, MA: Jones and Bartlett Learning.

The Sphere Project. 2011. *Humanitarian charter and minimum standards in humanitarian response.* Geneva: The Sphere Project. http://www.sphereproject.org/handbook/.

United Nations General Assembly. 1948. Universal declaration of human rights. http://www.ohchr.org/EN/UDHR/Pages/SearchByLang.aspx.

———. 1991. Resolution 46/119. Principles for the protection of persons with mental illness and the improvement of mental health care. 17 December. http://www2.ohchr.org/english/law/principles.htm.

———. 2006. Convention on the rights of persons with disabilities. http://www.un.org/disabilities/convention/news.shtml.

World Health Organization. 2008. mhGAP: Mental Health Gap Action Programme: Scaling up care for mental, neurological, and substance use disorders. Geneva: World Health Organization. http://www.who.int/mental_health/mhgap_final_english.pdf.

———. 2009a. Improving health systems and services for mental health. Geneva: World Health Organization. http://www.who.int/mental_health/policy/services/mhsystems/en/index.html.

———. 2009b. "WHO: Mental Health." (video) http://www.youtube.com/watch?v=L8iRjEOH41c.

———. 2010a. Mental health and development: Targeting people with mental health conditions as a vulnerable group. Geneva: World Health Organization. http://www.who.int/mental_health/policy/mhtargeting/en/index.html.

———. 2010b. Mental health: Strengthening our response. Fact sheet 220. http://www.who.int/mediacentre/factsheets/fs220/en/index.html.

————. 2010c. mhGAP Intervention guide for mental, neurological and substance use disorders in non-specialized health settings. Geneva: World Health Organization. http://www.who.int/mental_health/evidence/mhGAP_intervention_guide/en/index.html.

————. 2010d. 10 facts on mental health. World Health Organization. http://www.who.int/features/factfiles/mental_health/mental_health_facts/en/index.html.

————. 2011. Mental health atlas 2011. Geneva: World Health Organization. http://www.who.int/mental_health/publications/mental_health_atlas_2011/en/index.html.

————. 2012a. Development of a global mental health action plan 2013–2020. World Health Organization. http://www.who.int/mental_health/mhgap/consultation_global_mh_action_plan_2013_2020/en/index.html.

————. 2012b. QualityRights project. World Health Organization. http://www.who.int/mental_health/policy/quality_rights/en/.

————. 2012c. The global burden of mental disorders and the need for a comprehensive, coordinated response from health and social sectors at the country level. World Health Organization. http://www.who.int/mental_health/WHA65.4_resolution.pdf.

————. 2013. Comprehensive Mental Health Action Plan 2013-2020. Geneva: World Health Organisation. http://www.who.int/mental_health/en/.

————, War Trauma Foundation, and World Vision International. 2011. *Psychological first aid: Guide for field workers.* Geneva: World Health Organization. http://whqlibdoc.who.int/publications/2011/9789241548205_eng.pdf.

————, and World Organization of Family Doctors. 2008. Integrating mental health into primary care: A Global perspective. Geneva: World Health Organization. http://www.who.int/mental_health/policy/services/mentalhealthintoprimarycare/en/index.html.

Editors' Notes

For perspectives and resources related to "mental health *as* mission" (mhM) see the Resource Update, September 2012, archived at http://www.membercareassociates.org. Here are some of the summary thoughts in this Update on the relevance of mental health for mission and vice versa.

"mhM extends member care's core emphasis of well-being/effectiveness for mission/aid workers and embodies the joint efforts to serve humanity via supportive resources in the mental health sciences/disciplines. **It involves increasing mhM awareness and skills . . .** One of the main applications of mhM is to further equip/support mission/aid workers who themselves are helping people/communities in areas like domestic violence, depression, substance abuse, traumatic stress, and emergency settings. Another application involves trained member care workers and health workers who provide and develop direct services for people/communities needing mental health and psychosocial support."

For more information about Member Care Associates: http://membercareassociates.org/.

Sources

O'Donnell, K. 2011. Global mental health: A resource map for connecting and contributing. *Psychology International* 22, no. 2 (July): 4–6. http://www.apa.org/international/pi/2011/07/global-health.aspx.

———. 2012a. Global mental health: Finding your niches and networks. *Psychology International* 23, no. 1 (March): 10–12. http://www.apa.org/international/pi/2012/03/global-health.aspx.

———. 2012b. Global mental health: A resource primer for exploring the domain. *International Perspectives in Psychology: Research, Practice, Consultation* 1, no. 3 (July): 191–205. doi:10.1037/a0029290.

All three of the source articles for this chapter are part of a collaborative project to research, organize, and share important GMH resources, including the GMH-Map website: https://sites.google.com/site/gmhmap/.

Related Resource

Videos: Centre for Global Mental Health (see the materials at the GMH Media Resources section). http://www.centreforglobalmentalhealth.org/global-mental-health-video-resources.

Collins, P., Insel, T., Chockalingan, A., Daar, A., & Maddox, Y. Grand challenges in global mental health: Integration in research, policy, and practice. *PLoS Medicine* 10(4): e1001434. doi:10.1371/journal.pmed.1001434 http://www.plosmedicine.org/article/info%3Adoi%2F10.1371%2Fjournal.pmed.1001434.

CHAPTER 22

Mental Health and Vulnerable Groups

MENTAL HEALTH AND DEVELOPMENT: TARGETING PEOPLE WITH MENTAL HEALTH CONDITIONS AS A VULNERABLE GROUP

World Health Organization

EXECUTIVE SUMMARY

This report presents compelling evidence that people with mental health conditions meet major criteria for vulnerability. The report also describes how vulnerability can lead to poor mental health, and how mental health conditions are widespread yet largely unaddressed among groups identified as vulnerable. It argues that mental health should be included in sectoral and broader development strategies and plans, and that development stakeholders have important roles to play in ensuring that people with mental health conditions are recognized as a vulnerable group and are not excluded from development opportunities. The recommended actions in this report provide a starting point to achieve these aims.

KEY MESSAGES OF THIS REPORT

- People with mental health conditions meet criteria for vulnerability.
- Because they are vulnerable, people with mental health conditions merit targeting by development strategies and plans.
- Different development stakeholders have important roles to play in designing and implementing policies and programmes for reaching people with mental health conditions, and in mainstreaming mental

health interventions into sectoral and broader national development
strategies and plans.
- Development programmes and their associated policies should protect
the human rights of people with mental health conditions and build
their capacity to participate in public affairs.
- The recommended actions in this report provide a starting point to
achieve these aims.

Introduction

Despite their vulnerability, people with mental health conditions—including schizophrenia, bipolar disorder, depression, epilepsy, alcohol and drug use disorders, child and adolescent mental health problems, and intellectual impairments—have been largely overlooked as a target of development work. This is despite the high prevalence of mental health conditions, their economic impact on families and communities, and the associated stigmatization, discrimination, and exclusion. The need for development efforts to target people with mental health conditions is further reinforced by the United Nations Convention on the Rights of Persons with Disabilities (CRPD), which requires the mainstreaming of disability issues into strategies for sustainable development.

Two development paradigms—the need to improve aid effectiveness and the use of a human rights approach—should be taken into consideration when reviewing actions that can be taken to ensure people with mental health conditions are included in development programmes.

The emphasis on improving aid effectiveness is changing the way development stakeholders are working: towards a greater focus on country-owned, sectoral, and broader national development planning, and increased harmonization and alignment among stakeholders on issues such as funding mechanisms. The increased emphasis on country-owned planning has highlighted the need for effective partnerships, for inclusive decision-making processes, and for a strong civil society to voice its issues and concerns. Never before has civil society had such an opportunity to directly influence national planning processes; full advantage must be taken of this development.

The human rights-based approach to development recognizes the protection and promotion of human rights as an explicit development objective. This approach, coupled with the CRPD, places a duty on countries to ensure that the rights of people with mental health conditions are protected, and that development efforts are inclusive of and accessible to people with disabilities.

People with Mental Health Conditions Comprise a Vulnerable Group

People with mental health conditions meet the major criteria for vulnerability as identified by an analysis of major development stakeholders' projects and publications. They are subjected to stigma and discrimination on a daily basis, and they experience extremely high rates of physical and sexual victimization. Frequently, people with mental health conditions encounter restrictions in the exercise of their political and civil rights, and in their ability to participate in public affairs. They also are restricted in their ability to access essential health and social care, including emergency relief services. Most people with mental health conditions face disproportionate barriers in attending school and finding employment. As a result of all these factors, people with mental health conditions are much more likely to experience disability and die prematurely, compared with the general population.

Other Vulnerable Groups Have High Rates of Mental Health Conditions

Looking at the situation from a different perspective, vulnerability can lead to poor mental health. Stigma and marginalization generate poor self-esteem, low self-confidence, reduced motivation, and less hope for the future. In addition, stigma and marginalization result in isolation, which is an important risk factor for future mental health conditions. Exposure to violence and abuse can cause serious mental health problems, including depression, anxiety, psychosomatic complaints, and substance use disorders. Similarly, mental health is impacted detrimentally when civil, cultural, economic, political, and social rights are infringed, or when people are excluded from income-generating opportunities or education. Addressing mental health problems in vulnerable groups more generally can facilitate development outcomes, including improved participation in economic, social, and civic activities.

Improving Development Outcomes: Principles and Actions

A number of principles and actions developed from best practices and consistent with the CRPD, if integrated into national development and sectoral strategies and plans, could substantially improve the lives of people with mental health conditions and thus improve development outcomes for these individuals, their families, and their communities.

As a starting point, people with mental health conditions must be recognized by development stakeholders as a vulnerable group and consulted in all issues affecting them. Targeted policies, strategies, and interventions for reaching people with mental health conditions should be developed, and mental health interventions should be mainstreamed into broader poverty reduction and development work. To make implementation a reality, adequate funds must be dedicated to mental health interventions and mainstreaming efforts, and recipients of development aid should be encouraged to address the needs of people with mental health conditions as part of their development work. At country level, people with mental health conditions should be sought and supported to participate in development opportunities in their communities.

A number of different actions can be taken at country level to improve the development outcomes of people with mental health conditions. Mental health services are cost effective and affordable, and should be provided in primary care settings and mainstreamed within general health services. At a broader level, mental health issues should be integrated in countries' health policies, implementation plans, and human resource development, as well as recognized as an important issue to consider in global and multisectoral efforts such as the International Health Partnership, the Global Health Workforce Alliance, and the Health Metrics Network. Other actions that can be taken at country level include the (re)construction of community-based mental health services (during and after emergencies), which can serve populations long beyond the immediate aftermath of an emergency situation. Strong links should be developed between mental health services, housing, and other social services, because mental health conditions often coexist with a number of other problems such as homelessness. Access to educational opportunities also is essential to improving the lives of people with mental health conditions. Development stakeholders have key roles in encouraging countries to enable access to educational opportunities, as well as supporting early childhood programmes that have been proven effective for vulnerable groups. Because mental health conditions are associated with high rates of unemployment, people with these conditions should be included in income-generating programmes. Grants and support for small business operations have demonstrated benefits, not only for people with mental health conditions, but also for their families and communities. It is also essential for development stakeholders to focus on improving human rights protection for people with mental health conditions, thereby creating enabling environments. Finally, building the capacity of people with mental health conditions will enable them to participate fully in public affairs.

All Development Stakeholders Have Important Roles to Play

Development stakeholders have important roles to play in facilitating the implementation of the principles and actions recommended in this report. Contributions by development stakeholders occur at the different levels of policy, planning, implementation, and funding of services at country level, as well as in advocacy of mental health priorities nationally and globally. One role common to all development stakeholders is promoting the implementation of the CRPD.

Civil society can play an important role in supporting people with mental health conditions to access needed resources and to integrate fully into the community through direct service provision and advocacy. Services provided by civil society can include health care, social services, education programmes, and livelihood (income-generation) projects. In addition, civil society can advocate to government and funders for the need to recognize and support people with mental health conditions.

Among all development stakeholders, governments have the most important role to play in creating enabling environments, reducing stigma and discrimination, promoting human rights, and improving the quality and quantity of services (education, health, social services, and poverty alleviation). In addition, they have a duty to implement commitments such as the Accra Agenda for Action, the CRPD, and other human rights conventions. In order to improve development outcomes, different parts of government need not only to integrate mental health in their own sector but also to work collaboratively with other parts of government and civil society. Like civil society, government can provide support to create and strengthen mental health service user groups, and offer opportunities for these groups to express their views and participate in decision making.

Academic and research institutions can help improve development outcomes by generating and synthesizing policy-relevant research findings, as well as by building capacity to conduct and interpret research at local levels. Research, when properly formulated and implemented, can inform the planning and implementation of development programmes, and the allocation of scarce human and financial resources. In addition to building and managing knowledge, academic and research institutions have a key role to play in building the capacity of policymakers, planners, and service providers from different sectors.

Bilateral agencies and international funding organizations, as key development partners of governments and civil society, can advocate for a range of mental health issues: recognition of people with mental health conditions as a vulnerable group, inclusion of mental health issues into development instruments, integration of mental health interventions into primary care, mainstreaming of mental health issues into other sectors such as education and social services, identification of people with mental health conditions as important recipients of poverty alleviation interventions, and legal and regulatory reform to protect the human rights of people with mental health conditions. They also can improve development outcomes by increasing outreach to and consultation with people with mental health conditions, supporting the establishment and development of service user groups, and funding these groups to participate in public affairs and advocacy work. In addition they have a very important role to play in ensuring that financial resources in the area of mental health are provided where this has been identified as a gap.

As a result of their diversity, UN and other multilateral organizations can play many different roles in improving development outcomes. At the global level, they have an important advocacy function to place mental health higher on the agenda and ensure that adequate funding is allocated. At the country level, they can encourage member states to ratify the CRPD, and support them in its implementation. UN reform at global and national levels requires the integration of work plans and budgets among agencies (e.g., UN Development Assistance Framework), which can facilitate the prioritization of this vulnerable group. Multilaterals are also well placed to advocate for mental health to be included into national and sectoral policies and plans, and identify where and how coordination among sectors can be improved through the roles they play with regards to national planning. These include reinforcing government capacity to prepare, develop, and review national development strategies, plans, budgets, and aid negotiations, and participating in the coordination of sector and other broad mechanisms for country support.

Improving development outcomes for vulnerable groups is an important stated priority of development programmes. All development stakeholders have the responsibility to ensure that people with mental health conditions, as a vulnerable group, are provided with the opportunity to improve their living conditions and lead fulfiling lives within their communities.

EDITORS' NOTES

For more information about the World Health Organization, Department of Mental Health and Substance Abuse: http://www.who.int/mental_health/en/.

SOURCE

World Health Organization. 2010. Mental health and development: Targeting people with mental health conditions as a vulnerable group, xxiv-xxviii. Geneva: World Health Organization. Reprinted by permission. http://www.who.int/mental_health/policy/mhtargeting/en/index.html.

RELATED RESOURCES

Video: The Banyan. *The Banyan* (about the work of the Banyan in Chennai, India). YouTube video, 4:26. http://www.youtube.com/watch?v=THdLdJDc6go.

Global Initiative on Psychiatry. 2010. Prioritizing mental health in development aid programs: Improving psychosocial and mental health care in transitional and developing countries. Hilversum, the Netherlands: Global Initiative on Psychiatry. http://www.gip-global.org/.

Hieber, L. 2001. Lifeline media: Reaching populations in crisis; A guide to developing media projects in conflict situations. Geneva: Media Action International. http://www.preventionweb.net/files/636_10303.pdf.

Hill, M., H. Hill, R. Bagge, and P. Miersma. 2005. *Healing the wounds of trauma: How the church can help.* Nairobi: Paulines Publications.

Public Library of Science (PLoS) Medicine. 2009. Packages of care for mental, neurological, and substance use disorders in low- and middle-income countries. Movement for Global Health. http://www.globalmentalhealth.org/news_events/news/plos-medicine-launched-new-series-reviews.

United Nations General Assembly. 1991. Resolution 46/119. Principles for the protection of persons with mental illness and the improvement of mental health care. 17 December. http://www2.ohchr.org/english/law/principles.htm.

———. 2006. Convention on the rights of persons with disabilities. http://www.un.org/disabilities/convention/news.shtml.

World Health Organization. 2012a. Risks to mental health: An overview of vulnerabilities and risk factors. Geneva: World Health Organization. http://www.who.int/mental_health/mhgap/risks_to_mental_health_EN_27_08_12.pdf.

———. 2012b. WHO quality rights tool kit: Assessing and improving quality and human rights in mental health and social care facilities. Geneva: World Health Organization. http://www.who.int/mental_health/policy/quality_rights/en/.

World Health Organization. 2013. *Building back better: Sustainable mental health care after emergencies.* Geneva, Author. http://www.who.int/mental_health/emergencies/building_back_better/en/index.html.

Mental Health and Psychosocial Support in Emergency Settings

IASC GUIDELINES ON MENTAL HEALTH AND PSYCHOSOCIAL SUPPORT IN EMERGENCY SETTINGS

Inter-Agency Standing Committee

Armed conflicts and natural disasters cause significant psychological and social suffering to affected populations. The psychological and social impacts of emergencies may be acute in the short term, but they can also undermine the long-term mental health and psychosocial well-being of the affected population. These impacts may threaten peace, human rights, and development. One of the priorities in emergencies is thus to protect and improve people's mental health and psychosocial well-being.

Achieving this priority requires coordinated action among all government and nongovernment humanitarian actors. A significant gap, however, has been the absence of a multisectoral, interagency framework that enables effective coordination, identifies useful practices and flags potentially harmful practices, and clarifies how different approaches to mental health and psychosocial support complement one another. This document aims to fill that gap.

These guidelines reflect the insights of practitioners from different geographic regions, disciplines, and sectors, and reflect an emerging consensus on good practice among practitioners. The core idea behind them is that, in the early phase of an emergency, social supports are essential to protect and support mental health and psychosocial well-being. In addition, the guidelines recommend selected psychological and psychiatric interventions for specific problems.

The composite term "mental health and psychosocial support" is used in this document to describe any type of local or outside support that aims to protect or promote psychosocial well-being and/or prevent or treat mental disorder. Although the terms *mental health* and *psychosocial support* are closely related and overlap, for many aid workers they reflect different, yet complementary, approaches.

Aid agencies outside the health sector tend to speak of *supporting psychosocial well-being*. Health-sector agencies tend to speak of mental health, yet historically have also used the terms *psychosocial rehabilitation* and *psychosocial treatment* to describe nonbiological interventions for people with mental disorders. Exact definitions of these terms vary between and within aid organisations, disciplines, and countries. As the current document covers intersectoral, inter-agency guidelines, the composite term *mental health and psychosocial support* (MHPSS) serves to unite as broad a group of actors as possible and underscores the need for diverse, complementary approaches in providing appropriate supports.

Scientific evidence regarding the mental health and psychosocial supports that prove most effective in emergency settings is still thin. Most research in this area has been conducted months or years after the end of the acute emergency phase. As this emerging field develops, the research base will grow, as will the base of practitioners' field experience. To incorporate emerging insights, this publication should be updated periodically.

MENTAL HEALTH AND PSYCHOSOCIAL IMPACT OF EMERGENCIES

Problems

Emergencies create a wide range of problems experienced at the individual, family, community, and societal levels. At every level, emergencies erode normally protective supports, increase the risks of diverse problems, and tend to amplify preexisting problems of social injustice and inequality. For example, natural disasters such as floods typically have a disproportionate impact on poor people, who may be living in relatively dangerous places.

Mental health and psychosocial problems in emergencies are highly interconnected, yet may be predominantly social or psychological in nature. Significant problems of a predominantly social nature include

- preexisting (preemergency) social problems (e.g., extreme poverty, belonging to a group that is discriminated against or marginalised, political oppression),
- emergency-induced social problems (e.g., family separation; disruption of social networks; destruction of community structures, resources, and trust; increased gender-based violence), and

- humanitarian aid-induced social problems (e.g., undermining of community structures or traditional support mechanisms).

Similarly, problems of a predominantly psychological nature include

- preexisting problems (e.g., severe mental disorder, alcohol abuse),
- emergency-induced problems (e.g., grief; nonpathological distress; depression; and anxiety disorders, including post-traumatic stress disorder (PTSD)), and
- humanitarian aid-related problems (e.g., anxiety due to a lack of information about food distribution).

Thus mental health and psychosocial problems in emergencies encompass far more than the experience of PTSD.

People at Increased Risk of Problems

In emergencies, not everyone has or develops significant psychological problems. Many people show resilience; that is, the ability to cope relatively well in situations of adversity. There are numerous interacting social, psychological, and biological factors that influence whether people develop psychological problems or exhibit resilience in the face of adversity.

Depending on the emergency context, particular groups of people are at increased risk of experiencing social and/or psychological problems. Although many key forms of support should be available to the emergency-affected population in general, good programming specifically includes the provision of relevant supports to the people at greatest risk, who need to be identified for each specific crisis.

All subgroups of a population can potentially be at risk, depending on the nature of the crisis. The following are groups of people who frequently have been shown to be at increased risk of various problems in diverse emergencies:

- women (e.g., pregnant women, mothers, single mothers, widows and, in some cultures, unmarried adult women and teenage girls)
- men (e.g., excombatants; idle men who have lost the means to take care of their families; young men at risk of detention, abduction, or being targets of violence)
- children (from newborn infants to young people eighteen years of age), such as separated or unaccompanied children (including

orphans), children recruited or used by armed forces or groups, trafficked children, children in conflict with the law, children engaged in dangerous labour, children who live or work on the streets, and undernourished/understimulated children

- elderly people (especially when they have lost family members who were caregivers)
- extremely poor people
- refugees, internally displaced persons (IDPs), and migrants in irregular situations (especially trafficked women and children without identification papers)
- people who have been exposed to extremely stressful events/trauma (e.g., people who have lost close family members or their entire livelihoods, rape and torture survivors, witnesses of atrocities, etc.)
- people in the community with preexisting, severe physical, neurological, or mental disabilities or disorders
- people in institutions (orphans, elderly people, people with neurological/mental disabilities or disorders)
- people experiencing severe social stigma (e.g., untouchables/Dalits, commercial sex workers, people with severe mental disorders, survivors of sexual violence)
- people at specific risk of human rights violations (e.g., political activists, ethnic or linguistic minorities, people in institutions or detention, people already exposed to human rights violations)

It is important to recognise that:

- There is large diversity of risks, problems, and resources within and across each of the groups mentioned above.
- Some individuals within an at-risk group may fare relatively well.
- Some groups (e.g., combatants) may be simultaneously at increased risk of some problems (e.g., substance abuse) and at reduced risk of other problems (e.g., starvation).
- Some groups may be at risk in one emergency, while being relatively privileged in another emergency.
- Where one group is at risk, other groups are often at risk as well (The Sphere Project 2004).

To identify people as "at risk" is not to suggest that they are passive victims. Although at-risk people need support, they often have capacities and social networks that enable them to contribute to their families and to be active in social, religious, and political life.

RESOURCES

Affected groups have assets or resources that support mental health and psychosocial well-being. The nature and extent of the resources available and accessible may vary with age, gender, the sociocultural context, and the emergency environment. A common error in work on mental health and psychosocial well-being is to ignore these resources and to focus solely on deficits—the weaknesses, suffering, and pathology—of the affected group.

Affected individuals have resources such as skills in problem solving, communication, negotiation, and earning a living. Examples of potentially supportive social resources include families, local government officers, community leaders, traditional healers (in many societies), community health workers, teachers, women's groups, youth clubs, and community planning groups, among many others. Affected communities may have economic resources such as savings, land, crops, and animals; educational resources such as schools and teachers; and health resources such as health posts and staff. Significant religious and spiritual resources include religious leaders, local healers, practices of prayer and worship, and cultural practices such as burial rites.

To plan an appropriate emergency response, it is important to know the nature of local resources, whether they are helpful or harmful, and the extent to which affected people can access them. Indeed some local practices—ranging from particular traditional cultural practices to care in many existing custodial institutions—may be harmful and may violate human rights principles.

THE GUIDELINES

Purpose of These Guidelines

The primary purpose of these guidelines is to enable humanitarian actors and communities to plan, establish, and coordinate a set of minimum multisectoral responses to protect and improve people's mental health and psychosocial well-being in the midst of an emergency. The focus of the guidelines is on implementing minimum responses, which are essential, high-priority responses that should be implemented as soon as possible in an emergency. Minimum responses are the first things that ought to be done; they are the essential first steps that lay the foundation for the more comprehensive efforts that may be needed (including during the stabilised phase and early reconstruction).

To complement the focus on minimum response, the guidelines also list concrete strategies for mental health and psychosocial support to be considered mainly before and after the acute emergency phase. These "before" (emergency preparedness) and "after" (comprehensive response) steps establish a context for the minimum response and emphasise that the minimum response is only the starting point for more comprehensive supports.

Although the guidelines have been written for low- and middle-income countries (where Inter-Agency Standing Committee (IASC) member agencies tend to work), the overall framework and many parts of the guidelines apply also to large-scale emergencies in high-income countries.

TARGET AUDIENCE

These guidelines were designed for use by all humanitarian actors, including community-based organisations, government authorities, United Nations organisations, nongovernment organisations (NGOs), and donors operating in emergency settings at local, national, and international levels.

The orientation of these guidelines is not towards individual agencies or projects. Implementation of the guidelines requires extensive collaboration among various humanitarian actors: no single community or agency is expected to have the capacity to implement all necessary minimum responses in the midst of an emergency.

The guidelines should be accessible to all humanitarian actors to organise collaboratively the necessary supports. Of particular importance is the active involvement at every stage of communities and local authorities, whose participation is essential for successful, coordinated action, the enhancement of local capacities, and sustainability. To maximise the engagement of local actors, the guidelines should be translated into the relevant local language(s).

These guidelines are not intended solely for mental health and psychosocial workers. Numerous action sheets in the guidelines outline social supports relevant to the core humanitarian domains, such as disaster management, human rights, protection, general health, education, water and sanitation, food security and nutrition, shelter, camp management, community development, and mass communication. Mental health professionals seldom work in these domains, but are encouraged to use this document to advocate with communities and colleagues from other disciplines to ensure that appropriate action is taken to address the social risk factors that affect mental health and psychosocial well-being. However, the clinical and specialised forms of psychological or psychiatric supports indicated in the guidelines should only be implemented under the leadership of mental health professionals.

CORE PRINCIPLES

1. Human Rights and Equity

Humanitarian actors should promote the human rights of all affected persons and protect individuals and groups who are at heightened risk of human rights violations. Humanitarian actors should also promote equity and nondiscrimination. That is, they should aim to *maximise fairness* in the availability and accessibility of mental health and psychosocial supports among affected populations, across gender, age groups, language groups, ethnic groups, and localities, according to identified needs.

2. Participation

Humanitarian action should maximise the participation of local, affected populations in the humanitarian response. In most emergency situations, significant numbers of people exhibit sufficient resilience to participate in relief and reconstruction efforts. Many key mental health and psychosocial supports come from affected communities themselves rather than from outside agencies. Affected communities include both displaced and host populations and typically consist of multiple groups, which may compete with one another. Participation should enable different subgroups of local people to retain or resume control over decisions that affect their lives, and to build the sense of local ownership that is important for achieving programme quality, equity, and sustainability. From the earliest phase of an emergency, local people should be involved to the greatest extent possible in the assessment, design, implementation, monitoring, and evaluation of assistance.

3. Do No Harm

Humanitarian aid is an important means of helping people affected by emergencies, but aid can also cause unintentional harm (Anderson 1999). Work on mental health and psychosocial support has the potential to cause harm because it deals with highly sensitive issues. Also, this work lacks the extensive scientific evidence that is available for some other disciplines. Humanitarian actors may reduce the risk of harm in various ways, such as

- participating in coordination groups to learn from others and to minimise duplication and gaps in response;
- designing interventions on the basis of sufficient information;
- committing to evaluation, openness to scrutiny, and external review;
- developing cultural sensitivity and competence in the areas in which they intervene/work;
- staying updated on the evidence base regarding effective practices; and
- developing an understanding of, and consistently reflecting on, universal human rights, power relations between outsiders and emergency-affected people, and the value of participatory approaches.

4. Building on Available Resources and Capacities

As described above, all affected groups have assets or resources that support mental health and psychosocial well-being. A key principle—even in the early stages of an emergency—is building local capacities, supporting self-help, and strengthening the resources already present. Externally driven and implemented programmes often lead to inappropriate MHPSS and frequently have limited sustainability. Where possible, it is important to build both government and civil society capacities. At each layer of the pyramid (see fig. 4), key tasks are to identify, mobilise, and strengthen the skills and capacities of individuals, families, communities, and society.

5. Integrated Support Systems

Activities and programming should be integrated as far as possible. The proliferation of stand-alone services, such as those dealing only with rape survivors or only with people with a specific diagnosis, such as PTSD, can create a highly fragmented care system. Activities that are integrated into wider systems (e.g., existing community support mechanisms, formal/nonformal school systems, general health services, general mental health services, social services, etc.) tend to reach more people, often are more sustainable, and tend to carry less stigma.

6. Multilayered Supports

In emergencies people are affected in different ways and require different kinds of supports. A key to organising mental health and psychosocial support is to develop a layered system of complementary supports that meets the needs of different groups. This may be illustrated by a pyramid (see fig. 1). All layers of the pyramid are important and should ideally be implemented concurrently.

i. Basic services and security.

The well-being of all people should be protected through the (re)establishment of security, adequate governance, and services that address basic physical needs (food, shelter, water, basic health care, control of communicable diseases). In most emergencies, specialists in sectors such as food, health, and shelter provide basic services. An MHPSS response to the need for basic services and security may include: advocating that these services are put in place with responsible actors, documenting their impact on mental health and psychosocial well-being, and influencing humanitarian actors to deliver them in a way that promotes mental health and psychosocial well-being. These basic services should be established in participatory, safe, and socially appropriate ways that protect local people's dignity, strengthen local social supports, and mobilise community networks.

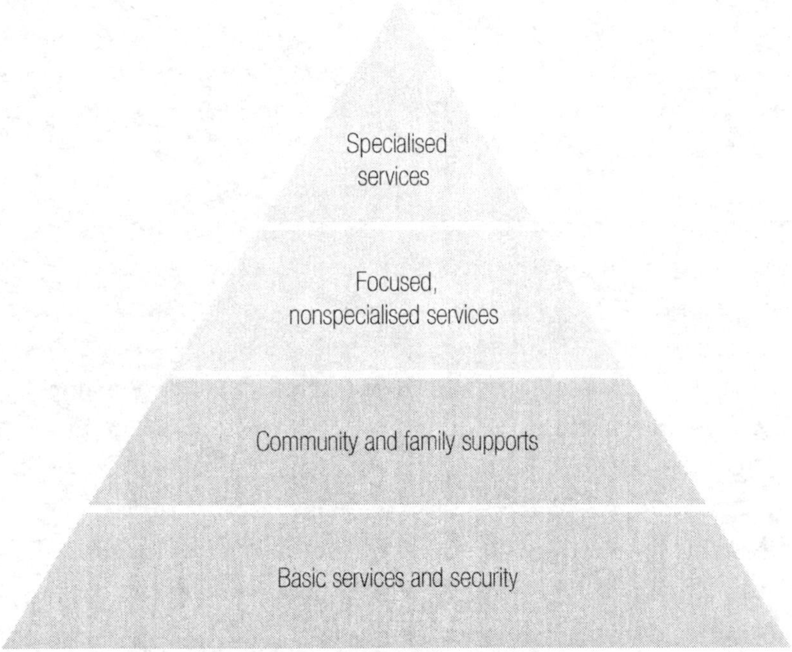

Figure 1
Intervention pyramid for mental health and psychosocial support in emergencies

ii. Community and family supports.

The second layer represents the emergency response for a smaller number of people who are able to maintain their mental health and psychosocial well-being if they receive help in accessing key community and family supports. In most emergencies, there are significant disruptions of family and community networks due to loss, displacement, family separation, community fears, and distrust. Moreover, even when family and community networks remain intact, people in emergencies will benefit from help in accessing greater community and family supports. Useful responses in this layer include family tracing and reunification, assisted mourning and communal healing ceremonies, mass communication on constructive coping methods, supportive parenting programmes, formal and nonformal educational activities, livelihood activities, and the activation of social networks, such as through women's groups and youth clubs.

iii. Focused, nonspecialised supports.

The third layer represents the supports necessary for the still smaller number of people who additionally require more focused individual, family, or group interventions by trained and supervised workers (but who may not have had years of training in specialised care). For example, survivors of gender-based violence might need a mixture of emotional and livelihood support from community workers. This layer also includes psychological first aid (PFA) and basic mental health care by primary health-care workers.

iv. Specialised services.

The top layer of the pyramid represents the additional support required for the small percentage of the population whose suffering, despite the supports already mentioned, is intolerable and who may have significant difficulties in basic daily functioning. This assistance should include psychological or psychiatric supports for people with severe mental disorders whenever their needs exceed the capacities of existing primary/general health services. Such problems require either (a) referral to specialised services if they exist, or (b) initiation of longer-term training and supervision of primary/general health-care providers. Although specialised services are needed only for a small percentage of the population, in most large emergencies this group amounts to thousands of individuals.

The uniqueness of each emergency and the diversity of cultures and sociohistorical contexts makes it challenging to identify universal prescriptions of good practice. Nevertheless, experience from many different emergencies indicates that some actions are advisable, whereas others should typically be avoided. These are identified below as "Do's" and "Don'ts" respectively:

DO'S	DON'TS
Establish one overall coordination group on mental health and psychosocial support.	Do not create separate groups on mental health or on psychosocial support that do not talk or coordinate with one another.
Support a coordinated response, participating in coordination meetings and adding value by complementing the work of others.	Do not work in isolation or without thinking how one's own work fits with that of others.
Collect and analyse information to determine whether a response is needed and, if so, what kind of response.	Do not conduct duplicate assessments or accept preliminary data in an uncritical manner.
Tailor assessment tools to the local context.	Do not use assessment tools not validated in the local, emergency-affected context.
Recognise that people are affected by emergencies in different ways. More resilient people may function well, whereas others may be severely affected and may need specialised supports.	Do not assume that everyone in an emergency is traumatised, or that people who appear resilient need no support.
Ask questions in the local language(s) and in a safe, supportive manner that respects confidentiality.	Do not duplicate assessments or ask very distressing questions without providing follow-up support.
Pay attention to gender differences.	Do not assume that emergencies affect men and women (or boys and girls) in exactly the same way, or that programmes designed for men will be of equal help or accessibility for women.
Check references in recruiting staff and volunteers and build the capacity of new personnel from the local and/or affected community.	Do not use recruiting practices that severely weaken existing local structures.

DO'S	DON'TS
After trainings on mental health and psycho-social support, provide follow-up supervision and monitoring to ensure that interventions are implemented correctly.	Do not use one-time, stand-alone trainings or very short trainings without follow-up if preparing people to perform complex psychological interventions.
Facilitate the development of community owned, managed, and run programmes.	Do not use a charity model that treats people in the community mainly as beneficiaries of services.
Build local capacities, supporting self-help and strengthening the resources already present in affected groups.	Do not organise supports that undermine or ignore local responsibilities and capacities.
Learn about and, where appropriate, use lo-cal cultural practices to support local people.	Do not assume that all local cultural practices are helpful or that all local people are sup-portive of particular practices.
Use methods from outside the culture where it is appropriate to do so.	Do not assume that methods from abroad are necessarily better or impose them on local people in ways that marginalise local sup-portive practices and beliefs.
Build government capacities and integrate mental health care for emergency survivors in general health services and, if available, in community mental health services.	Do not create parallel mental health services for specific subpopulations.
Organise access to a range of supports, including psychological first aid, to people in acute distress after exposure to an extreme stressor.	Do not provide one-off, single-session psychological debriefing for people in the general population as an early intervention after exposure to conflict or natural disaster.

DO'S	DON'TS
Train and supervise primary/general health-care workers in good prescription practices and in basic psychological support.	Do not provide psychotropic medication or psychological support without training and supervision.
Use generic medications that are on the essential drug list of the country.	Do not introduce new, branded medications in contexts where such medications are not widely used.
Establish effective systems for referring and supporting severely affected people.	Do not establish screening for people with mental disorders without having in place appropriate and accessible services to care for identified persons.
Develop locally appropriate care solutions for people at risk of being institutionalised.	Do not institutionalise people (unless an institution is temporarily an indisputable last resort for basic care and protection).
Use agency communication officers to promote two-way communication with the affected population as well as with the outside world.	Do not use agency communication officers to communicate only with the outside world.
Use channels such as the media to provide accurate information that reduces stress and enables people to access humanitarian services.	Do not create or show media images that sensationalise people's suffering or put people at risk.
Seek to integrate psychosocial considerations as relevant into all sectors of humanitarian assistance.	Do not focus solely on clinical activities in the absence of a multisectoral response.

REFERENCES

Anderson, M. (1999). *Do No Harm: How aid can support peace – or war*. Boulder, CO: Lynne Rienner.

IASC. (2003). Guidelines for HIV/AIDS Interventions in Emergency Settings. Geneva: IASC. http://www.humanitarianinfo.org/iasc/content/products/docs/FinalGuidelines-17Nov2003.pdf.

IASC. (2005). Guidelines on Gender-Based Violence Interventions in Humanitarian Settings. Geneva: IASC.http://www.humanitarianinfo.org/iasc/content/products/docs/tfgender_GBVGuidelines2005.pdf.

Sphere Project (2004). Humanitarian Charter and Minimum Standards in Disaster Response.

Geneva: Sphere Project. http://www.sphereproject.org/handbook/.

EDITORS' NOTES

For more information about the Inter-Agency Standing Committee: http://www.humanitarianinfo.org/iasc/pageloader.aspx.

SOURCE

Inter-Agency Standing Committee. 2007. IASC guidelines on mental health and psychosocial support in emergency settings. Geneva: Inter-Agency Standing Committee, 1–15. Reprinted by permission. http://www.who.int/mental_health/emergencies/guidelines_iasc_mental_health_psychosocial_april_2008.pdf.

RELATED RESOURCES

Video: National Geographic. "Hope in Hell." National Geographic. http://ngm.nationalgeographic.com/ngm/0512/sights_n_sounds/index.html.

AlertNet (resources, news, and video features). http://www.trust.org/alertnet/.

Carroll, C., and E. Girardet. 2005. Hope in hell: When disasters strike nations and aid agencies rally to help. *National Geographic*. http://ngm.nationalgeographic.com/2005/12/hope-in-hell/girardet-text.

Inter-Agency Standing Committee. 2010. IASC guidelines for mental health and psychosocial support in emergency setting: What should humanitarian health actors know. Geneva: Inter-Agency Standing Committee. http://www.who.int/mental_health/emergencies/en/.

International Federation of Red Cross and Red Crescent Societies. 2001. Psychological support: Best practices from Red Cross and Red Crescent programmes. Geneva: International Federation of Red Cross and Red Crescent Societies. http://helid.digicollection.org/en/d/Js2902e/.

————. 2012. World disasters report 2011: Focus on hunger and malnutrition. Geneva: International Federation of Red Cross and Red Crescent Societies. http://www.ifrc.org/publications-and-reports/world-disasters-report/.

International Federation Reference Centre for Psychosocial Support, and International Federation of Red Cross and Red Crescent Societies. 2009. Community-based psychosocial support: Trainer's book; A training kit. Copenhagen, Denmark: International Federation of Red Cross and Red Crescent Societies Reference Centre for Psychosocial Support. http://psp.drk.dk/sw40688.asp.

Jacobs, G. 2007. The development and maturation of humanitarian psychology. *American Psychologist* 62: 932–41.

Marsella, A., J. Johnson, P. Watson, and J. Gryczynski, eds. 2008. *Ethnocultural perspectives on disasters and trauma.* New York: Springer.

Mental Health and Psychosocial Support Network. http://mhpss.net/.

United Nations Children's Fund. 2011. Inter-agency guide to the evaluation of psychosocial programming in humanitarian crises. New York: Author. http://mhpss.net/wp-content/uploads/group-documents/67/1323249691-InteragencyPSSEvaluationGuidefinal.pdf.

United Nations High Commissioner for Refugees. 2013. *UNHCR's mental health and psychosocial support for persons of concern.* Geneva, Switzerland: Author. http://www.unhcr.org/51bec3359.html.

United Nations Office for the Coordination of Humanitarian Affairs (OCHA). OCHA in 2012 and 2013: Plan and budget. Geneva: United Nations. http://ochanet.unocha.org/p/Documents/OCHA_in_2012_13.pdf.

World Health Organization and United Nations High Commissioner for Refugees. 2012. Assessing mental health and psychosocial needs and resources: Toolkit for humanitarian settings. Geneva, Switzerland: Authors. http://www.who.int/mental_health/resources/toolkit_mh_emergencies/en/index.html.

World Health Organization. Mental health and psychosocial support in emergencies (resources). http://www.who.int/mental_health/emergencies/en/.

CHAPTER 24

Psychological First Aid

PSYCHOLOGICAL FIRST AID: GUIDE FOR FIELD WORKERS

World Health Organization, War Trauma Foundation, and World Vision International

When terrible things happen in our communities, countries, and the world, we want to reach out a helping hand to those who are affected. This guide covers *psychological first aid* (PFA), which involves humane, supportive, and practical help to fellow human beings suffering serious crisis events. It is written for people in a position to help others who have experienced an extremely distressing event. It gives a framework for supporting people in ways that respect their dignity, culture, and abilities. Despite its name, psychological first aid covers both social and psychological support.

Perhaps you are called upon as a staff member or volunteer to help in a major disaster, or you find yourself at the scene of an accident where people are hurt. Perhaps you are a teacher or health worker talking with someone from your community who has just witnessed the violent death of a loved one. This guide will help you to know the most supportive things to say and do for people who are very distressed. It will also give you information on how to approach a new situation safely for yourself and others, and not to cause harm by your actions.

Psychological first aid has been recommended by many international and national expert groups, including the Inter-Agency Standing Committee (IASC) and the Sphere Project. Psychological first aid is an alternative to psychological debriefing. In 2009 the World Health Organization's (WHO) mhGAP Guidelines Development Group evaluated the evidence for psychological first aid and psychological debriefing. They concluded that psychological first aid, rather than psychological debriefing, should be offered to people in severe distress after being recently exposed to a traumatic event.

This guide was developed in order to have widely agreed-upon psychological first-aid materials for use in low- and middle-income countries. The information we have given here is a model only. You will need to adapt it appropriately to the local context and the culture of the people you will help. This guide—endorsed by many international agencies—reflects the emerging science and international consensus on how to support people in the immediate aftermath of extremely stressful events.

UNDERSTANDING PFA (CHAPTER 1)

How Do Crisis Events Affect People?

Different kinds of distressing events happen in the world, such as war, natural disasters, accidents, fires, and interpersonal violence (for example, sexual violence). Individuals, families, or entire communities may be affected. People may lose their homes or loved ones, be separated from family and community, or may witness violence, destruction, or death.

Although everyone is affected in some way by these events, there are a wide range of reactions and feelings each person can have. Many people may feel overwhelmed, confused, or very uncertain about what is happening. They can feel very fearful or anxious, or numb and detached. Some people may have mild reactions, whereas others may have more severe reactions. How someone reacts depends on many factors, including:

- the nature and severity of the event(s) they experience,
- their experience with previous distressing events,
- the support they have in their life from others,
- their physical health,
- their personal and family history of mental health problems,
- their cultural background and traditions, and
- their age (for example, children of different age groups react differently).

Every person has strengths and abilities to help them cope with life challenges. However, some people are particularly vulnerable in a crisis situation and may need extra help. This includes people who may be at risk or need additional support because of their age (children, elderly), because they have a mental or physical disability, or because they belong to groups who may be marginalized or targeted for violence. Section 3.5 [of this source] provides guidance for helping vulnerable people.

WHAT IS PFA?

According to the Sphere Project (2011) and the Inter-Agency Standing Committee (2007), PFA describes a humane, supportive response to a fellow human being who is suffering and who may need support. PFA involves the following themes:

- providing practical care and support which does not intrude
- assessing needs and concerns
- helping people to address basic needs (for example, food, water, information)
- listening to people, but not pressuring them to talk
- comforting people and helping them to feel calm
- helping people connect to information, services, and social supports
- protecting people from further harm

It is also important to understand what PFA is not:
- It is not something that only professionals can do.
- It is not professional counseling.
- It is not "psychological debriefing,"[69] in that PFA does not necessarily involve a detailed discussion of the event that caused the distress.
- It is not asking someone to analyse what happened to them or to put time and events in order.
- Although PFA involves being available to listen to people's stories, it is not about pressuring people to tell you their feelings and reactions to an event.

PFA is an alternative to "psychological debriefing," which has been found to be ineffective. In contrast, PFA involves factors that seem to be most helpful to people's long-term recovery (according to various studies and the consensus of many crisis helpers[70]). These include

---

69   The World Health Organization (2010) and the Sphere Project (2011) describe psychological debriefing as promoting ventilation by asking a person to briefly but systematically recount their perceptions, thoughts, and emotional reactions during a recent stressful event. This intervention is not recommended. This is distinct from routine operational debriefing of aid workers used by some organizations at the end of a mission or work task.

70   See Hobfoll et al. (2007) and Bisson and Lewis (2009).

- feeling safe, connected to others, calm, and hopeful;
- having access to social, physical, and emotional support; and
- feeling able to help themselves as individuals and communities.

PFA : Who, When, and Where?

Who is PFA for?

PFA is for distressed people who have been recently exposed to a serious crisis event. You can provide help to both children and adults. However, not everyone who experiences a crisis event will need or want PFA. Do not force help on people who do not want it, but make yourself easily available to those who may want support.

There may be situations when someone needs much more advanced support than PFA alone. Know your limits and get help from others, such as medical personnel (if available), your colleagues, or other people in the area—local authorities or community and religious leaders. In the following box we have listed people who need more immediate advanced support. People in these situations need medical or other help as a priority to save life.

People who need more immediate advanced support:

- people with serious, life-threatening injuries who need emergency medical care
- people who are so upset that they cannot care for themselves or their children
- people who may hurt themselves
- people who may hurt others

When is PFA provided?

Although people may need access to help and support for a long time after an event, PFA is aimed at helping people who have been very recently affected by a crisis event. You can provide PFA when you first have contact with very distressed people. This is usually during or immediately after an event. However, it may sometimes be days or weeks after, depending on how long the event lasted and how severe it was.

Where is PFA provided?

You can offer PFA wherever it is safe enough for you to do so. This is often in community settings, such as at the scene of an accident; or places where distressed people are served, such as health centres, shelters or camps, schools, and distribution sites for food or other types of help. Ideally, try to provide PFA where you can have some privacy to talk with the person when appropriate. For people who have been exposed to certain types of crisis events, such as sexual violence, privacy is essential for confidentiality and to respect the person's dignity.

HOW TO HELP RESPONSIBLY (CHAPTER 2)

Respect Safety, Dignity, and Rights

When you take on the responsibility to help in situations where people have been affected by a distressing event, it is important to act in ways that respect the safety, dignity, and rights of the people you are helping. The following principles apply to any person or agency involved in humanitarian response, including those who provide PFA.

RESPECT PEOPLE'S . . .

Safety

- Avoid putting people at further risk of harm as a result of your actions.
- Make sure, to the best of your ability, that the adults and children you help are safe, and protect them from physical or psychological harm.

Dignity

- Treat people with respect and according to their cultural and social norms.

Rights

- Make sure people can access help fairly and without discrimination.
- Help people to claim their rights and access available support.
- Act only in the best interest of any person you encounter.

Keep these principles in mind in all of your actions and with all people you encounter, whatever their age, gender, or ethnic background. Consider what these principles mean in terms of your cultural context. Know and follow your agency codes of conduct at all times if you work or volunteer for an agency that has these codes.

We offer the following Ethical Do's and Don'ts as guidance to avoid causing further harm to the person, to provide the best care possible, and to act only in their best interest.

DO'S	DON'TS
Be honest and trustworthy.	Don't exploit your relationship as a helper.
Respect people's right to make their own decisions.	Don't ask the person for any money or favour for helping them.
Be aware of and set aside your own biases and prejudices.	Don't make false promises or give false information.
Make it clear to people that even if they refuse help now, they can still access help in the future.	Don't exaggerate your skills.
Respect privacy and keep the person's story confidential, if this is appropriate.	Don't force help on people, and don't be intrusive or pushy.
Behave appropriately by considering the person's culture, age, and gender.	Don't pressure people to tell you their story.
	Don't share the person's story with others.
	Don't judge the person for their actions or feelings.

ADAPT WHAT YOU DO TO TAKE ACCOUNT OF THE PERSON'S CULTURE

Consider the following questions as you prepare to offer PFA in different cultures:

Dress
- Do I need to dress a certain way to be respectful?
- Will impacted people be in need of certain clothing items to keep their dignity and customs?

Language
- What is the customary way of greeting people in this culture?
- What language do they speak?

Gender, Age, and Power
- Should affected women only be approached by women helpers?
- Who may I approach? (In other words, the head of the family or community?)

Touching and Behaviour
- What are the usual customs around touching people?
- Is it all right to hold someone's hand or touch their shoulder?
- Are there special things to consider in terms of behaviour around the elderly, children, women, or others?

Beliefs and Religion
- Who are the different ethnic and religious groups among the affected people?
- What beliefs or practices are important to the people affected?
- How might they understand or explain what has happened?

Whenever there is a crisis event, there are often people of various cultural backgrounds among the affected population, including minorities or others who may be marginalized. Culture determines how we relate to people, and what is all right and not all right to say and do. For example, in some cultures it is not customary for a person to share feelings with someone outside their family. Or it may only be appropriate for women to speak with other women, or perhaps certain ways of dressing or covering oneself are very important.

You may find yourself working with people of backgrounds different from your own. As a helper, it is important to be aware of your own cultural background and beliefs so you can set aside your own biases. Offer help in ways that are most appropriate and comfortable to the people you are supporting.

Each crisis situation is unique. Adapt this guide to the context, considering local social and cultural norms. See the following box for questions you can consider in providing PFA in different cultures.

BE AWARE OF OTHER EMERGENCY RESPONSE MEASURES

PFA is part of a broader response to large humanitarian emergencies (Inter-Agency Standing Committee 2007). When hundreds or thousands of people are affected, different types of emergency response measures take place, such as search-and-rescue operations, emergency health care, shelter, food distribution, and family tracing and child protection activities.

Often it is challenging for aid workers and volunteers to know exactly what services are available where. This is true during mass disasters and in places which do not already have a functioning infrastructure for health and other services.

Try to be aware of what services and supports may be available so you can share information with people you are helping and tell them how to access practical help.

Whenever possible in responding to a crisis situation:

- follow the direction of relevant authorities managing the crisis;
- learn what emergency responses are being organized and what resources are available to help people, if any;
- don't get in the way of search-and-rescue or emergency medical personnel; and
- know your role and the limits of your role.

It is not necessary to have a "psychosocial" background in order to offer PFA. However, if you want to help in crisis settings, we recommend that you work through an organization or community group. If you act on your own, you may put yourself at risk, it may have a negative effect on coordination efforts, and you are unlikely to be able to link affected people with the resources and support they need.

Look After Yourself

Helping responsibly also means taking care of your own health and well-being. As a helper, you may be affected by what you experience in a crisis situation, or you or your family may be directly affected by the event. It is important to pay extra attention to your own well-being and be sure that you are physically and emotionally able to help others. Take care of yourself so that you can best care for others. If working in a team, be aware of the well-being of your fellow helpers as well. (See chapter 4 [of this source] for more on caring for caregivers.)

Practise What You Have Learned (chapter 5)

The following case scenarios are examples of crisis events you may deal with in your role as a helper. As you read these scenarios, imagine:

- What would you need most urgently if something like this happened to you?
- What would you find most helpful?

Keep in mind the PFA action principles of look, listen, and link as you imagine how you would respond to people in each scenario. We have included some important questions to help you think through what to consider and ways to respond.

Case Scenario 1: Natural Disaster

You hear that a large earthquake has suddenly hit the centre of the city in the middle of the working day. Many people have been affected and buildings have fallen. You and your colleagues felt the shaking, but are okay. The extent of the damage is unclear. The agency you work for has asked you and your colleagues to help survivors, and to support any severely affected people you encounter.

As you prepare to help, ask yourself the following questions:

- Am I ready to help? What personal concerns might be important?
- What information do I have about the crisis situation?
- Will I travel alone or together with colleagues? Why or why not?

Things to consider:

- When going to help in a crisis situation—particularly immediately after a mass disaster—consider the advantages of working in a team or in pairs.
- Working in teams will help you to have support and back-up in difficult situations and is important for your safety. You can also be more effective in a team. For example, one person can stay with someone who is distressed while the other person can focus on finding special help such as medical care, if needed. If possible, try to have a "buddy system" where you and a fellow helper can check in with each other for support and help.
- Some agencies may be able to give you support, such as supplies, transportation, communication equipment, updated information about the situation or security issues, and coordination with other team members or services.

As you move about the city, what should you look for?

- Is it safe enough to be at the crisis site?
- What services and supports are available?
- Are there people with obvious, urgent basic needs?
- Are there people with obvious, serious emotional reactions?
- Who may likely be in need of special help?
- Where can I provide PFA?

As you approach people, how can you best listen to their concerns and give comfort?

- What basic needs may affected people have?
- How will I identify and introduce myself to offer support?
- What does it mean in this situation to help keep affected people safe from harm?
- How will I ask people about their needs and concerns?
- How can I best support and comfort affected people?

Sample Conversation with a Distressed Adult

In this conversation, you have come to a woman standing outside the rubble of a fallen building. She is crying and shaking, although she does not appear to be physically injured.

You: Hello, my name is __. I'm working with the agency __. May I talk with you?

Woman: It's terrible! I was going into the building when it started shaking! I don't understand what's happening!

You: Yes, it was an earthquake, and I can imagine it was terrible for you. What is your name?

Woman: I'm Jasmina—Jasmina Salem. I'm very scared! *[shaking, crying]* I wonder if I should go in there and try to find my colleagues? I don't know if they're all right!

You: Ms. Salem, it's not safe at all to go in the building now, you may get hurt. If you like, we can talk just over there where the area is safer and I can sit with you for a while. Would you like that?

Woman: Yes, please. [You move to a quieter place a short distance away from the scene of the fallen building where rescue and medical people are working.]

You: Can I get you some water? [If available, offer practical comfort like water or a blanket.]

Woman: I just want to sit here a moment.

[You sit quietly near the woman in silence for two to three minutes, until she begins to speak again.]

Woman: I feel terrible! I should have stayed in the building to help people!

You: I can understand that.

Woman: I ran outside. But I feel so badly for the other people!

You: It's difficult to know what to do in a situation like this. But it sounds as though you acted on good instincts when you ran from the building, or you might have been injured.

Woman: I saw them take a body out of the rubble. I think it was my friend! *[crying]*

You: I'm so sorry. There is a rescue team working, and we will find out later how the people are who were in the building. [The conversation continues for another ten minutes with you listening to the woman's story and asking for her needs and concerns. The conversation wraps up as follows:]

Woman: I need to find out if my family is all right, but I lost my phone when the shaking started, and I don't know how to get home.

You: I can help you call your family, and then we can figure out together how you can get to them.

Woman: Thank you. That would help a lot.

In this sample conversation, notice that you

- introduced yourself by name and told the person the agency you work for;
- asked the person if they would like to talk;
- addressed the person by their name, respectfully using the last name;
- protected the distressed person from further harm by moving to a safer place;
- offered the distressed person some comfort (for example, some water);
- listened and stayed near the person, without forcing them to talk;
- reflected back to the person ways they had acted appropriately;
- took the time to listen;
- identified the person's needs and concerns;
- acknowledged the person's worry over the possible loss of colleagues;
- offered to help connect the person with their family members.

What can you do to link people with information and practical support?

- What challenges might there be in this situation to finding out about available resources (food, shelter, water) or services for affected people?
- What worries and concerns may be on people's minds? What practical suggestions could I give to help them address their problems?
- What information will affected people want? Where will I find updated and reliable information about the crisis event?
- What can I do to connect people with their loved ones or services? What challenges might there be? What may children and adolescents or people with health conditions need? How can I help link vulnerable people with loved ones and services?

References

Bisson, J. I., and C. Lewis. 2009. Systematic review of psychological first aid. Commissioned by the World Health Organization. http://mhpss.net/wp-content/uploads/group-documents/178/1350270188-PFASystematicReviewBissonCatrin.pdf?9d7bd4.

Hobfoll, S. E., P. Watson, C. C. Bell, R. A. Bryant, M. J. Brymer, M. J. Friedman, M. Friedman, B. P. Gersons, J. T. de Jong, C. M. Layne, S. Maguen, Y. Neria, A. E. Norwood, R. S. Pynoos, D. Reissman, J. I. Ruzek, A. Y. Shalev, Z. Solomon, A. M. Steinberg, and R. J. Ursano. 2007. Five essential elements of immediate and mid-term mass trauma intervention: Empirical evidence. *Psychiatry* 70, no. 4: 283–315.

Inter-Agency Standing Committee. 2007. IASC guidelines on mental health and psychosocial support in emergency settings. Geneva: Inter-Agency Standing Committee. http://www.who.int/mental_health/emergencies/guidelines_iasc_mental_health_psychosocial_april 2008.pdf

The Sphere Project. 2011. Humanitarian charter and minimum standards in humanitarian response. Geneva: The Sphere Project. http://www.sphereproject.org/.

World Health Organization. 2010. mhGAP intervention guide for mental, neurological and substance use disorders in non-specialized health settings. Geneva: World Health Organization. http://www.who.int/mental_health/mhgap.

Editors' Notes

For more information on the World Health Organization (Department of Mental Health and Substance Abuse), War Trauma Foundation, and World Vision International: http://www.who.int/mental_health/en/, http://www.wartrauma.nl/en/, and http://www.wvi.org/.

Source

World Health Organization, World Vision International, and War Trauma Foundation. 2011. Psychological first aid: Guide for field workers, ii, 2–12, 42–46. Geneva: World Health Organization. Reprinted by permission. http://whqlibdoc.who.int/publications/2011/9789241548205_eng.pdf.

Related Resource

Chicago Department of Public Health. 2012. *Psychological first aid basics*. http://www.youtube.com/watch?v=kFe1pFJEO3E.

Also see the listing for chapter 23.

CHAPTER 25

Culturally Competent Care in Mental Health

CRITICAL ISSUES FOR MENTAL HEALTH PROFESSIONALS

WORKING WITH ETHNOCULTURALLY DIVERSE POPULATIONS

Anthony Marsella, Professor Emeritus, University of Hawaii

Our global era increasingly brings together ethnoculturally diverse individuals, families, communities, and nations that differ in religion, economy, beliefs, and histories. Often, these groups also come together under conditions that are plagued by anger, fear, and distrust. Mental health services are the crucible in which many of the issues different groups face must be addressed. Services occur in a broad arena of settings, including hospitals, clinics, courts, prisons, police forces, schools, and workplaces. It is essential that all parties involved in the delivery of mental health services recognize the critical issues that must be considered when encountering international, ethnocultural diversity.

1. Variations between Professional and Patient

At one point in the history of mental services in the United States, professionals and patients were mainly from the same ethnocultural groups, with variations in social class, education, and gender emerging as the major sources of concern in service provision decisions. In today's global era, however, mental health services must now consider a new spectrum of patient and professional ethnocultural variations. These new realities require careful attention to cultural sensitivities and competencies and include a variety of dimensions, such as ethnic background, gender, gender preference, age, language preference and fluency, and religion.

2. A New Spectrum of Patients

Many unfamiliar high "risk" and high "vulnerability" statuses, identities, and roles are becoming commonplace among mental health services settings, including migratory workers, international workers (skilled and unskilled), immigrants, temporary immigrants, undocumented immigrants, refugees, asylum seekers (war victims, torture victims), and international students. Patients in each of these bring unique needs and problems requiring complex service resources that must be accessible and acceptable. There are problems with culture shock, acculturation, assimilation, uprooting, language competency, and scores of economic, housing, and medical problems. Many service centers are ill-prepared to address and treat these problems.

3. Assessment and Testing Methods

For valid clinical and psychological assessment to occur, it is essential that there be linguistic, conceptual, scale, and normative equivalence for the clients being tested or assessed. The use of standardized "Western" assessment instruments poses many risks. It is not simply an issue of language, but rather whether concepts are similar, scales (e.g., true/false) are appropriate, and norms are suitable for other populations. Without this equivalence, there can be many errors in service provision decisions, especially those related to classification, diagnosis, therapy, and medications. The issue of culture-bound or culture-specific disorders and therapies looms as a special problem because of the detrimental consequences of erroneous clinical conclusions. Therapists should ask themselves a few questions: (1) Do I know the range of normal behavior for my patient's group? (2) Do I know the patterns of disorder for my patient's group? (3) Do I know what my patient's group considers the cause of disorder to be? (4) Do I know what treatment preferences my patient may have and whether alternatives are available? In my years of experience, I came to find that the best beginning to any assessment responsibility is to ask the patient to tell you his or her story—patient narration in their own words, at their own pace, and with their own priorities.

4. Cultural Competency

Excessive reliance on the delivery of mental health services rooted within Western assumptions, knowledge, and practices can have pernicious consequences. Indeed, these can often produce a range of iatrogenic (i.e., treatment-induced) problems. It is essential that mental services be responsive to ethnocultural differences in etiological and causal models of health and disorder, patterns of disorder, standards of normality, and treatment alternatives. Table 1 lists a brief cultural competency checklist that can assist the therapist / health professional in evaluating the adequacy of their preparation for transcultural mental health work.

5. Locations for Services

CLIENT'S ETHNO-CULTURAL GROUP: _____

Rate yourself on the following items of this scale to determine your "cultural competence" for this client:

Very True	True	Somewhat True	Not True	Unsure
4	3	2	1	U

1. _____ Knowledge of group's history
2. _____ Knowledge of group's family structures, gender roles, dynamics
3. _____ Knowledge of group's response to illness (i.e., awareness, biases)
4. _____ Knowledge of help-seeking behavior patterns of group
5. _____ Ability to evaluate your view and group view of illness
6. _____ Ability to feel empathy and understanding toward group
7. _____ Ability to develop a culturally responsive treatment program
8. _____ Ability to understand group's compliance with treatment
9. _____ Ability to develop culturally responsive prevention program for group
10. _____ Knowledge of group's "culture-specific" disorders
11. _____ Knowledge of group's explanatory models of illness
12. _____ Knowledge of group's indigenous healing methods and traditions
13. _____ Knowledge of group's indigenous healers and their contact ease
14. _____ Knowledge of communication patterns and styles (e.g., non-verbal)
15. _____ Knowledge of group's language
16. _____ Knowledge of group's ethnic identification and acculturation situation
17. _____ Knowledge of how one's own health practices are rooted in culture
18. _____ Knowledge of impact of group's religious beliefs on health and illness
19. _____ Desire to learn group's culture
20. _____ Desire to travel to group's national location, neighborhood

TOTAL SCORE: _____   **TOTAL # of U's:** _____
80-65 = Competent;   *(If this number is above 8,*
65-40 = Near Competent;   *more self-reflection is need)*
40 Below = Incompetent

Your Age: _____   **Your Gender:** _____
Your Religion: _____   **Your Ethnicity** _____

© AJM (2009) Atlanta, Georgia. Free use with acknowledgement and citation. Based on Marsella, Kaplan, & Suarez, 2000; Yamada, Marsella, & Yamada, 1998; Yamada, Marsella, & Atuel, 2002; Hanson, Pepitone, Green (2000). Contact: marsella@hawaii.edu

Table 1
Cultural Competence Self-Evaluation Form (CCSE)

While the office, clinic, and hospital were once conventional locations for the provision of mental health services, pressing problems, including funds and personnel shortages, now require services be delivered under challenging locations such as refugee camps, disaster crisis centers, street corners, homeless shelters, and rural outreach centers. These services are often faced with critical challenges because of patient crises, trauma, and emergency needs, as well as the pressures of time, medical complications, and threats to life. New training is needed for rendering effective services in these locations, especially the circumstances under which the services must be delivered.

6. Society as Patient

Most mental services are provided to individual patients, and the problems are located and intervened at intrapsychic and intracellular levels. However, transcultural mental health professionals are often in a position to see that the patients they are required to treat are also victims of societal circumstances such as prejudice, racism, oppression, persecution, marginalization, and poverty. These circumstances are often unacknowledged and so the sociopolitical determinants are ignored. The danger is that the individual becomes a victim who cannot address the very life contexts that are creating their problems and conflicts. In these instances, society is the patient in need of treatment. Transcultural mental health professionals are in a unique position to identify, question, and pursue the resolution of the problems via social activism. Through activism they can change and influence policies, policy makers, government officials, and business leaders. In many respects the transcultural mental health professional has a variety of roles and functions to fulfill that go far beyond treating individual patients from different diverse cultural traditions. The sociopolitical dimension may be new for mental health services, but it cannot be ignored. Table 2 lists a code of behavior for the transcultural mental health professional. It is not simply about ethics. Rather, it is about accepting one's role as a way of life.

THE TRANSCULTURAL MENTAL HEALTH PROFESSIONAL CODE

- It is not an 8:00–5:00 job. It is a way of life.
- It is a worldview rooted in empathy, justice, and conscience.
- It is committed to diversity, social justice, and activism.
- It is concerned with promoting and optimizing communication and understanding across ethnocultural boundaries.
- It is concerned with empowering individuals, groups, and cultures.
- It is concerned with offering hope, opportunity, and optimism to patients in need.
- It is concerned with addressing major societal problems including poverty, oppression, racism, sexism, violence, abuse, and inequality. It locates these problems within the societal contexts in which they are generated, empowered, and sustained.
- It is ecological, historical, interactional, and contextual.
- It acknowledges the complexity of problems and encourages multicultural, multidisciplinary, multisectoral, and multinational understanding and action.
- It is political, revolutionary, and progressive. Injustice is neither tolerated nor accepted.

Table 2
The Transcultural Mental Health Professional Code

7. Treatment Must Tap Positive Resources

For many patients from diverse ethnocultural backgrounds, effective treatment will require linkages to ethnocultural community services and resources. If these services are not present, the transcultural mental professional should attempt to develop them by working with community leaders. Community-based ethnocultural services are an essential part of the provision of mental health services. Weekly office or clinic visits are insufficient. A strong social support and community-based network must be a goal of treatment and care when working with ethnoculturally diverse patient populations. The challenge, of course, is whether the needed social and community supports are present given the typical problems of poverty and marginalization.

8. Prevention

More needs to be done in the area of prevention for ethnoculturally diverse patients. Prevention is often assigned the last priority due to the burdens of understaffing and underfunding. Yet the old adage "a pound of prevention is worth a ton of cure" remains true. One of the best examples of this is the extensive costs for running our correctional systems when so much more could have been done to prevent many of the problems that characterize the inmates. The three popular levels of prevention remain a standard: (1) educate to prevent, (2) identify problems early, and (3) treat problems effectively once they emerge. In the case of transcultural mental health services, more must be done to develop and offer a full spectrum of patient services (e.g., education, employment training, crisis counseling, meeting emergency needs).

9. Available, Accessible, and Acceptable Mental Health Services

Because much of the ethnocultural diversity that mental health services encounter are going to be dealing with poor, undereducated, non-English language speakers who are in urgent need of many services, the therapy encounter must be prepared to render a broad spectrum of services including medical, educational, financial, transportation, and housing. The service delivery system must be set up to offer services that are available, accessible, and acceptable. Too often the needed services are not available, and when they are available, they are not accessible (e.g., traveling miles to obtain a service). There is then the issue of acceptability, which requires that careful attention be given to the sensitivities of cultural variations in terms of service providers, settings, and demands on the patient. While this concern applies to all mental health patients, the ethnocultural therapy encounter is especially demanding.

10. Legal Complications

Accountability is becoming an increasing concern for mental health care because of increasing legal actions. When we accept ethnoculturally diverse patients, we accept the responsibility to know and to understand them so we do not make serious errors in care. Errors in diagnosis, assessment, treatment, and medications are frequent outcomes for which we must be held accountable, especially when patients suffer painful and harmful consequences. It is essential we work with culture brokers and culture consultants if we are unfamiliar with a patient's culture. Mental health professionals have the responsibility to know the limitations of their competencies. Good intentions are not enough.

11. Feminization of the Mental Health Professions

A popularly held view is that the gender of the therapist does not matter in determining therapy success or effectiveness. However, the reality of the situation is that there are a number of gender-related factors that call this assumption into question, including: (1) comfort in discussing certain topics, (2) communication and expressive styles, (3) empathy and understanding, (4) unconscious parental conflicts, (5) preferences for certain therapies or healing principles, (6) gender role perceptions and expectations, and (7) perceptions that therapists may be biased against men. While all of these factors are subject to debate, they assume critical implications when ethnocultural variations may be present because of the importance of patriarchal cultural norms and expectations. The status of women varies across cultures, and adherences to certain religious or traditional beliefs can present a conflict. The reality of the mental health professions today is that women now dominate all the professions (i.e., psychiatric nursing, social work, teaching, counseling, marriage and family counselors, and psychology). Graduate programs in psychology now have a much higher percentage of female students, and this trend appears likely to increase. Thus it may be necessary to consider this issue in transcultural locations and settings.

12. Transcultural Mental Health Research and Training

Conventional mental health research and training methods often create problems among ethnocultural groups. Under the illusion of "good intentions," dominant populations in charge of mental health services see their goal as preparing the ethnocultural patient to accept, adopt, and live according to the dominant group's standards of normality and expectation. In today's world, however, these goals must be reconsidered since they seek to homogenize diversity, and in doing so, destroy critical ethnic identity resources. Indeed the task of healing may be to help a patient discover their ethnocultural heritage and roots, and to join their culture's community groups. Emphasis upon using dominant culture norms and expectations can distort, deny, hide, or contribute to patient problems, and interfere with the service needs of minority and marginalized groups.

NOTES

This list in this article is intended to be open-ended. There are more than twelve critical issues that can be identified and discussed. Others may add their suggestions in an effort to develop a more comprehensive listing.

SOURCE

Marsella, A. 2011. Twelve critical issues for mental health professionals working with ethnoculturally diverse populations. *Psychology International* 22, no. 3 (October): 7–10. http://www.apa.org/international/pi/2011/10/critical-issues.aspx. Reprinted by permission.

RELATED RESOURCES

Video: World Health Organization. "Mental Health: Global Overview." World Health Organization. http://www.youtube.com/watch?v=L8iRjEOH41c.

Berry, J., Y. Poortinga, S. Breugelmans, A. Chastiosis, and D. Sam, eds. 2011. *Cross-cultural psychology: Research and applications*, 3rd ed. Cambridge: Cambridge University Press.

Casto, F., M. Barrera, and L. Steiker. 2010. Issues and challenges in the design of culturally adapted evidence-based interventions. *Annual Review of Clinical Psychology* 6: 213–39.

Dana, R., and J. Allen, eds. 2008. *Cultural competence training in a global society*. New York: Springer.

Gropper, R. 1996. *Culture and the clinical encounter: An intercultural sensitizer for the health professions*. Yarmouth, ME: Intercultural Press.

Judy Hall and Elizabeth Altmaier. 2008. *Global Promise: Quality Assurance and Accountability in Professional Psychology*. Oxford, UK: Oxford University Press.

International Union of Psychological Science, and International Association of Applied Psychology. 2008. Universal declaration of ethical principles for psychologists. International Union of Psychological Science. http://www.am.org/iupsys/resources/ethics/univdecl2008.html.

Kitayama, S., and D. Cohen, eds. 2007. *Handbook of cultural psychology*. New York: Guilford Press.

McGill University. Division of Social and Transcultural Psychiatry. http://www.mcgill.ca/tcpsych/. [Note: There are a growing number of academic programs in the health sciences that include cross-cultural courses and components in their training. Multicultural competence is increasingly becoming a necessary and required skill.]

Rose, P. 2013. *Cultural competency for the health professional*. Burlington, MA: Jones and Bartlett Learning.

World Federation for Mental Health. 2007. World mental health day—October 10, 2007: Mental health in a changing world; The impact of culture and diversity. World Federation for Mental Health. http://www.wfmh.org/PDF/Englishversion2007.pdf.

Good Practice in the Human Resource Sector

CONNECTIONS AND CONTRIBUTIONS FOR SERVING HUMANITY

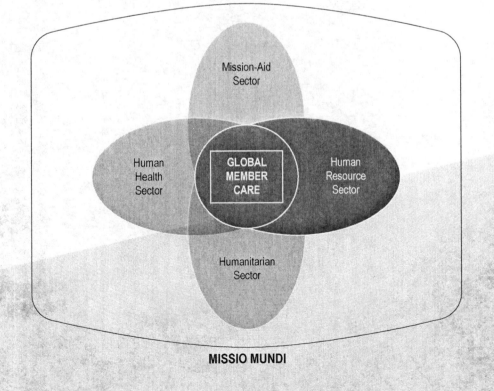

MISSIO DEI

Mission-Aid
Sector

Human
Health
Sector

GLOBAL
MEMBER
CARE

Human
Resource
Sector

Humanitarian
Sector

MISSIO MUNDI

APPLICATIONS FOR PART FOUR

*Keep in mind these five goals for crossing sectors
as you go through the material.*

In what ways could you connect and contribute?

- To support mission/aid workers in their well-being and effectiveness
- To support colleagues in other sectors via materials in the member care field
- To equip mission/aid workers with tools and opportunities for their work with others
- To equip member caregivers who directly work with vulnerable populations and others
- To stay informed as global citizens about current and crucial issues facing humanity

CHAPTER 26

Strengthening Human Resource Systems

HUMAN RESOURCE MANAGEMENT RAPID ASSESSMENT TOOL FOR HEALTH ORGANIZATIONS: A GUIDE FOR STRENGTHENING HRM SYSTEMS

Management Sciences for Health

INTRODUCTION

The Human Resource Management (HRM) Rapid Assessment Tool offers a method for assessing what an organization's Human Resource Management system consists of and how well it functions. The HRM Rapid Assessment Tool helps users to develop strategies to improve the human resource system and make it as effective as possible. It can also serve as a basis for focusing discussions, brainstorming, and strategic planning. It is designed to be used in public and private-sector health organizations.

For newly formed organizations, the tool can serve as a guide for developing an optimal HRM system. For established organizations facing changes, such as contracting out services, decentralizing, downsizing, or expansion, the tool can serve as a reference for the types of HRM issues that must be addressed in order to manage change successfully.

For optimal benefit to the organization, it is important that the use of this tool be fully supported by the leadership of the organization. Units within an organization can also benefit from using the tool as a guide for improving human resource components that they can influence directly.

DEVELOPING AN EFFECTIVE HUMAN RESOURCE SYSTEM

Human Resource Management is defined as *the integrated use of procedures, policies, and practices to recruit, maintain, and develop employees in order for the organiza-*

tion to meet its desired goals. It includes five broad areas: human resources capacity, personnel policy and practice, human resources data, performance management, and training.

HRM is most effective in an organization when its authority is located at the senior management level. A system that functions effectively can assist the organization in developing a set of policies, practices, and systems that advance the skills and increase the motivation of staff in order to achieve the highest possible level of performance over time.

Benefits of an Effective Human Resource System

- encourages systematic planning to support organizational mission
- increases capacity of the organization to achieve its goals
- provides a clear definition of each employee's responsibilities and a link to the organization's mission
- encourages greater equity between compensation and level of responsibility
- defines levels of supervision and management support
- increases level of performance and the efficient utilization of employees skills and knowledge
- results in cost savings through improved efficiency and productivity
- increases the organization's ability to manage change

The HRM Rapid Assessment Tool

The HRM Rapid Assessment Tool is intended to provide users with a rapid assessment tool to identify the characteristics and capacity of an organization's human resource system and help users form an action plan for improving the human resource system in the organization. The instrument itself consists of a matrix that includes:

- twenty-two human resource components that fall within five broad areas of human resource management;
- four stages of human resource development;
- characteristics that describe each human resource component at each stage of development; and
- blank spaces for users to write a brief statement, or indicator, to show that the organization fits a particular stage of development.

Human Resource Components

The twenty-two human resource components assessed by this tool fall within five broad areas of human resource management and represent the core functions of an effective human resource system. Based on a set of characteristics describing stages of human resource development, the tool provides a process through which an organization can assess how well it is functioning in relation to each of these twenty-two components, and determine what steps it can take to function more effectively.

HUMAN RESOURCE COMPONENTS ASSESSED BY THE HRM TOOL

HRM Capacity
HRM Staff
HRM Budget
HRM Planning

HRM Data
Employee Data
Computerization of Data
Personnel Files

Personnel Policy and Practice
Job Classification System
Compensation and Benefits System
Recruitment, Hiring, Transfer, and Promotion
Orientation Program
Policy Manual
Discipline, Termination, and Grievance Procedures
HIV/AIDS Workplace Prevention Program
Relationships with Unions
Labor Law Compliance

Performance Management
Staff Retention
Job Descriptions
Staff Supervision
Work Planning and Performance Review

Training and Staff Development
Staff Training
Management and Leadership Development
Links to External Preservice Training

Stages of Development

As organizations grow, strengthen, and mature, they evolve through several stages of development. Organizations pass through these stages at different rates and tend to remain at a particular stage until they have developed a clear mission, good management structures and systems, and skilled managers and staff who use these structures and systems effectively. Most organizations are at different stages of development for different human resource components at any given time, because the components have received different levels of attention as the organization developed. The numbers at the top of the HRM Tool refer to these four stages of development.[71]

Human Resource Characteristics

For each human resource component, the Tool provides a statement that describes the common characteristics of organizations at each stage of development. These characteristics build on the characteristics of the previous stage(s). At the first stage, the characteristics describe an organization that is either just beginning to develop a human resource system or has not paid very much attention to that component. At the fourth stage, the characteristics describe an organization that is operating extremely effectively with regard to that component and may need to direct its energies to components that are at lower stages of development.

Evidence

Because the users of this tool will come from many parts of the organization, they often differ in their perceptions of whether or not the organization meets all the characteristics of a particular stage. To help resolve these different views, users should write one or two indicators that they believe show that the organization fits the characteristics of the stage they have selected. The Tool provides a blank space in the far right column for these statements or indicators.

What Constitutes Evidence?

Many types of evidence—not simply quantitative data—may support participants' assessments. This Tool defines evidence as a fact or concrete observation that supports the identified stage of development. Convincing evidence answers the question, "What can we see or hear that tells us our assessment is accurate?" For example, a participant who places her organization at Stage 2 for a workplace prevention program for HIV/AIDS can point to a program that was developed, but not yet implemented.

---

71   See the full version of the Tool to access the matrices for the HRM components as well as interpretation and action plan suggestions. For more information about Management Sciences for Health: http://www.msh.org/.

Using the HRM Rapid Assessment Tool

This tool is best administered by a committee of staff internal to the organization, such as representatives from senior staff from different levels, programs, and units. It is often useful but not necessary for an external consultant to facilitate the process. The HRM Tool is organized according to the twenty-two human resource components in a matrix showing four stages of development. The characteristics that describe each stage provide information that is useful in developing a plan of action for improving the human resource areas that need strengthening.

Conducting the Self-assessment

First, each person in the group should individually assess each human resource component in the matrix by reviewing the characteristics of each component at each stage of development. There is no scoring involved. For each human resource component, each person circles the characteristic that he or she believes best represents the current status of the human resource system. If only part of the statement applies to the current human resource system in the organization, you should circle the previous characteristic. In the blank box in the right hand column, in the row marked "Evidence," write one or two specific, concrete observations that provide evidence that the organization fulfills the characteristic you have chosen.

After this individual exercise, people share their assessments with the whole group (taking one component at a time), discuss their indicators, and work together to come to agreement on the appropriate stage. The group should be able to move through the process at a good pace, spending more time discussing those components where there is a wide divergence of opinion.

Reaching Consensus

Consensus is based on two assumptions. The first is that no single member of an organization possesses the complete truth—that every person at all levels of the organization possesses some part of the truth, and that an accurate picture is best obtained by pooling these individual perceptions. The second assumption is that carefully chosen indicators can provide convincing factual evidence and allow a group of people to come to agreement on what may initially seem to be incompatible viewpoints.

The organization reaches consensus not by voting but by patiently sorting through all opinions and coming to a decision that each member can accept and work with, even if it does not completely match his or her preference.

Once the assessment is complete, the group should discuss the results, agree on the areas that need strengthening, and formulate an action plan that includes specific activities, with time lines, to improve these areas. You may find it helpful to review the documents listed below to inform the discussion.

Complementing the Self-assessment with a Review of Documents

The assessment work could be complemented by direct observation of the organization's human resource practices and a review of relevant HRM and personnel documents. The following documents may prove useful to you to complete the self-assessment:

- Personnel Files and Review
- Job Descriptions and Work Plans
- Financial/Payroll Records
- Labor Law
- Employee Policy Statement or Manual
- Organizational Mission Statement
- Strategic Plans

DEFINING THE IMPORTANCE OF THE HRM COMPONENTS

The following chart provides a summary of how each HRM component fits in the overall management of the organization and its particular relevance to the human resource system.

HRM AREA AND COMPONENT	IMPORTANCE
HRM Capacity	
HRM Staff	Staff dedicated to HRM are essential to policy development and implementation.
HRM Budget	Allows for consistent HR planning and for relating costs to results.
HR Planning	Allows HRM resources to be used efficiently in support of organization goals.

HRM AREA AND COMPONENT	IMPORTANCE
Personnel Policy and Practice	
Job Classification System	Allows organization to standardize the jobs and types of skills it requires.
Compensation and Benefits System	Allows for equity in employee salary and benefits, tied to local economy.
Recruitment, Hiring, Transfer, Promotion	Assures fair and open process based on candidates' job qualifications.
Orientation Program	Helps new employees to identify with the organization and its goals/values.
Policy Manual	Provides rules and regulations that govern how employees work and what to expect.
Discipline, Termination, Grievance Procedures	Provides fair and consistent guidelines for addressing performance problems.
HIV/AIDS Workplace Prevention Programs	Assures that all staff have the systems and knowledge required to prevent the spread of HIV/AIDS.
Relationships with Unions	Promotes understanding of common goals and decreases adversarial behaviours.
Labor Law Compliance	Allows organization to function legally and avoid litigation.
HRM Data	
Employee Data	Allows for appropriate allocation and training of staff, tracking, and personnel costs.
Computerization of Data	Accessible, accurate, and timely data is essential for good planning.
Personnel Files	Provide essential data on employee's work history in organization.

HRM AREA AND COMPONENT	IMPORTANCE
Performance Management	
Staff Retention	Ensures that the organization views staff as a strategic resource. High employee turnover can be very costly and lower internal morale.
Job Descriptions	Define what people do and how they work together.
Staff Supervision	Provides a system to develop work plans and monitor performance.
Work Planning and Performance Review	Provides information to staff about job duties and level of performance.
Training and Staff Development	
Staff Training	A cost-effective way to develop staff and organizational capacity.
Management and Leadership Development	Leadership and good management are keys to sustainability.
Links to External Preservice Training	Preservice training based on skills needed in the workplace is cost-effective.

SOURCE

Management Sciences for Health. 2009. *Human resource management rapid assessment tool for health organizations: A guide for strengthening HRM systems,* 2nd ed. Cambridge, MA: Management Sciences for Health. Reprinted by permission. http://erc.msh.org/toolkit/toolkitfiles/file/HRM%20tool%202009%20final_intranet.pdf.

See also: Society for Human Resource Management (website with resources), http://www.shrm.org.

RELATED RESOURCES

Video: RSA Animate. "The Surprising Truth about What Motivates Us." RSA Animate. http://www.youtube.com/watch?v=u6XAPnuFjJc.

Handy, C. 1988. *Understanding voluntary organisations*. London: Penguin Books.

Henry, J. 2004a. Understanding HR in the humanitarian sector: Handbook 1. London: People In Aid.

———. 2004b. Enhancing quality in HR management in the humanitarian sector. Handbook 2. London: People In Aid.

Johnson, L., ed. 2006. *HR magazine guide to managing people: 47 tools to help managers*. Alexandria, VA: Society for Human Resource Management.

Mattis, R., and J. Johnson. 2011. *Human resource management*, 13th ed. Mason, OH: Southwestern Cengage Learning.

People In Aid. 2013. The state of HR in international humanitarian and development organisations 2013. London: People In Aid. http://www.peopleinaid.org/publications/stateofhr2013.aspx.

CHAPTER 27

Ethics in Human Resource Management

HRPA Code of Ethics

Human Resources Professionals Association

The *Scope of HR Practice* is the creation and implementation of all policies, practices, and processes to effectively organize and manage all human capital resources in the workplace in service of the ultimate goal of enhancing business outcomes. Human Resources Management involves maintaining or changing relations between employees, between employers or between employers and employees.

The **Practice of Human Resources Management** includes, but is not limited to, one or more of the following:

1. The development and implementation of human resources policies and procedures;
2. Consultation in the area of human resources management;
3. Providing advice to clients, managers, and employees in matters pertaining to management of human resources;
4. The representation of clients and organizations in proceedings related to human resources management;
5. Program development and evaluation in the area of human resources management;
6. The supervision of other Human Resources professionals whether registered or non-registered;
7. Coaching of employees, managers, and other individuals in matters relating to work and employment;

8. The conduct of research in the area of human resources management;
9. Teaching in the area of human resources management.

THE HRPA CODE OF ETHICS

The HRPA Code of Ethics comprises seven principles. These principles are: Competence, Legal requirements, Dignity in the workplace, Balancing interests, Confidentiality, Conflict of interest, Professional growth and support of other professionals.

DIVISION I—Competence

Principle:

HR practitioners must maintain competence in carrying out professional responsibilities and provide services in an honest and diligent manner. They must ensure that activities engaged in are within the limits of their knowledge, experience, and skill. When providing services outside one's level of competence, or the profession, the necessary assistance must be sought so as not to compromise professional responsibility. Specifically,

1. A member shall discharge his or her professional obligations with competence and integrity. A member shall provide professional services of a high quality.
2. A member shall practice the profession of Human Resources Management in keeping with generally recognized standards of practice and all applicable laws.
3. A member shall bear in mind the limitations of his or her skills, knowledge, and the means at his or her disposal. Members shall avoid, in particular:
   (1) undertaking work for which the members are not sufficiently prepared without obtaining the necessary assistance or information;
   (2) accepting an engagement in respect of which the member has not acquired or is unable to acquire, in the proper time, the necessary competence.

4. A member shall not accept a number of engagements or tasks in excess of that which the interest of his or her clients or the respect of his or her professional obligations may allow.

5. A member may not practice or perform certain professional acts under conditions or in situations which could impair the dignity of the profession or the quality of services the member provides.

6. A member shall prevent the inappropriate use and application by others of the tools, techniques, and processes used in the practice of Human Resources Management.

7. A member shall take the necessary means to maintain his or her knowledge and skills up to date including full participation in HRPA recertification program to maintain his or her designation.

DIVISION II—Legal Requirements

Principle:

HR practitioners must adhere to any statutory acts, regulations or by-laws which relate to the field of Human Resources Management, as well as all civil and criminal laws, regulations and statutes that apply in their jurisdiction. They must not knowingly or otherwise engage in or condone any activity or attempt to circumvent the clear intention of the law. Specifically,

1. A member shall not act in a manner that is dishonest, fraudulent, criminal, or illegal, or with the intent of circumventing the law.

2. In developing Human Resources programs and policies, whether as the individual responsible for the program or policy, or as a consultant to an organization, the member shall not implement, or allow to be implemented, Human Resources programs and policies that are dishonest, fraudulent, criminal, or illegal.

3. When advising an employer or client, a member shall not knowingly assist in or encourage dishonesty, fraud, crime, or illegal conduct, or instruct the employer or client on how to violate or circumvent the law.

4. A member who discovers that dishonesty, fraud, crime, or illegal conduct has been occurring in an organization shall take every appropriate step to attempt to stop the dishonest, fraudulent, criminal or illegal conduct.

5. A member shall not:
    (1) Retaliate in any way against employees that are exercising their right to launch a complaint or grievance;
    (2) Knowingly participate in or condone any act of retaliation on the part of the organization that employs them or to which they are providing service against employees who are exercising their right to launch a complaint or grievance.

DIVISION III—Dignity in the Workplace

Principle:

HR practitioners support, promote and apply the legislative requirements and the principles of human rights, equity, dignity and respect in the workplace, within the profession and in society as a whole. Specifically,

1. In the practice of Human Resources Management, a member shall:
    (1) act in such a way as to respect the rights of all individuals involved;
    (2) act in such a way as to protect the dignity of all individuals involved;
    (3) ensure that human resources policies and practices respect the rights and protect the dignity of all individuals involved.
2. A member shall, as far as the member is able, contribute to the furthering of human rights, equity, dignity and respect in the workplace.
3. In the practice of Human Resources Management, a member shall bear in mind:
    (1) the importance of work and the work environment for the psychological well-being of individuals;
    (2) the necessary health and safety measures in the work environment in which the member practices his or her profession;
    (3) the protection of the physical and mental health of the persons under his or her authority or supervision;
    (4) the importance of courses and programs for the advancement, training, development or promotion of the persons under his or her authority or supervision;
    (5) the confidentiality of the records of persons under his or her authority or supervision and of the confidential information

concerning these persons and that becomes known to him in the practice of his or her profession.

4. Under no circumstances, in the practice of Human Resources Management, shall a member engage in, or condone:

    (1) any acts of harassment or intimidation;

    (2) any acts of physical or psychological violence;

    (3) any acts of discrimination on the grounds of race, ancestry, place of origin, colour, ethnic origin, citizenship, creed, sex, sexual orientation, age, record of offences, marital status, family status, or disability as noted in the Ontario Human Rights Code.

5. A member shall not commit acts derogatory to the dignity of the profession. Specifically, members should avoid the following:

    (1) advising or encouraging someone to commit a discriminatory, fraudulent, or illegal act;

    (2) refusing to counsel or to represent a person on the sole ground that the person lodged a complaint against another member of the Association under section 4 (1)(d) of the Human Resources Professionals Association Act, 1990, or that the person filed a claim against another member of the Association;

    (3) failing to notify the Registrar of the Association that the member has reasonable grounds to believe that another member of the Association has contravened the HRPA Code of Ethics or the HRPA Rules of Professional Conduct;

    (4) drawing up a declaration or report the member knows to be incomplete, without mention of any restriction, or that the member knows to be false; and

    (5) allowing a person not registered with HRPA to pass themselves off as a member of the HRPA or allowing a person who has not been granted a professional designation by the Association to use such title or initials reserved for the members of the Association who have been granted such designation;

    (6) not informing the Registrar of the Association at the proper time that a person who is not registered with HRPA has passed themselves off as a member of HRPA or that a person who has not been granted the Certified Human Resources Professional designation has passed themselves off as having the designation.

DIVISION IV—Balancing Interests

Principle:

HR practitioners must strive to balance organizational and employee needs and interests in the practice of their profession. Specifically,

1. A member must understand that while they may be employed or retained by one concern, he or she has a duty to parties other than their employer or their client.

    (1) A member must respect the dignity of all individuals;

    (2) A member must respect the legal rights of all employees, including the rights of individuals who were previously employees of an organization and those pursuing employment with an organization;

    (3) In adversarial situations or in situations with competing interests, a member is required to act in good faith towards all parties at all times;

    (4) When a member is engaged to act as a mediator, whether formally or informally, the member shall act in an impartial and unbiased manner;

    (5) A member must not use the power of their position, especially the access to personal information, to gain unfair advantage in any situation.

DIVISION V—Confidentiality

Principle:

HR practitioners must hold in strict confidence all confidential information acquired in the course of the performance of their duties and not divulge confidential information unless required by law and/or where serious harm is imminent. As part of their practices as Human Resource Management Professionals, members will have access to and be responsible for much personal information. Human Resources professionals have specific duties with respect to such information. Human Resources professionals have duties with respect to (1) the handling and management of files and records related to the management of the Human Resources function; (2) the kind of information that is shared by employees of an organization in confidence, and (3) the respect of all laws pertaining to the protection of personal information.

Human Resources Professionals must treat the handling of confidential, personal, or privileged information with the utmost importance as it is core to the credibility of the profession. Specifically,

1. A member shall ensure that files and records that contain personal information are handled appropriately in accordance with accepted professional practice and in accordance with all appropriate laws. This requirement applies regardless of the medium on which the information is stored:
   (1) all records and files containing personal information must be secure;
   (2) access to such records and files must be limited to those individuals who have a legitimate need to know;
   (3) the policies regarding access to files and records must be stated explicitly and communicated to those on whom the information is collected upon demand;
   (4) systems and processes need to be in place to ensure the accuracy of the records and files;
   (5) employees shall not be denied access to their files and records.

2. Because of the nature of their role, information is shared with Human Resources professionals in confidence. In such situations, a member must exercise caution:
   (1) in dealing with information provided in confidence, a member must be guided by the desire to find a resolution that is acceptable to all parties. If a member believes that he or she cannot play a constructive role in the matter, the member must inform the party or parties that this is the case;
   (2) as appropriate, a member must inform relevant parties of the limits of confidentiality;
   (3) as applicable, a member must notify individuals that information suggesting that there is imminent risk to an identifiable person, or group, of death, or serious bodily harm, including serious psychological harm that substantially interferes with health or well-being cannot be held in confidence;
   (4) as applicable, a member must notify individuals that information regarding acts that may be criminal or otherwise illegal cannot be held in confidence.

3. For the purposes of preserving the secrecy of confidential information brought to his or her knowledge in the practice of his or her profession, a member shall:

    (1) refrain from using such information with a view to obtaining a direct or indirect benefit for himself or herself or for another person;

    (2) take the necessary measures to prevent his or her colleagues and the persons under his or her authority or supervision from disclosing or making use of such information that becomes known to them in the performance of their duties; and

    (3) avoid holding or participating in indiscreet conversations concerning an employer or client or employee and the services provided to such employer or client or employee.

4. When required by law or by order of a tribunal of competent jurisdiction, a member shall disclose confidential information, but the member shall not disclose more information than is required.

5. When a member believes upon reasonable grounds that there is imminent risk to an identifiable person, or group, of death, or serious bodily harm, including serious psychological harm that substantially interferes with health or well-being, the member must disclose confidential information where it is necessary to do so in order to prevent death or harm, but shall not disclose more information than is required.

DIVISION VI—Conflict of Interest

Principle:

HR practitioners must either avoid, or disclose a potential conflict of interest that might influence or might be perceived to influence, personal actions or judgments. Specifically,

1. A member shall safeguard his or her professional independence at all times. The member shall, in particular:

    (1) ignore any intervention by a third party which could influence the fulfillment of his or her professional obligations to the detriment of his or her employer or client;

(2) avoid carrying out a task contrary to his or her conscience or to the principles governing the practice of his or her profession; or

(3) avoid any situation in which the member would be in conflict of interest.

2. A member must not allow personal interest to cloud his or her judgment or to cause him or her to act in an unprofessional manner.

3. A member may represent an employer or client, notwithstanding his or her personal opinion on the employer's or client's position in the matter.

4. Generally, a member shall only act, in the same matter, for a party representing similar interests. If a member's professional duties require that the member represent different interests in the same matter, the member shall specify the nature of his or her duties or responsibilities and shall inform the parties concerned that he or she will cease to act if the situation becomes irreconcilable with his or her duty to be independent.

5. A member called upon to work with another person, in particular a member of the Association or a member of another professional Association, shall preserve his or her professional independence.

6. A member shall not receive, other than the remuneration to which the member is entitled, any benefit, commission or rebate relative to the practice of his or her profession.

7. As soon as a member ascertains that the member is in conflict of interest, this member shall notify the employer or client of this conflict of interest and request his or her authorization to continue carrying out the engagement.

DIVISION VII—Professional Growth and Support of Other Professionals

Principle:

HR practitioners must maintain personal and professional growth in Human Resources Management by engaging in activities that enhance the credibility and value of the profession. Specifically,

1. A member shall, in order to maintain certification, participate fully in all mandatory aspects of the Association's Recertification program.

2. A member shall, as far as the member is able, contribute to the development of his or her profession by sharing his or her knowledge and experience with other members of the Association and students and by taking part in activities, courses and continuing training sessions organized for the members of the Association.
3. A member shall not take credit for work performed by another.

EDITORS' NOTES

For more information about the Human Resources Professional Association: http://www.hrpa.ca.

SOURCE

Human Resources Professionals Association (HRPA). (2010). Rules of professional conduct (incorporating the HRPA Code of Ethics, 7–16). Ontario, Canada: Author. Retrieved from http://www.hrpa.ca/OfficeOfTheRegistrar/Documents/HRPA%20Rules%20of%20Professional%20Conduct%20August%202010_V5.pdf. Reprinted by permission.

RELATED RESOURCES

Video: Focus on HR. Society for Human Resource Management (bi-weekly video updates/information).
http://www.shrm.org/multimedia/video/focusonhr/.
Gusdorf., M. (2010). Ethics in human resource management. Alexandria, VA: Society for Human Resource management [instructor's guide with five case studies]. Retrieved from http://www.shrm.org/education/hreducation/documents/gusdorf_ethics%20in%20human%20resource%20management_im_final.pdf.
O'Donnell, K. (2011). Ethics and human rights in member care: Developing guidelines in mission/aid (Part three). In *Global member care: The pearls and perils of good practice*. Pasadena, CA: William Carey Library.
Society for Human Resource Management. (2001). The code of ethics toolkit: A guide to developing your organization's code of ethics. Retrieved from http://www.shrm.org/about/Documents/organization-coe.pdf.
Society for Human Resource Management. *HR magazine*. Retrieved from http://www.shrm.org/Publications/hrmagazine/Pages/default.aspx.
Society for Human Resource Management. Code of ethical and professional standards in human resource management. Retrieved from http://www.shrm.org/.
World Federation of People Management Associations. *Worldlink magazine: Linking people management professionals around the globe*. Retrieved from http://www.wfpma.com/worldlink.

CHAPTER 28

HIV/AIDS in the Workplace

ILO Code of Practice on HIV/AIDS and the World of Work

International Labour Organization

The HIV/AIDS epidemic is now a global crisis, and constitutes one of the most formidable challenges to development and social progress. In the most affected countries, the epidemic is eroding decades of development gains, undermining economies, threatening security, and destabilizing societies. In sub-Saharan Africa, where the epidemic has already had a devastating impact, the crisis has created a state of emergency.

Beyond the suffering it imposes on individuals and their families, the epidemic is profoundly affecting the social and economic fabric of societies. HIV/AIDS is a major threat to the world of work: it is affecting the most productive segment of the labour force and reducing earnings, and it is imposing huge costs on enterprises in all sectors through declining productivity, increasing labour costs, and loss of skills and experience. In addition, HIV/AIDS is affecting fundamental rights at work, particularly with respect to discrimination and stigmatization aimed at workers and people living with and affected by HIV/AIDS. The epidemic and its impact strike hardest at vulnerable groups including women and children, thereby increasing existing gender inequalities and exacerbating the problem of child labour.

This is why the ILO is committed to making a strong statement through a code of practice on HIV/AIDS and the world of work. The code will be instrumental in helping to prevent the spread of the epidemic, mitigate its impact on workers and their families, and provide social protection to help cope with the disease. It covers key principles, such as the recognition of HIV/AIDS as a workplace issue, nondiscrimination in employment, gender equality, screening and confidentiality, social dialogue, prevention, and care and support, as the basis for addressing the epidemic in the workplace.

This code is the product of collaboration between the ILO and its tripartite constituents, as well as cooperation with its international partners. It provides invaluable practical guidance to policy makers, employers' and workers' organizations, and other social partners for formulating and implementing appropriate workplace policy, prevention, and care programmes, and for establishing strategies to address workers in the informal sector.

This is an important ILO contribution to the global effort to fight HIV/AIDS. The code will help to secure conditions of decent work in the face of a major humanitarian and development crisis. Already, valuable lessons have been learned in attempting to deal with this crisis. A few countries have achieved a degree of success in slowing down the spread of the infection and mitigating its effects on individuals and their communities.

The best practices have included committed leadership, multisectoral approaches, partnership with civil society, including people living with HIV/AIDS, and education. These elements are reflected in the key principles of the code and its reliance on the mobilization of the social partners for effective implementation.

This is a forward-looking and pioneering document which addresses present problems and anticipates future consequences of the epidemic and its impact on the world of work. Through this code the ILO will increase its support for international and national commitments to protect the rights and dignity of workers and all people living with HIV/AIDS.

Objective

The objective of this code is to provide a set of guidelines to address the HIV/AIDS epidemic in the world of work and within the framework of the promotion of decent work. The guidelines cover the following key areas of action:

(a) prevention of HIV/AIDS
(b) management and mitigation of the impact of HIV/AIDS on the world of work
(c) care and support of workers infected and affected by HIV/AIDS
(d) elimination of stigma and discrimination on the basis of real or perceived HIV status

Use

This code should be used to:

(a) develop concrete responses at enterprise, community, regional, sectoral, national, and international levels;

(b) promote processes of dialogue, consultations, negotiations, and all forms of cooperation between governments, employers and workers and their representatives, occupational health personnel, specialists in HIV/AIDS issues, and all relevant stakeholders (which may include community-based and nongovernmental organizations [NGOs]); and

(c) give effect to its contents in consultation with the social partners:
- in national laws, policies, and programmes of action;
- in workplace/enterprise agreements; and
- in workplace policies and plans of action.

KEY PRINCIPLES

1. Recognition of HIV/AIDS as a Workplace Issue

HIV/AIDS is a workplace issue and should be treated like any other serious illness/condition in the workplace. This is necessary not only because it affects the workforce, but also because the workplace, being part of the local community, has a role to play in the wider struggle to limit the spread and effects of the epidemic.

2. Nondiscrimination

In the spirit of decent work and respect for the human rights and dignity of persons infected or affected by HIV/AIDS, there should be no discrimination against workers on the basis of real or perceived HIV status. Discrimination and stigmatization of people living with HIV/AIDS inhibits efforts aimed at promoting HIV/AIDS prevention.

3. Gender Equality

The gender dimensions of HIV/AIDS should be recognized. Women are more likely to become infected and are more often adversely affected by the HIV/AIDS epidemic than men due to biological, sociocultural, and economic reasons. The greater the gender discrimination in societies and the lower the position of women, the more negatively they are affected by HIV. Therefore, more equal gender relations and the empowerment of women are vital to successfully prevent the spread of HIV infection and enable women to cope with HIV/AIDS.

4. Healthy Work Environment

The work environment should be healthy and safe, so far as is practicable, for all concerned parties in order to prevent transmission of HIV, in accordance with the provisions of the Occupational Safety and Health Convention, 1981 (no. 155). A healthy work environment facilitates optimal physical and mental health in relation to work and adaptation of work to the capabilities of workers in light of their state of physical and mental health.

5. Social Dialogue

The successful implementation of an HIV/AIDS policy and programme requires cooperation and trust between employers, workers, and their representatives and government, where appropriate, with the active involvement of workers infected and affected by HIV/AIDS.

6. Screening for Purposes of Exclusion from Employment or Work Processes

HIV/AIDS screening should not be required of job applicants or persons in employment.

7. Confidentiality

There is no justification for asking job applicants or workers to disclose HIV-related personal information. Nor should coworkers be obliged to reveal such personal information about fellow workers. Access to personal data relating to a worker's HIV status should be bound by the rules of confidentiality consistent with the ILO's code of practice on the protection of workers' personal data, 1997.

8. Continuation of Employment Relationship

HIV infection is not a cause for termination of employment. As with many other conditions, persons with HIV-related illnesses should be able to work for as long as medically fit in available, appropriate work.

9. Prevention

HIV infection is preventable. Prevention of all means of transmission can be achieved through a variety of strategies which are appropriately targeted to national conditions and which are culturally sensitive. Prevention can be furthered through changes in behaviour, knowledge, treatment, and the creation of a nondiscriminatory environment. The social partners are in a unique position to promote prevention efforts, particularly in relation to changing attitudes and behaviours through the provision of information and education, and in addressing socioeconomic factors.

10. Care and Support

Solidarity, care, and support should guide the response to HIV/AIDS in the world of work. All workers, including workers with HIV, are entitled to affordable health services. There should be no discrimination against them and their dependants in access to and receipt of benefits from statutory social security programmes and occupational schemes.

EDITORS' NOTES

For more information about the International Labour Organization: http://www.ilo.org/.

SOURCE

International Labour Organization. 2001. *An ILO code of practice on HIV/AIDS and the world of work*. Geneva: International Labour Organization, preface and 1–4. Reprinted by permission. http://www.ilo.org/aids/Publications/WCMS_113783/lang--en/index.htm. © International Labour Organization.

RELATED RESOURCES

Videos: International Labour Organization (several videos on HIV/AIDS in various work settings). http://www.youtube.com/playlist?list=PL7011D7879AA663AD&feature=plcp.

International Aids Society. 2012. *IAS News*, June–July. http://www.iasociety.org/Default. aspx?pageId=147.

International Labour Organization. 2010. Recommendation concerning HIV and AIDS and the world of Work, 2010 (No.200). Geneva: International Labour Organization. http://www. ilo.org/wcmsp5/groups/public/---ed_protect/---protrav/---ilo_aids/documents/ normativein- strument/wcms_142706.pdf. (See also the PowerPoint/pdf overview: http://www.ilo.org/aids/ Publications/WCMS_153555/lang--en/index.htm.)

UNAIDS. 2011. UNAIDS world AIDS day report 2011. Geneva: UNAIDS. http://www.unaids.org/en/media/unaids/contentassets/documents/unaidspublication/2011/JC2216_WorldAIDSday_report_2011_en.pdf.

UNESCO, and International Labour Organization. 2006. An HIV and AIDS workplace policy for the education sector in Southern Africa. Geneva: International Labour Organization and UNESCO. http://unesdoc.unesco.org/images/0014/001469/146933E.pdf.

United Nations. 2011. UN Cares 10 minimum standards with indicators. UN Cares. http://www.uncares.org/UNAIDS2/workplace/min_standards.shtml.

CHAPTER 29

Managing and Supporting Staff

CODE OF GOOD PRACTICE IN THE MANAGEMENT AND SUPPORT OF AID PERSONNEL

People In Aid

The People In Aid Code is an important resource for the aid community around the world. It grew from the collaborative effort of relief and development agencies committed to improving the quality of the assistance provided to communities affected by poverty and disaster. The intention of the Code is to improve agencies' support and management of their staff and volunteers.

Background

The mission of most relief and development agencies is to work with those who are poor, distressed, affected by conflict, vulnerable, displaced, disadvantaged, and worried about their future. In 1994, worried that these descriptions also applied to their own staff, a group of agencies commissioned a survey. Concentrating on aid workers as employees, Rebecca McNair (n.d.) found that they felt poorly managed and unsupported. This led the sector to ask how human resources among relief and development agencies could be improved. The answer was the "People In Aid Code of Best Practice in the management and support of aid personnel."

In our sector we rely a great deal on the expertise and experience of people. Evaluations of the sector's work consistently show that it is staff and volunteers that make the difference between effective humanitarian aid or development assistance and inadequate fulfilment of an NGO's mission. As stated in the 2003 annual review of ALNAP (Active Learning Network for Accountability and Performance in Humanitarian Action), "One of the central factors in the success of humanitarian action has been the dedication of staff—ordinary people doing extraordinary things, despite working in disenabling bureaucracies."

NGOs openly and often acknowledge their accountability to two main stake-holders: donors and beneficiaries. People In Aid maintains that to truly satisfy their accountability to these two groups they must also be accountable to those who deliver their missions: their staff and volunteers.

People In Aid was created by the sector with a single remit: to encourage improvements in the way that staff are managed and supported. We were also created as a network of members, so that NGOs committed to improving their human resource management could do so together and had a central resource to assist them.

GUIDING PRINCIPLE

PEOPLE ARE CENTRAL TO THE ACHIEVEMENT OF OUR MISSION.

Our approach to the people who work for us is fundamental to the achievement of our mission. We recognise that the people who work for us merit respect and proper management, and that the effectiveness and success of our operations depend on the contributions of all salaried and contract staff, and volunteers.

Why a "Guiding Principle"?

It is no secret that evaluation after evaluation of relief and development work concludes by emphasising the centrality of people in delivering organisational and programme objectives. This is something People In Aid has been championing since its beginnings in 1995. It is therefore appropriate that, with this revision of the Code, a guiding principle reflects the importance of staff and volunteers in achieving the organisational mission.

The guiding principle makes explicit what is generally accepted, and each of the seven principles that follow assumes the centrality of people to the organisational mission. The principles of the Code of Good Practice provide a sound framework for responding to the challenge of delivering effective human resource management. Those that implement the Code demonstrate their belief in this guiding principle and their commitment to staff and volunteers.

We would hope that those agencies which do not have a corporate value related to their people might consider adopting this guiding principle. We would also hope that when writing in their annual reports, chief executives, presidents, or chairs might reaffirm the guiding principle and recognise the contribution of their colleagues. For those who choose to implement the Code of Good Practice, the guiding principle will become a reality in plans, budgets, training programmes, consultation mechanisms, and the other processes which the Code's principles enlarge upon. The benefits will be felt by your agency, your beneficiaries, your donors, and your colleagues.

PRINCIPLE ONE:
HUMAN RESOURCE STRATEGY

HUMAN RESOURCES ARE AN INTEGRAL PART OF OUR STRATEGIC
AND OPERATIONAL PLANS.

Our human resources strategy is central to our organisational strategy. Our human resources strategy is long term and encompasses every part of the organisation.

Indicators

1. Our organisational strategy or business plan explicitly values staff for their contribution to organisational and operational objectives.
2. The organisational strategy allocates sufficient human and financial resources to achieve the objectives of the human resources strategy.
3. Operational plans and budgets aim to reflect fully our responsibilities for staff management, support, development, and well-being. The monitoring of these plans and budgets feeds into any necessary improvements.
4. Our human resources strategy reflects our commitment to promote inclusiveness and diversity.

PRINCIPLE TWO:
STAFF POLICIES AND PRACTICES

OUR HUMAN RESOURCES POLICIES AIM TO BE EFFECTIVE, FAIR,
AND TRANSPARENT.

We recognise that our policies must enable us to achieve both effectiveness in our work and good quality of working life for our staff. We do not aim to respond solely to minimum legal, professional, or donor requirements.

Indicators

1. Policies and practices that relate to staff employment are set out in writing and are monitored and reviewed, particularly when significant changes in the legal or working environment take place.
2. The policies and practices we implement are consistent in their application to all staff, except while taking into account relevant legal provisions and cultural norms.
3. Staff are familiarised with policies and practices that affect them.
4. Appropriate guidance is provided to managers so that they are equipped to implement policies effectively.
5. The rewards and benefits for each role are clearly identified and applied in a fair and consistent manner.
6. Policies and practices are monitored according to how well they meet:
   - organisational and programme aims; and
   - reasonable considerations of effectiveness, fairness, and transparency.

Principle Three:
Managing People

Good support, management, and leadership of our staff is
key to our effectiveness.

Our staff have a right to expect management which prepares them to do their job so we can, together, achieve our mission. Our management policies, procedures, and training equip our managers to prepare and support staff in carrying out their role effectively, to develop their potential, and to encourage and recognise good performance.

Indicators

1. Relevant training, support, and resources are provided to managers to fulfil their responsibilities. Leadership is a part of this training.
2. Staff have clear work objectives and performance standards, and know whom they report to and what management support they will

receive. A mechanism for reviewing staff performance exists and is clearly understood by all staff.

3.   In assessing performance, managers will adhere to the organisation's procedures and values.

4.   All staff are aware of grievance and disciplinary procedures.

PRINCIPLE FOUR:
CONSULTATION AND COMMUNICATION

DIALOGUE WITH STAFF ON MATTERS LIKELY TO AFFECT THEIR
EMPLOYMENT ENHANCES THE QUALITY AND EFFECTIVENESS OF OUR
POLICIES AND PRACTICES.

We recognise that effective development, implementation, and monitoring of human resources policies and practices rely on appropriate consultation and communication with the people who work for us. We aim to include all staff, whether salaried or contract, and volunteers in these processes.

Indicators

1.   Staff are informed and adequately consulted when we develop or review human resources policies or practices that affect them.

2.   Managers and staff understand the scope of consultation and how to participate, individually or collectively.

PRINCIPLE FIVE:
RECRUITMENT AND SELECTION

OUR POLICIES AND PRACTICES AIM TO ATTRACT AND SELECT A
DIVERSE WORKFORCE WITH THE SKILLS AND CAPABILITIES TO
FULFIL OUR REQUIREMENTS.

Our recruitment and selection process tells candidates about our agency. How we recruit and select our staff significantly influences how effective they are in fulfilling our objectives.

Indicators

1.   Written policies and procedures outline how staff are recruited and selected to positions in our organisation.
2.   Recruitment methods aim to attract the widest pool of suitably qualified candidates.
3.   Our selection process is fair, transparent, and consistent to ensure the most appropriate person is appointed.
4.   Appropriate documentation is maintained and responses are given to candidates regarding their selection/nonselection to posts. We will provide feedback if necessary.
5.   The effectiveness and fairness of our recruitment and selection procedures are monitored.

PRINCIPLE SIX:
LEARNING, TRAINING, AND DEVELOPMENT

LEARNING, TRAINING, AND STAFF DEVELOPMENT ARE PROMOTED

THROUGHOUT THE ORGANISATION.

We recognise the importance of relevant training, development, and learning opportunities, both personal and professional, to help staff work effectively and professionally. We aim to instil a culture of learning in the organisation so that we and the staff can share our learning and develop together.

Indicators

1.   Adequate induction, and briefing specific to each role, is given to all staff.
2.   Written policies outline the training, development, and learning opportunities staff can expect from the organisation.
3.   Plans and budgets are explicit about training provision. Relevant training is provided to all staff.
4.   Managers know how to assess the learning needs of staff so they can facilitate individual development. Where appropriate, training and development will be linked to external qualifications.
5.   The methods we have in place to monitor learning and training ensure that the organisation also learns. They also monitor the

effectiveness of learning and training in meeting organisational and programme aims as well as staff expectations of fairness and transparency.

PRINCIPLE SEVEN:
HEALTH, SAFETY, AND SECURITY

THE SECURITY, GOOD HEALTH, AND SAFETY OF OUR STAFF ARE A PRIME RESPONSIBILITY OF OUR ORGANISATION.

We recognise that the work of relief and development agencies often places great demands on staff in conditions of complexity and risk. We have a duty of care to ensure the physical and emotional well-being of our staff before, during, and on completion.

Indicators

1. Written policies are available to staff on security, individual health, care and support, health and safety.
2. Programme plans include written assessment of security, travel, and health risks specific to the country or region, reviewed at appropriate intervals.
3. Before an international assignment, all staff receive health clearance. In addition they and accompanying dependants receive verbal and written briefing on all risks relevant to the role to be undertaken, and the measures in place to mitigate those risks, including insurance. Agency obligations and individual responsibilities in relation to possible risks are clearly communicated. Briefings are updated when new equipment, procedures, or risks are identified.
4. Security plans, with evacuation procedures, are reviewed regularly.
5. Records are maintained of work-related injuries, sickness, accidents, and fatalities, and are monitored to help assess and reduce future risk to staff.
6. Work plans do not require more hours work than are set out in individual contracts. Time off and leave periods, based on written policies, are mandatory.
7. All staff have a debriefing or exit interview at the end of any contract or assignment. Health checks, personal counseling, and careers

advice are available. Managers are trained to ensure these services are provided.

8. In the case of staff on emergency rosters, managers should ensure that health clearance, immunisations, and procedures for obtaining the correct prophylaxes and other essential supplies are arranged well in advance.

REFERENCES

McNair, R. n.d. Room for Improvement. *Relief and Rehabilitation Network Paper 10.* London: Overseas Development Institute.

EDITORS' NOTES

For more information about People In Aid: http://www.peopleinaid.org/. See their extensive resources related to human resource management in humanitarian assistance.

SOURCE

People In Aid. 2003. Code of good practice in the management and support of aid personnel, 2, 3, 7, 8, 10, 12, 14, 16, 18, 20. London: People In Aid. Reprinted by permission. http://www.peopleinaid.org/pool/files/code/code-en.pdf.

RELATED RESOURCES

Video: Russ, Catherine. 2012. "Global Survey on Humanitarian Professionalisation." 14 March. Enhancing Learning and Research for Humanitarian Assistance (ELRHA) video, 6:59. http://www.elrha.org/news/elrha/globalsurvey.

Global Connections. n.d. Guidelines for good practice in member care. Global Connections. http://www.globalconnections.co.uk/resources/codesandstandards/membercareguidelines.

Missions Interlink NZ. 2012. Guidelines for good practice in member care. Missions Interlink NZ. http://www.missions.org.nz/images/guidelines%20mc%2017%20july%202012.pdf.

People In Aid. Case studies. http://www.peopleinaid.org/resources/casestudies.aspx.

Russ, C. 2011. Global survey on humanitarian professionalism. With support from D. Smith. Enhancing Learning and Research for Humanitarian Assistance. http://www.elrha.org/uploads/Global%20Humanitarian%20Professionalisation%20Survey.pdf.

Also see the listing for chapter 30.

CHAPTER 30

Staff Care in Organizations

Approaches to Staff Care in International NGOs

Benjamin Porter and Ben Emmens,
InterHealth and People In Aid

As the reach of humanitarian aid organisations expands into increasingly insecure and dangerous environments, we hear and read reports of elevated rates of injuries and death. From kidnappings, to vehicle accidents, to targeted killings, to disease, aid workers ranging from short-term missions to long-term development projects are at risk in several locations around the world. For People In Aid and InterHealth the importance of staff care is undeniable, more so now than ever before. In this research, organisations acknowledged their clear role to care for their workers in these unpredictable environments, yet many felt unsure how to build a holistic system of support amidst the new and complex situations in which aid workers find themselves today.

For the past ten years, People In Aid has been supporting NGOs around the world through advising, consulting, networking, training, and through its internationally recognised Code of Good Practice in the Management and Support of Aid Personnel (2003). For the past twenty years, InterHealth has been supporting organisations and churches sending workers to some of the most treacherous places in the world through research, writing, and professional clinical services in the areas of occupational, psychological, and physical/travel health services. In recent strategic reviews, both organisations affirmed their commitment to international outreach as core to their ongoing service delivery. We are very pleased with the partnership between People In Aid and InterHealth and the new opportunities for synergising key initiatives and maximising our potential through separate skills but similar goals and values.

The effects of working in the humanitarian and development sector have been well documented, but there is little research into how organisations mitigate the negative consequences and enhance staff care practice. This review is the first step in a process of discovery which will ultimately include separate reviews of staff care practice, and approaches to in-country staff care provision for national or locally hired staff. The twenty organisations interviewed (nineteen international nongovernmental organisations and one international organisation) cover a broad spectrum, with some working exclusively in emergency/insecure contexts, and others exclusively in a nonemergency context. Some work through advocacy or consulting, others through partnership, secondments, or direct implementation. As such this research should be read as *indicative* of the diverse and innovative approaches to staff care that exists, and not necessarily a representative comparison between organisations.

EXECUTIVE SUMMARY

Background to This Research

Increasingly, humanitarian and development work is undertaken in insecure and sometimes treacherous environments. With a deeper understanding of human vulnerabilities, and a growing appreciation of the risks associated with the work they do, humanitarian and development organisations are realising the growing extent of their duty of care towards the people that deliver their projects and pro-grammes, whether they be full-time or part-time staff, volunteers or consultants, international or local.

In recent years many International NGOs (INGOs) have strengthened the extent and nature of their staff care support. Spurred on by greater awareness and recognition of the benefits, and in the context of various codes and guidelines, there has been a marked increase in investment in staff wellness programmes, counselors, and specialist staff.

There is plenty of anecdotal evidence to suggest this investment is bringing dividends, but organisational approaches vary dramatically, from the ad hoc to the consistently high quality. The diversity of staff care practice identified by this brief report alone demonstrates the high levels of creativity and the depth of critical thinking within organisations as they respond to the unique stressors of humanitarian and development workers in unfamiliar environments. Yet at the same time little has been formally documented regarding the nature and extent of staff care practices across the sector. Through sharing these organisations' experiences of staff care, it is our hope that this piece of research will contribute towards a deeper overall understanding of the current approaches to staff care within the humanitarian and development sector, and encourage organisations to network and take tangible steps towards improving their provision. Several disciplines and factors are involved in developing a comprehensive staff care systems (e.g., health and travel medicine, occupational health and employment law, human resource and management systems), and while several of these disciplines are interwoven in this report, the research focused on mechanisms for emotional and psychological well-being of staff.

In early 2009 People In Aid and InterHealth came together to research the provision of psychological and medical care for international staff and frequent travelers. The focus of this report is on psychological care.

Key Findings

1. Staff care practices appear to be inconsistent, and existing guidelines (or minimum standards) tend not to be adhered to. The questionnaire for this study is based on existing sector guidelines and standards. However, more specific guidelines for staff care are needed to comprehensively guide staff care practice.

2. All organisations have some policies in place covering aspects of staff care, but only one third of the organisations interviewed had a distinct and specific staff care policy. Several organisations are in the process of developing country/programme-specific staff care policy.

3. There are no consistent definitions relating to staff care practices in the humanitarian and development sector, and the scope of staff care provision within agencies is also inconsistent. Organisations expressed interest in determining staff care according to staff types, duration of contract, and context, yet clear definitions for these categories have not been developed.

4. Significant progress has been made with respect to the standardisation of induction. Sixty percent of organisations have a standardised induction process, and 30 percent are actively revamping their induction system.

5. Several organisations have developed robust peer support programmes. The embedded nature of support provides continuity and access to on-the-ground crisis response, but organisations warn that it is not a quick fix.

6. Almost half of the organisations do not have a standard procedure for staff to receive a medical checkup at a travel clinic/hospital,

and only one-quarter of those interviewed require (or strongly encourage) a postassignment psychological review or debriefing upon return. End-of-assignment is a period of rapid transition for the organisation and the staff. A thorough reentry process assists in a smooth transition of organisational knowledge, ensures that continuing or leaving staff are healthy, provides closure, and protects the organisation in the event of subsequent illness.

7. In the current economic environment, staff care is at risk for further cuts, and face-to face interaction may decrease.

8. Less than one-third of the organisations interviewed evaluate their staff care practice. No organisations have conducted research (publicly available) on staff care. Highly developed monitoring and evaluation systems have been developed across the INGO sector to capture the impact of implementation with beneficiaries. Yet the same rigour has not been applied to the evaluation of staff care practices. By providing scientific evidence on the effects of staff care, organisations can determine the effects of the intervention on the staff (positive or negative), as well as the return on investment.

CONCLUSION

The humanitarian and development sector has made considerable progress with respect to staff care in the last ten to fifteen years. Organisations are taking a posture of curiosity and experimentation that is centred in concern for the well-being of staff. Diverse operational models, stemming from diverse organisational missions and visions, have made staff care development an organisation-by-organisation endeavour.

Throughout an individual's life with the organisation, there are three distinct opportunities to offer support: predeparture, on-assignment, and postassignment.

Of the organisations interviewed, there has been significant effort in preparing staff to enter the field. The majority of organisations have implemented standardized inductions, and linkages between the regional/headquarters and the field are strengthening, and this is to be commended.

The on-assignment period continues to be extremely diverse. This is primarily due to various models of operation, but this research shows that many organisations continue to engage with staff illness and distress on an ad hoc basis, which is unsatisfactory. There is opportunity for learning and experience to be shared more systematically at a local level through networking and collaboration. And coordination within and between organisations in country programmes could be more fully explored.

The area where most improvements can be made is that of postassignment/ reentry. In a sector where one assignment/deployment flows into another, and international staff return to massively different contexts without systematic regional or headquarter debriefings, some international staff may "fall through the cracks," risking their personal health and well-being, and putting the organisation at risk of liability.

In addition to taking tangible steps to improve staff care at all stages of an employee's relationship with the organisation, an important next step for the sector is to gain a clear understanding of the impact and effectiveness of staff care initiatives. Evaluations based on outcomes, and measuring indicators such as wellness/sickness absence, productivity, satisfaction, and retention will guide organisations in building a healthy workforce, and will also clearly articulate the return on investment and justify any need for further funding.

A FRAMEWORK FOR ACTION

The report raises many questions relating to staff care; we conclude this summary by highlighting a few of the key questions which we hope will catalyse valuable discussion and thus help any organisation embarking on a review of their approach to staff care:

1. Who is responsible for staff care? Where is the balance between individual and corporate responsibility? To what extent should any policy be proactive or reactive?
2. Who falls under the scope of a staff care policy? What are the differences (if any) in your policy for full-time staff, consultants, and volunteers, and how do they vary by context or location?
3. How can specific staff care practices be developed for the variety of types of staff, duration of contract, and context of work?
4. What are the benefits and limitations of in-house medical or psychological staff care personnel?
5. Which aspects, if any, can be "outsourced"? Has your organisation investigated the appropriate insurance providers, taking into account the specific needs of international aid workers?

6.   In what ways can your organisation coordinate or collaborate with other actors in sharing the costs of staff care?

7.   Should your organisation consider developing a monitoring and evaluation system for current staff care practice, or joining with another organisation in producing an efficacy study?

EDITORS' NOTES

For more information about InterHealth and People In Aid: http://www.interhealth.org.uk/ and http://www.peopleinaid.org/.

SOURCE

Porter, B., and B. Emmens. 2009. Approaches to staff care in international NGOs. London: InterHealth and People In Aid, 3, 7–9. Reprinted by permission. http://www.peopleinaid.org/ pool/files/pubs/approaches-to-staff-care-in-international-ngos.pdf.

RELATED RESOURCES

Video: Centers for Disease Control and Prevention. "Stress Management for Emergency Responders." Antares Foundation. http://www.antaresfoundation.org/podcast/podcasts_on_ stress_management_for_emergency_responders.htm.

Antares Foundation. 2012. *Managing stress in humanitarian workers: Guidelines for good practice*, 3rd ed. Amsterdam, the Netherlands: Antares Foundation. http://www.antaresfounda-tion.org/guidelines.htm.

Danieli, Y., ed. 2002. *Sharing the front line and the back hills: Peacekeepers, humanitarian aid workers, and the media in the midst of crisis.* Amityville, NY: Baywood.

Ehrenreich, J. H. 2002. A guide for humanitarian, health care, and human rights workers: Caring for others, caring for yourself. Hepatitis and AIDS Research Trust. http://www.heart-intl.net/HEART/102504/GuideHumanitarianHeal.pdf.

Fawcett, J., ed. 2003. *Stress and trauma handbook: Strategies for flourishing in demanding environments.* Monrovia, CA: World Vision International.

Hay, R., V. Lim, D. Blocher, J. Ketelaar, and S. Hay. 2007. *Worth keeping: Global perspectives on best practice in missionary retention.* Pasadena: William Carey Library.

International Federation of Red Cross and Red Crescent Societies. 2001. Psychological support programme for delegates. In *Psychological support: Best practices from Red Cross and Red Crescent programmes*, 18–21. Geneva: International Federation of Red Cross and Red Crescent Societies. http://helid.digicollection.org/en/d/Js2902e/5.html.

———. 2009. *Managing stress in the field*, 4th ed. Geneva: International Federation of Red Cross and Red Crescent Societies. http://www.ifrc.org/Global/Publications/Health/managing-stress-en.pdf.

International Labor Organization. 2012. Stress prevention at work checkpoints: Practical improvements for stress prevention in the workplace. Geneva: International Labor Organization. http://www.ilo.org/wcmsp5/groups/public/---dgreports/---dcomm/---publ/documents / publication/wcms_168053.pdf.

Member Care Associates. Organisational links. http://membercareassociates. org/?page_id=28.

O'Donnell, K., ed. 2002. *Doing member care well: Perspectives and practices from around the world.* Pasadena: William Carey Library.

———. 2011. *Global member care: The pearls and perils of good practice.* Pasadena: William Carey Library.

United Nations High Commissioner for Refugees. 2000. Too high a price? *Refugee* 4, no. 121. http://www.unhcr.org/3b69138b2.html.

CHAPTER 31

Resilience, Risk, and Responsibility

CARING FOR VOLUNTEERS: A PSYCHOSOCIAL SUPPORT TOOLKIT

International Federation of Red Cross and Red Crescent Societies'
Reference Centre for Psychosocial Support

FOREWORD

2011. Mass shooting in Norway, earthquakes in New Zealand, civil unrest in the Middle East, and a gigantic earthquake, tsunami, and nuclear scare in Japan: all were major disasters and dramatic events where Red Cross and Red Crescent (RCRC) staff and volunteers were asked to provide psychosocial support to survivors and family members. Some National Societies were well prepared; others realized they were not. Occasions like these caused every society to reflect on how they could improve their preparedness.

Staff and volunteers across the globe provide important psychosocial support every day. Not only in response to disasters, armed conflicts, and mass shootings, but also in social programmes for slum-dwellers, with victims of violence or accidents, with elderly and isolated people, with people stigmatized because of illness and prejudice, and with refugees and asylum seekers.

Clear Message

During the psychosocial support workshop at the IFRC General Assembly in Geneva in November 2011, a number of National Societies spoke about their experiences and work. And their message was clear: we need to be much better in training and preparing our staff and volunteers for the important work of helping our beneficiaries—and to help ourselves and each other.

The role of volunteers in emergencies is increasingly complex. In the emergency environment, staff and volunteers are exposed to trauma, loss and devastation, injury, and even death. They may find themselves comforting survivors in the initial phases of shock and grief, or providing survivors of violence with their first encounter with someone who can understand and give a human perspective to inhumane actions.

FIRST AID NOT ENOUGH

Volunteers may work long hours in challenging emergency environments, often putting aside their own needs. At the end of the day they often feel inadequate to help beneficiaries with the tragedy they are facing. Additionally, as members of affected communities, volunteers often work close to home and may experience the same losses and grief in their families and communities as the beneficiaries they are supporting. Basic first-aid training or being part of a disaster response team is not enough to prepare volunteers for these emotional experiences. It is of course difficult to prepare for every type of event and to include every single volunteer.

But it is possible to be prepared, both for supporting the well-being of staff and volunteers, as well as for the many other aspects of disaster response. A 2009 report with nineteen participating National Societies showed that preparedness for psychosocial support to volunteers had often been developed *after* a major disaster, but that most had wished they had had plans in place *before*. In other words, and as is said on planes every day, "Put on your own oxygen mask first, before you assist others."

SMALL MEASURES, BIG IMPACT

This toolkit will help you do exactly that. Other materials available from the IFRC Reference Centre on Psychosocial Support (the PS Centre) mainly deal with assisting beneficiaries, whereas this toolkit has been written especially to help you assist volunteers—before, during, and after a crisis.

Although the focus is on volunteers, "Caring for Volunteers" will also provide useful tools for staff to use. Whether yours is a large or small society, whether you are often involved in emergencies or mainly work through social programmes, you can adapt the information in this toolkit to suit your own particular needs.

This toolkit supplements the main manual for "Volunteers in Emergencies," to be published by the IFRC in late 2012. It will help you tailor your guidelines for psychosocial support in ways that

- are feasible for your National Society,
- are adequate to the responsibilities and risks your volunteers may face, and
- make best use of your Society's capacities and resources.

RESILIENCE, RISK, AND RESPONSIBILITY (CHAPTER 1)

Understanding Resilience

Resilience is a person's ability to cope with challenges and difficulties, and to restore and maintain a new balance when the old one is challenged or destroyed. It is often described as the ability to "absorb shocks and bounce back."

How each person responds to stress—whether they develop psychological problems or show resilience—is influenced by many factors, including the nature and severity of the crisis event, personality and personal history, and available support systems. Volunteers who are personally impacted by the crisis in which they are helping may have an additional vulnerability to stress, but they—as well as all volunteers—may benefit from training and support from peers and the organization.

The interacting social, psychological, and biological factors that keep people resilient are called protective factors. They reduce the likelihood of severe psychological effects when encountering hardship or suffering. Belonging to a caring family or community, maintaining traditions and cultures, and having a strong religious belief or political ideology are all examples of protective factors. For volunteers working in emergency settings, other protective factors may include the motivation to help others, a good social support system, being able to leave work behind and take a rest, and the ability to give support to and receive support from team members.

For example, after the bomb and shootings in Norway in July 2011, the Red Cross encouraged volunteers to talk openly about their reactions, and regular debriefings were organized. A special programme was implemented to train and assist staff and volunteers in local branches to provide support to affected young people and their relatives returning home after the tragedy.

Providing clear information about and easy access to available support is also essential. Knowing there is support available, if and when it is needed, provides a safety net to volunteers and emergency response teams as they take on the difficult tasks of helping others in crisis.

Fostering Resilience

National Societies can create conditions that foster resilience in individual volunteers and response teams. For example, consider these helpful measures:

- Encourage reasonable working conditions through policies and strategies.
- Provide accessible guidance and support from managers and peers.
- Create an organizational culture where people can talk openly and share problems, and respect the principle of confidentiality.
- Arrange regular meetings which bring all staff and/or volunteers together and foster a feeling of belonging to a team.
- Create a work culture where getting together after a critical event is the norm; e.g., a peer support system.
- Show appreciation for the work of volunteers.

Risks to Volunteer Well-being

In choosing to assist in difficult situations, volunteers may be exposed to destruction, death, stories of loss and grieving of survivors, and sometimes insecurity in the crisis environment. In addition, the traditional heroic role of RCRC staff and volunteers includes expectations that they are selfless, tireless, and somehow superhuman, even in the face of overwhelming tragedy. The demands of the situation may far exceed their capacity to help, and at the end of the day they often feel they have not done enough.

But it is not the exposure to trauma or extreme circumstances that most often causes stress for volunteers. Those who act as helpers often find meaning in their work, and through this they are able to cope with the situations they are exposed to. Instead, volunteers (and staff) face a more frequent kind of stress that comes from working conditions and organizational issues. Let us look more closely at some of the main risks to the psychological well-being of volunteers:

- exposure to traumatic events and stories
- unrealistic expectations
- heroic aspirations
- working conditions
- organizational issues

Exposure to traumatic events and stories.

Exposure to certain terrible things—such as graphic scenes of destruction, or injury or death of children—are particularly difficult for any responder. Volunteers may feel guilt at the death of someone they take care of, and must cope with their own fears about death and suffering as they assist others. Some volunteers may work in close proximity to the crisis event—on the "front lines" of helping people very recently or severely affected.

Being a witness to traumatic events—or hearing stories of trauma and loss of survivors—can be very distressing for the volunteer. In addition, as volunteers often come from affected communities, the crisis may have impacted them and their families directly. They may have lost relatives, or their property may be destroyed. Volunteers may have the same needs for assistance as the beneficiaries they are helping.

Unrealistic expectations.

Volunteers are often poorly prepared for their own emotional reactions to the impact of their experiences when providing care and relief to others. In their compassion for those who are suffering, volunteers may expect themselves to deny their own needs and work tirelessly. Their own situation and problems are pushed into the background. For example, they may feel it is not alright for them to go to their home for rest when others have lost their homes, or to enjoy seeing their families when survivors have lost loved ones. Of course these expectations are unrealistic and easily lead to high levels of stress. Volunteers' own needs and reactions must be addressed at some point.

Heroic aspirations.

In addition, some volunteers are motivated by the idea they can "save the world." When they are unable to meet the overwhelming needs of beneficiaries in crisis, they may feel inadequate. Some beneficiaries may also have unrealistic expectations of what the volunteer can do for them. Volunteers may be unprepared for facing the frustration and anger of beneficiaries who feel their needs are not being met.

Working conditions.

Harsh working conditions related to the nature of the emergency can cause chronic stress for volunteers. They may perform physically difficult, exhausting, and sometimes dangerous tasks, or be expected (or expect themselves) to work long hours in difficult circumstances. Volunteers may find themselves working in a prolonged crisis and becoming increasingly detached from their own family and home life. If they become part of a collective crisis—such as a massive natural disaster—or if they face moral and ethical dilemmas, their stress is increased. They may feel inadequate to deal with the task, or overwhelmed by the needs of the people they are trying to help.

Organizational issues.

Organizational issues have a very big impact on the stress and well-being of volunteers and staff. Stress can be caused by the following kinds of organizational issues:

- unclear or nonexistent job description, or unclear role in the team
- lack of information about the crisis
- poor preparation and briefing for the task
- lack of boundaries between work and rest
- inconsistent or inadequate supervision
- an atmosphere at the workplace where volunteer well-being is not valued and where their efforts are not being acknowledged and appreciated

WHEN STRESS FROM WORKING CONDITIONS AND ORGANIZATIONAL ISSUES IS NOT ADDRESSED, VOLUNTEER WELL-BEING AND THE QUALITY OF THEIR WORK CAN BE AFFECTED.

Burnout.

Chronic work-related stress from all of these factors puts volunteers at special risk of *burnout*. Burnout is an emotional state due to long-term stress, characterized by chronic emotional exhaustion, depleted energy, impaired enthusiasm and motivation to work, diminished work efficiency, a diminished sense of personal accomplishment, and pessimism and cynicism.

A survey of the well-being of the volunteers who assisted after Cyclone Nargis in Myanmar in 2008 was conducted in cooperation with Yangon University. It showed that almost one in ten volunteers was feeling extremely depressed or burned out. One of the reasons was lack of appreciation. The Myanmar Red Cross took serious action and began organizing appreciation ceremonies for the volunteers, as well as encouraging hubs/branches to be more aware of the volunteers' well-being and to support those who needed it. Among the initiatives was an international photo exhibition highlighting the work and stories of twenty-five of the volunteers.

Burnout implies that stress factors have taken over and that the person is so exhausted they are no longer able to distance themselves from their situation. They may forget about their own needs for rest and recreation, and eventually find that they have no more energy available, and thus no more to give in the form of support to others. Often the affected person is the last one to realize what is happening. For this reason, it is important for the whole team to understand the causes of stress and burnout and to be able to recognize the signs early on.

Warning Signs of Burnout

Look out for warning signs that volunteers could be close to burnout:

- physical symptoms, such as headaches or sleep difficulties
- behaviour changes, such as risk-taking or drinking too much alcohol
- relational problems, such as temper outbursts or withdrawing from colleagues
- becoming less efficient at work or having difficulty concentrating
- developing a negative attitude toward the job or organization, or toward beneficiaries themselves
- emotional distress, such as continuous feelings of sadness

BEING RESPONSIBLE FOR VOLUNTEER WELL-BEING

Volunteers work within the framework of National Societies as they help in emergency responses. That framework can be supportive and protective for volunteers when everyone in the system understands the risks of the job and actively supports resilience and well-being. Thus volunteers well-being is everyone's responsibility— managers, staff, and the volunteers themselves. However, each group has different responsibilities, and we will elaborate on these later.

One way to increase the resilience of volunteers and response teams is to ensure everyone understands what they are likely to encounter in emergencies and how it can affect their psychological well-being. If a manager, for example, does not understand and value the importance of supporting staff and volunteers through the risks of the job, he or she may not create a supportive and reasonable working environment for the team. The system of support then breaks down, affecting the whole team. To avoid burnout, everyone involved in the work must be aware of and respect personal and practical limitations, and take responsibility to treat each other with respect. Everyone plays a role in keeping the team and themselves healthy and functioning well together.

NATIONAL SOCIETIES HAVE AN OBLIGATION TO SUPPORT THE WELL-BEING
OF THEIR VOLUNTEERS BEFORE, DURING, AND AFTER THE EMERGENCY RESPONSE.

At these key points, measures can be taken to reduce the likelihood that volunteers will develop stress-related problems. Equipped with information and support from the National Society, volunteers are then better able to:

- manage their stress;
- work effectively in a team;
- seek help when they need it; and
- sustain their own well-being through the demands of the job.

Before the emergency response, the primary intervention consists of good, solid information about the tasks at hand, about stress, and about how to cope with emotional reactions to difficult situations. Such information prepares helpers to detect their own reactions and offers options for self-care and peer support.

During the emergency response, it is important to remember that the needs of volunteers and staff are often similar to the needs of those they are supporting. They too benefit from support that reduces the likelihood of developing stress-related problems. A supportive environment is one of the many crucial factors in minimizing stress.

After the response is over, volunteers need appraisal of their work and signs from others that they and their work have been valued. Reflecting together with a supervisor or peers after the response can help volunteers to understand and come to terms with their experiences.

In addition, it may take some time for volunteers and staff to process what they have seen and heard during the crisis—and what they were and were not able to do for others.

It is helpful to follow up with volunteers over time to assess their needs for support.

After the armed conflict in 2011, the Libyan Red Crescent recorded the experiences of some of the volunteers there. The National Society realized that it had not been well prepared to handle the reactions of young volunteers being sent into conflict areas as ambulance drivers or first aiders. The lessons learned have now formed the foundation of a new psychosocial programme in Libya, supported by a number of movement partners like the Danish and Italian Red Cross and the Palestine Red Crescent.

In prolonged crises or massive events, the personal situation for the volunteer may continue to be challenging. At times volunteers and staff may show signs of serious stress reactions or other mental health problems. Each programme should have a *referral mechanism for individuals in need of professional support.*

All of these measures—before, during, and after—not only assist the well-being and recovery for volunteers as community members themselves, it also helps to keep volunteers motivated and engaged.

Managers and Volunteer Resilience

Managers play an important role in creating a supportive team dynamic by showing concern for the well-being of individual volunteers and the team as a whole. They can

- ensure reasonable working hours and conditions for volunteers,
- prepare job descriptions or make clear what is expected,
- prepare and train volunteers for their task in the field,
- check in with volunteers to see how they are coping during the emergency response,
- have regular team meetings during the emergency to check in with the team and offer support,
- encourage volunteer work to be carried out in pairs,
- set up peer support or buddy systems,
- offer information about stress and its impacts,
- encourage good coping strategies,
- support volunteers who have experienced especially difficult events, and
- show appreciation and let volunteers know they are valued members of the team.

EDITORS' NOTES

For more information about the International Federation of Red Cross and Red Crescent Societies: http://www.ifrc.org/.

SOURCE

International Federation of Red Cross and Red Crescent Societies' Reference Centre for Psychosocial Support. 2012. *Caring for volunteers: A psychosocial support toolkit.* Copenhagen, Denmark: International Federation of Red Cross and Red Crescent Societies, 1–19. Reprinted by permission. http://ifrc.org/psychosocial.

RELATED RESOURCES

Video: International Federation Reference Centre for Psychosocial Support. "Rebuilding Hope." International Federation of Red Cross and Red Crescent Societies. http://psp.drk.dk/sw40692.asp.

Foyle, M. 2001. *Honourably wounded: Stress among Christian workers,* rev. ed. London: Monarch.

Handy, C. 1988. *Understanding voluntary organisations: How to make them function effectively.* London: Penguin Books.

Levine, S., A. Pain, S. Bailey, and L. Fan. 2012. The relevance of 'resilience'? *HPG Policy Brief 49* (September). http://www.odi.org.uk/sites/odi.org.uk/files/odi-assets/publications-opinion-files/7818.pdf.

Stoddard, A., A. Harmer, and V. DiDomenico. 2009. Providing aid in insecure environments: 2009 update; Trends in violence against aid workers and the operational response. *HPG Policy Brief 34* (April). http://www.odi.org.uk/resources/docs/4243.pdf.

Williamson, C. 2010. Personnel management and security. *Humanitarian Exchange 47* (June): 14–17. http://www.odihpn.org/humanitarian-exchange-magazine/issue-47/personnel-management-and-security.

Also see the listing for chapter 30.

CHAPTER 32

Strengthening Organizational Culture and Effectiveness

THE STATE OF THE UNHCR's ORGANIZATION CULTURE

Barb Wigley, United Nations High Commissioner for Refugees

The Office of the United Nations High Commissioner for Refugees (UNHCR) was established in 1950 by the United Nations General Assembly. The agency is mandated to lead and coordinate international action to protect refugees and resolve refugee problems worldwide. Its primary purpose is to safeguard the rights and well-being of refugees. It strives to ensure that everyone can exercise the right to seek asylum and find safe refuge in another State, with the option to return home voluntarily, integrate locally, or resettle in a third country. It also has a mandate to help stateless people. In more than five decades, the agency has helped tens of millions of people restart their lives. Today, a staff of some 6,600 people in more than 110 countries continues to help about 34 million persons.

EXECUTIVE SUMMARY

"The State of UNHCR's Organization Culture" is the report of a research project undertaken in collaboration between the Staff Development Section, and the Evaluation and Policy Analysis Unit of UNHCR, and the University of Melbourne in Australia. The study was developed independently of any other existing processes or reviews, and the data was primarily gathered between November 2003 and April 2004.

The report essentially argues that the *culture and climate* of this organization have a significant impact on organizational performance and outcomes.

- **Organization culture** consists of commonly held overt and unspoken assumptions or understandings that are learned and passed on to new members and which serve as guides to acceptable and unacceptable perceptions, thoughts, feelings, and behaviours.
- **Organization climate** refers to employees' perceptions about the way in which their workplace functions, including their experience of, for example, leadership and managerial practices, key policies, interpersonal dynamics and communication, and the emotional tenor of the workplace.

... The research analysed a wide range of organizational issues from the perspective of their interaction with organization culture, climate, and dynamics. Taking this perspective as the central theme, it should be noted that the report does not set out to provide a definitive assessment of the organization as a whole; for example, it does not provide analysis of operations from a technical, financial, or political standpoint, although these factors are considered in as much as they influence or are influenced by organizational culture and climate.

... The report emphasises that lack of attention to cultural factors:

- ensures limited success in any change endeavours,
- lowers organizational morale, and
- reduces the overall effectiveness of the organization.

The research was conducted utilising a qualitative approach in line with established methodology in the research of culture arising from anthropology and systems psycho-dynamic frameworks. It draws upon ethnographic, in-depth interview and participant observation techniques, along with some documentation review. The rigor of the approach lies in the number of people participating in individual or group interviews (over one hundred), the length of time spent immersed in the organization (around five months in the data-gathering phase and a further three months validating the findings) and the number of country operations visited (thirteen, including HQ). A number of staff assisted in the development and refinement of the final report by providing responses to their reading of the first drafts, which were subsequently incorporated into the final product.

In conducting this broad analysis of staff experience and perceptions of UNHCR, the intention has been to provide the organization with additional means by which it may solve some of the persistent problems it faces. The report is presented largely as a resource to augment, inform, and tie together other processes and reviews currently underway or being planned. It offers a unique perspective and insights that aim to enable both a greater understanding of the underlying dynamics that currently get in the way of successful change management and problem solving in many areas, and a broader range of options for planning and the development of strategies for action.

In addition to the specific recommendations summarised below, it is hoped that as a consequence of wide access to the details of the report, common dynamics and patterns of interaction within the organization, and particularly those that staff find problematic, may be brought to conscious attention and stimulate reflection, discussion, and debate. Through heightened awareness of, for example, the roles all members of the organization play in sustaining, creating, and perpetuating dynamics that most are unhappy with, it becomes possible on an interpersonal and local level to facilitate some degree of incremental change.

It is not sufficient to merely "blame others" either inside or outside the organization, or to locate the responsibility for change solely at the feet of senior management. This report aims to demonstrate how culture is shaped and embedded at every level and sustained by everyone in different ways. From this perspective it is therefore also possible to imagine that, in small and large ways, anyone in the organization has the potential to contribute to a gradual shift of the culture in more positive directions.

Overview of Findings

Strengths

The report discusses a number of organizational strengths that are related to its culture, and emphasises that at the same time that it struggles with conflict and dysfunction, UNHCR is also immensely strong, intelligent, and successful. Some key organizational strengths related to culture that are outlined in the report are as follows:

- The mandate
- The commitment and talent of many staff
- Satisfaction with being able to directly help refugees and "make a difference"
- Many strong bonds and positive relationships
- Many talented managers and leaders

- A firm conviction that the organization should and could be doing better
- A common understanding at all levels of the organization's shortcomings
- A high degree of idealism and commitment to the cause
- Skills in dealing with all levels of operations from governmental politics to relationships with refugees
- A strong belief in democracy
- Ability to mobilise resources/emergency capability
- Training and learning
- Diversity
- A high level of capacity to think analytically

UNHCR has a clear core purpose, or "primary task," expressed through its mission statement and its mandate. It achieves this task fully or partially much of the time through the efforts of many talented and skilled staff. As with any other organization, UNHCR also has a number of other secondary and auxiliary tasks that it must attend to in the service of the wider organizational goals. For a number of reasons, these secondary tasks can have a tendency to gain precedence over the actual primary task, distract focus from the core purpose, and at times even undermine its achievement, thus contributing to a considerable degree of internal stress and dissatisfaction. In this case, it can be considered that the secondary or auxiliary tasks have gained a prominence disproportionate to the actual primary task, becoming alternative primary tasks. In UNHCR the major alternative primary task appears to be self-perpetuation, with a preoccupation with becoming and remaining "organized." For example, reporting requirements and the complex processes and impact of rotating international staff take significant time and energy away from the core work of safeguarding the rights and well-being of refugees.

Hindrances

Much of what gets in the way of the organization achieving its goals and functioning as effectively as it might originates through the anxiety created by the enormity and complexity of the work and the desire to exert some control and predictability over an environment that is extremely difficult to control or predict. For example, the organization must deal with the trauma and desperate circumstances of the refugees in its care, the high expectations of a global community reflected primarily through donors, complex politics, and a high degree of risk where much is at stake. Some of the outcomes of these tensions are as follows:

- UNHCR comprises an uncomfortable mix of two seemingly opposite and incongruent styles of operation. On the one hand, it is drawn on many levels to crisis and short-term modes of operation that are not always necessary or appropriate and which lead to a lack of effective reflection and long-term planning. On the other hand, the organization has developed a bureaucratic style of operation that is in part a result of the organization engaged in the alternative primary task of self-perpetuation and "organization." The evolution of a highly bureaucratic style is an expression of attempts to control and contain. Without a clear thinking through of what should be controlled and contained and in what way, however, this mode of operation largely fails to do this successfully, and instead, for example, impedes UNHCR's ability to adapt sufficiently rapidly to the current environment of competition for funding, slows action and decision making, diffuses accountability, and creates a high degree of frustration. Some specific examples of this are as follows:
  - The volume of frameworks, guidelines, and reporting requirements imposed by HQ on the field in part represents a response to concern regarding the capabilities of staff and the magnitude of the task, and exacerbates conflict and distance between HQ and the field.
  - The organization avoids problems of accountability and poor performance, and along with lack of mechanisms to reward good performance, this undermines its potential.
  - The rotation policy as it is currently structured and implemented serves an aspect of the alternative primary task of the organization; that is, to remain preoccupied with the organizing of the organization and to distract from achievement of the stated primary task.
- There are many strong and well-regarded leaders throughout UNHCR, but as a result of complex organizational dynamics and defences, UNHCR experiences a lack of cohesive leadership, direction, and containing authority; and leadership is often unclear and undermined at all levels. The scene is set at the senior management level and

influences how leadership is taken up and perceived throughout the organization.

- UNHCR has developed some organizational defences against the anxiety created by its primary task that create significant conflict and get in the way of growth, reflection, change, and the fulfilment of task. For example:
  - There is a complex relationship between UNHCR workers and refugees, which can cause workers, without adequate training and support, to defend themselves against the very people they are there to assist.
  - An unquestioned underlying assumption in UNHCR that "fairness" should take precedence over most other issues in decision and policy making is an organizational defence and an unachievable aim that leads to the suppression of difference and to the treating of people equally unfairly.
  - Conflict and difference between sub and interest groups across the organization express organizational defences such as splitting, competition, and envy, where stories of the "other" reflect, for example, racial and gender stereotypes and perceptions of threat, exclusion, and "nepotism."
  - The organization fails to adequately meet the support and welfare needs of its staff through managerial, psychological, staff development, and organizational support mechanisms.
  - The deep level of commitment to the cause and the mandate of the organization, while an underlying strength, also presents a vulnerability to exploitation in terms of personal sacrifice and reduces the incentives within the organization to resolve structural and organizational problems.
  - The internal dynamics and relationships of the organization in many ways can be found reproduced in its relationships with donors, implementing partners, and peer agencies. Over the past few years UNHCR has commissioned a number of internal and external reviews on a range of issues of concern to the organization (not necessarily specifically concerned with organization culture) that contain many similar findings and recommendations to those included in this report. Aspects of organization culture, including many of those discussed in the report, may

provide clues as to what often gets in the way of the organization acting upon what it knows to be problematic, even in the face of repeated evidence and the existence of clear recommendations for change. It should be noted also, however, that a number of recent initiatives are aiming to address aspects of organizational functioning raised through this research. The perspectives offered in this report aim to provide some additional resources to assist in the successful implementation of these.

OVERVIEW OF RECOMMENDATIONS

The primary recommendations focus upon five key areas of most relevance to the subject matter. A second section of recommendations included in the main report offers supplementary thoughts and issues of concerns that were raised in the report, in less developed format, as a resource. A summary of the recommendations related to the five key areas are as follows:

Leadership and Authority

The report argues that it is critical that UNHCR values and supports the development of its leaders and managers and, in particular, the development of a positive managerial culture and a higher consistency of people management skills. Much research in the field of organizations has emphasised the primary impact that improvements in the quality of leadership and management practices have on organizational well-being, morale and, ultimately, functioning. In the UNHCR context this could involve, for example:

- increased cohesion at the most senior levels;
- high-profile support and reinforcement for participation in management learning processes, and at the same time there needs to be a broad-ranging approach to the development of management skills that is designed to complement, while not entirely relying upon, in-house management learning programmes;
- active supervision and support of leaders and managers in their roles by line managers; and
- development of mechanisms to select and "groom" potential managers with the highest degree of aptitude for the role.

Planning and the Primary Task

Lack of planning and reflection have an impact on outcomes and ability to learn from experience. A greater formalisation and modeling of the value of thinking and planning would institutionalise planning practices further and allow the organization to incorporate much of what it learns through the numerous evaluations and reports generated each year in a more structured and reliable way. It is recommended that UNHCR:

- develop means by which long-range planning and thinking can occur collaboratively at a senior level,
- use improved planning and reviewing processes to develop clearer parameters and guidance regarding the primary task of the organization,
- build in formal and regular planning and reflection opportunities throughout various and strategic sections of the organization,
- encourage local managers to enable regular team-based reflection and discussion opportunities, and
- ensure that ground-level practice informs strategy through opportunities for the field to have input into planning processes.

Conflict and Competition

There are some approaches that might be used for tackling problems of conflict and competition directly; however, they may also be reduced through a number of indirect means that seek to address underlying causes rather than just the symptoms. Problematic organizational defences, such as conflict and competition, are stimulated by a range of other factors that contribute to a less-integrated method of functioning in the organization. Therefore it makes sense to suggest that, if some of the source problems can be ameliorated, their negative side effects may also be reduced somewhat. For example, through:

- strengthening of leadership at all levels of the organization as one of the primary interventions, as mentioned above;
- mobilisation of energy around primary task and refocusing the attention of workgroups to more clearly defined goals;
- attention to an increase in accountability mechanisms;
- some sensitisation to racial, gender, and sexual stereotyping in the organization; and
- strengthening of staff welfare and support services.

Culture of Sacrifice

The findings of this research encourage a rethinking of the systems that ask too much of people, as both staff and refugees stand to benefit in the long run. Such an aim might be worked towards through, for example:

- leadership from senior levels to place reasonable boundaries around what people do;
- an acknowledgment of difference within the organization, and reflection within appropriate forums regarding ways in which different needs and life stages might be accommodated more effectively;
- a challenging of many of the underlying assumptions, such as "everyone should be exactly the same" and dynamics that restrict thinking and options;
- addressing the need for some form of career management structures;
- greater access to staff welfare services, as mentioned above, and taking up of the findings regarding health problems in the organization may assist people to find more ways to balance their own needs with those of the organization.

Relationships with Refugees

There needs to be a greater degree of support within the organization for the development of skills in managing the face-to-face challenges of working with refugees, rather than relying upon a belief that goodwill and a passion for the work is enough. Through, for example:

- establishing policy and an expectation that all workers with hands-on roles with refugees are given access to regular supervision and support by their managers;
- possible establishment of team or peer support and skill-development strategies, such as a buddy system and regular team discussion/reflection opportunities; and
- ensuring that all staff who work for UNHCR in hands-on roles have access to training and education regarding managing refugee relationships and situations of trauma, aggression, etc.

SOME EXCERPTS FROM THE REPORT

4. From November 2003 until early January 2004 and for a short time in March 2004, I was based at headquarters in Geneva. I joined the Staff Development Section and participated in the daily life of the organization and of that section in particular. I sought to interview as many people throughout HQ as I could gain access to during that time, and met with people at every level of the organization and from as many backgrounds, programme areas, and roles as possible. I attended meetings, forums, and staff gatherings.

5. From late January until mid-March 2004 and then between mid-April and early May 2004, I visited the field in Africa, the Balkans, and Southeast Asia. In total I visited the operations of twelve countries outside headquarters. In each country I spent time at the branch office in the capital city and then visited at least one suboffice, except where there were none, and whenever possible I also visited refugee camps or settlements. The length of time I spent in each location varied between a few hours to a week. I met with as many staff members as I could, either individually or in groups, from the drivers to the representatives. I also attempted to participate in or observe as many aspects of the day-to-day operations in the field as feasible at each location, which included attending meeting with donors and implementing partners, tagging along with field officers working in the camps or traveling to remote areas to access beneficiaries.

6. Following is the list of questions that I generally used in each interview, both in HQ and field settings. While these were not rigidly adhered to every time, they formed a loose framework and were raised in the majority. I particularly attempted to ensure each time that both strengths and weaknesses were asked about, so as not to lead people solely into a discussion of the negative.

Demographics:
- Current role, length of service, brief work history, and what led you to work for UNHCR.

The Organization:
- What do you see as the greatest strengths of UNHCR?
- What are its most significant weaknesses in your view?
- Where are the main conflicts or tensions in the organization?
- How well is the organization in tune with the needs of its staff, in both field and HQ settings?

- What are the greatest support needs of staff in the field?
- How would you describe leadership and management in UNHCR?
- How does the organization manage difference? For example, in gender and culture.
- In general, how would you characterize the relationship between UNHCR and the refugees it works with?
- If you were High Commissioner for a week and you could be sure of success, what one or two things would you change as the highest priority?

8. My intention is to be vague about exactly which offices I visited, as the purpose was to saturate myself in the overall culture of the organization to an extent that I might be able to discover general findings that apply to the organization as a whole. While I learnt a great deal about the specific challenges and situations in different areas, I was clear with project participants that my report would not identify their particular regions or analyse locally specific problems, as tempting as that might be. My concern was that the report not be seen as a critique of specific operations and teams, but rather I was in a unique position to experience some of what happens in the organization as a whole.

9. I also took the opportunity whenever possible to meet, on my own or just with an interpreter, with refugees, implementing partners, peer agencies, and donors, to discuss their perspectives regarding UNHCR. It should be stressed, however, that my main focus has been on the views and experience of those within the organization, and the data related to external stakeholders is limited, and discussion of these external perspectives is brief by comparison.

10. Since submitting the first draft of the report in mid-2004, a detailed process of feedback and further data gathering has been undertaken. Initial comments were incorporated to shape a second draft, which was then distributed amongst the Senior Management Committee and a number of other staff members who have key areas of expertise, for further discussion. This has constituted an ongoing process between September and December 2004 of dialogue and data verification.

The Report

20. While there are many struggles and complexities across UNHCR that contribute to the stress levels of the staff and impact on the nature of the work and its outcomes, it has to be said that it is an organization with enormous strengths and charisma and which serves a critical and immensely valuable service to the world.

My intention in telling stories of this organization, that necessitate discussing some aspects of its "darker side," is as an offering for reflection and insight, as a means to stimulate thought and dialogue that may assist a strong and worthy organization to become even better. It is not my intention to "pathologise the behaviour and functioning of the institution and its individual members without giving true regard to the effectiveness with which the conscious real-world tasks of the organization are being pursued" (Mosse 1994, 7). UNHCR is both immensely strong, intelligent, and successful, and beset by conflict, weakness, drama, pain, and dysfunction. I hope that I have done justice to its strengths, while acknowledging that I spend more time on the aspects of the organization that cause distress and undermine its performance.

My Experience on the Project

23. Thus the writing of the report has been a labour of both affection and anxiety. My experience of such generosity and openness gives data as to a strength of the organizational culture, and contributed very much to my own sense of attachment and regard for the organization. My anxiety rests partly around the enormity of the task that I got myself into, a sense of being overwhelmed, perhaps paralleling in some ways the enormity of the task of the organization as a whole. And it also resides around my desire to "do the right thing"—to honour the knowledge and experience that has been so generously entrusted to me.

Staff Support

212. Organization culture has a role in determining values about the approach to work and how stress might be managed within that organization. A number of research studies have found workplace design and dynamics (such as interactions and the nature of relationships) to be more important than personal coping mechanisms in determining health or ill health. The methods that workers use to cope with their own stress are influenced and shaped by what happens between people and the experiences that they share within particular organizational contexts. These processes occur predominantly outside conscious awareness, where people unwittingly join together in reproducing social structures and interactions that may be experienced as distressing. These structures also often mirror social and political power structures in the wider society. Many examples in UNHCR have already been discussed.

213. Research within the humanitarian aid field has found that both exposure to traumatic events and organizational and interpersonal issues were among the greatest sources of stress for workers (Bierens de Haan 2002; Macnair 1995). A study entitled

"Stress, Coping and Burnout" was conducted within UNHCR by the University of Bristol in 2001–2. In line with similar research elsewhere in the humanitarian field, they found that the major source of stress and burnout in UNHCR was systemic in nature, with the factors reported to cause the most stress being work overload and lack of resources. They suggested that while critical incident stress as a result of difficult or dangerous field postings had been addressed by the organization to some extent, it was important to recognise that high levels of emotional exhaustion and burnout were being reported throughout a range of duty stations, including HQ, and not just those in hazardous locations.

214. Workload and lack of resources also came up anecdotally as significant sources of stress in this research. Some staff commented that people are expected to complete unrealistic workloads and feel that they have to keep working until the work is completed. This is compounded in the field by the number of posts being cut and the consequent increase in workload for those remaining.

REFERENCES

Bierens de Haan, DB, Van Beerendonk, H., Michel, N., Mulli, J.-C. 2002, 'Le Programme de soutien psychologique des intervenants humanitaires du Comite International de la Croix-Rouge', *Revue Francaise de Psychiatre et de Psychologie Medicale* 53, no. 6.

Macnair, R. 1995. *Room For Improvement: The Management and Support of Relief and Development Workers*, Overseas Development Institute, London.

EDITORS' NOTES

See also the follow-up study: Wigley, B. 2006. The state of the UNHCR's organisation culture: What now? Geneva: United Nations High Commissioner for Refugees, Evaluation and Policy Analysis Unit. http://www.unhcr.org/43eb6a862.pdf.

For more information about the UNHCR: http://www.unhcr.org/.

SOURCE

Wigley, B. 2005. *The state of UNHCR's organization culture*. Geneva: United Nations High Commissioner for Refugees, Evaluation and Policy Analysis Unit, Executive Summary.) Reprinted by permission. http://www.unhcr.org/cgibin/texis/vtx/home/opendocPDFViewer. html?docid=428db1d62&query=Barb%20Wigley.

RELATED RESOURCES

Videos: UNHCR Video Galleries (various topics and current issues). http://www.unhcr.org/pages/4ac9fdae6.html.

Bennis, W., D. Goleman, J. O'Toole, and P. Biederman. 2008. *Transparency: How leaders create a culture of candor*. San Francisco: Jossey-Bass.

Holbeche, L. and G. Matthews. 2012. *Engaged: Unleashing your organization's potential through employee engagement*. San Francisco, CA: John Wiley & Sons.

Johnson, L., ed. 2006. *HR magazine guide to managing people: 47 tools to help managers*. Alexandria, VA: Society for Human Resource Management.

United Nations High Commissioner for Refugees. 2012. *UNHCR 2011 global report. Geneva: United Nations High Commissioner for Refugees*. http://www.unhcr.org/gr11/index.xml.

United Nations High Commissioner for Refugees. 2013. *UNHCR's mental health and psychosocial support for staff*. Geneva, Switzerland: Author. http://www.unhcr.org/51f67bdc9.pdf.

Williams, M. 2007. *Fit in: The unofficial guide to corporate culture*. Herndon, VA: Capital Books.

CHAPTER 33

Humans Abusing Humans: Smuggling, Trafficking, and Abduction

UNHCR HANDBOOK FOR THE PROTECTION OF WOMEN AND GIRLS

United Nations High Commissioner for Refugees

The international community has made particularly concerted efforts since the early 1990s to promote and protect the rights of women and girls. Of critical importance has been the recognition that

- women's and girl's rights are human rights;
- violence against women and girls, whether in war, in peace, at the hands of family members, the community, or the State, is a human rights violation that should incur individual criminal responsibility;
- States and other actors, including UN agencies such as the United Nations High Commissioner for Refugees (UNHCR), have clear responsibilities to ensure that these are respected; and
- the extent to which women and girls are able to enjoy one right or set of rights often affects their enjoyment of other rights.

Everyone who is displaced is likely to find their right to personal liberty and security violated, perhaps in numerous ways. Although all displaced persons and returnees are at risk of becoming victims of sexual and gender-based violence (SGBV), smuggling, trafficking, and abduction, women and girls are most frequently targeted. They, along with men and boys, may also have their right to freedom of movement violated and may be forcibly recruited into armed groups.

SMUGGLING, TRAFFICKING, AND ABDUCTION

Smuggling, trafficking, and abduction each endanger the physical liberty and security of women and girls of concern. If they are fleeing conflict and persecution, they, like men and boys, are increasingly obliged to pay people-smugglers and undertake perilous journeys if they are to reach a country where they can claim asylum.

The trafficking of people, particularly women and children, is also a growing phenomenon. Victims are tricked or coerced into various exploitative situations, including prostitution, other forms of sexual exploitation, forced labour, begging, and slavery. Women and girls may be targeted by traffickers because of their ethnicity, race, or poverty. Once displaced, whether internally or as refugees, women's and girls' often-uncertain status also exposes them to greater risk of abduction and trafficking.

> When our boat sank we felt we were going to die. Everyone . . .
> screamed—"God, God, please help us, save us please" . . . I can
> never forget the unbelievable pictures in front of my eyes. Some
> people . . . in the water, some swallowing the water and choking
> and choking. I will never forget the bodies lying on the sea. And
> the moment that pushed me into . . . the . . . water and . . . I saw
> my son fighting for his life as well . . . finding a piece of wood, my
> son started to scream, "Mum, Mum, we will choke, we will die.
> God please save us." At this point, I was anxious to get where my
> son was, but I saw a dead woman's body beside me. And with my
> heart burning, I feeling very scared and try to hold the hand of
> the dead body to support myself to swim to my son's side. Thank
> God I could arrive near my son. We kissed each other . . . Some
> other people were still fighting for their lives. The screaming still
> rings in my ears . . . My friend who was holding onto a piece of
> wood had all her children's dead bodies floating around her. Next
> morning while we were still waiting for death, the Indonesian
> fishermen help us and save us." (Amal Basry, survivor of the
> sinking of SIEV-X in Australia's border-protection surveillance
> zone on 19 October 2001, in which 353 people, including 146
> children and 142 women, drowned. Amal was one of fewer than
> fifty survivors, of whom only a dozen were women and children,

adrift in the water for around twenty hours before they were rescued by Indonesian fishing boats.)[72]

Challenge: Smuggling

Women and girls who pay smugglers to take them out of their country may be hoping to escape conflict and human rights violations or may be seeking better economic prospects, but they can all too easily find themselves in dangerous and/or degrading situations. Unlike trafficking, smuggling is essentially a voluntary act—at least initially—involving the payment of a fee to the smuggler to provide a specific service.

Women and girls may nevertheless end up being raped and/or exposed to other violence and/or abuse during the journey, including at the hands of those supposed to bring them to safety, pirates, and the authorities, if detected. They may be abandoned in a country en route without papers or any kind of support. Their position in society means they may be less able than men to negotiate safe passage. If unable to meet further demands or pay additional fees or bribes, they may also end up being trafficked or drawn into other abusive situations.

Initial consent or cooperation to smuggling may be nullified or vitiated by subsequent coercive, abusive, or exploitative circumstances and thus become trafficking.[73]

> Khin is a 13-year-old Muslim girl who lives in a refugee camp near Mae Sot with her mother and three siblings. Khin reported that her father and stepmother took her to Bangkok, where, for approximately a year, she was forced to sell tissues on the street. If she did not make at least 200 baht (US$5) a day, she was beaten. Her father and stepmother then forced her to go back out to the

---

72 Amal's son survived, largely because when Amal was first rescued, she persuaded the fishermen to keep searching for him and other survivors. Eight months later, the Australian government allowed her and her son into the country on a temporary visa, even though her husband was already living there as a recognized refugee. Three years after that, in mid-2005, she was granted a permanent refugee visa. She died of cancer in March 2006. See http://sievx. com/. As one male survivor testified: "The bottom level of the boat had women and children, the middle level had families, and the top level had men only. No one survived from the bottom level." See http://sievxmemorial.org/accounts.htm. See also Human Rights Watch, "By Invitation Only: Australian Asylum Policy," 2002.

73 See UN Office of Drugs and Crime, *Toolkit to Combat Trafficking in Persons*, 2006, xiii–xviii, at http://www.unodc.org/unodc/en/humantrafficking/publications.html and 2000 Protocol to Prevent, Suppress and Punish Trafficking in Persons, especially Women and Children, Article 3(b).

streets until she brought the required amount of profits home. Eventually, Khin was picked up by the Thai police and taken to a government-run shelter for trafficking victims. Later, the police returned her to the border near Mae Sot where she was reunited with her mother and siblings. At that point, a local NGO asked the refugee community in the camp to take in Khin, her mother, and her siblings and care for them, because her mother had few means of generating income. This had been a contributing factor that had compelled Khin to live with her father and, while her mother was unaware of the abuses, left Khin vulnerable to being trafficked. (From "Abuse without End: Burmese Refugee Women and Children at Risk of Trafficking")[74]

I have five children, but one is missing. She is thirteen years old. In the evening, a girl had come and went away with my daughter. Someone saw her at [the open border crossing between Nepal and India]. After a long interval, there was a call from the Mumbai police. This information was given to others, to UNHCR and the [Refugee Coordination Unit implementing government policy in the camps]. No one has come to speak to me. I feel she won't know how to come back home, she doesn't know how to read. Days pass, at night I can't sleep. Children don't know how much we love them. (Lilal B., a refugee in Nepal)[75]

Challenge: Trafficking

The trafficking of people is a modern form of slavery that treats human beings as a commodity to be bought and sold.[76] Eighty percent of all people trafficked are women and girls.[77]

They are given false promises of a new and better life, but can end up in highly exploitative and hazardous situations, including prostitution, domestic service, beg-

---

74   Women's Commission for Refugee Women and Children, "Abuse without End: Burmese Refugee Women and Children at Risk of Trafficking," January 2006, 22.

75   From Human Rights Watch, "Trapped by Inequality: Bhutanese Refugee Women in Nepal," September 2003, 58–59.

76   For a definition see, 2000 Protocol to Prevent, Suppress, and Punish Trafficking in Persons, especially Women and Children, Article 3.

77   OCHA, "Violence Threatens Women in All Stages of Life," 9 December 2005.

ging, and other forced labour, such as child labour. They may be forced to work for a pittance or for nothing at all. Fear of deportation, seizure of papers, and incarceration are all factors exploited by traffickers to keep their victims under their control.

Women and girls may be at particular risk of being trafficked from their homes and villages of origin if they are poor, have disabilities, have been subject to other forms of SGBV, are separated from their family or other support networks, are part of a single-headed household, and/or because they are stateless or of a particular religion, caste, or ethnicity.

Challenge: Danger of Trafficking during Displacement

In addition, women and girls may be fleeing persecution and may have paid smugglers to bring them across borders, but then find that their uncertain situation leads to forced labour, debt bondage, and/or trafficking. They may have fled their homes to escape conflict and human rights abuses only to be abducted and/or trafficked from camps or the streets. If women and girls lack adequate protection, assistance, and/or livelihood opportunities, they are also at greater risk of abuse and trafficking.

During ongoing conflict and uncertain peace, past trauma and/or abuse can lead to ostracism, while education to raise awareness about this rights violation may be lacking or inadequate. Both of these factors can increase the risk of trafficking.

Challenge: Securing Protection for Victims of Trafficking

Where trafficked women and girls manage to escape those who have trafficked them and/or those to whom they have been sold, or if they are discovered, the authorities may view the case primarily as a criminal matter. As a result, victims may be summarily returned with no, or inadequate, consideration of their protection needs. This can, in turn, lead to a cycle of renewed trafficking and abuse.

Trafficked women and girls may be unaware of their rights, may lack access to information and advice, and may face obstacles to gaining access to mechanisms that protect those rights. They may find themselves without personal identity documents and be unable to establish their nationality status, leaving them *de facto* stateless. If they are able to seek asylum, they may find that procedures are not sufficiently age- and gender-sensitive to recognize their claim. Staff and local authorities' attitudes and prejudices can hinder their access to procedures and to protection.

Challenge: Abduction

"Abduction is the removal, seizure, apprehension, taking custody, detention or capture of a child (under 18 years) temporarily or permanently by force, threat or deception for involvement in armed forces or armed groups, for participation in hostilities, for sexual exploitation and forced labour."[78]

This working definition has been adopted by both the UN Task Force on this issue and interagency consultations in the context of their efforts to enhance the protection of children in armed conflict. Outside this context, individuals may also be abducted for sexual exploitation, child or early marriage, forced marriage, forced adoption, or forced labour.

Women and girls may, for instance, be abducted and pressed into prostitution, sexual slavery, child or forced marriage, female genital mutilation, or domestic labour. Boys are more vulnerable to abduction for forced military recruitment, but girls may be abducted for this purpose, too. When young girls disappear from camps for days, some label their disappearance "elopement." In fact, it is more likely that the girls have been trafficked or abducted for child or forced marriage.

Women and girls may be abducted in places where they are isolated or alone, when, for example, they are walking to and from school or the marketplace, or when fetching firewood and water. Even if rescued and returned to their communities, women and girls who have been abducted may face social stigma and discrimination, including by their families, particularly if they have been forced into marriage or sexual slavery and/or to take part in armed conflict.[79]

Challenge: Abduction in Internal Displacement

Internally displaced women and girls living in remote areas are also more vulnerable to armed attack by raiders and are at heightened risk of abduction, rape, and sexual abuse.

In northern Uganda, for instance, tens of thousands of girls and boys living in isolated settlements are obliged to walk several kilometres each night to find the relative safety of towns. Known as "night commuters," they are seeking to avoid the danger of being abducted by armed militia for use as child soldiers, sex slaves, and porters. Some are, in fact, twice displaced.

---

78   See, "Rights of the Child: Report of the UNHCHR on the abduction of children in Africa," E/CN.4/2006/65, 8 February 2006. para. 10.

79   See UN Commission on Human Rights, resolution 2005/43, requesting OHCHR, relevant UN agencies, international organizations, and NGOs to undertake a comprehensive assessment of the situation of the abduction of children throughout Africa; World Vision International, "Abduction of Children in Africa," January 2006.

First they are forced to leave their home as a result of the conflict, and then they are uprooted from their place of refuge by rebel incursions. Night commuting may also take place in camps for the internally displaced. Children whose huts are on the periphery may sleep near public service buildings in the centre of the camp for shelter, as the lack of security prevents monitoring of the camps by night.[80]

INTERNATIONAL LEGAL STANDARDS AND GUIDELINES

Trafficking is a crime under international law and in many countries.[81] It is a form of enslavement[82] and, in some circumstances, a crime against humanity or a war crime. Trafficking violates a range of women's and girls' rights: their rights to liberty and security of person, to be treated with humanity and respect for their inherent human dignity, their right not to be held in slavery, and sometimes their right to life. Child trafficking violates the right of a child to be free from all forms of abuse and exploitation.[83]

The focus of international efforts to combat human trafficking, including those under the 2000 Palermo Trafficking Protocol, has been on prevention, prosecution, and protection. Equally important are measures to rescue, rehabilitate, and reintegrate victims of trafficking.[84]

Smuggling and abduction are also crimes that can result in serious violations of women's and girls' rights, including their right to life.[85] In addition, even though smuggling is initially a voluntary arrangement, it may later become trafficking. Abduction is recognized by the secretary-general as one of the six grave violations of the rights of children in armed conflict that require particular monitoring.[86]

---

80   UNICEF, The State of the World's Children 2005, 48–49.

81   See 2000 Protocol to Prevent, Suppress and Punish Trafficking in Persons, especially Women and Children.

82   See 1998 Rome Statute of the International Criminal Court, Article 7(2)(c).

83   See 1989 Convention on the Rights of the Child, Articles 19, 34, 35, and 36.

84   See 2005 Council of Europe Convention on Action against Trafficking in Human Beings. See also International Organization for Migration (IOM), The IOM Handbook on Direct Assistance for Victims of Trafficking, 2007, especially chapter 3 on referral and reintegration assistance.

85   See, "Rights of the Child: Report of the UNHCHR on the Abduction of Children in Africa," E/CN.4/2006/65, 8 February 2006. para. 52.

86   See "Report of the Secretary-General on Children and Armed Conflict," A/59/695–S/2005/72, 9 February 2005, para. 68.

RESPONSIBILITY: STATES

States have a responsibility to prevent and combat trafficking in persons, including in particular women and children, to protect and assist victims of trafficking in full respect for their human rights, and to promote cooperation among other States to do so.[87]

They must safeguard the rights of individuals who have been smuggled, including in relation to any possible return to the country of origin, and must "take into account the special needs of women and children."[88]

States are obliged to take measures to provide "special protection and assistance" to children, including girls, if they are deprived of their family environment and to protect them from economic exploitation, sexual exploitation and abuse, abduction, and trafficking.[89]

States party to the 1951 Refugee Convention also have a responsibility to provide international protection to victims of trafficking or individuals fearing being trafficked who have a well-founded fear of persecution within the meaning of the Convention if returned to their country of origin.[90]

RESPONSIBILITY: UNHCR

UNHCR has a responsibility:

- to ensure women and girls of concern do not fall victim to trafficking;
- to advocate with asylum decision-making authorities to ensure that victims of trafficking or individuals fearing being trafficked who have a well-founded fear of persecution, within the meaning of the Convention, if returned to their country of origin, are recognized as

---

87   2000 Protocol to Prevent, Suppress and Punish Trafficking in Persons supplementing the Convention against Transnational Organized Crime, Article 2. See also CEDAW, Articles 2, 6, 11; CRC, Article 35. The Human Rights Committee, in its review of States' implementation of Article 8 of the 1966 International Covenant on Civil and Political Rights, has interpreted the prohibition of slavery and the slave trade as encompassing trafficking.

88   2000 Protocol against the Smuggling of Migrants by Land, Sea and Air supplementing the Convention against Transnational Organized Crime, Articles 9, 16 and 18.

89   CRC, Articles 11, 16, 19–22, 32, 34, 35, 36, 37, 38, 39.

90   See, UNHCR, "Guidelines on International Protection: The Application of Article 1A(2) of the 1951 Convention and/or 1967 Protocol relating to the Status of Refugees to Victims of Trafficking and Persons at Risk of being Trafficked," HCR/GIP/06/07, April 2006; ExCom Conclusion No. 107 (LVIII), 2007, para. (g)(viii).

refugees and afforded international protection and, where the Office undertakes refugee status determination itself to be aware and take account of these issues;[91] and

- to work with partners to ensure that States assume their responsibilities to protect women and girls of concern who have been smuggled or abducted, and to ensure States bring smugglers and abductors to justice.

How to Respond

Suggestions for actions which UNHCR, together with local, national, and international partners, should carry out in order to protect women and girls from smuggling, trafficking, and abduction include:

RESPONSE	ACTIONS
Coordinate	• Work with government partners, civil society, and in multisectoral teams, including protection and community service staff, social workers, and health-care providers, to identify and provide health care, psychosocial support, legal advice, and other assistance to women and girls of concern to the Office who have been smuggled, trafficked, or abducted.
	• Coordinate with government partners and other agencies, including UNICEF and the International Organization for Migration (IOM) to raise awareness of the potential international protection needs of women and girls who have been trafficked to another country.[1]
	• Support the efforts of governments and of other UN agencies to provide legal assistance to victims of trafficking and to establish victim-support and witness-protection schemes so that perpetrators can be brought to justice.
	• Support these efforts by working with partners to promote education and vocational training for victims of trafficking to help reintegration and rehabilitation and thereby reduce the risk that they will be trafficked again.

---

91   UNHCR, "Guidelines on International Protection: The Application of Article 1A(2) of the 1951 Convention and/or 1967 Protocol relating to the Status of Refugees to Victims of Trafficking and Persons at Risk of being Trafficked," HCR/GIP/06/07, April 2006, para. 5.

RESPONSE	ACTIONS
Assess, analyse, and design	• Ensure registration identifies displaced women and girls most at risk of trafficking and abduction and monitor their situation regularly. • Work with key partners, including UNICEF, the International Organization for Migration, the Organization for Security and Cooperation in Europe (OSCE), and governments and support programmes to – provide access to safe houses; – provide health care, psychosocial counseling, legal advice, and reintegration assistance to women and girls of concern who have been trafficked and/or abducted;[2] – help them deal with health problems, including post-traumatic stress disorder (PTSD), which they may face; – include support for longer-term solutions such as skills training and livelihood opportunities; and – ensure access to asylum procedures for those who fear being persecuted if returned to their country of origin.
Intervene to protect	• If a victim of trafficking would enjoy protection in the country of origin and return is the desired outcome, promote cooperation among States to verify his or her identity and nationality status as a means to prevent *de facto* statelessness.[3] • If victims of trafficking express a fear of return, ensure that their claim can be assessed to determine whether they require international protection and that asylum procedures take into account the age, gender, and specific needs of victims of trafficking. This includes providing legal counseling and, for girls, a best-interests determination and appointment of a guardian to support her through the procedure.[4] • Work with the local authorities and local NGOs to ensure safe and secure accommodation for victims of trafficking who are persons of concern and are witnesses in prosecution cases.

RESPONSE	ACTIONS
Strengthen national capacity	• Support law enforcement measures that prevent, deter, and combat trafficking. Lobby government ministries and parliamentarians to ensure that measures to criminalize trafficking and bring perpetrators to justice also include explicit safeguards in antitrafficking legislation to ensure victims of trafficking can be identified, assisted, counseled, allowed a reflection period, and have access to asylum procedures before any decision on return to the country of origin is taken.[5] • Work with government authorities, agencies, and other partners to organize training for border guards, police, and immigration and camp officials to raise their awareness of protection concerns related to trafficking and enable them to identify and profile victims and potential victims of trafficking. • Ensure information is available at the border in relevant languages for victims of trafficking, explaining how to seek support and approach UNHCR if they fear return to their country of origin. • Support national antitrafficking initiatives and ensure that the authorities are aware that victims of trafficking may fear return to their country of origin and may have a claim for asylum. • Promote use of UNHCR's Guidelines on International Protection on trafficking[6] by decision makers in asylum procedures to raise awareness of the potential international protection needs of victims of trafficking and ensure that those falling within the refugee definition are accorded such protection. Where victims of trafficking are otherwise in need of international protection, promote the granting of complementary forms of protection.

RESPONSE	ACTIONS
Strengthen community capacity to support solutions	• Raise awareness among the displaced community (e.g., through radio programmes, leaflets, songs, and drama) of the dangers of being smuggled, trafficked, or abducted and the kinds of tactics used to deceive potential victims. • Launch information campaigns for women and girls through women's groups and schools to tell them about the dangers of trafficking and how false information may be given by foreigners or female friends, who have been abroad for a time and returned unusually wealthy, including offers of, and advertisements for, marriage or jobs. • Work with parents in the displaced or returnee community to change the belief that girls are inferior to boys and that girls' main purpose is marriage. • Establish centres where displaced children from urban or rural areas, who would otherwise risk abduction at night, can safely stay overnight.
Monitor, report, and evaluate	• Establish reporting and monitoring mechanisms with partners to ensure – a coordinated and ongoing response to the needs of victims of trafficking; – those expressing fear of return are channelled into asylum procedures; and – measures, such as allocation of guardians and strengthened coordination between relevant authorities, are in place to prevent those admitted to such procedures from disappearing while their claim is being assessed.

EDITORS' NOTES

This chapter is an important reminder of how human beings (not simply "human resources") are massively abused throughout the world. Whether it be children working in sweatshops, people relegated to indentured servitude, or forced prostitution, millions of human beings work and live as virtual slaves of others. Human resources as a sector must continue to acknowledge and confront this most egregious side of human resource "management."

For more information on the United Nations High Commissioner for Refugees (UNHCR). http://www.unhcr.org/.

SOURCE

United Nations High Commissioner for Refugees. 2008. UNHCR handbook for the protection of women and girls. Geneva: United Nations High Commissioner for Refugees, 175, 199, 218–24. Reprinted by permission. http://www.unhcr.org/protect/PROTECTION/47cfae612.html.

RELATED RESOURCES

Video: Viva Network and Asha Forum. "Child Trafficking and Women in Poverty." YouTube. http://www.youtube.com/watch?v=BG3kc1F5jmk.

Cockburn, A. 2003. 21st century slaves. *National Geographic* 204, no. 3: 2–25.

Global Protection Cluster. 2012. Minimum standards for child protection in humanitarian action. http://cpwg.net/minimum-standards/.

International Committee of the Red Cross. 2004. Children in war. Geneva: International Committee of the Red Cross. http://www.icrc.org/eng/assets/files/other/icrc_002_0577k_children_in_war_kit.pdf.

Keeping Children Safe Coalition. 2006. Keeping children safe: A toolkit for child protection. London: Keeping Children Safe. http://www.keepingchildrensafe.org.uk/toolkit.

United Nations. 1989. Convention on the rights of the child. http://www.unicef.org/crc/.

United Nations Office on Drugs and Crime. 2009. Global report on trafficking in persons. United Nations Office on Drugs and Crime. http://www.unodc.org/unodc/en/human-trafficking/global-report-on-trafficking-in-persons.html.

CHAPTER 34

Human Rights and Work

ILO DECLARATION ON FUNDAMENTAL PRINCIPLES AND RIGHTS AT WORK

International Labour Organization

Adopted in 1998, the Declaration commits Member States [governments] to respect and promote principles and rights in four categories, whether or not they have ratified the relevant Conventions [international binding agreements]. These categories are: freedom of association and the effective recognition of the right to collective bargaining, the elimination of forced or compulsory labour, the abolition of child labour, and the elimination of discrimination in respect of employment and occupation.

The Declaration makes it clear that these rights are universal, and that they apply to all people in all States—regardless of the level of economic development. It particularly mentions groups with special needs, including the unemployed and migrant workers. It recognizes that economic growth alone is not enough to ensure equity, social progress, and to eradicate poverty (International Labour Organization n.d.).

ADOPTED BY THE INTERNATIONAL LABOUR CONFERENCE AT ITS EIGHTY-SIXTH SESSION, GENEVA, 18 JUNE 1998 (ANNEX REVISED 15 JUNE 2010)

Whereas the ILO was founded in the conviction that social justice is essential to universal and lasting peace;

Whereas economic growth is essential but not sufficient to ensure equity, social progress, and the eradication of poverty, confirming the need for the ILO to promote strong social policies, justice, and democratic institutions;

Whereas the ILO should, now more than ever, draw upon all its standard-setting, technical cooperation and research resources in all its areas of competence, in particular employment, vocational training, and working conditions, to ensure that, in the context of a global strategy for economic and social development, economic and social policies are mutually reinforcing components in order to create broad-based sustainable development;

Whereas the ILO should give special attention to the problems of persons with special social needs, particularly the unemployed and migrant workers, and mobilize and encourage international, regional, and national efforts aimed at resolving their problems, and promote effective policies aimed at job creation;

Whereas, in seeking to maintain the link between social progress and economic growth, the guarantee of fundamental principles and rights at work is of particular significance in that it enables the persons concerned to claim freely and on the basis of equality of opportunity their fair share of the wealth which they have helped to generate, and to achieve fully their human potential;

Whereas the ILO is the constitutionally mandated international organization and the competent body to set and deal with international labour standards, and enjoys universal support and acknowledgment in promoting Fundamental Rights at Work as the expression of its constitutional principles;

Whereas it is urgent, in a situation of growing economic interdependence, to reaffirm the immutable nature of the fundamental principles and rights embodied in the Constitution of the Organization and to promote their universal application;

THE INTERNATIONAL LABOUR CONFERENCE

1. Recalls:
    (a) that in freely joining the ILO, all Members have endorsed the principles and rights set out in its Constitution and in the Declaration of Philadelphia, and have undertaken to work towards attaining the overall objectives of the Organization to the best of their resources and fully in line with their specific circumstances;
    (b) that these principles and rights have been expressed and developed in the form of specific rights and obligations in Conventions recognized as fundamental both inside and outside the Organization.
2. Declares that all Members, even if they have not ratified the Conventions in question, have an obligation arising from the very fact of membership in the Organization to respect, to promote, and to

realize, in good faith and in accordance with the Constitution, the principles concerning the fundamental rights which are the subject of those Conventions, namely:

(a) freedom of association and the effective recognition of the right to collective bargaining,

(b) the elimination of all forms of forced or compulsory labour,

(c) the effective abolition of child labour, and

(d) the elimination of discrimination in respect of employment and occupation.

3. Recognizes the obligation on the Organization to assist its Members, in response to their established and expressed needs, in order to attain these objectives by making full use of its constitutional, operational, and budgetary resources, including, by the mobilization of external resources and support, as well as by encouraging other international organizations with which the ILO has established relations, pursuant to article 12 of its Constitution, to support these efforts:

(a) by offering technical cooperation and advisory services to promote the ratification and implementation of the fundamental Conventions;

(a) by assisting those Members not yet in a position to ratify some or all of these Conventions in their efforts to respect, to promote, and to realize the principles concerning fundamental rights which are the subject of these Conventions; and

(b) by helping the Members in their efforts to create a climate for economic and social development.

4. Decides that, to give full effect to this Declaration, a promotional follow-up, which is meaningful and effective, shall be implemented in accordance with the measures specified in the annex hereto, which shall be considered as an integral part of this Declaration.

5. Stresses that labour standards should not be used for protectionist trade purposes, and that nothing in this Declaration and its follow-up shall be invoked or otherwise used for such purposes; in addition, the comparative advantage of any country should in no way be called into question by this Declaration and its follow-up.

REFERENCES

International Labour Organization. n.d. About the declaration. International Labour Organization. http://www.ilo.org/declaration/thedeclaration/lang--en/index.htm. ©1998 International Labour Organization.

EDITORS' NOTES

For more information about the International Labour Organization: http://www.ilo.org/.

SOURCE

International Labour Organization. 1998. ILO declaration on fundamental principles and rights at work. International Labour Organization. Reprinted by permission. http://www.ilo.org/declaration/lang--en/index.htm.

RELATED RESOURCES

Videos: International Labour Organization (various topics from around the world). http://www.ilo.org/global/about-the-ilo/multimedia/video/lang--en/index.htm.

Bjork, J., and A. Gulzar. 2010. 10 things you need to know about labour trafficking in the Greater Meking Sub-region. World Vision International. http://www.wvasiapacific.org/down-loads/publications/10Things_labour_trafficking.pdf.

FRONTERA. 2007. Motivating staff and volunteers working in NGOs in the South. London: People In Aid. http://www.peopleinaid.org/pool/files/pubs/motivating-staff-and-volunteers-working-in-ngos-in-the-south.pdf.

International Labour Organisation. 2011. *Electronic library on occupational safety and health* (DVD-ROM). http://www.ilo.org/global/publications/ilo-bookstore/order-online/books/WCMS_169013/lang--en/index.htm.

United Nations. 1966. International covenant on economic, social, and political rights. http://www2.ohchr.org/english/law/cescr.htm.

World Health Organization. 2010. Healthy workplaces: A model for action; For employers, workers, policy-makers, and practitioners. Geneva: World Health Organization. http://www.who.int/occupational_health/publications/healthy_workplaces_model_action.pdf.

World Health ORganisation, 2010. WHO Global Code of Practice on the International Recruitment of Health Personnel. Geenva, Author. http://www.who.int/hrh/migration/code/WHO_global_code_of_practice_EN.pdf

CHAPTER 35

Serving Well

David Mazel

IT WAS TERRIBLY EMBARRASSING
TO HAVE MY NOBLE WISH SO GENTLY REFUSED,
TO HAVE MY EYES OPENED TO SEE THAT ONE PERSON
COULD ACTUALLY THRIVE ON WHAT STRUCK ANOTHER
AS BEING SO UTTERLY WRETCHED.

On the street in Brooklyn where I grew up, there lived a woman by the name of Sadie Josephson. When she was seventy-five her husband died, leaving her only a little insurance and an old house. What could she do? She went into business for herself, the only business she really knew after fifty years of marriage. She became a laundress. And a good one, too.

For blocks around, the housewives who didn't have their own washing machine preferred her to the local laundromat ten to one. She got the laundry clean clear through, not just on the surface. She also ironed it, and she didn't cost that big a penny more, either. Even the housewives who had their own washer and dryer would now and then turn to Sadie to get the sparkle and warmth, the human touch, that no machine could give. For Sadie did everything by hand.

She would pick up the bundle of laundry in a bright-red toy wagon, the same one in which her three boys, now middle-aged and far away, had ridden, and then she would tow it back to her house. There, in the basement, she would fill as many of her four sturdy oaken washtubs as she needed with steaming water; take up her washboard and bar of strong yellow soap; and getting down on her knees, commence to scrub away.

She was a little woman, only five feet tall, with wispy-white hair and thin arms and small hands. But she never let that hair get in her eyes, and in those arms she had great strength. Nor did she ever scrimp it. She scrubbed a sock just as hard as she scrubbed a towel or a sheet. You could say that in the tubs all laundry became equal.

After the scrubbing Sadie would pull the corks out of the tubs, letting foamy rivers dash down the drain, and then she would plunge the big, dripping clumps into tubs of fresh water and rinse each piece over and over until it was soapless. Then, with a wicker basket heaped full, up the stairs and out she'd go to the greenhouse in her backyard. Here her husband had once grown many kinds of flowers. Now the flowers were gone, and dozens of clotheslines, with hundreds of wooden clothespins clinging to them like little birds, stretched from one end to the other.

In a corner of this greenhouse was a coal-burning stove that cast a circle of warmth. And within this circle stood Sadie's ironing board, looking like a faithful, spindly-legged horse, and on top of it, plugged into a long extension cord, her heavy iron. Here she would stand for hour after hour, pressing the iron down hard on the board as if to leave her mark on some stubborn surface, not singing, not even humming, but just ironing in a green, almost devout quiet.

When someone's laundry was ready to come home, ordinarily Sadie would bring it in the red wagon. But my mother always sent me to fetch ours, to save the old woman the journey. And always, seeing that greenhouse of laden clotheslines, I would feel what a shame it was, what a wrong, that someone so old should have to work so hard. It seemed to me that the lot of the laundress could only be described by the first big word I had ever learned in school—"servitude."

One day, as she placed the stack of immaculate laundry in my arms, I could no longer refrain from letting the old woman know how my spirit cried out against this lot of hers. "Sadie," I said, "I wish I was rich. I would deliver you from this servitude this very moment."

She bent down and kissed me on the head. "Would you, darling?" she said. "That is sweet. But you see, I don't want to be delivered! I am quite happy to do my laundry. I feel good in my heart, and I'm a burden to nobody."

I blushed deeply. It was terribly embarrassing to have one's noble wish so gently refused, to have one's eyes opened to the truth that one person could actually thrive on what struck another as so utterly wretched. Sadie saw this, and comforted me with her philosophy:

"God, He lights two candles in each of us," she said. "One is strength, and the other is hope. Sometimes a big wind comes along and blows out one or the other— *only one or the other, because God never allows the wind to blow out both. And so,* when the strength is blown out, we relight it with the hope; and when the hope is blown out, we relight it with the strength. In me, today, both candles are burning. They will always burn."

Then with a brisk nod and a smile, she shooed me off into my day.

SOURCE

Mazel, D. 1985. Sadie. *My heart's world, pp. 44–46.* Wild Rose, WI: Phunn Publishers. Reprinted by permission. More stories by David Mazel: http://www.ufollow.com/search/fulltext/mazel/facet/author/david.mazel/. For copies of this book, contact: Phunn Publishers, S5707 US Highway; Viroqua, WI 54665–8606 USA.

Afterword

What lies ahead for the member care field, and indeed for our world at large? What are our future challenges and opportunities for member care in mission/aid and beyond, into all humanity care?

Our developing field needs "good learners-practitioners" who are growing in their character (virtues), competency (skills), and compassion (love). We need to be willing to integrate our lives more globally: to cross many new boundaries, work cooperatively across sectors, and journey through "deserts" (our internal and external places of difficulty). We must grow together through the hard times, inspired by the vision to see member care develop globally in culturally relevant ways—for all peoples and from all peoples.

As a diverse, resilient, international community of member care workers, we will need to have clear ethical commitments in order to provide/develop quality services to mission/aid workers in many settings, often in unstable locations permeated with conflict, calamity, and corruption. And as earthen vessels we must develop the personal resiliency and mature faith that can sustain us as we take risks to do good and to resolutely confront evil in its many forms.

The material in this book and the historical flow of our field are intentionally heading us towards an ultimate destination. Our destination is also the foundation and motivation for our field: resilient love. Sacrificial and celebratory love. Love flowing from duty and desire. Agape.

Amo neniam pereas.
Love never fails.

Index